DATE DUE FOR

THE LOCAL
HISTORIAN'S
ENCYCLOPEDIA

John Richardson

HISTORICAL PUBLICATIONS

Historical Publications Ltd
Orchard House
54, Station Road
New Barnet, Herts

Copyright John Richardson

First published 1974
Reprinted 1975 with minor revisions
Reprinted 1977
Reprinted 1981 with minor revisions
Reprinted 1983
Reprinted 1985

ISBN 0 9503656 0 2

Printed by Eyre and Spottiswoode Ltd
at the Grosvenor Press

311830

FOREWORD

An Encyclopedia for local historians seems an unlikely publication. A local history can, after all, be written without reference to events outside the community concerned — and frequently is — but it is less valuable because of this.

Local history is more than the famous residents, the finer buildings, the folk-lore and the Church. None of these things shapes a community today and it would be a mistake to over-estimate their importance centuries ago. National legislation, county and local administration, the law, the development of public life, all, on the face of it, more pedestrian, were quite often greater influences than parochial factors.

This Encyclopedia sets out to give a local history researcher basic information in a wide range of subjects, including the 'non-parochial' fields mentioned above. It is divided into sections which, usually, provide an historical progression of events. Hopefully it is also so arranged as to introduce the researcher into entirely new fields of study. It gives a glossary of terms in a number of subjects, the date and intent of legislation that touched on most parishes in the land, and is a guide to those who need to use the county and national archives.

Markets and Fairs, very important elements in local life up to the 19th century, are given a disproportionate amount of space, but only because the information given is not easily obtainable elsewhere.

John Richardson

CONTENTS

Part 1 — Land Measurement

Part 2 — Field Names and Geographical Features

Part 3 — Open Field Farming, Commons and Enclosures

Part 4 — Tenants and Tenures

Part 5 — The Transfer and Inheritance of Land

Part 6 — Agricultural History

Part 7 — Farm houses and buildings

Part 8 — Miscellaneous

Part One — Land Measurement

1 General

Measurement of area and distance in Old English and medieval times varied considerably over the country and within any one region. The Hide, for example, was an area which was assumed to support a peasant family for a year and, therefore, its size depended on the quality of the soil.

Generally the main units of measurement bore the same relationship to each other over England, but even so there were many exceptions. The normal relationship was:

1 Hide, Carucate or Ploughland	= 4 Virgates or Yardlands
1 Virgate or Yardland	= 2 Bovates or Oxgangs
1 Bovate or Oxgang	= 2 Farthingdales
1 Farthingdale	= 10 Acres
1 Acre	= 4 Rods x 40 Rods

2 Acre

The Acre, originally a stretch of land of no particular size or nature, came to mean land cleared for cultivation or grazing. In open-field farming it then came to mean as large a strip as could be ploughed by a yoke of oxen in a day. Edward I standardised the Acre at 40 Rods long x 4 Rods wide, or 4840 sq. yds. Even so, for a long time, there were regional variations and the Acre could mean in Ireland 7840 sq. yds., Westmorland 6760 sq. yds. and Scotland 6084 sq. yds.

It was also a lineal measure in some Midland counties of between 22 and 32 yards.

3 Acreland

An area varying from 8 to 20 acres.

4 Acreme

Ten acres approximately, similar to a Farthingdale. Late medieval term.

5 Arpen(t)

A vineyard measure derived from France. Between 100 and 160 sq. yds.

6 Bescia

A medieval, variable dimension, used for turf-cutting in the fens. It seems to have meant the amount of land that could be dug by one man with a spade between May 1st and August 1st each year.

7 Bovate
A variable measure related to the amount of land an ox could plough in a year and the soil quality. Generally reckoned to be one-eighth of a Hide (qv) and consisting of between 7 to 32 acres. In some areas it would contradict the normal measurement relationship and be equal to 1 Virgate (qv) instead of one half. Alternatively known as an Oxgang.

8 Broad Oxgang
Double a normal Oxgang (qv); quarter of a Hide or equivalent to a Yardland or a Virgate.

9 Carucate
Alternative name for Hide (qv).

10 Couture
Equivalent to a Furlong (qv). Derived from the coulter blade on the plough.

11 Davoch
A Scottish measure supposed to have averaged 416 acres.

12 Day-Math
A Cheshire term for approximately twice a statute acre, or a day's mowing for one man.

13 Day-Work
In some areas in Yorks, Lancs and Lincs, 3 roods of land.

14 Erws
The Welsh term for acre.

15 Fardel
Equivalent to a Farthingdale (qv); 10 acres.

16 Farthingdale/Farthinghold
Generally used as meaning a quarter of a Virgate — 10 acres, but could also mean a quarter of an acre.

Also known as a Fardel and Ferling.

17 Ferendell
A quarter of an acre.

18 Ferling
Equivalent to a Farthingdale (qv).

19 Flat(t)
Equivalent to a Furlong (qv).

20 Furlong
Originally meant a furrow length in the open fields and sometimes a measurement of area, i.e., a rectangular block of strips. Eventually standardised as a measurement of length—one-eighth of a mile, 220 yards. Also known as a Couture, Flat(t) or Quarentena.

21 Hide
Originally the amount of land which could be ploughed in a year using one plough and support a family. It could therefore vary in area with the soil quality — generally between 60 and 180 acres. It usually held 4 Virgates, but it could also contain 2, 3, 5, 6, 7 or 8 Virgates depending on the local interpretation of the word. Alternatively called Ploughland, Carucate, Husbandland, Sulung, Ploughgate.

22 Hill
A Sussex land measure, amounting to half an acre.

23 Hop Acre
The area occupied by a thousand hop plants — about half an acre.

24 Husbandland
Generally the equivalent of a Hide but in some northern and Scottish areas could be as little as 20 acres.

25 Irish Mile
The old measurement, before standardisation, was 6,720 feet.

26 Knight's Fee/Knight's Service
In this context, a variable measurement depending on the quality of the soil, and thought to be the amount of land which could support a knight and his family for a year. It could vary between 4 and 48 Hides.

27 Landyard
A Somerset measure for a rod.

28 League
Generally 3 miles (15,840 feet) but could vary between 7,500 feet and 10,000 feet.

29 Librate
A measurement which could vary two ways. It was an amount of land worth £1; its area therefore depended on the value of the pound and on the soil quality.

30 Markland
An area varying between 1 and 3 acres.

31 Math
Approximately 1 acre, or the amount of land that one man could mow in a day. A Herefordshire term.

32 Mile
Before standardisation it could vary between 4,854 feet and 6,600 feet. The old Scottish Mile was often 5,928 feet and the Irish Mile 6,720 feet.

33 Narrow Oxgang
Equivalent to an Oxgang (qv). In opposition to a Broad Oxgang which was twice the size.

34 Nook
Two Farthingdales (qv) or 20 acres. A Scottish or north of England term.

35 Oxgang/Oxgate/Oxland
A variable measure depending on the soil quality. Originally the amount of land that could be cultivated using one ox, and could vary between 7 and 50 acres. Normally it was reckoned to be one-eighth of a Hide (qv). Alternatively called a Bovate.

36 Pace
Approximately 5 feet, or two steps.

37 Perch
Could vary between 9 and 26 feet but later standardised at 16½ feet.

38 Ploughgate/Ploughland
Equivalent to a Hide (qv).

39 Quarentena
Equivalent to a Furlong (qv).

40 Scottish Mile
The old measurement, before standardisation, was usually 5,928 feet.

41 Stadium
A Furlong (qv).

42 Stang
A Welsh measure varying between a Rod and a Customary Acre.

43 Sulung
A Kent term, equivalent to a Hide (qv). A variable measure depending on the soil quality, and was the amount of land that could be cultivated using an 8-ox plough team. It was divided into 4 Yokes, and was also used as a unit for tax assessment.

44 Tenantry Acre
A variable measure but usually three-quarters of an acre.

45 Verge
In this context, a variable area of land between 15 and 30 acres.

46 Virgate

A variable measure depending on the soil quality. A quarter of a Hide (qv), and could be from 15 to 60 acres. Normally about 30 acres. Also known as a Yardland, Wista or Yoke.

47 Wista
A Sussex term for a Virgate (qv).

48 Wood Acre
A measure of land three-eighths larger than a statute acre.

49 Yardland
Equivalent to a Virgate (qv).

50 Yoke
A Kent term for a Virgate (qv).

Part Two — Field Names and Geographical Features

51 Ait
A widespread term for an island in a river; an osier bed.

52 Amad
A haymead.

53 Applegarth
A Yorkshire term for an orchard.

54 Assart
Originally an enclosure, but then more particularly a clearing or enclosure in a forest, and more rarely in other waste land. If forest land was involved permission was required from the Crown.

55 Bache/Batch
A stream.

56 Bang/Bank/Bong
A low bank serving as a boundary or else a slope in an otherwise flat field.

57 Barken
See Barton.

58 Barrow
In this context, a grove or copse.

59 Barth
A sheltered pasture for young animals.

60 Barton/Berton/Burton/Barken
a) barley enclosure (OE bere-tun bere=barley).
b) a farmyard.
c) especially in Devonshire, the demesne lands of a manor.
d) a chicken coop.

61 Batch
See Bache.

62 Bawn
The Irish word for a yard or cattle enclosure, but previously meant a fortified enclosure.

63 Beck
A Danelaw county term for a stream.

64 Berneshawe
A barnyard.

65 Berton
See Barton.

66 Bong
See Bang.

67 Booly/Booley
A temporary enclosure used by Irish herdsmen who moved about with their herds in the summer months.

68 Bottom
A hollow or dell.

69 Bourne/Burn
A stream. Burn is used mainly in Scotland, Ireland and the north of England.

70 Brake
Wasteland covered with brushwood.

71 Breach/Breech
Land newly cultivated.

72 Breck
Land enclosed from the waste of forest, usually on a temporary basis. Alternatively called Break or Breckland.

73 Burgage
A small field, usually less than half an acre, a short distance from the farmhouse.

74 Burton
See Barton.

75 Burn
See Bourne.

76 Butland
Waste land.

77 Byes
The corners or ends of fields which could not be reached by a plough and had to be dug by hand.

78 Cam
A ridge on a hill, or an earthbank.

79 Cangle
An enclosure.

80 Cantle
A projecting corner of land.

81 Car(r)
Marshy land. A north-country and midland term.

82 Catchland
Boundary land which did not belong to any parish. The land's tithe went to the first cleric who claimed it. Alternatively called Catchpole Acre.

83 Catch-meadow
A meadow irrigated by water from a nearby slope.

84 Catchpole Acre
See Catchland.

85 Chase
Land formerly reserved for hunting by the local lord or by the Crown.

86 Cleugh/Clough
A deep valley or ravine.

87 Close
Originally meant an enclosure from the open fields.

88 Cockshoot/Cockshut
A clearing cut through a wood which might be used for shooting game as it went through it.

89 Coldharbour
An exposed place, or else a shelter from an exposed place.

90 Conyger
A rabbit warren. There were strict laws against killing rabbits and not until the Ground Game Act 1880 were farmers able to kill rabbits on their own land. Alternatively called: conygree, conyearth, conygarth, conyhole, conywarren, cunner.

91 Co(o)mb
A narrow valley, or hollow in the side of a hill.

92 Crew(e)
A small enclosure for cattle.

93 Croat/Croft/Croud/Crowd
a) Enclosed meadow or arable land, usually adjacent to the house. b) In the Highlands and Islands of Scotland, a smallholding farmed by peasant tenants. The crofting areas were Inverness, Orkney and Shetland, Ross, Argyll, Sutherland and Caithness.

94 Demesne
Land retained by the lord of the manor for his own use and upon which tenants gave free service according to the customs of the

manor. Land which was part of the main farm of the manor.

95 Denn
A pasture, usually for pigs.

96 Dolver
An East Anglian term for land reclaimed from the fens or, more generally, marshy land.

97 Down
A hill or an expanse of hills.

98 Dumble
A north country and midland term for a wooded valley, or a ravine containing a stream.

99 Ed(d)ish/Etch
An enclosure

100 End
The outlying part of an estate.

101 Ersh
A ploughed field.

102 Essart
See Assart.

103 Etch
See Eddish.

104 Ffridd
The Welsh term for fenced-in land nearest to the farmstead.

105 Fit
Grassland near to a river.

106 Flash
A shallow pool.

107 Flockrake
A Scottish term for a sheep pasture.

108 Flonk
Enclosure in front of a pig-sty.

109 Fold
A small enclosure or else a pen for animals.

110 Forschel
A strip of land adjacent to the highway.

111 Forstal
A small piece of waste land; a paddock or farmyard.

112 Foss(e)
A ditch or trench.

113 Freeth
A west country and Welsh term for a hedge, especially a wattled hedge. It could also mean a gap in a hedge filled with wattle.

114 Frith
A wooded area or a clearing in a wood.

115 Furrow
A strip of arable land.

116 Gainage
See Innings.

117 Gair
A northern and Scottish term for a Gore (qv).

118 Gall
A widespread term for agriculturally inferior land, usually marshy.

119 Garston
An enclosed yard for cattle.

120 Gill
A wooded valley, usually with a stream running through it.

121 Gore
A triangular or irregularly-shaped

piece of land in the open fields, sometimes called a Gore Acre.

122 Gospel Tree
A tree that marked the boundary of a parish or manor.

123 Gr(e)ave/Greeve
A grove.

124 Grip
A widespread term for a ditch or small watercourse.

125 Ground
A large area of grassland lying at a distance from the farm.

126 Gut
A stream.

127 Gypsey
A stream temporarily running through a normally dry valley.

128 Hade
A midland term for a headland (qv).

129 Hafod
A Welsh term for a summer or upland pasture.

130 Hag(g)
A wood, sometimes enclosed.

131 Hale/Hall
A small corner of land.

132 Half
A half-acre; a moiety.

133 Half-year Close
A close used for pasture in the winter.

134 Ham
In this context, an enclosure, usually for pasture.

135 Hamstal/Homestal
A field adjacent to the farm-house.

136 Hanger
A wooded hill.

137 Hanging Field
A field on a slope.

138 Hant
A feeding-place for cattle.

139 Harden
See Headland.

140 Harve
An Essex term for a small enclosed piece of land near the house.

141 Hatch
A fenced piece of land.

142 Hatchet
A field to which access is gained through a wicket gate.

143 Haughland
A Scottish or north of England term for a low-lying riverside meadow.

144 Haw
An enclosed piece of land near the house; a small yard.

145 Hay
A small, enclosed field. A term found in south-west England, south Wales and Northumberland.

146 Headland
A strip of land at the end of a ploughed field upon which the plough turned; the headland was

afterwards ploughed at right-angles. Alternatively called Hade, Harden.

147 Heaf
A northern term for sheep pasture.

148 Heater
An East Anglian term for a triangular piece of land.

149 Hempland
Land, in medieval times, for the cultivation of hemp.

150 Hendre
A Welsh term for the land on which cattle and owners spent the winter months.

151 Hern/Hirn/Hyrne
An oddshaped, small piece of land, or else land in the bend of a river.

152 Hield
A slope.

153 Holm(e)
A water meadow.

154 Holt
A grove or copse.

155 Home Close
Either the field nearest the farmhouse or the close in which the farmhouse is built.

156 Hop(e)
An enclosed piece of land, especially in marshy areas.

157 Hoppet
A small enclosure.

158 Horselease
A widespread term for meadow

land kept for horses.

159 How(e)
A tumulus or natural mound.

160 In-by Land
A northern term for the enclosed land nearest to the farmhouse. The term stems from the Scandinavian word 'by' meaning farm. Alternatively called Infield.

161 Infield-Outfield
A farming method in which the arable field, the infield, of a locality is continuously under cultivation, and parts of the outlying land, the outfield, are occasionally cultivated. and parts of outlying land, the outfield are occasionally cultivated.

162 Inhams/Inhomes
Land enclosed from the waste.

163 Inland
a) Land near to the farmhouse cultivated by the owner.
b) Land enclosed and cultivated as opposed to waste or common land.

164 Inlandes
Parts of demesne land rented out to tenants.

165 Innings
The taking in of marshland or flooded land, or else the actual land reclaimed. When profitable it was called Gainage in some areas.

166 Intake
A piece of land which had been enclosed, generally from a moor, but also from a common or waterway.

167 Inwood
A wood on demesne land.

168 Jack
Waste land.

169 Keld
A northern term for a spring or a marshy area.

170 Knap(p)
A hillock.

171 Lache
A pond.

172 Ladder Farm
Also called a striped farm, it consisted of holdings of small ribboned fields.

173 Laighton
A northern term for a garden. Alternatively spelt Leighton.

174 Lake
A widespread term for a stream.

175 Langat(e)
A long strip of land.

176 Laystall
An area where dung or refuse is laid.

177 Lea
Grassland, but quite often arable land newly laid for pasture, then ploughed up again. Alternatively spelt lay, ley, leah, lee, ley.

178 Lease/Leaze
Meadow, usually common.

179 Leasow
Enclosed pasture.

180 Leat/Leet
An artificial waterway to provide water for industrial and domestic purposes.

181 Leighton
See Laighton

182 Levant
A stream temporarily running through a normally dry valley.

183 Ley
a) a meadow.
b) untilled land.

184 Mailing
A northern term for a land-holding.

185 Mains
A northern and Scottish term for demesne land.

186 March
A border or boundary.

187 Marksoil
A boundary mark, such as a stone.

188 Merestake/Merestone
A boundary stake or stone.

189 Nailbourne
A stream running through a normally dry valley.

190 Nook
A triangular, or secluded piece of land.

191 Oldland
Land which was once arable but now used for pasture.

192 Outfield
A northern and Scottish term for land not kept in cultivation all the time, but occasionally used for crops.

193 Paddle
A Lincolnshire term for a pasture.

194 Park
a) Land enclosed to keep beasts for hunting, a privilege granted by

the Crown.
b) In Scotland and Ireland, enclosed land for grazing or cultivation.
c) Demesne land, sometimes used for ornamental purposes.

195 Parrock
A paddock or small enclosure.

196 Pendicle
A Scottish term for a small piece of land, sometimes attached to a large estate.

197 Pightel
A small piece of land in the open fields, or else a small enclosed plot Alternatively spelt: pightle, pigtail, pingle.

198 Pike
A triangular piece of land.

199 Piking
A Worcestershire term for a triangular piece of land.

200 Pilch
A triangular piece of land.

201 Pill
A waterway, especially in Monmouthshire.

202 Pin Fallow
Land left fallow for only part of a year, between harvest in autumn and sowing the next springtime. Also called Bastard Fallow.

203 Pingle
A midland term for a small piece of land in the open fields, or small enclosed field.

204 Plack/Plackett
A small field.

205 Plashet
A marshy piece of land.

206 Pleck
A small piece of land.

207 Purlieu
Land once added unlawfully to an ancient forest; it might well have since been disafforested.

208 Quarter
An allotment.

209 Quillet
A widespread term for a narrow strip of land, or small croft.

210 Rand
A Lincs term for a strip of marshy land lying between a river bank and an artificial embankment running parallel to it.

211 Rap
A west country term for a thin strip of land.

212 Reading/Reeding/Ridding
A clearing in a wood; assart; land taken in from the waste and cultivated.

213 Reen
A major field drain which collects from smaller drains.

214 Royd
A northern term for a clearing in a wood.

215 Scoot
A small, oddly-shaped parcel of land.

216 Screed
A narrow strip of land.

217 Sentry Field
A west country term for a field near a church which at one time had the right of Sanctuary (qv).

218 Sherd/Shord
A clearing in a wood.

219 Shieling
A Scottish term for pasture land or else for the hut built on such

pasture.

220 Shoot
A nook of land projecting beyond another.

221 Sike
A northern term for a stream, one that usually runs dry in the summer.

222 Slade
A valley.

223 Slai(gh)t/Slei(gh)t
Sheep pasture.

224 Slang/Sling
A narrow strip of land between fields. The word is found in the Midlands, south-west England and south Wales.

225 Sling
A curved field.

226 Slip
A narrow strip of land.

227 Slough
A marshy piece of land.

228 Snowhill
A hill facing north which retains snow longer than other places.

229 Spong
A midland and East Anglian term for a narrow strip of land.

230 Spot
A small piece of land.

231 Stubb/Stubbing
Land covered with tree-stumps.

232 Swale
Meadow land, especially in marshy areas.

233 Thwaite
A clearing in a wood or forest.

234 Townland
The enclosed or infield part of a farm in Scotland.

235 Township
In this context, a farm which was occupied by two farmers who worked together, or divided the land between them.

236 Tye
A small enclosure, often where three roads met.

237 Tyning
Enclosed land.

238 Vaccary
Pasture for cows.

239 Velge
Fallow land.

240 Voryer
A west country and Welsh term for a strip of land, unploughed, around the edges of an arable field.

241 Wath
A ford, or a stream that can be forded.

242 Waver
A village pond.

243 Weald
A term in Kent, Surrey and Sussex for wooded country.

244 Went/Wentin
A west country term for a part of a field, too large or hilly to be ploughed in a continuous furrow. It could also be a small part of a field separated from the rest by some barrier such as a road.

245 Wick
In this context, a dairy farm.

246 Wong
Enclosed meadow land; low-lying land, often marshy.

247 Wray/Wroe
A nook of land.

Part Three — Open Field Farming, Commons and Enclosures

248 General

The Open Field system, introduced by the Saxons, is believed to have replaced the Celtic enclosed fields over most of the country excepting in the west, Wales and the north of England. As a rule each locality operated the three-field method, that is, each had three large, open fields, divided into strips of approximately 1 acre each. Only two fields could be cultivated in any one year; the remaining field would lie fallow. For example, one field would yield barley the first year, wheat the next, and lie fallow in the third year.

There were no hedges surrounding the fields or between the individual strips. Each farmer had strips, usually called selions (and a variety of other names as well), scattered all over the three fields. One likely reason for this seemingly odd distribution of land is that strips were given to the farmers making up the ploughing team as they gradually came under cultivation. Another reason advanced is that the various farmers were given a share of both good and bad land.

The Open Field system had many drawbacks. Time was wasted by farmers moving from one strip to another in the two vast, cultivated fields, and access was sometimes difficult for a plough and an 8-ox team. The lack of hedges gave no protection against the spread of weeds or stray cattle. The multi-occupation of a field could lead to boundary disputes and gave no incentive to an individual to improve drainage or farming methods. Also, the continuous growth of cereals exhausted the land. Furthermore, keeping a field fallow all year was wasteful.

In hand with the Open Field system was the Commons system. The farmers grazed their cattle and otherwise supplemented their income on what was in fact the lord's land, but used commonally.

Terms

249 Acre

In this context, an individually held arable strip in the common field.

250 Ade/Aid

A Shropshire term for a gutter or ditch to help with irrigation across an open arable field.

251 Approvement

The enclosure of common land.

252 Balks/Baulks

In the open fields, thin unploughed lengths of land between each man's strip. These gave access to the cultivated strips, and were either at right-angles to them (called waybalks or headlands), or else parallel to them (called sidebalks).

The more prominent balks between fields served as grass roads and were sometimes called the common or town balks.

Alternatively called edge, linch(et), mear, meer, mere, rean and wall.

253 Broad

A wide strip of land in the common arable field.

254 Butt

A piece of land in an open arable field which, because of the irregular shape of the field, was shorter than the normal strip.

255 Carr
Common land, usually marshy.

256 Cavel
A north country and Lincs term for a division of land, or a strip in the open arable field.

257 Champion
Open field land as opposed to land held by an individual in un-shared tenure.

258 Chart
A Kent and Surrey term for a rough common.

259 Co-aration
The cultivation of open fields by the community of farmers.

260 Commons
The Commons were an integral part of the rural economy. While the tenants worked the arable fields in strips, they supplemented their livelihood by grazing their cattle on the common pasture. Common land consisted of meadows, waste land and roadside strips. Encroachment was allowed by the Statute of Merton 1235 and by subsequent legislation.

Cattle were not allowed to graze on the common meadows from Candlemas (Feb 2) until Lammas Day (Aug 1) when the meadows were cropped.

261 Dales/Doles
Portions of the common meadows divided among the occupiers of the related open arable fields. The shares were sometimes allotted yearly by lot or rotation and tenants were entitled to the hay from their portions.

262 Dalt
Share of the common field.

263 Dell
A group of Selions (qv).

264 Doat/Dote
A share of the common field.

265 Edge
See Balk.

266 Engrossment
The drawing of two or more holdings into one.

267 Fardel
A group of Selions (qv).

268 Farren
A west country term for a division of land in an open field.

269 Field
The present-day fields are, more properly, closes. Before enclosures a field was a large stretch of open land subdivided into strips.

270 Field Garden Allotments
Parts of a common, not more than a quarter of an acre each, let to the poor of the parish.

271 Flat(t)
A strip in an open field, or a piece of level ground.

272 Folk Land
Common land.

273 Fore-Acre/Forical
A Kent term for the headland on which the plough was turned.

274 Fother
An odd piece of land in the open field.

275 Furhead
The headland of a field on which the plough was turned.

276 Furlong
In this context, the main division of an open field; a group of Selions (qv) of the same length. Could also mean a strip of ploughed land, a furrow in length. Less commonly it

could mean a headland on which the plough turned.

277 Gait/Gate
The north country term for Stint (qv).

278 Half-Year Land
See Lammas Land.

279 Ham
In this context, a common pasture.

280 Headland
Untilled land, usually held in common at the head of strips upon which the plough turned. Some headlands came to form the winding routes between the fields, forerunner of today's winding lanes.

281 Hitched Land
Part of the common arable field used especially for a different sort of crop such as turnips etc.

282 Huvvers
A Lincs term for ridges separating one tenant's land from another in the open fields.

283 Ings
Common meadows.

284 Inhook
Land which was for a time enclosed in its fallow year.

285 Inter-Commoning
The pasturing of cattle belonging to two or more villages on common land which was not the property of a single owner.

286 Jack's Land
See Noman's Land

287 Laine
A southern England term for an open field.

288 Lammas Lands

The farmers of the open fields were entitled to graze their cattle on the common pasture from Lammas Day (August 1st now) until sowing time. The term could also apply to the arable land as well but more rarely.

289 Land
A Selion.

290 Lawn
A Selion.

291 Lease/Leaze
Commonland subject to the rights of pasturage of the tenants.

292 Linchet
A Balk.

293 Loon
A Selion.

294 Lot Meadow
A common meadow the portions of which were distributed annually by lot to the tenants of the related open-field strips. Alternatively called Rotation Meadow.

295 Marrows
A partnership in ploughing open field strips.

296 Mear/Meer/Mere
A Balk (qv), though usually meaning the more prominent kind, dividing fields or marking boundaries. Could also mean waste or poor land.

297 Ming Land
A midland term for land of different owners lying intermixed in the open fields.

298 Minnis
A south country term for a high common, or tract of moor.

299 Moss Rooms
A Cheshire term for strips of

peat moss fields held in common.

300 Noman's Land
A small piece of common land without an owner. Alternatively called Jack's Land.

301 Paull
A Selion (qv).

302 Playstow
A village green, mainly for recreation.

303 Pleck
Waste or common land.

304 Quillet
An open stretch of land farmed jointly by several farmers.

305 Rap .
A Selion (qv).

306 Rean
A Balk (qv); a thin, untilled strip between fields.

307 Ridge/Rig(g)
A Selion (qv).

308 Rig and Rennal
A Scottish term for an open-field system.

309 Rotation Meadow
See Lot Meadow

310 Score
A term used in Cheshire and Lancs to describe common pasture.

311 Selion
A cultivated strip in an open field, consisting of a ridge with a furrow on either side. Also called land, loon, paull, rap, ridge, rigg, shot, stetch and stitch.

312 Several
A piece of common assigned for a period to a particular occupier.

313 Sheath
A north country term for a group of strips in the open field.

314 Shifting Severalties
The system of changing the occupancy of portions of the common meadow by lot or rotation.

315 Shot
A Selion (qv).

316 Squatter
A person who encloses common land and builds without permission of the lord.

317 Stetch/Stitch
A Selion (qv)

318 Stint
The number of cattle which a holder of common right is allowed to put on to the common pasture. A term used in the south of England. In the north Gate is more. usual.

319 Stitch-meal
Land in separated pieces; groupings of stitches.

320 Strip Farming
See General section on Open-Field Farming (248).

321 Surcharge
To overstock the common pasture with cattle.

322 Tenantry Field
A commonly held field.

323 Tye
A south country term for a large common.

324 Wall
A Balk or Mere; a thin untilled strip of land between fields.

325 Wandale
A Yorkshire term for a strip of

an open arable field.

326 Ward
The closing of the common meadows so that sowing may begin.

327 Waste
Inferior land used commonally.

328 Wong
In the Scandinavian counties a furrow length in the open fields; alternatively, enclosed land among open strips.

Common Rights

329 Adjustment of Rights
As used in the Commons Act 1876, meant the determination of common rights and any modification of them.

330 Bote
The Old English term for the right to take material from the common lands for the tenant's use. The term was superseded by Estover (qv). See Firebote, Foldbote, Haybote, Housebote, Ploughbote, Cartbote.

331 Cartbote
The Old English term for the right to take wood from the commons to make or repair carts.

332 Cattlegait/Cattlegate
The right to graze a fixed number of beasts on the common or else on private land in which the owner of the beasts has no monetary interest. Each eligible tenant of the manor was given a fixed 'gate' on the common, that is, the number of beasts he was allowed to graze.
The word 'gate' was mainly used in the north; 'stint' was used in the south.
Alternatively called Beastgate, Cowgate, Horsegate, Kinegate, Oxgate, Sheepgate.

333 Common Appendant
The right to the use of a common that is attached to the occupancy of a piece of land. This arose frequently in the case of freehold tenants.

334 Common Appurtenant
The right to the use of a common based on possession of land or houses but not resting on actual tenure. This could extend over several lordships and was a right normally obtained by special grant. It could also allow the grazing of normally non-commonable animals such as pigs and goats.

335 Common in Gross
The right to the use of a common which was annexed to a man's person; it had no connection with his occupancy of house or land. This could apply to tenants in adjoining manors.

336 Common of Pasture
The right of pasturing cattle on the common land.

337 Common of Piscary
The right to fish in manorial waters.

338 Common of Shack
The right of tenants responsible for the yearly crop to turn their beasts on to the fields after the crop had been harvested.

339 Common of Turbary
The right to dig peat or turf for fuel on the common lands.

340 Common of Vicinage
Where two manors lie together and where the tenants have intercommoned, the permissive right to have one's cattle stray on to the other manor's land without molestation.

341 Commons
The right of pasturing beasts on the common land.

342 Cowgate
See Cattlegate.

343 Cow Leaze
In this context the right to pasture cattle on the common lands.

344 Driving
The annual right of the lord to examine the beasts pastured on the common lands to make sure that only those of his tenants with common rights are using the commons.

345 Estovers
The Norman-French term for the right to carry wood from the common lands for the repair of house and implements, and for fuel. Estover superseded the word bote.

346 Falcage
A Scottish term for the right of mowing.

347 Ferbote/Firebote
The Old English term for the right to take wood from the commons for fuel.

348 Foldbote
The Old English term for the right to take wood from the commons to make sheep folds.

349 Freedom
The right of pasturing cattle on the common lands.

350 Gait/Gate
See Cattlegait.

351 Haybote/Heybote/Hedgebote
The Old English term for the right to take wood from the commons to make or repair fences.

352 Horsegate

See Cattlegate

353 Housebote
The Old English term for the right to take wood from the commons to make or repair houses.

354 Levant and Couchant
The right of pasturing cattle on the common lands.

355 Ploughbote
The Old English term for the right to take wood from the common lands to make or repair ploughs.

356 Sheepgate
See Cattlegate.

357 Stint
See Cattlegate.

358 Stray
The right of allowing one's cattle to stray on to the common land.

Enclosure Legislation

359 1235 Statute of Merton
This authorised manorial lords to enclose portions of the waste provided that sufficient pasture was left for his tenants.

360 1285 Statute of Westminster
This authorised enclosure of manorial waste where the common rights belonged to tenants from other manors.

361 1607 — First private Enclosure Act
The first known private act dealt with some parishes in Herefordshire.

362 1760-1797 Enclosure Acts
During this period about 1500 private Enclosure Acts were passed through Parliament.

363 1801 — General Enclosure Act
Private Enclosure Acts were expensive and occupied a great deal

of Parliamentary time. This Act streamlined the procedure. The rate of enclosure was stimulated by the need to improve agriculture.

364 1836 — Enclosure by consent
Legislation allowed enclosure without private legislation if two-thirds of the interested parties agreed.

365 1845 — Enclosure Act
This authorised Enclosure Commissioners to consider applications for enclosure; their views were reported to Parliament. This legislation also gave the Commissioners the power to allocate land for 'exercise and recreation'.

366 1876 — Curtailment of enclosures
Legislation barred enclosure of common land unless the Enclosure Commissioners considered this to be of benefit to the community.

367 1899 — Commons Act
This authorised the care of commons by district councils if the lord of the manor, or tenants representing one-third in value of the common right holders, agreed.

368 1925 — Law of Property Act
This legislation gave the public right of access to any common or waste land in borough or urban districts.

369 1965 — Commons Registration Act
This Act required the registration of all common lands and village greens in England and Wales before January 2nd, 1970.

Part Four — Tenants and Tenures

370 Agist
Land let out in the summer to graze cattle at a fixed price per head.

371 Al(l)odium
A term to describe some estates in Hampshire, Kent, Surrey, Sussex and Berkshire. It is thought by some authorities that the description, found in Domesday Book, referred to holdings which were not subject to an overlord, and for which no services were given. Professor Maitland in his 'Domesday Book and Beyond' however, puts this theory in doubt and maintains that it has scant evidence.

372 Allotment
In this context, usually refers to land distributed by the Enclosure Commissioners in exchange for rights and holdings held in the open-field system. Can also mean land given to a parish or manor official.

373 Ancient Demesne
The manors which belonged to the Crown during the reigns of Edward the Confessor and William I; they are described as 'terrae regis (Eduardi)' in Domesday Book. The tenants were exempt from the jurisdiction of the shire reeve and were not liable to serve on juries and inquests outside the manor. They were not taxed for the upkeep of roads and bridges and were free from market tolls. The tenants could only be sued or sue on matters affecting their lands in the Court of Common Pleas or the Court of Ancient Demesne of the manor. Abolished 1925.

374 Basket Tenure
The tenant of this holding was required to make baskets for the Crown.

375 Bond Tenants

A name sometimes given to copy-holders or other customary tenants.

376 Bookland
A Saxon term for land held by title from the Crown. The tenants were probably exempt from a number of public services such as defence and bridge-building. Alternatively called Charter-land and Deed-land.

377 Borough English
A widespread form of tenure where it was customary for the youngest son to inherit. It was abolished in 1924.

378 Burgage
A tenure in an ancient borough which was held of the Crown or the lords of the borough. In Saxon times the rent was called a landgable or hawgable. The land or tenement was held subject to the customary rents and services of the borough.

It was sometimes called Burgage Holding in Scotland.

379 Charter Land
See Bookland.

380 Chivalry
An alternative name for a Knight's Fee (qv).

381 Copyhold
Originally a tenure dependent upon custom and the lord's will, and carrying with it obligations to perform certain services for the lord. The Black Death and the scarcity of labour hastened the prevalence of copyhold tenure with the services commuted to money payments. The tenant was protected not by national law but by title written into the court rolls. To transfer the property the tenant surrendered to the lord, who held the fee-simple, and who then admitted the new tenant. Copyhold tenure was abolished in 1926.

Alternatively called Tenancy by Copy and Tenancy by the Verge.

382 Cottier
An annual tenure, the main feature being that the land was let direct to a labourer who made the highest public bid for it.

383 Customary Freehold
Land held by custom and not by the will of the lord, by which it differed from Copyhold tenure (qv) and Leasehold. It was abolished in 1922. Alternatively called Frank Tenure.

384 Deed Land
See Bookland.

385 Demesne
Land of the manor held in the lord's own hands. The villein tenants, as part of their obligations in return for their holdings, had to work regularly on the demesne lands.

386 Farm
Before its modern agricultural meaning, it denoted land let on lease.

387 Fee
Land or freehold property which can be inherited.

388 Fee-Farm Rents
In this context, describes a group of Crown revenues, amongst which borough rents are the most significant. The chief residents of the borough would pay the Exchequer a fixed sum for the privilege of collecting the borough's revenues and retaining them.

389 Frankalmoin
Land granted by a layman to an ecclesiastical establishment which would acquire its income. Usually the gift was conditional upon the provision of a chantry after the

donor's death with obits and prayers being offered for his soul. The tenure was free of manorial services except for the Trinoda Necessitas (qv). Abolished in 1925.

390 Frank Fee
A tenure which required no services. Sometimes called an Improper Feud.

391 Frankmarriage
A tenure with an entailed interest. It arose in cases where a landowner granted land to the man marrying his daughter or sister. The couple possessed the land exempt from any services to the donor and this applied until the fourth generation had held the tenure.

392 Frank Tenement
See Freehold.

393 Freehold
A free tenure and not subject to the custom of the manor or the will of the lord. Its disposal after death was without restriction. Alternatively called Frank Tenement or Freeland.

394 Freeland
See Freehold.

395 Free Socage
See Socage.

396 Free Warren
A franchise obtained from the Crown empowering the grantees to kill game and beasts and also to preserve them.

397 Glebe
Land assigned to the Incumbent of a parish as part of his benefice and the endowment of the church.

398 In Capite

Tenant-in-Chief who held his land immediately of the Crown.

399 King's Widow
A widow of a Tenant-in-Chief (qv); she was unable to marry again without the Crown's permission.

400 Knight's Fee
A feudal tenure which obliged the holder to provide military assistance to the Crown. This military service would normally require a fully-armed knight and his servants for 40 days a year. The tenure was quite often commuted to a money payment, and finally abolished in 1660 by the Tenures Abolition Act.

401 Lay Fee
Land held of a lay lord as opposed to an ecclesiastical one.

402 Mesnalty
An estate held by a mesne lord, who held the land direct from the king and who was above other lords.

403 Mortmain
A term meaning dead hand, in this case, of the Church. Land held by ecclesiastical bodies and granted to them by laymen (see Frankalmoin), gave its tenants freedom from escheats and reliefs etc. This resulted in a financial loss to the manorial lords. The dead hand was thus on the potential income of the lords.
Henry III revised the Magna Carta in 1217 and prohibited the transfer of land to an ecclesiastical body without the lord's permission and further legislation in 1279 added penalties for causing land to come under Mortmain.

404 Overland
A west country term for a tenure which had no common rights.

405 Plight

A holding of land.

406 Purpresture

In theory an illegal tenure usually occurring when Crown lands were encroached upon. The offence could mean the forfeiture of the encroacher's land, but quite often the offence was merely noted and the general Eyre levied a rent or fine that was paid to the sheriff.

407 Reveland

Crown land in the hands of a sheriff, reeve, bailiff or other deputy.

408 Sac and Soc

A jurisdiction claimed by lords as part of their manorial tenure. It included a right to hold a court which the lord controlled, and to receive manorial profits and services.

409 Seisin

A term meaning possession rather than ownership. It probably dates from before the Norman Conquest and was amplified by Novel Disseisin (qv). A grant of land was only valid when the tenant had given the lord livery of seisin — usually a symbolic gift; a tenant was then 'seised in deed'. Before the gift, the heir to the land was 'seised in law'.

410 Seize

A freeholder was said to be seized of his land if he possessed it. He was disseized when dispossessed.

411 Serjeanty

A term covering tenures dependent upon a wide variety of services, some grand and some petty. Grand Serjeants did military service and paid fines; most serjeants performed personal services for their lord; the king, for example, might make serjeants of his tailor, physician or gamekeeper.

412 Severalty

Land held by an individual as opposed to land held in common.

413 Socage

A free tenure without the obligation of military service. The holding could be alienated by the tenant and inherited without restriction, although primogeniture gradually became common. The heir paid a fee for entry to the land. Socage was of two kinds: free socage, where the services were honourable and fixed, and villein socage where the services were of a humbler nature and fixed. Abolished 1660.

414 Tenancy at Will

A tenure granted by the lord and at his disposal. It was mainly used by the Crown to reward servants.

415 Tenant by Copy

See Copyhold.

416 Tenant by the Verge

See Copyhold.

417 Tenant-in-Chief

A tenant who held land immediately of the Crown. Alternatively called Tenant In Capite.

Part Five — The Transfer and Inheritance of Land

418 Conveyancing of Freehold Property

Freehold tenures were conveyed in earlier times by 'livery of seisin'. It was the custom for the vendor, before a witness, to hand over a piece of turf from the holding to the purchaser. It was unnecessary to mark the conveyance with a deed, called a Feoffment or Deed of Gift, but usual, and after 1677, compulsory.

A relief, (an entry fee), was payable by the purchaser to the Crown or feudal tenant-in-chief. To escape this it was common for the freeholder to convey the property to several people who, ostensibly, were the owners, but who held it for the use of the original freeholder. Theoretically the nominees could take the income from the land themselves, in which case the real owner could take them to the Court of Chancery.

This procedure caused a loss of revenue to the Crown and the Statute of Uses 1535 restricted it by making the original freeholder the actual owner and liable for the relief. In the same year the Statute of Enrolments made compulsory the enrolment of conveyances so as to prohibit secret conveyancing.

Alternatively, the freeholder could lease his land, usually for a year, to an occupier who had entered it by a deed of grant (a Release), holding for himself a future interest (a Reversion) which was an incorporeal hereditament, and which could be conveyed without livery of seisin.

Eventually a freeholder was able to sell his reversion to the purchaser without the necessity for a relief.

The Lease and Release procedure was in general use until 1841.

419 Conveyance of entailed land

There were two kinds of freehold tenure, the first being fee simple in which the owner could dispose of his property freely. The second kind was Fee Simple Conditional which restricted inheritance to a particular class of heirs, for example, male heirs. The owner could not sell his land until he had male heirs. In 1285 this kind of tenure was made entailed, and the owner was unable to sell it at all.

This situation led to fictitious legal actions so that entailed land could be sold.

Firstly, the proposed purchaser declared to the court that the vendor had agreed to convey the land and had failed to do so. On his part the vendor admitted that the land did belong to the prospective purchaser anyway. A fine was then made out, (a document detailing the conveyance), written three times, one part — the foot — retained by the court.

An alternative fictitious arrangement was the Common Recovery. The purchaser stated in court that he had been ejected from the vendor's land wrongfully by a fictitious third person. The vendor, appearing at court as the tenant, then called upon another person, a vouchee, who was said to be the owner of the land and who was there to vouch that the tenant (the actual vendor) was entitled to be there. It was then the custom for the plaintiff and the vouchee to withdraw from the court to negotiate, and for only the plaintiff to return. The vouchee was then deemed to be in contempt of court by his absence. Therefore the tenant had no evidence to support his title and the plaintiff was awarded the the estate in fee simple.

420 Conveyance of Copyhold Land

The conveyance of copyhold land had to be noted in the manor court rolls, although the conveyance need not necessarily have taken place in the manor court.

A copyholder 'surrendered' his property, and a mortgage of copyhold land was called a Conditional Surrender. In cases of mortgage the action was recorded in the court rolls but the mortgagee was not admitted to the land. On repayment of the mortgage a warrant of satisfaction was given to the mortgagor.

Terms

421 Alienation

The transfer of a holding by sale rather than by inheritance. A feudal tenant was unable to alienate without licence from the lord who would collect a fee for granting the transfer. If alienation took place without his permission he was empowered to seize the property until he gave his consent, upon which he could levy a fine as well.

Similarly a lord could not alienate his estate without licence from the Crown who also collected licence fees and fines for 'pardons'. The Crown appointed deputies to collect this revenue and, as a body, were known as the Alienation Office, the functions of which were eventually transferred to the Treasury.

422 Borough English

A custom whereby the youngest son was considered the rightful heir.

423 Conditional Surrender

A term usually applied to the mortgage of copyhold land.

424 Corporeal Hereditaments

Tangible estate such as land, buildings etc. as contrasted with Incorporeal hereditaments such as rights and privileges.

425 Curtesy of England

This allowed the widower to hold his deceased wife's land if they had a child still to attain his majority. The husband was allowed to retain the holding even if he remarried in the meantime.

426 Demise

A term to denote the transfer of a right or landholding, usually in the form of a lease.

427 Dower

Before the 12th century Dower meant the gift from a husband to his bride on the morning of their marriage. It later came to mean that part of the estate the widow had the right to claim for life or until her remarriage. This portion was usually one-third, and sometimes one-half.

A Dower House is the term for a house allocated to the widow.

428 Enfeoff

Either to put a tenant legally in possession of a holding, or to surrender a holding.

429 Escheat

The reversion to the lord or the Crown of an estate. This occurred when the tenant died without heirs, or where the heir had not yet attained his majority, or else where the tenant had committed a felony and forfeited his estate as a consequence.

The Crown appointed Escheators to collect any revenues from Escheats. These officers were introduced in 1195 mainly as a check on the sheriffs, and after a period of limited activity, they were later appointed for each county or group of counties.

Escheats were abolished in 1925.

430 Farleu/Farley

A money payment made instead of a Heriot (qv).

431 Feodary

An officer concerned with the inheritance of land.

432 Fine

A money payment made by a tenant to his lord on the transfer of property to him.

433 Freebench

A widow's dower in the case of copyhold (qv) land.

434 Gavelkind

A custom by which a tenant's

inheritance, other than the widow's dower which could be a half, was divided equally among his sons, or for want of sons among his daughters. This arrangement was most prevalent in Kent but was also known in Middlesex, Dorset and Wales.

The other main characteristics of the tenure were that a tenant was of age by 15, and the estate could not be escheated when the tenant was found guilty of a felony. It could only be escheated when there were no heirs.

Gavelkind was abolished in 1925.

435 Grasson/Grassum
A fine paid on the transfer of a copyhold estate.

436 Harrial
A Cumberland term for Heriot (qv).

437 Hereyeld
A Scottish term for Heriot (qv).

438 Heriot
An obligation, derived from Saxon times, on an heir to return to the lord the war apparel of the deceased tenant which had been originally supplied by the lord. The military gear, depending on the status of the tenant, included a horse, harness and weapons. This obligation applied to both freeman and villein. At about the time of the Norman Conquest the custom was being superseded by a tenant's heir giving his lord the best beast of the dead tenant, and later this became simply a money payment and, in effect, a fee to enter into the estate.

439 Incorporeal Hereditaments
See Corporeal Hereditaments.

440 Infeoff

See Enfeoff.

441 Inquisition Post Mortem
An inquiry into the possessions, services and succession of a deceased person who held land of the Crown

442 Last Heir
The person who received land by Escheat (qv). Usually the Crown or a lord.

443 Livery of Seisin
The infant heir of a tenant-in-chief (qv) of the Crown had to sue Livery of Seisin, in order to obtain possession of his father's estate.

444 Moiety
Usually a half-portion of an estate but not necessarily as much.

445 Mort D'Ancestor, Assize of
A system originating from the Assize of Northampton 1176, which ensured that lords admitted a tenant's heirs on the death of the tenant. At this time only close relatives were eligible to inherit automatically, but this was modified in the 13th century when more distant relations were entitled to plead at the Assize for admittance.

446 Primer Seisin
The right of the Crown to take from the heir of a tenant-in-chief one full year's profits if the heir were of full age.

447 Primogeniture
The system by which the eldest son, or his issue, was heir to the estate of his father to the exclusion of other brothers and sisters in cases of intestacy. This right was abolished in 1925.

448 Quia Emptores
A Statute passed in 1289/90

which ensured that land alienated by a lord of the manor was said to be held of the Crown.

449 Regrant
The term commonly used in court rolls where a lord gives back land to the heirs of a deceased tenant. This regranting was normally accompanied by some form of payment by the incoming tenant, such as a Relief (qv).

450 Relief
A payment made by an incoming tenant to succeed to his ancestor's land. In Saxon and early Norman times the term was generally used where land had military obligations attached, such as a Knight's Fee (qv). The payment varied with the size of the estate — eg. 100s for a Knight's Fee, or a year's rent for a smaller holding. The practice was abused by Crown and tenants-in-chief alike and eventually regulated in the Magna Carta. Reliefs were collected until 1661.

451 Soul Scot
An ecclesiastical heriot (qv). In some parishes after the lord had taken his heriot, usually the best chattel, the parish Church was entitled to take the second best chattel.

452 Surrender
A term commonly used to denote a yielding up of copyhold lands by alienation.

453 Wardship and Marriage
The Crown was entitled to hold the land of a tenant-in-chief upon his death if the heir had not attained a majority, (for a boy this was 21, for a girl 14, except in the case of a Gavelkind (qv) tenure), and to draw from its revenues. Quite often this wardship was farmed out to the highest bidder, sometimes leading to abuse and corruption of the estate management. The Crown was also entitled to control the marriage of a ward as well as that of the widow.

454 Widow Bench
See Dower.

Part 6 — Agricultural History

455

17th cent:	Potatoes, turnips and red clover introduced.
c1700	Jethro Tull's seed drill and horse hoes.
c1710	James Miekle's winnowing fans in Scotland.
1716	Turnips grown on large scale in Scotland.
1747	Sugar extracted from beet, in Germany.
1767	Francis Moore's steam engine for ploughing.
c1770	James Sharp's winnowing machine.
1786	Mangolds introduced from France.
1804	Guano introduced for fertilising.
1822	Rotary digging machine.
1836	Combine harvesters in USA.
1850	Horses work buttermaking churns.
1851	Reapers introduced.
1879	Mechanical separators for milk.
1880-95	Milking machines introduced.
1882	Bacillus of bovine TB discovered.
1886	Control of anthrax initiated.
1896	Bacillus of contagious abortion of cattle discovered.
1899	Oil-driven tractor introduced.
1910	King Edward potato introduced.

456 Agricultural Organisations

1774	Bath and West of England Agricultural Society.
1791	Veterinary College in London.
1793	Board of Agriculture.
1798	Smithfield Show.
1822	Board of Agriculture wound up.
1833	Royal Jersey Agricultural and Horticultural Society.
1838	English Agricultural Society, later the Royal Agricultural Society of England.
1842	Farmers' Club.
1843	Rothamsted Experimental Station.
1845	Royal Agricultural College at Cirencester.
1872	National Agricultural Labourers' Union.
1878	English Jersey Cattle Society.
1889	New Board of Agriculture
1907	National Cattle Breeders' Association.
1908	Lincs Farmers' Union which within a year was to develop into the National Farmers' Union.
1909	British Friesian Cattle Society.
1919	Board of Agriculture becomes Ministry of Agriculture.

Part 7 — Houses and Farm Buildings

457 Ancient Messuage

Theoretically a house erected before the time of legal memory, that is before the reign of Richard I. However, it was used quite commonly to describe houses built before living memory.

458 Barn

Originally meant barley-house and derived from the OE word 'bern'.

459 Bield

A stone shelter in the fields; a Yorkshire term.

460 Biggin

A Scottish and north of England term for a rough house or cottage.

461 Booth

A northern and Scottish term for a cow-house.

462 Bottle

A northern term for a house.

463 Bow

A northern and Scottish term for a house or cattle fold.

464 Capital Messuage

A large house.

465 Claybiggin

A widespread term for a rough cottage or hut made of clay and wood.

466 Cob/Cot House

A cottage built of clay and straw (cob).

467 Cote

A cottage or hut. In northern counties a term for an animal shed. An isolated farm house.

468 Courtledge

A west-country term for the yard and outbuildings of a house.

469 Curtilage

A widespread term for the yard and outbuildings of a house.

470 Erding

A Middle Ages term for a dwelling. Also spelt Earding.

471 Garth
A yard or enclosure.

472 Garthstead
A house and its land.

473 Hallhouse
A dwelling.

474 Lathe
A widespread term for a barn.

475 Messuage
A house, its outbuildings and yard and, in some instances, the garden as well.

476 Onstead
A northern term for a group of farm buildings.

477 Tallet
A stable loft; a widespread southern term for the space beneath a roof that has no ceiling.

478 Toft
A house or the land where one has stood. Common rights might still attach to the house even though it had long disappeared.

479 Town Place
The buildings and cottages belonging to a farm.

Part 8 — Miscellaneous

480 1285 Statute of Winchester
This Statute stipulated that the wall or fence of a park should be 200ft. from the king's highway and that the intermediate area be cleared of bush and undergrowth so that ambush was made more difficult.

481 1589 Legislation on Cottages
It was enacted that no cottage could be built for a land labourer unless it possessed 4 acres of land — this area assessed as being sufficient to provide sustenance for one family.

In addition, a family in such a cottage was not allowed to give board and lodging to people other than family, and neither could a cottage be divided into two tenements.

This legislation was repealed in 1775.

482 1778 Catholic Relief Acts
Roman Catholics were allowed, after taking the Oath of Allegiance, to own land once more.

483 Historic Buildings Preservation
The first legislation to protect ancient buildings or structures was the Ancient Monuments Protection Act 1882, and this was amplified in 1900. In 1918 the Ancient Monuments Consolidation and Amendment Act set up advisory boards for England, Wales and Scotland and these published their first lists in 1921.

The Historic Buildings and Ancient Monuments Act 1933 empowered the Ministry of Works to issue interim preservation notices on the recommendation of his Ancient Monument Boards.

In 1944 the Town and Country Planning Act began a system by which the Ministry of Town and Country Planning prepared lists of historic buildings for local authorities and classified the buildings in grades of importance.

Those grades are:

Grade 1: of such great value and interest that in no circumstances should demolition be allowed.

Grade 2: not to be demolished without very good reason.

Grade 3: generally applies to more modest buildings.

The Local Authority (Historic Buildings) Act 1962 enabled local authorities to make grants for the upkeep of historic buildings whether graded or not.

SECTION B

THE LOCAL COMMUNITY AND ITS ADMINISTRATION

Part 1 — Types of Area and Administration

Part 2 — Local officials

Part 3 — Classes of Society

Part 4 — Manor Customs and Procedures

Part 5 — Borough Charters

Part 6 — Local Government Franchise

Part One — Types of Area and Administration

1 Bailiwick
An area under the jurisdiction of a bailiff.

2 Barmote
A Derbyshire court which managed the affairs of the lead mines.

3 Barony
The Irish equivalent of the English Hundred (qv). Baronies existed before the Norman Conquest and were small kingdoms that later became divisions of counties in medieval times.

4 Bedellary
An area under the supervision of a beadle.

5 Berewick
A wick (qv) in which barley was grown. A subsidiary or outlying estate.

6 Borough
Up to 1835 most boroughs had achieved their status by charter, mainly in the 16th and 17th centuries, although others may have obtained their charter in medieval times from the Crown or a baron. Each borough usually had the right to levy a toll at the market, to send a representative to the House of Commons, and to hold a court which dealt with civil and some criminal matters.

The control of a borough lay, quite often, in a self-perpetuating body, filling vacancies by co-option. This meant that power lay with the land-owning, Church of England classes.

The Municipal Corporations Act 1835 laid down that councillors were to be elected for three years with aldermen elected by the councillors for six years. The vote was given to ratepayers who had lived in the borough for three years. This legislation applied to 178 boroughs. Additional corporations, including Manchester and Birmingham, were established by the Crown later. Legislation was refined and consolidated by the Municipal

Corporations Act 1882.

7 Burgh
The Scottish equivalent of the English Borough, having its own charter. A Burgh could be royal, or owe its charter to a lord of regality or to a baron. Up to 1832 only royal burghs could return members to Parliament.

8 Burh
An Old English word for a fortified area — either a town or dwelling.

9 Byelaw
A north country term for a district having its own byelaw court.

10 Cantrev
The Welsh equivalent of the English Hundred (qv). In its turn it was divided into Commote, Maenol, Trev and Gavel.

11 Castelry
In medieval times an area which was organised for the protection of its castle.

12 Churchtown
A west country term for a town, village or hamlet, which contained a church.

13 Clachan
In Scotland and Ireland a village containing a church.

14 Close Parish
A term to describe a parish which took particular care to bar itinerant strangers from obtaining settlement certificates there. Under the Poor Law regulations once a settlement was granted the person could, if necessary, apply for support from the parishioners.

15 Close Vestry
See Select Vestry

16 Colonia
There were four Coloniae in Roman Britain — Colchester, Gloucester, Lincoln and York. They were centres in which retired Roman soldiers were given land as a pension. A Colonia had full Roman citizenship, a privilege not given to a native township

17 Constablewick
A township or tithing under the jurisdiction of a constable.

18 Cot-town
A small village containing residents dependent on the main local farm.

19 County
The term County, via the French comte, was introduced by the Normans, eventually replacing the Old English 'shire'. Many shires had followed the boundaries of the Old English kingdoms and provinces. In the 8th and 9th centuries Wessex was divided into shires, Mercia in the 10th century.

Most of the other shires were formed by the time of the Conquest; six counties were created after then, London being the last in 1888.

Wessex included Hants, Wilts, Berks, Somerset and Dorset and perhaps also parts of Oxon.

Mercia at one time included Derby, Glos, Leics, Northants, Notts, Rutland, Staffs, Warks and Worcs and perhaps also parts of Beds, Bucks and Oxon.

Norfolk and Suffolk are divisions of the old East Anglian kingdoms. Sussex, Essex, Kent and Middlesex were Teutonic kingdoms, and Yorkshire roughly corresponds to the Danish kingdom of York. Cumberland was Cumbria (land of the Welsh), Northumberland a part of the old kingdom of Northumbria.

Durham was granted to St Cuthbert in 685 and held by bishops as a palatine from the Conquest to

Welsh counties were created under Henry VIII

Cheshire was a Roman province. Lancashire was the Honor of Lancaster. In 1071 the northern part was in Yorkshire, the southern was crown property in the time of Edward the Confessor. Westmorland, under the Normans, was held as two baronies each divided into two wards

Rutland was a soke in Northamptonshire given as dower to the Queen of England in John's reign. Monmouth became an English county in 1535.

The Scottish counties in the Lowlands were established by Malcolm III in the 11th century, and those in the Highlands between the 16th and 17th centuries. The Welsh counties, in their present form, were created under Henry VIII.

Each county was in the charge of a peer or great landowner who usually combined the office of Lord Lieutenant and Keeper of the Records (custos rotulorum). Beneath him was the High Sheriff appointed by the Crown.

The High Sheriff entrusted the bulk of his work to a professional Under-Sheriff who was usually reappointed by each new Sheriff. The Under-Sheriff was also the County Clerk.

Until 1832 each English county returned 2 members to Parliament except Yorkshire which, since 1521, had returned 4. The Reform Act 1832 readjusted representation to allow for population changes. Welsh counties had, since their formation, returned one member.

20 County Councils

These were established by the Local Government Act 1888. The administrative functions of Quarter Sessions were transferred to them.

21 Court Baron

A manorial court which enforced the customs of the manor. It was part of the property of the lord and was a private jurisdiction. Originally the Homage or Jury had to consist of at least two or three freeholders as a minimum, but with the decline of this form of tenure, copyhold tenants formed the Homage and the Court Baron became a Customary Court Baron.

The main business of the Court consisted of escheats (qv), surrenders of land, dower administration, the use of the common fields and wastes, and the related rights of lord and tenants.

The Court appointed a reeve and beadle who were responsible for collecting the lord's dues, (amongst other things), a hayward to look after the commons, and at times, minor posts such as a woodward, swineherd and common driver.

The Court was presided over by the lord or his steward. The names of those owing suit were read out, those with apologies for absence — essoins — noted, and those without sufficient excuse for absence were fined. The Homage was sworn in and business proceeded. The decisions were recorded on Court rolls.

22 Court Leet

This usually refers to a manorial court although it also applied to some Hundred courts. It dealt with petty offences such as common nuisances, highway or ditch disrepair, breaking the Assize of Bread and Ale etc. Indictable offences went to the Assizes.

It was a court of record and a public jurisdiction. It was presided over by the lord or his steward. Each male over the age of 12 in some places and 16 in others, with a residence of one year and a day, was obliged to attend although, in practice, only the main tenants and especially the Chief Pledges (qv) attended.

The Court met, in theory, twice a year, and as well as considering allegations of offences, elected the constable, aletaster, pinder and any other minor officials to enforce the bye-laws the Court was empowered to make. It appointed two affeerers who fixed the penalty for any proved offence.

The Court also included the View of Frankpledge (qv).

Alternatively called Halmot Court, Soke Court, Forest Court, Lawday and Swainmoot.

23 District Councils

These were established by the Local Government Act 1894. Counties were divided into county boroughs and District Councils, either urban or rural.

24 Extra-Parochial

An area outside the jurisdiction of the adjoining civil or ecclesiastical parish. It therefore paid no poor or church rates, and usually no tithes. In theory the tithe money went to the Crown instead. In 1894 all Extra-Parochial areas were made into parishes or incorporated into existing ones.

25 Fief

An area held by grant from a superior. A manor or fee (qv).

26 Field Jury

In some manors a jury was elected to manage the usage of the common fields.

27 Fifteen

A Select Vestry (qv).

28 Five Boroughs

The headquarters of the Danish armies in the 9th century. They consisted of Derby, Lincoln, Nottingham, Leicester and Stamford, the first four of which gave their names to shires (which are referred to as Danelaw counties). There is also evidence to suggest that Torksey and York were additional garrison towns. The Five Boroughs formed a federation with a general assembly as its court.

29 Frankpledge

Under the Saxons each vill or area was divided into associations of tithings — ten men. The members of each tithing were bound to stand security for the others' good behaviour. This system was called Frankpledge. The View of Frankpledge, the actual inspection by the authorities to make sure that it existed, was held, after the Conquest, at the twice-yearly Sheriff's Tourn, but later almost always at the manorial Court Leet (qv).

Some areas, such as Westmorland, did not adopt the system, and some classes of society — knights and clerks for example, were exempt. Inhabitants were bound to produce offenders or they would themselves be liable to make good any damage. Those people who had no such local surety had to find their own.

Representatives of tithings were called tithingmen, headboroughs, thirdboroughs and borsholders.

Collective responsibility for apprehending offenders was a dominant part of English life until the development of police forces, and was reinforced by the Hue and Cry system (qv).

30 Gemote

A Saxon term meaning a court or assembly.

31 Green Village

A village in which the houses are grouped around a common village green, as opposed to a village along a central road.

32 Halmot/Hallmote/Hallmoot

A Court Baron or Court Leet

(qv).

33 Ham
A house or village. Hamlet is the diminutive.

34 Hamil
A north country term for hamlet or village.

35 Hamlet
A small village, usually without a church and under the jurisdiction of, and in the same parish as, another village or town. It had neither a constable nor an overseer and did not levy a separate rate.

36 Hardwick
A pastoral settlement.

37 Home
A Shropshire term for a parish consisting of several hamlets.

38 Honor
A grouping of several knight's fees (qv), lordships or manors, under the administration of a lord and honorial court. The court consisted of the honorial barons who were the chief under-tenants. This grouping normally occurred around a castle, but in some cases the land could be widely scattered around England. Royal honors were still to be found in the 16th century.

39 Hundred
1) A division of a shire especially important in Saxon and Norman times. There are several theories still held as to its origin. One is that it consisted of a hundred families, or ten tithings. Another is that it was an amount of land which contained 100 geld hides.
The Hundred was probably established in the 10th century. Its court was presided over by the Hundred Reeve acting on behalf of the King. The court meetings, held monthly, usually began in the open

air at a place distinguished by some feature such as a boundary stone, barrow, tree or cross roads. The court, consisting of freeholders, considered criminal and minor ecclesiastical matters and private pleas. It also levied taxes.

The influence of the Hundred declined from medieval times as parochial and manorial administration became stronger, and the Justices of the Peace increased their status. As a unit of government it formally existed until late in the 19th century. The Local Government Act 1894 set up district councils which are the successors to the Hundred Courts.

Alternatively called Wapentakes in the Danelaw counties, Lathes in Kent, Rapes in Sussex, Leets in East Anglia and Wards in Cumberland, Westmorland, Durham and Northumberland.

Hundred names and areas are detailed in the Victoria County History series and their derivations in the English Place Names series.

2) A division of a Wapentake in Derbyshire, Leicestershire, Lincolnshire and Nottinghamshire (Danelaw counties), or a division of a Lathe (a Hundred) in Kent.

40 Husting
Now used in connection with meetings before a parliamentary election, although Old English Hustings had some legal business to pursue. As a form of administration the word is preserved in the City of London's Court of Husting which was established before the Conquest. This was in the nature of a county court. Similar courts, which recorded deeds and wills, existed elsewhere eg. Boston and Winchester.

41 Joclet
A Kent term for a small manor or farm.

42 Kintra

A Scottish term for a region or district.

43 Kirk Clachan/Kirktoun
A Scottish village containing a church.

44 Knight's Fee
An area held by a knight for which he was obliged to give military service to his immediate overlord.

45 Lady Court
The court of a lady of the manor.

46 Lathe
In Kent an administrative area equivalent to the Hundred (qv). Confusingly it was itself divided into Hundreds. In Norman times there were six Lathes but this was later reduced to five.

47 Lawday
See Court Leet

48 Leet
See Court Leet.

49 Liberty
1) An area situated outside the borough in which the freemen had certain rights of pasture etc.

2) A group of manors, the lord of which held certain privileges granted by the Crown. The sheriff's authority was excluded and the lord had the return of writs.

3) In the Isle of Wight another name for a Hundred (qv).

50 Lordship
A manorial holding.

51 Manor
The land held by a lord. The various types of tenure allowed for a wide variety of customs, rights and obligations in each manor. The lord was usually empowered to hold a Court Baron (qv), or failing that a Customary Court Baron, and also a Court Leet (qv). The manor could be a subdivision of a parish but could also spread over two parishes.

52 Moot
An assembly of people which formed a legislative court, especially important in Saxon times. There were gemots, witangemots, burg-motes, hundred-motes etc.

53 Open Parish
As opposed to a Close Parish (qv), one in which it was relatively easy for a stranger to obtain a settlement certificate.

54 Open Vestry
A general meeting of all rate-paying inhabitants to take decisions which affected the organisation of the parish. This is in contrast to a Select Vestry (qv) where power, undemocratically, was vested in a few, or to a modern borough council where affairs are managed by representatives of those entitled to vote.

Open Vestries in large urban areas in the 19th century became unmanageable and liable to mob leadership. Some took advantage of the powers allowed in the Surges Bourne Act 1819, and elected a Parish Committee which, confusingly, was often called a Select Vestry.

55 Palatinate
An area administered by an earl or a bishop.

56 Parish
Originally the area served by a parson from the parish church, and to whom it paid its tithes and other ecclesiastical dues.

Successive Acts of Parliament, especially in the 16th and 17th centuries, promoted the parish as an area for secular administration, gradually superseding the manorial courts which fell into decay except in respect of their right to regulate the transfer and inheritance of estates. At times there was an overlapping of powers between parish vestries and manor courts.

The Parish vestry had always been able to levy a church rate and it was a logical step for it to impose a rate for other social purposes. With the relief of the poor and the management of highways made over to them, the parish took over any remaining responsibilities in these fields still held by the manors.

Parishes did not necessarily follow the manorial boundaries; sometimes even the county boundaries were crossed. Furthermore, just as some parishes contained several townships, each with their own customs, so did some boroughs contain several parishes. The arrangements were confused, the power distribution depending on local factors.

The Vestry appointed parish officers such as churchwardens, sexton etc., but the choice of Overseer of the Poor, Surveyor of Highways and Constable was not theirs, although in many parishes they recommended names for these posts which could hardly be refused by the Justices of the Peace. Obligation to serve as a parish officer was constantly avoided by money payments or by devices such as the Tyburn Ticket (qv).

The significance of the parish as a local government authority came to an end in the 19th century with reforms which created municipal and county boroughs and rural councils. Parish councils, established by the Local Government Act 1894, still exist and have limited adoptive powers.

57 Parish Councils

Parish Councils were established under the Local Government Act 1894. Councils were to be elected in rural areas with a population of over 300. In parishes where the population numbered between 200 and 300 a council could be elected if a parish meeting decided so. In areas with an even smaller population a council could be elected if the county council agreed.

Each rural parish was required to have a parish meeting at least once a year.

58 Part
See Riding.

59 Port
In the Old English period, a market town whether on the coast or inland.

60 Quarter
A section of a parish divided for administrative purposes in the implementation of the Poor Law regulations. This division usually occurred in the larger parishes.

61 Rape
The Sussex equivalent of a Hundred (qv). There were six Rapes each with a castle and a harbour. It was a unit of local government and assessed for taxation.

62 Regality
A Scottish term for a territorial jurisdiction granted by the Crown.

63 Reguard
A forest court held every three years to safeguard the bounds of a forest and the Crown's rights in it. It consisted of 12 knights and their findings were reported to the Justices.

64 Riding
A third of a shire, from the Old Norse 'thrithing'. Yorkshire was divided into Ridings by the Danes and they each had their town courts which were intermediate between the shire and the wapentake (qv). A similar division took place in Lincolnshire where the thirds are

known as Parts or Divisions.

65 Royalty
A Scottish and north of England term for an area under the jurisdiction of the Crown. An example of this would be a royal palace and its estate.

66 Seigniory
A lord's holding of land, usually a manor.

67 Seigniorial Borough
A borough which received its charter from an earl or lord, and not from the Crown.

68 Select Vestry
1) The governing body of a parish, not elected by the parishioners, but perpetuating itself by co-option. It acted, as far as the national government was concerned, on behalf of its parish, but these spokesmen were not in any way answerable to the parishioners.

The Close Vestries, as they were sometimes called, were of several kinds. Some claimed their authority from custom, others were created by Church Building Acts or Local Acts of Parliament in the 19th century when new parishes were devised to cope with areas in which the population had outgrown the old parish facilities

The Select Vestry generally had 12 to 24 members, appointed for life. It performed the usual functions of the Open Vestry; it elected churchwardens, managed the financial affairs of the parish and its property, and collected the rates.

In common with an Open Vestry it had the same ambiguous relationship to the Justices of the Peace as three of the most important parish officers were appointed, usually on the Vestry's recommendation, by the Justices.

Alternatively called: Masters of the Parish, Twelve, Fifteen, Sixteen, Company of Four and Twenty, Ancients, Elders, Twenty and Gentlemen.

69 Shire
See County.

70 Soke
A Danelaw county term for a jurisdiction over a number of estates and villages. (There were 32 such townships in the Soke of Peterborough). It is thought that the townships were settled by Danish soldiers who owed personal allegiance to a lord and a court. The land of any particular Soke could be in a number of manors which meant that some villages and farms were under divided lordship. The Soke was the lord's private jurisdiction and he was entitled to hold a Soke Court. His tenants were freemen.

The word was also generally used for a private jurisdiction, whether owned by barons, religious houses or gilds.

71 Swainmoot
See Court Leet.

72 Swanimote
A forest court which met three times a year to arrange for the use of the Crown's woodland.

A fortnight before Michaelmas it would regulate the pasturing of pigs; about St Martin's Day it would meet to collect dues for this. It also met just before Midsummer when the forest was closed while the beasts fawned.

73 Team/Theam
A Crown grant to the lord of the manor to have jurisdiction over the punishment of offenders within his manor.

74 Tithing

A group of ten men who stood security for each other. In Saxon to medieval times every man over the age of 12 was obliged to be a member.

75 Township
A vague term denoting a group of houses which formed a unit of local administration. Generally the term was superseded, after the Conquest, by Vill (qv).

76 View of Frankpledge
See Frankpledge.

77 Vill
A settlement which could be a parish, manor or tithing.

78 Wick
A village, or else a marsh. In areas where salt was obtained by evaporation of water in bays the word came to be used in place names, as in Droitwich etc.

Part Two — Local Officials

79 Affeerers
Officers, (usually two), appointed by a manorial court to fix the penalties for proven offences.

80 Agister
A royal forest official who received payment for the pannage of commoners' pigs. In the New Forest this title survives as an officer in charge of the ponies etc.

81 Alderman
In its modern sense, one who governs a local authority whether county or borough, together with the mayor, chairman and councillors. See also Ealdorman

82 Aletaster

A manorial official who tested the quality of ale and beer sold within the manor. He was responsible for ensuring that these commodities were sold to the proper weight and measure. He was the forerunner of the Inspector of Weights and Measures. Alternatively called Alefounder or Aleconner.

83 Almanac Man
A Lincolnshire officer, appointed by the Court of Sewers, who was responsible for warning inhabitants near the Trent when high tides were expected.

84 Amen Clerk
A Parish Clerk (qv).

85 A(u)lnager
An officer in a port or market town responsible for ensuring that any cloth sold was woven to the correct length and width as laid down by statute. He stamped approved cloth with the town seal.

86 Bailiff
One of the lord's representatives, beneath the rank of Steward.

87 Bang-Beggar
See Beggar-Banger

88 Beadle
A parish officer with duties varying in each locality. At times he was a messenger, town crier, assistant to the constable, common driver or mace bearer. His origin was probably that of bidding people to parish meetings and quite often had a special dress together with a whip or 'wand' which was not only a symbol of his authority but enabled him to drive dogs from the vestry meetings.
Alternatively called Beadman. Beagle, Bydel, Bedell.

89 Bedman

A west country term for a sexton.

90 Bedral
A minor church official in Scotland who would be a Clerk, beadle or sexton.

91 Beggar-Banger
A parish officer responsible for controlling the length of stay of any stranger. In some places he was synonymous with the constable or beadle.

Alternatively called Bang-Beggar.

92 Bellman
A town crier.

93 Besswarden
An officer appointed by the parish to look after its beasts.

94 Boonmaster
See Surveyor of Highways.

95 Borsholder
See Constable.

96 Bozzler
A southern term for a sheriff's officer or a parish constable.

97 Burleyman
A manorial officer appointed to enforce byelaws, but could also be a petty constable or tithingman (qv). Alternatively called Bylawman.

98 Chief Pledge
See Constable.

99 Churchman
See Churchwarden.

100 Churchmaster
See Churchwarden.

101 Church Reeve
See Churchwarden.

102 Churchwarden
A parish post of great antiquity. He was elected by the vestry, usually on Easter Tuesday. He was a temporal officer and although the Archdeacon later swore him in he had no power to disallow the appointment. The Churchwarden had many duties, some specific to a particular period in history. They included:

a) custodian of the parish property and income.

b) representing the parishioners in matters of collective obligations and in any collective action they might wish to take.

c) the upkeep of the church fabric.

d) providing the facilities and allocating pews for worship.

e) ensuring that parishioners attended church regularly and brought their children for baptism.

f) attending the Archdeacon's court.

g) accounting for the expenditure of the church rate.

h) helping to keep the parish register.

i) reporting, if necessary, on any failing in duty by the Incumbent.

j) supervising the education and relief of the poor.

k) arranging for the burial of unknown strangers and the baptism of foundlings.

l) caring for the parish arms and paying the soldiers.

m) being responsible for the extinction of vermin.

n) presenting offences within the cognizance of the church courts.

Parishes appointed at least two churchwardens and sometimes four. Frequently there would be one to represent each of the townships, vills or manors in the parish, although the authority of any one of the wardens would extend over the entire parish — unlike the constable who had authority only in his own manor.

Alternatively called Churchman, Churchmaster, Church Reeve, Kirkmaster.

103 Clapman
A town crier.

104 Collector
The suppression of the monasteries in 1547 and the lack of any consistent substitute method for helping the poor obliged some parishes to appoint Collectors of the parish alms. Their necessity was emphasised by the first Poor Law Act of Elizabeth in 1563 which enacted that 'two able persons or more shall be appointed gatherers and collectors of the charitable alms of all the residue of the people inhabiting in the parish'.

The Collectors had to account to the parish meetings each quarter. A fine of twenty shillings was imposed on any parishioner who refused to act in this post. The office was combined with that of Overseer of the Poor in 1597/8.

105 Constable
It is thought that the office of Constable is more ancient than that of Churchwarden. While the manorial courts were strong he was appointed by the Courts Leet (qv) but later the vestries made the nominations and the Justices of the Peace confirmed the appointments. In some places the Justices were entirely responsible for the appointments. The Vestries officially received this responsibility in 1842.

A Constable appointed by the Leet had authority only in that Leet's manor; in the rest of the parish other constables were responsible.

His duties, some for certain periods of history, included:

a) supervising the provision of Watch and Ward (qv) as specified by the Statute of Winchester 1285.

b) ensuring the upkeep of local means of punishment and imprisonment, such as stocks and cage.

c) inspecting alehouses and suppressing gaming-houses.

d) apprenticing pauper children.

e) supervising the settlement or removal of itinerant strangers and beggars.

f) seeing to the welfare of the poor.

g) collecting the county rate and acting as agent for the collection of special national taxes.

h) managing the parish economy.

i) supervising the military arms supply and the provision of training for the local militia.

j) convening parish meetings.

k) assisting the churchwarden in presenting those parishioners who did not attend church regularly.

l) caring for the parish bull.

m) helping at shipwrecks in coastal areas.

Generally the position of constable was not welcomed by parishioners whose turn it was to be appointed. There was a widespread practice of paying someone else to do the job.

An Act of 1662 empowered the Constable to levy a local rate to meet his expenses.

Alternatively called Borsholder, Bozzler, Chief Pledge, Headborough, Petty Constable, Thirdborough, Tithingman, Verderer.

106 Coroner
The office dates back to the late 12th century for certain, and possibly before that. He had a number of duties which included inquests, treasure trove, deodands etc., but his main task now is to hold inquests. He was a royal officer and gradually developed into a county official. Up to the Local Government Act 1888 he was appointed by the freeholders of the county, but at this date his appointment was put in the hands of the county council.

107 Countour

In the 13th and 14th centuries the officer who helped to collect and audit the county rates.

108 Decimer
See Dozener.

109 Distributor
An assistant to the Overseer of the Poor (qv).

110 Dozener
In some old boroughs he was elected by the householders of each street to represent them at the borough's Court Leet (qv). Also called Decimer.

111 Ealdorman
A royal official, sometimes related to the king, who presided over civil matters at the old shire courts. He was the chief personage in the county or group of counties in which he acted as the king's deputy. In Cnut's time he received the 'earl's penny', a third penny from the judicial profits of the shire court.

After the Norman Conquest the term became gradually shortened to Earl and became more a title than a position. His administrative functions were largely taken over by the Sheriff (qv).

112 Factor
A Scottish term for the steward of an estate responsible for the management and collection of the rents of the land.

113 Field Master
A manorial officer who managed the collective use of the common fields. He was sometimes synonymous with the Hayward or the Reeve.

Alternatively called Fieldman, Field Reeve, Foreman of the Fields, Messor.

114 Gauger
An officer responsible for assessing and collecting excise duty.

115 Guardians of the Poor
Boards of Guardians of the Poor were established by the 1834 Poor Law Amendment Act which compulsorily amalgamated parishes into 'unions' to provide for the poor. The Guardians were the local instrument for Poor Law administration. They were required to have a property qualification and were elected by voters who also needed a local property qualification. The Guardians were abolished in 1929.

116 Franklin
A steward or bailiff.

117 Hayward
An officer, appointed by the manor, vill or parish, to supervise the good repair of fences and enclosures so that cattle should not stray on to the common fields. He looked after the common stock and impounded stray cattle, putting them in the care of the Pinder (qv) if there was one.

In some parishes the Hayward acted as Field Master (qv), supervising the agriculture of the common fields.

Alternatively called Hedge-looker.

118 Headborough
The head person in the Frankpledge (qv) or tithing. A constable or deputy constable.

119 Hedge-looker
See Hayward.

120 High Constable
An officer of the Hundred (qv) responsible for law and order and the performance of the petty constables. He was appointed by the Court Leet of the Hundred, or by the Justices of the' Peace. His appointment is dealt with by the Statute of Winchester 1285 but it is

clear that the office was already in existence.

Alternatively called Hundred Constable.

121 Hogringer

An officer appointed by the manor Court Leet and responsible for ensuring that all pigs using the common had rings through their noses to prevent them rooting up the turf. He had power to impound pigs which were not so treated and to charge for ringing them subsequently.

122 Hundred Constable

See High Constable.

123 Incumbent

The Incumbent's influence depended upon the strength of the vestry as opposed to the manor courts. Generally speaking, although the Government required him to keep the parish registers, make recommendations on fit people to run alehouses, countersign constables' reports etc., he was not required to be too involved in the civil administration. He was automatically on the vestry and, by custom, in the chair.

124 Kirkmaster

1) A churchwarden. Alternatively called a Kirkwarden.

2) In some parishes indicates a Select Vestryman. (See Vestryman).

125 Lord Lieutenant

The Lord Lieutenant was a crown appointment, at first known merely as a Lieutenant in Tudor times. His main concern was with the county militia but in many ways was the principal officer of the county. He assumed the office of Custos Rotulorum — the keeper of the records, for the county. His duties nowadays are mostly of a ceremonial nature.

126 Master of the Parish

A Select Vestryman.

127 Mayor

The first Mayor was probably that of London, in 1191. By the middle of the 13th century it was general for boroughs to appoint one. His powers were governed by the provisions of the borough charters.

Legislation in 1835 and 1882 relieved mayors of many of their executive duties. An Act of 1882 allowed the appointment of a deputy mayor.

128 Mayor's Brethren

A body of 24 Aldermen governing a town together with 48 other residents who formed a Common Council.

129 Meresman

A parish officer appointed to maintain the boundaries of the parish, but could also be involved in the upkeep of roads, bridges and waterways.

130 Messor

See Field Master.

131 Moss Reeve

A bailiff who received and dealt with claims for land on swamps and mossy areas.

132 Murenger

A Shropshire and Cheshire term for an officer appointed to supervise the upkeep of city walls.

133 Mysgather

A tax collector.

134 Myslayer

An assessor of taxes.

135 Neatherd

A cowherd appointed by the community to prevent cattle straying.

136 Overseer of the Highways
See Surveyor of the Highways.

137 Overseer of the Poor
This office was established by the Poor Law Act 1597/8 and made obligatory by the Poor Relief Act 1601. It superseded the less formal office of Collector (qv).

At least two persons were appointed yearly by each vestry with approval from the Justices of the Peace where necessary, to levy a poor rate and to supervise its distribution.

The duties of the Overseers were given to the Guardians of the Poor in 1834 and the Overseers became just assessors and collectors. The office was abolished by the Rating and Valuation Act 1925.

138 Parish Clerk
The post was a temporal one although he would normally be appointed by the Incumbent and quite frequently, in earlier times, be in holy orders himself. A Parish Clerk could arrange for baptisms and communions, act as sexton, ring the church bell for service and even lead the responses at services.

He was paid from the church funds and was normally appointed for life.

139 Parker
An officer responsible for the care of the game on 'imparked' land.

140 Pavior
A man paid by a town to see to the upkeep of the paving stones.

141 Petty Constable
See Constable.

142 Pinder/Pinfold
A manorial or parish officer in charge of the pound or pinfold into which stray animals were put, and later released on payment of a fine.

Alternatively called Poundkeeper, Punder.

143 Ponderator
An early inspector of weights and measures, especially in market towns.

144 Poundkeeper
See Pinder.

145 Precentor
A Yorkshire term for an officer responsible for the upkeep of public footpaths.

146. Provost
An official, elected by the manor, and responsible for the husbandry. Walter of Henley's 13th century 'Husbandrie' remarks that he 'must cause all the hairs of the avers (cattle) to be gathered to make ropes, and have hemp sown in the court for wagon-ropes, harness etc., allowance paid for anyone who could make them'. He was also responsible for repairing hedges, ditches etc., the issue of the mares in the manor, and for stock losses.

His duties were roughly similar in some manors to those of a constable.

In Scotland he is the chief magistrate of a burgh.

147 Punder
See Pinder.

148 Reeve
Strictly speaking, a deputy. In the case of a manor, usually a man of villein status elected by his fellow tenants to organise the daily business of the manor. Because of this he was quite often the spokesman for the manor in negotiations with the lord or his steward.

The Reeve received a money payment exacted from the villagers and sometimes a remission of rent, special grants of grazing land for that year, and a remission of feudal dues.

He was, where no other officer was appointed, such as a Field Master (qv), in charge of the agricultural policy and its implementation in the manor, as well as responsible for the prosperity of the livestock.

The extent of his duties varied from parish to parish and he would in certain areas being doing work that in others would be done by a specially appointed Hayward, Field Master or Beadle.

A Reeve could be chosen either by rotation or else be a person owning a particular piece of land.

149 Scaleraker
A north country term for a town scavenger.

150 Scavelman
A southern term for a man employed to scour waterways.

151 Scavenger
A man employed to clear refuse off the streets.

Alternatively called Scaleraker or Sheldrake.

152 Selectman
A member of a Select Vestry (qv); a Vestryman (qv).

153 Seneschal
A steward. According to Walter of Henley's 'Husbandrie' (13th century) a Seneschal had supervision of several manors, which he toured at least three times a year. 'He should have lands of demesne measures, should know by the perch of the country how many acres in each field for sowing (wheat, rye, barley, oats, peas, beans and dredge), ploughing (each plough should plough 9 score acres — 60 for winter seed, for spring seed and in fallow), also how many acres to be ploughed by boon custom and how many by

the demesne ploughs; reaping (how many acres by boon and custom and how many for money), meadows and pastures (how much hay is needed, how much stock can be kept on pastures and on common. Also how stock is kept and improved. Fines imposed if loss or damage due to want of guard. No under or over stocking of manors; if lord needs money for debts, Seneschal should see from which manor he can have money at greatest advantage and smallest loss'.

154 Sexton
A paid official appointed by the Vestry, Incumbent or Churchwardens. He could be responsible for gravedigging, bellringing, cleaning the church, opening the pews and other odd jobs.

155 Sheldrake
A Cumberland term for a Scavenger (qv).

156 Sheriff
A Shire-reeve. He became, as the Crown's deputy, the most important figure in each county in the 11th century. As Ealdormen (qv) became men with titles but not office the Sheriffs took over most of the county administration. Until the 14th century, when the Justices of the Peace developed, the Sheriff was the main instrument of the King's courts. He accounted for royal revenues in the shire, and was in charge of the county militia.

In 1170 an enquiry was held into the malpractices of Sheriffs and this led to the appointment of coroners (qv) and the rise of the Justices to curb the Sheriffs' powers.

A modern Sheriff has ceremonial and minor judicial powers.

157 Stoneman/Stonewarden
See Survey of Highways.

158 Surveyor of Highways

A parish officer created by the Highway Act 1555. He was unpaid and appointed by the parishioners. In 1691 the law was altered so that the inhabitants merely gave the Justices a list of landowners eligible to be Surveyor, and the Justices chose, usually by rotation.

He was obliged to survey the highways three times a year and organise the statute labour that was provided by landowners to repair the roads, or else collect any commutations.

Alternatively called Boonmaster, Overseer of the Highways, Stoneman, Stonewarden, Waymaker, Waywarden, Wayman.

159 Steward
The lord's manorial representative. He often presided over, and kept the records of, the manorial courts. He looked after the business of land transfers and rents.

160 Swineherd
A man employed by the community to prevent the pigs from straying off the common.

161 Thirdborough
A Constable (qv) or his deputy. The word is probably a corruption of the Middle English 'fridborgh' — peace pledge.

162 Tithingman
A term which probably originated before the Conquest when a tithing — an association of ten men who stood security for each other — elected a representative as their spokesman. After the Conquest it was a term meaning Constable or deputy constable.

163 Town Husband
A colloquial term for a parish officer who collected money for the maintenance of illegitimate children from their parents.

164 Verderer
1) An officer responsible for the preservation of the King's forest. It is thought that the post dates back to the early 11th century. There were four Verderers to each forest, elected by freeholders in the county court. The office was held for life. The Verderers attended the Court of Attachment held every 40 days and punished minor offences.
2) In the south-west he could be a petty constable.

165 Water Bailiff
An officer in seaport towns who was empowered to search ships for contraband etc.

166 Waymaker/Wayman/Waywarden
See Surveyor of Highways.

167 Webster
Mentioned in Walter of Henley's 13th century 'Husbandrie' as a bailiff, steward or major-domo or a great medieval lord, holding high military command.

168 Wellmaster
An officer appointed by the Court Leet (qv) who was responsible for the adequate and clean water supply for the area.

169 Wood Reeve/Woodward
A forest keeper.

Part Three — Classes of Society

170 Alien
A medieval alien who had not been granted privileges by the Crown, was not able to hold or inherit land.

171 Atheling
The Anglo-Saxon term for a member of the royal family and, as a consequence, in control of large areas.

172 Bordar

A villein cottager and therefore one of the lowest ranks in the feudal system. He was allowed to cultivate some land to give him subsistence but he was obliged to perform menial work for the lord either free or for a fixed sum.

173 Carl/Carlot

See Ceorl.

174 Ceorl

A free peasant in Old English times. He ranked above a serf but below the thane or gesith (qv). His wergild (qv) was normally 200 shillings and he was liable to military service and the upkeep of bridges and defences. After the Norman Conquest the Ceorl's status diminished to that of a bordar, cottar or villein.

Alternatively called Carl, Carlot, Churl.

175 Cottar

A cottager, sometimes with a small landholding — usually 5-8 acres. He was obliged to provide labour on the lord's farm either free or at a fixed rate.

176 Electioner

A person eligible to be elected as a parish officer.

177 Eorl

An Anglo-Saxon aristocrat.

178 Franklin

A freeholder, usually of the wealthier sort.

179 Freeman/Free Peasant

Simplified, a tenant who held his land ,from the lord at a fixed rent, as opposed to a villein who had to give labour and produce services for his holding. His position in the community varied through-out the country. A situation could exist in which a poor freeman might be employed by a villein, or else a villein could be farming freeland. Freemen were more common in East Anglia and the Midlands and less common in the west country.

180 Freeman

Before the Municipal Corporations Act 1835 a Freeman, in this sense, was a citizen of the borough or the city, who was able to claim revenues from the city profits and exemption from tolls.

The title is now an honourary one conferred at the wish of the city or corporation.

181 Gebur

An Old English term for a free peasant, within the strata of society called ceorls (qv). He was, in status, between the geneat and cottar. His wergild (qv) was 200 shillings.

The word came later to be shortened to 'boor' — an uncomplimentary reference to a peasant.

182 Geneat

An Old English term for a free peasant, within the strata of society called ceorls (qv). He was superior to a gebur. His wergild (qv) was 200 shillings and he was liable for some military service. In the Middle Ages his equivalent was a Radknight (qv).

183 Gesith

Literally, a companion, in this case to the king. He was part of the king's household and warband, and given land in reward for these services. In the Teutonic kingdoms except Kent, the gesiths were the aristocracy, but by the 9th century the term was replaced by Thane (qv). The Gesith had a wergild (qv) of 1200 shillings.

184 Glebae Adscriptitii

Villein tenants who could not be removed from their holdings as long as they performed the services due from them.

185 Hold
A Scandinavian term, used in Northumbria in the 10th and 11th centuries, to mean a nobleman.

186 Husbandman
This term usually referred to a tenant farmer.

187 Lackland
A person who owned no land.

188 Laet
A social group in Kent in Anglo-Saxon times between free and servile. Its members had the rights of a free peasant but had to perform some villein services to the lord.

189 Laird
A Scottish and northern England term for a lord or large landowner.

190 Mesne Lord
A lord who held land direct from the Crown and who was above other lords.

191 Neife
A villein (qv).

192 Peder
A Lincolnshire term for a cottar (qv) or cottager.

193 Radknight
A tenant who gave service on horseback for his lord, as an obligation of his land-holding.

194 Regardant Villein
A person who performed the lowest manorial services and was assumed to be annexed to the manor rather than to the lord's person. He was distinct from a villein in gross who was transferable from one owner to another.

195 Socman/Sokeman
A free tenant.

196 Thane/Thegn
An Old English term for one who was part of the king's household or his military elite. The word also applied to one of a lord's household or military supporters, but the king's thane had a higher status. The word seems to have superseded Gesith in the 9th century. The Thane had a wergild (qv) of 1200 shillings.

197 Theow
The Anglo-Saxon term for a slave who could be either a conquered native or an Anglo-Saxon felon. He had no rights whatsoever.

198 Thrall
A slave.

199 Vavassor
A term dating from the Norman Conquest to denote a free tenant of high status but with less land than a baron; he had military obligations to his lord. The word was particularly used in Scandinavian counties. He was the forerunner of the Knight.

200 Villein
A general term to describe an unfree tenant who had a share in the agricultural system of the manor. He was above the status of a slave but was assumed (excepting the Regardant Villein (qv)), to be annexed to the lord's person. In return for his landholding he was obliged to perform a variety of services and pay a range of fines. His holding was at the will of the lord and he could be deposed from it. His daughter could not marry without the payment of a fine (merchet), he could not acquire land that would not be taxed, and upon his death a fine (heriot) was paid by his heirs.

His social bargaining position became better after the Black Death and in many cases the services were commuted to a money payment. His usual holding would be about 30 acres.

201 Villein in Gross
A villein annexed to the lord's person who could be transferred to another owner by deed. He was distinct from a Regardant Villein (qv) who was annexed to the manor.

202 Yeoman
A general term but one which usually referred to a freeholder farming his own land, normally worth 40 shillings or more a year. He was qualified to serve on juries and vote for shire representatives.

Part Four — Manor Customs and Procedures

203 Allegiance
It was necessary for the medieval tenant to pay homage and swear allegiance to his manorial lord.

204 Amercement
The common term to denote a fine in a manorial court.

205 Bannering
A Shropshire term for Perambulating the Bounds (qv) of a parish.

206 Beating the Bounds
See Perambulating the Bounds.

207 Biscot
A 16th and 17th century fine on landholders who did not repair waterways running through their lands.

208 Borchalpening
A half-penny fine paid at the View of Frankpledge (qv).

209 Censure
The name for the custom in some manors in Cornwall and Devon for all persons over 16 years to pay homage and pay 11d per poll and 1d each subsequent court.

210 Court Roll
A written document recording decisions taken at the manorial courts.

211 Customal
A written statement of the customs of the manor, the services owed by free and unfree tenants, the duties of the town burgesses, and the rights and obligations of their lord. This was periodically read out at manor courts.

212 Doom
A judgement made by the jury of a manorial court.

213 Essoin
To offer an excuse for non-attendance at court, the excuse itself, or the person making it. This term applied to law courts as well as to the manor courts.
Alternatively called Forfal.

214 Estray
An animal found wandering in the manor and for whom no owner could be found. Proclamation was made of its finding and if no owner claimed it within a year and a day, it became the Crown's property, usually in the person of the lord. If an owner did claim the Estray he had to pay for its past upkeep and release.

215 Extents
An enlargement of the Customal (qv) and included a statement of the extent and valuation of the manor lands and tenancies.

216 Forfal
See Essoin.

217 Homage
Either the pledge or loyalty by tenants to their lord, or the assembled body of such tenants. Acceptance of a tenant into the homage also obliged the lord to warrant him.

218 House Row
The system whereby parish officers were chosen by rotation. It was also used when deciding which house should take a parish apprentice. It was simply a method in which houses were chosen in the order in which they stood.

219 Perambulation of the Bounds.
It was the custom in Ascension week to walk and redefine the boundaries of the parish. The ceremony was carried out by the Incumbent, Churchwardens and parishioners. The custom is known to date from the end of the 9th century at least.
Alternatively called Bannering, Beating the Bounds, Possessioning, Processioning.

220 Possessioning/Processioning
See Perambulation of the Bounds.

221 Pinfold/Pound
An enclosure in which stray cattle were impounded and released on payment of a fine. The Pound was kept by the manor or parish.

222 Scot Ale
A dinner given to tenants when they paid their rents.

223 Suit of Court
The attendance which a tenant was obliged to give at the lord's court.

Part Five — Chartered Boroughs

224
The following boroughs were granted charters between the years 1042 and 1660. Details of the charters, the dates, grantors, extents etc. may be found in the most authoritative work on Borough Charters, 'British Borough Charters 1042-1660), in 3 volumes, by Adolphus Ballard, J. Tait and H. Weinbaum.

Beds
Bedford, Dunstable.

Berks
Abingdon, Newbury, Reading Wallingford, Windsor (New), Wokingham.

Bucks
Aylesbury, Buckingham, Colnbrook, Wycombe.

Cambs
Cambridge, Wisbech.

Cheshire
Altrincham, Chester, Congleton, Ellesmere, Frodsham, Knutsford, Macclesfield, Nantwich, Stockport.

Cornwall
Bodmin, Camelford, Dunheved, Grampound, Helston, Launceston, Liskeard, Looe (East), Looe (West) Lostwithiel, Marazion, Penknight, Penryn, Penzance, St. Ives, Saltash, Tintagel, Gregony, Truro.

Cumberland
Carlisle, Egremont, Kirkby Johannis, Skynburgh.

Derby
Bakewell, Chesterfield, Derby.

Devon

Barnstaple, Bideford, Bradninch, Dartmouth, Exeter, Okehampton, Plymouth, Plympton, South Molton, Tiverton, Torrington, Totnes.

Dorset
Blandford Forum, Bridport, Dorchester, Lyme Regis, Melcombe Regis, Nova Villa (Newton), Poole, Shaftesbury, Sherborne, Weymouth.

Durham
Barnard Castle, Durham, Elvet, Gateshead, Hartlepool, Stockton-on-Tees, Sunderland, Wearmouth.

Essex
Colchester, Great Dunmow, Harwich, Maldon, Saffron Walden, Thaxted.

Glos
Berkeley, Bristol, Chipping Campden, Chipping Sodbury, Cirencester, Gloucester, St Briavels, Tewkesbury, Wotton-under-Edge.

Hants
Andover, Basingstoke, Christchurch, Petersfield, Portsmouth, Romsey, Southampton, Whitchurch, Winchester.

Hereford
Hereford, Leominster.

Herts
Berkhamstead, Hemel Hempstead Hertford, St Albans.

Hunts
Godmanchester, Huntingdon.

Isle of Wight
Brading, Frauncheville, Newport, Newtown, Yarmouth.

Kent
Canterbury, Dover, Faversham, Cinque Ports, Folkestone. Fordwich, Gravesend, Hythe, Lydd, Maidstone, Queensborough, Rochester, Romney, Sandwich, Tenterden.

Lancs
Bolton, Clitheroe, Kirkham, Lancaster, Liverpool, Manchester, Ormskirk, Preston, Roby, Salford, Ulverston, Warrington, Warton, Wigan.

Leics
Leicester.

Lincs
Boston, Gainsborough, Grantham, Grimsby, Lincoln, Louth, Stamford, Torksey, Wainfleet.

Norfolk
Great Yarmouth, Kings Lynn, Norwich, Thetford.

Northants
Daventry, Higham Ferrers, Northampton.

Northumberland
Alnwick, Bamburgh, Berwick-upon-Tweed, Corbridge, Morpeth, Newcastle-upon-Tyne, Norham, Warenmouth.

Notts
Newark, Nottingham, Retford East, Southwell.

Oxon
Banbury, Burford, Chipping Norton, Eynsham, Henley-on-Thames, Oxford, Woodstock.

Shropshire
Baschurch, Bishops Castle, Bridgnorth, Burford, Clun, Ludlow, Newport, Oswestry, Ruyton, Shrewsbury, Wenlock.

Somerset
Axbridge, Bàth, Bridgwater, Chard, Dunster, Ilchester, Langport Estover, Milborne Port, Nether Weare, Taunton, Wells, Yeovil.

Staffs
Abbots Bromley, Agardsley, Burton-on-Trent, Kinver, Leek, Lichfield, Newcastle-under-Lyme, Sta-

fford, Tamworth, Uttoxeter, Walsall.

Suffolk
Aldborough, Bury St Edmunds, Dunwich, Eye, Hadleigh, Ipswich, Lydham, Orford, Southwold, Sudbury.

Surrey
Farnham, Godalming, Guildford, Kingston-upon-Thames.

Sussex
Arundel, Cinque Ports, Chichester, Hastings, Lewes, Pevensey, Rye, Seaford, Winchelsea (New).

Warks
Coventry, Stratford-upon-Avon, Sutton Coldfield, Warwick.

Westmorland
Appleby, Kendal.

Wilts
Calne, Chippenham, Cricklade, Devizes, Marlborough, Salisbury (New), Salisbury (Old), Wilton, Wootton Bassett.

Worcs
Bewdley, Clifton, Droitwich, Evesham, Kidderminster, Worcester.

Yorks
Beverley, Doncaster, Hedon, Helmsley, Hull, Leeds, Pontefract, Ravenserod, Richmond, Ripon, Scarborough, Sheffield, York.

Wales
Aberavon, Abergavenny, Aberystwyth, Bala, Beaumaris, Bere, Brecon, Builth, Caergwrle, Caerleon, Caerwys, Cardiff, Cardigan, Carmarthen, Caernarvon, Conway, Cowbridge, Criccieth, Deganwy, Denbigh, Dryslwyn, Flint, Harlech, Haverfordwest, Holt, Hope, Kenfig, Kidwelly, Laugharne, Llandovery, Llanfyllin, Llantrissaint, Monmouth, Montgomery, Neath, Nevin, Newborough, Newport (Mon), Newport (Pem), Newtown by Dinefwr, Newtown, Pembroke, Pwllhelli, Radnor (New) Rhuddlan, Ruthin, St Clears, Swansea, Tenby, Usk, Welshpool.

Part Six — Local Government Franchise

Municipal Corporations

225   Municipal Corporations Act 1835
The Reform Act 1832 had swept away what, in Parliamentary terms, had been rotten boroughs. Those areas returning members to Parliament disproportionate to their present population had their voting powers diminished and vestries with large, mainly industrial, populations were raised to the status of parliamentary boroughs.

The reform of local government representation in the boroughs was long overdue and the new franchise conditions laid down in the 1835 Act were generally those used in the 1832 Act.

The franchise was extended to each male person over 21 who occupied as owner or tenant any house or place of business, if he had occupied the premises for 2½ years, had paid the rates, or had lived within 7 miles of the borough for the previous six months.

Those towns with over 6000 inhabitants were divided into wards for voting purposes.

Those qualified for election were:
a) in towns divided into 4 or more wards, owning estate or property worth £1000, or occupying land assessed at £30 or more per annum
b) elsewhere, possessing estate or property worth £500 or occupying land assessed at £15 or more per annum.

Voting was by signed voting papers. A tenant paying his rates via his landlord was not necessarily given the vote. Usually he had to apply for his name to be substituted for that of his landlord to obtain the vote. The voting right of a tenant in this situation was the subject of a protracted legal debate for many years. The Small Tenements Rating Act 1850 rated owners rather than occupiers of property assessed at less than £6 per annum; the Representation of the People Act 1867 reversed this, making voting for the tenant easier but the collection of rates harder, and the Assessed Rates Act 1869 restored the 1850 position although updating the rateable value qualification.

226 Representation of the People Act 1918

This Act established a common franchise for county councils, boroughs, parishes and urban and district councils:

Men — six months occupancy of premises or land within the area.

Women — as for men, or else as the wife of a man qualified to vote, if she was over 30.

227 Representation of the People Act 1928

Women over 21 were allowed to vote at local elections.

228 Representation of the People Act 1945

This Act extended the franchise in local government elections to all those registered for Parliamentary elections.

Vestries

229 General

Until well into the 19th century those areas which weren't boroughs were governed by parish vestries. The vestry's legal position was confused and obscure and the right to

take part in its meetings was denied in some areas to certain classes of residents and automatically assumed in others.

The vestry's origin was the calling together of parishioners to discuss church business and was basically an ecclesiastical organisation. The 1601 Poor Law made the Overseers of the Poor, appointed by the vestry, responsible for local Poor Law administration. Later Acts made the vestry itself responsible.

With the growth of towns the parish vestry, with even more civil duties loaded upon it, and working in partnership with the Justices of the Peace, became outmoded. Most vestries were 'open', that is, most ratepayers could attend and take part. Meetings a thousand-strong could and did occur; leadership fell into the hands of the mob or a clique. There appeared to be no inclination or procedure for the open vestry to appoint a small number to represent them and administer the affairs of the parish.

Elsewhere some parishes since the 17th century had been 'select' or 'close' vestries. They were self-perpetuating bodies, subject to no control or audit and generally consisting of the larger land occupiers. The basis for their right to govern in this manner might well be a grant from a bishop or a Private Act of Parliament. The system, inevitably, led to corruption but despite prolonged criticism of the more notorious vestries, could still be found in the late 19th century.

In open vestries the general rule was one man — one vote, a state of affairs which disconcerted the major landowners, for it was they who supplied most of the ever increasing costs of poor relief. After the Speenhamland system (qv) became common, (under which insufficient wages were augmented by poor relief), it was in the interests of the tenant farmers — the employers of cheap labour — for the poor relief sum to increase for, by and large, this came out of the pockets of their landlords.

It was not surprising that in this situation Parliament, itself mainly composed of the larger landowners, passed the Sturges Bourne Acts of 1818 and 1819 — the Vestries Act and the Poor Relief Act. These established the right of larger landowners to have more votes at vestry meetings.

230 Vestries Act 1818 (Sturges Bourne Act)

This Act, which did not apply to areas governed by 'select' or 'close' bodies, established the system of voting according to landownership. The scale of voting was as follows:

Assessed for Poor Rate at over £150 — 6 votes.

Assessed for Poor Rate at over £125 — 5 votes.

Assessed for Poor Rate at over £100 — 4 votes.

Assessed for Poor Rate at over £75 — 3 votes.

Assessed for Poor Rate at over £50 — 2 votes.

Assessed for Poor Rate at under £50 — 1 vote.

231 Poor Relief Act 1819 (Sturges Bourne Act)

This was an adoptive Act which enabled open vestries to appoint a representative vestry or Poor Law Committee. The voting powers were defined as those of the 1818 Act. Those elected were to be substantial householders or occupiers. The incumbent, churchwardens and overseers were ex-officio.

232 Vestries Act 1831 (Hobhouse's Act)

This Act, a breakthrough for democratic ideas, was adoptive and mainly intended for those vestries whose population had grown enor-

mously with industrialisation, and where it had become impossible to govern through large open vestries.

Consequently this Act was largely ignored outside London. It provided for the election of a Select Vestry (in the sense of being chosen), and introduced the provision for a secret ballot if it was asked for by 5 ratepayers.

All parishioners rated for one year could cast one vote for each vacancy.

The qualifications for being a vestryman were established as being a resident householder assessed at £40 or more in London, and in parishes with over 3000 householders. Elsewhere a vestryman had to be assessed at £10 or more. One third of the elected representatives retired each year.

233 Metropolis Management Act 1855

This Act, applicable to London only, established the Metropolitan Board of Works as the overall local authority for the metropolis and was a development from the 1831 Vestries Act.

In the election of vestries the franchise was the same — all parishioners rated for one year. Similarly the qualification for election remained as being a householder assessed at £40 or more. Each voter had one vote for each vacancy. The ballot could be secret if asked for by 5 ratepayers. District Boards underneath the MBW were set up and their membership elected by the vestries. The MBW was elected by the District Boards and the larger vestries.

234 Local Government Act 1894

This Bill transferred the civil functions of the vestries to new parish councils and parish meetings. It also created Rural and Urban District Councils. All county and parliamentary electors were given one vote each.

In rural parishes an open meeting known as the parish meeting (to which all ratepayers and lodgers might come), would convene and in the larger parishes elect a committee to govern. Those electors, including women, who had been resident for 12 months were eligible for election.

235   Local Government Act 1899

This Act converted the London vestries established by the 1855 Act, into borough councils. Women were ineligible for membership, and aldermen were co-opted by the councillors.

236   Qualification of Women (County and Borough Councils) Act 1907

This Act enabled women to become councillors.

Franchise in parish councils is then covered by the Representation of the People Acts of 1918, 1928 and 1945, as described above.

Poor Law Administration

237 1782 Gilbert's Act

Franchise was restricted, in the election of Guardians, to owners or occupiers of premises assessed at £5 or more, but this qualification did not apply in those areas where it would mean that less than ten people would be qualified to vote.

238 Poor Relief Act 1819

See 231.

239 Poor Law Amendment Act 1834

This Act defined the conditions for the elections of Guardians in Unions of parishes. The franchise was extended to owners of land in the parishes and to those ratepayers rated for one year. The owners were allowed votes as for the 1818 Vestries Act. Ratepayers were allowed votes as follows:

Assessed at less than £200 — 1 vote
Assessed at less than £400 — 2 votes
Assessed at above £400 — 3 votes

The Justices of the Peace were ex officio.

240 Poor Law Amendment Act 1844

Owners and ratepayers were allowed votes in the election of Guardians as follows:

Assessed at less than £50 — 1 vote
Assessed at less than £100 — 2 votes
Assessed at less than £150 — 3 votes
Assessed at less than £200 — 4 votes
Assessed at less than £250 — 5 votes
Assessed at above £250 — 6 votes

Public Health Boards

241 Public Health Act 1848

This provided for the election of local Public Health Boards. The franchise was extended to all landowners and ratepayers. Votes were allowed as under the Poor Law Amendment Act 1844 (see above). Members of the Boards had to live in the area or within 7 miles. In boroughs the councils acted as the Boards.

Burial Boards

242 Burial Act 1852

This Act applied to London. The Boards were elected by the vestries. Members had to be ratepayers.

243 Burial Act 1853

This Act extended the 1852 Act to parishes outside London.

School Boards

244 Education Act 1870

This Act allowed for the election of School Boards. The franchise, in boroughs, was extended to all burgesses, in London to all parishioners rated for one year, and elsewhere to all ratepayers. Each voter had one vote for each vacancy and if he chose could cast all his votes for one candidate.

SECTION C

TAXES, SERVICES, RENTS, RATES AND OTHER DUES

Part 1 — Local

Part 2 — Ecclesiastical

Part 3 — National

Part One — Local

1 Accapitare
The act of becoming vassal to a lord.

2 Aids
Originally Aids were regarded as free gifts from the free tenant to his lord — these were feudal Aids. Also Gracious Aids were paid by lords and tenants-in-chief to the Crown. The practice was much abused and it was curtailed, in theory, by the Magna Carta in 1215. It was laid down that a lord might only exact an Aid on three occasions: to pay the ransom on the lord's body, to make the lord's eldest son a knight, and when the lord's eldest daughter was married. The amount of the Aid was not, however, specified.

The Statute of Westminster 1275 forbade feudal Aids being taken until the eldest son was fifteen and the eldest daughter was seven. Gracious Aids were restricted to 20 shillings for a Knight's Fee (qv) or 20 shillings for £20 worth of rented land.

Feudal Aids were abolished by the Statute of Tenures 1660.

3 Amober
In Wales and the border counties a tax to waive the lord's right to have sexual intercourse with the betrothed daughter before the wedding-day.

4 Arrentation
The commutation of services to rent.

5 Avenage
A produce rent in oats paid by a tenant to his lord.

6 Average
A service due from a tenant to his lord in which he did work using his beasts (avers).

7 Bailie-Days
See **Bind Days.**

8 Beaconage
Money paid towards the upkeep of the local beacon.

9 Bede
A service performed by a tenant for his lord. Hence Bedemad (mowing service), Bederepe (reaping service) Bedewed (hoeing service) etc.

10 Benerth
A feudal service owed by a tenant to, his lord, using plough and cart.

11 Berbiage

A rent paid for pasturing sheep.

12 Beverches
Services performed by unfree tenants at the lord's bidding.

13 Bind Days
The days on which tenants were bound to work for their lord as an obligation of their tenure. Alternatively called Bailie-Days.

14 Blancheferme
A rent or due paid to the Hundred sheriff.

15 Bondage
A service given by a tenant to his lord as an obligation of tenure.

16 Boon
A service in kind or labour given by a tenant to his lord.

17 Boonwork
A day's work performed by tenants for their lord on special occasions.

18 Bord Lode
A labour service carried out by a bordar (qv) by carrying timber from the wood to the lord's house.

19 Brigbote
Money paid for the upkeep of the local bridges.

20 Burgbote
Money paid for the upkeep of the borough's walls.

21 Cane
A Scottish and north country term for a rent paid with produce.

22 Cess
A widespread term meaning a tax.

23 Chevage
An annual payment made by tenants to their lord.

24 Chief Rents
Customary rents paid by freeholders to the lord.

25 Childwite
A fine paid by the father of an illegitimate child to the lord. This was regarded as compensation to the lord for cheapening the value of one of his bondswomen.

26 Chiminage
A toll to pass through the lord's forest on a track cleared by him.

27 Common Fine
Money paid by tenants to their lord. Alternatively called Headsilver.

28 Cornage
A rent paid by tenants to their lord based on the number of horned cattle they possessed. Alternatively called Horngeld, Neatgeld.

29 County Rate
To take the place of a number of rates raised at county level for a number of purposes, the County Rate Act 1739 allowed for one general rate to be levied.

30 Driftland
An annual rent paid by tenants for driving their cattle through a manor to a market.

31 Dry Boon
A colloquial term to describe an obligatory period of service given by tenants to their lord which was rewarded only with water instead of ale.

32 Farm
A rent or a service paid for a landholding.

33 Feudal Incidents
A general term for the obligations arising from feudal tenure, such as services, payment of aids and reliefs etc.

34 Fines
Moneys or other benefits which accrued to the lord from his tenants or his possession of the manor.

35 Foldage
The lord's right to insist that his tenants' sheep graze on his demesne land for a period so as to manure it. The lord was obliged to provide a sheep fold.

36 Fold Course
The lord's right to graze his sheep on his tenants' land.

37 Free Services
These were honourable services performed by free tenants, such as military aid, or a money payment.

38 Furnage
A sum paid by tenants to use the lord's baking oven or, alternatively,. a price paid for the privilege of owning their own equipment.

39 Gable/Gafol/Gavol
The Saxon term for money or service due from a tenant to his lord.

40 Gale
Rent. Paid on Gale Days.

41 Gavelacre
A reaping service performed by tenants for their lord. The term also applied to land ploughed by tenants for their lord.

42 Gavelerthe
A ploughing service performed by tenants for their lord.

43 Gavelsed
A threshing service performed by tenants for their lord.

44 Geld
A Saxon term for money or tribute as compensation for a crime. A north country term for a tax.

45 Groundage
a) a tax paid for ground on which a ship stood when docked.
b) a Yorkshire term for the ground rent of a leasehold property.

46 Harrage
A variation of Average (qv).

47 Hawgable
See Landgable.

48 Hock Day
One of the days of the year on which rent was paid. Hock Day was the second Tuesday after Easter Sunday.

49 Horngeld
See Cornage.

50 Knight's Service
Originally the military support and other obligations owed by a tenant occupying a Knight's Fee (qv). This later became commuted to money payments.

51 Landgable
A rent paid by a tenant in ancient boroughs. Alternatively called Hawgable.

52 Mail
A Scottish and north country term for rent.

53 Marchet/Merchet
A fine paid by a tenant upon the marriage of a daughter, to his lord. In some cases the fine was taken on the marriage of a son.

54 Millsoke
The tenant's obligation and consequently, the payment, to grind his corn at the lord's mill, sometimes called the Thirling Mill. Alternatively called Suit of Mill.

55 Multure
A toll paid to a miller for grinding corn.

56 Murage
A tax to pay for the upkeep of the town or city walls.

57 Neatgeld
See Cornage.

58 Pannage
A payment made by tenants to their lord for the right to pasture their pigs in the lord's woods.

59 Passage
A toll on the passage of goods or passengers.

60 Pavage
A tax to pay for the upkeep of paved roadways.

61 Plough Duty
The obligation of landed tenants to repair highways using their ploughs and beasts.

62 Pontage
A toll paid to cross a bridge.

63 Quarterage
County Rates.

64 Quit Rent
A payment made by tenants to their lord to excuse themselves from the customary manor services. Abolished 1922.

65 Scot
A local tax as opposed to a national one.

66 Scot and Lot
Payments made by town dwellers for the upkeep of the various borough facilities — the forerunner of present-day rates. In some boroughs the contributors were allowed to vote in Parliamentary elections and these rights were preserved by the Representation of the People Act 1832.

67 Selver
A feudal term for a payment or toll.

68 Service
A general term for a duty, obligation or due resulting from a tenant's occupancy of land or buildings belonging to a manorial lord. Freeholders were obliged to give military service, or to pay a fixed rent, and to grind their corn at the lord's mill.
A villein, or unfree tenant. gave labour service for the number of days customary in the manor and gave produce, usually corn or barley, in lieu of rent. He would pay various other dues, such as a fine when his daughter married, or when his son went to school or into the Church.
In some parts of the country Service obligations were at a very early date commuted to a fixed money payment.

69 Service Silver
A payment made by feudal tenants to their lord when his heir attained his majority.

70 Sessions Money
The County Rate.

71 Suit of Mill
See Millsoke.

72 Tallage
A tax, usually paid at Michaelmas, exacted by the lord on his unfree tenants. It was abolished in the 14th century as it was superseded by other forms of local taxation. Tallage was also exacted by the Crown on towns and boroughs on Ancient Demesne (qv) land.

73 Third Penny
A Saxon term for a third part of the profits of the shire court claimed by the ealdorman.

74 Toll

Originally the right to levy dues and later described the dues themselves. Tolls were levied at markets and for the upkeep of roads and bridges. Freedom from tolls could be purchased.

75 Trinoda Necessitas

A term to describe the basic obligations of all villeins in the Dark and Middle Ages. It consisted of fyrd-bote (military support), burgh-bote (the maintenance of fortresses) and bridge-bote (the upkeep of roads and bridges).

76 Water-Gavil

A rent paid for fishing in the lord's river.

77 Wet Boon

A colloquial term to describe an obligatory service period given by tenants to their lord which was rewarded with ale.

78 Wite

A feudal term for a fine.

79 Wood Penny

A payment made to the lord for the right to take wood from the commons and wastes.

Part Two — Ecclesiastical

80 Altarage

A general term covering mortuaries (qv), surplice fees (qv) and other minor church income.

81 Annates

The first year's revenues from an ecclesiastical benefice which were paid to the Pope. Henry VIII suspended their payment in 1532 as a bargaining gesture in his divorce dispute and they were annexed to the Crown in 1534. In 1704 they were paid into the Queen Anne's Bounty (qv).

82 Appropriation

An ecclesiastical benefice whose tithes would normally go to the Incumbent, but which have been appropriated by a religious body or personage.

83 Church Rates

These were levied on real property whether owned or leased and were based on the amount of land held. Compulsory payment was abolished in 1868.

84 Conductio Sedilium

Pew rents.

85 Easter Dues

The Church Rates paid at Easter.

86 Fabric Lands

Lands given to provide funds for the upkeep of the local church.

87 Godbote

A church fine for an offence against God.

88 Great Tithes

See Tithes.

89 Hearth Penny

A penny paid by free householders on the Thursday before Easter to the Minster church.

90 Heritor

A Scottish term to describe a landholder who was obliged to pay tithes (alternatively called teinds) for the upkeep of the minister and his church.

91 Lamplands

A Yorkshire term to describe those lands whose rents were used for the upkeep of the church altar lights.

92 Leun/Lewn(e)
A Church Rate.

93 Mainport
A small offering, perhaps bread, paid to the rector instead of certain tithes.

94 Mixed Tithes
See **Tithes.**

95 Mortuary
In effect, an ecclesiastical heriot (qv). When a tenant died his second best chattel was taken by the Church as recompense for the tithes and other dues supposedly unpaid in his lifetime. In 1529 Parliament limited Mortuaries to moderate amounts.

96 Parsonage
In this context, the established revenue for the upkeep of the Incumbent.

97 Pentecostals
See **Peter's Pence.**

98 Personal Tithes
See **Tithes.**

99 Peter's Pence
A tax, established in 787, paid to the Pope. After a dormant period it was revived by William I and not abolished until 1534 when it was appropriated by the Crown. Alternatively called Pentecostals, Romescot and Smoke Farthings. See Annates and **Queen Anne's Bounty.**

100 Pit Money
A burial fee.

101 Plough Alms
Until medieval times a penny paid by each plough team to the parish priest. It was collected within a fortnight of Easter.

102 Praedial Tithes

See **Tithes.**

103 Queen Anne's Bounty
A fund established by Queen Anne in 1704 to receive and use the annates and tenths previously confiscated by Henry VIII. Generally the revenues were used to supplement the incomes of the poorer clergy.
The fund was made responsible by the Tithe Act 1925 for the collection of tithe rent charges. These were abolished by the Tithe Act 1936 and Government Stock was received in compensation. In 1948 Queen Anne's Bounty and the Ecclesiastical Commission were formed into the Church Commission for England.

104 Rectorial Tithes
See **Tithes.**

105 Romescot
See **Peter's Pence.**

106 Sheaf
A Rectorial Tithe (qv).

107 Small Tithe
See **Tithe.**

108 Smoke Farthings
See **Peter's Pence.**

109 Soul-scot
A gift made from the estate of a deceased person to the parish priest. Later became known as a Mortuary (qv).

110 Spiritualities
The sources of income to a bishop or an ecclesiastical establishment exempt from secular control.

111 Surplice Fees
Fees paid to the Incumbent at marriages and burials.

112 Temporalities
Ecclesiastical holdings subject to

secular control.

113 Tithes

A tenth part of the main produce of the land (corn, oats, wood etc.), known as a Praedial Tithe, and a tenth part of the produce of both stock and labour such as wool, pigs, milk etc., known as a Mixed Tithe, were paid to the local church.

A tenth part of the profits of labour, called a Personal Tithe, was also paid.

In addition tithes were divided into Great or Rectorial Tithes, and Small or Vicarial Tithes in parishes where the Rector and Incumbent were different people. Under the Appropriation (qv) system a Rector, either an ecclesiastical dignitary or a layman, could appropriate the tithes of a parish but in practice took only tithes from corn, hay, wood etc. It is reckoned that after the Dissolution one-third of the Rectors were laymen. The Incumbent (the Vicar), had the tithes most troublesome to collect — from the minor produce and labour.

Under the Tithe Commutation Act 1836 tithes could be commuted to a rent-charge based on the prevailing price of corn. The Tithe Act 1925 abolished the rent-charge and the Tithe Act 1936 extinguished them altogether, giving the Queen Anne's Bounty (qv) Government Stock instead.

114 Vicarial Tithes

See Tithes.

Part Three — Some National Taxes

115 Armorial Bearings

A tax on Armorial Bearings was imposed from 1793-1882.

116 Carriage Tax

A tax levied from 1747 to 1782 on the possession of a carriage.

117 Carucage

A tax first levied in 1194 on each carucate (hide) of land held, based on the information in the Domesday Book. In areas where the term Hide was used the tax was called Hideage, or Hidegeld. It was discontinued in 1224.

118 Clocks and Watches

A tax was levied on the possession of clocks and watches from 1797-8.

119 Danegeld

A tax raised, certainly by 991, to give as tribute to the Danes to prevent them invading England. It was based upon the amount of land in each shire. Cnut later levied the tax, calling it Heregeld, to maintain a standing army, but it was abolished in 1051. William I revived the right to tax for his own revenue. In 1083/4 he raised a levy of 72 pence on each hide or carucate of land. Professor Maitland's book 'Domesday and Beyond' gives a list of each county's contribution in the middle of the 12th century. The tax was discontinued in 1163.

120 Dogs

A tax was imposed on the possession of dogs from 1796 to 1882.

121 Escuage

See Scutage.

122 Female Servants Tax

A tax was imposed on households employing female servants from 1785 to 1792.

123 Fifteenth

See Movables.

124 Food Rents

In Old English times each area was obliged to make sufficient provision for the maintenance of the king and his household for a day. Generally, this obligation had been commuted to a money payment by the time of the Norman Conquest.

125 Fumage
A Saxon tax on the number of chimneys on a house.

126 Game Duty
From 1784 to 1807 all persons qualified to kill or sell game, including the manorial gamekeepers, registered with the Clerk of the Peace who issued a certificate for which they paid a fee.

127 Geld
An Old English term for an extraordinary tax based on the amount of land possessed. See Danegeld.

128 Guns
A tax was levied on the possession of guns from 1870-82.

129 Hair Powder Duty
From 1795 to 1798 it was required that people using hair-powder should pay duty and obtain a licence.

130 Hearth Tax
This tax was levied from 1662 until 1689. Its records are very important for local historians as they provide an indication of the size of houses at that time. Those in receipt of poor relief or in houses worth less than 20 shillings per annum not paying parish rates were exempt, but otherwise residents were required to pay 2 shillings per hearth. The parish constable compiled lists of householders and numbers of hearths and gave these to the Justices of the Peace in Quarter Sessions. The tax was collected twice a year at Michaelmas and Lady Day. It was still levied in Scotland until 1690.

131 Heregeld
See Danegeld.

132 Hideage/Hidegeld
See Carucage.

133 Horses
A tax was levied on the possession of horses from 1784 to 1874.

134 House-Duty
A tax levied on inhabited houses from 1851 to 1924. It replaced the Window Tax.

135 Income Tax
This was first levied in 1799 to pay for the war against the French, at the rate of 2 shillings in the £. It was abolished in 1802 but revived in 1803.

136 Land Tax
This was collected from 1692 to 1831, being made perpetual in 1797. The usual rate was 4 shillings in the £.

137 Male Servants Tax
This was levied on households employing male servants from 1777 to 1852. The Society of Genealogists holds the returns of 1780 which give the names of 24,750 people paying tax on 50,000 unnamed servants.

138 Moveables Tax
A tax levied on a person's belongings which began in 1181 with the so-called Saladin Tithe at a rate of one-tenth, and was standardised later at one-tenth for towns and one-fifteenth elsewhere. Sometimes the tax collectors relied on the sworn declaration of the individual and at others on the assessments arrived at by Jurors. It was last collected in 1623. Alternatively called Tenth or Fifteenth.

139 Poll Tax

Although a form of personal tax had been levied since 1222, it became a more regular and prominent tax as from 1663.

Dating from the Restoration period until its abolition in 1698, everyone over 16 not in receipt of poor relief had to pay, theoretically, 1 per cent of the value of their estate.

140 Purveyance

The right of the Crown to exact from a locality provisions at a rate below the market price. This applied as the Court travelled round the country. Parish constables were normally responsible for managing the transactions, and also handled the collections of the money to buy exemption from this irritating imposition.

141 Racehorses

A tax was levied on the possession of racehorses from 1784 to 1874.

142 Registration Tax

In 1694 Parliament taxed births, marriages, burials as registered in the parish records, and also widowers without children and bachelors, in order to provide war revenue. They appointed assessors to do this. After 5 years the tax was discontinued.

In 1783 a tax was placed on entries in the three parts of the parish register. This caused an immediate reduction in the number of registrations. The Act was repealed in 1794.

143 Saladin Tithe

See **Moveables Tax**.

144 Scutage

By the 11th century it was becoming increasingly difficult to enforce the obligation of each tenant-in-chief to provide a military force in support of the Crown. Scutage, a tax meaning 'shield-money', was introduced so that the tenants could commute the obligation. It was fixed at 20 shillings per Knight's Fee (qv) and this was recovered by the tenant-in-chief from his tenants.

145 Silver Plate Tax

A tax was levied on the possession of silver-plate from 1756 to 1777.

146 Tenth

See **Moveables Tax**.

147 Window Tax

Imposed by Parliament in 1696, replacing the Hearth Tax (qv), to help meet the cost of reminting the damaged coinage. After 1792 houses with between 7 and 9 windows were taxed at 2 shillings, and from 10 to 19 windows at 4 shillings. In 1825 houses with less than eight windows were exempt. The tax was abolished in 1851. Scotland was exempted altogether in 1707.

SECTION D

ARCHIVES, DOCUMENTS AND PRINTED RECORDS

Part 1 — General Terms

Part 2 — Parish Registers and Registration

Part 3 — Non-Parochial Registers and Records

Part 4 — County and Quarter Sessions Records

Part 5 — Civil Records

Part 6 — State Records

Part 7 — Army and Navy Records

Part 8 — Other Records

Part 9 — Maps and Mapmakers

Part 10 — County Record Offices, Societies and Periodicals

Part 11 — National Societies and Periodicals

Part 12 — Specialist Libraries

Part 13 — The Calendar

Part 14 — Regnal Years

Part 15 — Latin

Part One — General Terms

1 Calendar
A list of documents with summaries of their contents.

2 Cartulary/Chartulary
A register of lands or privileges, occasionally in rolls but more often in book form.

3 Charter
A document recording a grant.

4 Deed Poll
Originally a deed where no duplicate was required and therefore had a straight (polled) edge. Nowadays the term is restricted to instruments for changing names.

5 Dorse

The back of a document. Information written on the back of a document is quite often known as an endorsement.

6 Estreat

An extract or copy of a record, especially of fines.

7 Folio

A leaf of a book or manuscript, although it can be a number of pages in some circumstances.

8 Indenture

Originally a document cut through the middle, the authenticity of one part being proved when matched with the other. The text of the document was written twice, above and below a word such as 'indenture' or a phrase from the Vulgate. A jagged cut was then made through this line or phrase. In Norman times and earlier, indentures were used for wills and later for contracts, title deeds etc. The word is now used in connection with apprenticeship articles and leases.

9 Inquest

a) an inquiry at which information on some local matter was sworn to agents of the central government.

b) the enquiry into a deceased person's assets and holdings.

10 Letters Close

Private letters.

11 Letters Patent

Open letters, usually embodying a grant of a holding or privilege.

12 Membrane

Part of a Roll (qv).

13 Pawn

A parchment strip containing a list of names.

14 Pell

A parchment document recording the payment or receipt of money.

15 Ragman

A name given to parchment rolls to which were attached a great many hanging seals.

16 Recto

The right hand page, or the front of a leaf.

17 Roll

A document consisting of a number of single sheets (membranes) attached end to end. The term can also be used to describe a single membrane.

18 Starr

A term applied, before the expulsion of the Jews in 1290, to contracts between Jews and Christians. They were written in both Latin and Norman-French with an acknowledgement at the foot in Hebrew.

19 Verso

The left hand page or back of a leaf.

Part Two — Parish Registers and Registration

20 1538 Mandate

This Mandate, formulated by Thomas Cromwell, instructed every parish to purchase a 'sure coffer', the parson to have one key, a churchwarden another. The minister was to enter into a book every marriage, christening and burial at which he had officiated, the entries to be made after the service on Sunday with a churchwarden as a witness. This book was then to be kept in the newly acquired parish chest.

There are approximately 1500 parishes in which register entries begin as early as 1538. In practice the entries were usually made on sheets of paper and written up in a book in 1598.

21 1563 Roman Catholic registers

The Roman Catholic church ordered that registers of marriages and christenings be kept.

22 1598 Provincial Constitution of Canterbury

This instructed that henceforth registers were to be in parchment books and that all previous entries made on sheets should be copied up first in the new books, and especially all those entries since the accession of Queen Elizabeth. Complying only with the latter part of the injunction led to so many registers beginning in the year 1558. Under the new ruling both church-wardens were to witness the entries which were to be read out each Sunday. Also the churchwardens were to transcribe a year's entries to send to the diocesan registry within a month after Easter. These copies are called Bishop's Transcripts.

23 1644/5

An ordinance instructed that when recording baptisms the date of birth should be noted and the parents' names. In the case of burials the date of death was to be inserted.

24 1653 Act

The Government (during the Interregnum) took unto itself the custody of the registers and appointed sometimes illiterate Parish Registers to keep the records. This legislation became obsolete at the Restoration in 1660. A number of civil registers for 1653-1660 are at Somerset House.

25 1667 and 1678 Burial in Wool Acts

Legislation in 1667, more strictly enforced after 1678, declared that 'no corpse of any person (except those who shall die of the plague) shall be buried in any shirt, shift, sheet or shroud or anything whatever made or mingled with flax, hemp, silk, hair, gold or silver or in any stuff or thing, other than what is made of sheep's wool only.' An affidavit was made at each burial that the law had been complied with. The law was intended to help the wool trade and a penalty of £5 was imposed, if wool was not used, on the estate of the deceased and on anyone connected with the burial. The Acts were repealed in 1814 but by then were in general disuse.

26 1694

A tax was levied for the French War on births, marriages and deaths. This was fixed at 2 shillings per birth, 2/6d per marriage and 4 shillings per burial of non-paupers. The duty was higher in the case of wealthy families. Births were to be notified to the incumbent within five days and he was to record them for a fee of 6d.

27 1711

An Act was passed ordering that proper register books be used with ruled and numbered pages.

28 1754 Hardwicke's Marriage Act

This Act, limited to England and Wales, was designed to end clandestine marriages. It declared that all weddings could only be solemnized after the publication of banns, which were recorded at the back of the register or in a separate book. The records were to be 'in proper books of vellum or good and durable paper'. Bound volumes of specially printed forms were introduced at this stage.

The Act laid down that no marriage could be performed except by a clergyman of the Church of England, although Jews and Quakers were excluded. It also provided that minors were to obtain the consent of parents or guardians.

29 1783 Stamp Act

A duty of 3d was imposed on every register entry of a marriage, birth or christening, and burial. The incumbent, who collected the duty, was given a 10% commission.

30 1812 George Rose's Act

This Act, enforceable from 1813, laid down that there should be three separate registers for births, marriages and burials, specially printed by the King's printers. The entries for baptisms were to include names, address and descriptions of the parents, and the burial entries to include the age, address and occupation of the deceased.

31 1823 Marriage Act

This Act declared clandestine marriages (i.e. those without banns or licence) valid, but the officiating minister a felon.

32 1836 Marriage Act

Superintendent registrars were empowered to issue licences for marriage in the office of a registrar or in a non-conformist church.

33 Marriage Licences

Licences to marry under special circumstances have been granted by bishops since the early 14th century. After Hardwicke's Marriage Act 1754 (qv) a licence enabled the parties to marry without the calling of banns or where both were away from their normal place of residence.

Normally the bishop of the diocese in which both parties lived issued the licence, but if two dioceses were involved the couple should have applied to the Vicar-General of the Archbishop of either the Province of Canterbury or York. If the parties lived in different Provinces they would have applied to the Archbishop of Canterbury's Master of Faculties.

The licence would give names, addresses, descriptions, ages, parishes, parents and their consent if the parties were under age, and the places where the marriage could take place.

A Marriage Bond was entered into with two sureties one of whom was often the groom. The sureties bound themselves to ensure that the couple married in a specified church or chapel. Few bonds exist before 1600 and they were unnecessary after 1823.

Original licences should be in the appropriate Diocesan or County Record office. Some have been printed or copied by the Society of Genealogists. York records are at the Borthwick Institute, York. Canterbury records from 1543 to 1869 are at Lambeth Palace.

34 Registration in England and Wales

Since July 1st 1837 copies of entries of births, marriages and deaths have had to be deposited at the General Register Office, now at St. Catherine's House, Kingsway, London W.C.2.

The marriage certificate gives the date and place of marriage, the names, ages, occupations, marital status and addresses of the couple, and the name and occupation of the father.

A birth certificate gives the place of birth, the parents' names and occupation of the father, the maiden name of the mother, their address, and details of the informant.

A death certificate gives the name, address, age and cause of death, and details of the person who submitted the information.

Searches can be made at St. Catherine's House in person. It costs nothing to search but a full certificate costs £4.00. A certificate by post which includes the cost of the staff doing the search, costs £8.50.

35   Adopted Children

Registers concerning adopted children began in 1927. The indexes to these are at St. Catherine's House, Kingsway, London W.C.2, but the actual registers are kept at the Titchfield, Hampshire, office of the General Register Office.

36   Divorces

Registers of divorces began in 1852. The records are at the Divorce Registry at Somerset House.

37   Registration in Scotland

The general registration of births, marriages and deaths began in 1855. The records are with the Registrar General, New Register House, Edinburgh 2.

38   Registration in Ireland

The general registration of births, marriages and deaths began in 1864 and, up to 1921, cover the whole of Ireland. They are in the care of the Registrar General, Custom House, Dublin, who also holds those pertaining to the Republic since that date. In Northern Ireland records since partition (1922) are with the Registrar General, Fermanagh House, Ormeau Avenue, Belfast.

39   Searching Parish Registers in England and Wales

A great many parish registers are in the hands of the County Record Offices and these should be consulted first. Alternatively the Society of Genealogists (qv) has a great many transcripts of registers and an Index of Parish Registers and their whereabouts.

If the registers are still in the care of the incumbent the fees fixed

under the Parochial Fees Order 1972 are 30p for the first year searched and 15p for each additional year. Researchers with a great many years to search may be able to negotiate a flat, but more economic fee.

40   Searching Parish Registers in Scotland

The Presbyterian Church of Scotland registers began in 1558 although there are very few surviving from the 16th century. These records are housed at New Register House, Edinburgh. Researchers should consult a 'Detailed List of Parochial Registers of Scotland' (1872).

41   Searching Parish Registers in Ireland

Only about one third of the old parish registers survived the 1922 disaster, and these, generally, had not then yet been deposited in Dublin. Catholic registers, which began around 1820, had not been deposited and also survived. These records may be consulted at the office of the Registrar General, Custom House, Dublin.

42   Bishop's Transcripts

In 1598 incumbents were instructed to send copies annually of the entries in their parish registers; these were to be sent within a month after Easter. A combination of sporadic attention to this order and the indifferent care of the returns at diocesan level has meant that the Transcripts are sometimes poor alternatives to the parish registers. Researchers should enquire at the Diocesan Office or else the County Record Office.

Part Three — Non-Parochial Registers and Records

This section deals with the registers which were not compiled by a minister of the Church of England,

and with the record repositories for the various religions.

43   Army and Navy Registers

St. Catherine's House, Kingsway, London WC2 has many old registers dealing with army and navy personnel and their families. These are dealt with more fully in the section called Army and Navy Records.

44 Baptist Registers and Records

The central repository for Baptist records is the Baptist Church House (Property and Trustee Dept.), 4 Southampton Row, London, W.C.1. Researchers should also enquire at the regional Baptist association.

Most early Baptist registers were deposited with the Registrar-General and are now at the Public Record Office. The earliest known registers are as follows:

Beds 1709, Berks 1764, Bucks 1773, Cambs 1778, Cheshire 1813, Cornwall 1760, Cumberland 1797, Derby 1753, Devon 1767, Dorset 1778, Durham 1768, Essex 1775, Glos 1651, Hants 1785, Hereford 1747, Herts 1717, Hunts 1789, Kent 1650, Lancs 1755, Leics 1752, Lincs 1703, London 1656, Middlesex 1783, Norfolk 1761, Northants 1755, Northumberland 1781, Notts 1742, Oxford 1647, Rutland 1768, Shrops 1766, Somerset 1679, Staffs 1793, Suffolk 1785, Surrey 1781, Sussex 1669, Warks 1750, Wilts 1767, Worcs 1756, Yorks 1685.

Anglesey 1789, Brecon 1822, Carmarthen 1783, Denbigh 1785, Flint 1827, Glamorgan 1773, Merioneth 1800, Montgomery 1832, Pembroke 1787.

Researchers should also consult the Baptist Magazine (from 1809) and the Baptist Handbooks.

45 Bible Christian Registers

The early registers were deposited with the Registrar-General and are now in the Public Record Office. The earliest known registers are:

Cornwall 1817, Devon 1818, Hants 1824, Kent 1820, Lancs 1800, London 1823, Somerset 1823, Surrey 1835, Sussex 1824.

46 Catholic Registers and Records

For the period from Elizabeth to William and Mary, the Recusant Rolls, usually in the County Record Offices, list a great many Catholics. Alternatively these may be in the Public Record Office.

In 1717 Papists had to register their names and landholdings, these being kept by the Clerk of the Peace. These records would normally be in the County Record Office.

Catholics kept unofficial registers with details of births, deaths and marriages, but most of these are no older than 1778 when the first Roman Catholic Relief Bill was passed. Catholic registers were not handed over to the Registrar-General and are still in the hands of the church.

The Catholic Record Society, founded 1904, at St Edward's, Sutton Park, Guildford, Surrey, has published registers and historical records dating from the 16th century. A list of those printed up to 1958 is contained in 'Texts and Calendars' by E.L.C. Mullins.

47 Cemetery Registers

A number of prominent cemeteries in which non-conformists could be buried kept registers. These were deposited with the Registrar-General and are now in the Public Record Office. These cemeteries were: Bunhill Fields (London) 1713-1854, Eccleshall, Sheffield 1836-38, Leeds 1835-37, Liverpool (Everton) 1825-37, Walworth South London Burial Ground 1829-37, and Victoria Park Cemetery, London, 1853-76.

48 Congregationalist Registers and Records

The central repository for records

is the Congregational Church of England and Wales, Memorial Hall, Farringdon Road, E.C.1. Alternatively other records may be found at regional level.

The old registers were handed in to the Registrar-General and are now at the Public Record Office.

The earliest known registers are: Beds 1730, Berks 1705, Bucks 1765, Cambs 1688, Cheshire 1709, Cornwall 1769, Cumberland 1700, Derby 1703, Devon 1697. Dorset 1741. Durham 1717, Essex 1707, Glos 1712, Hants 1691, Hereford 1690, Herts 1748, Hunts 1742, Kent 1646, Lancs 1717, Leics 1733, Lincs 1774, London 1644, Middlesex 1758, Norfolk 1692, Northants 1692, Northumberland 1746, Notts 1706, Oxford 1685, Rutland 1785, Shrops 1767, Somerset 1681, Staffs 1777, Suffolk 1689, Surrey 1698, Sussex 1698, Warks 1688, Westmorland 1757, Wilts 1723, Worcs 1699, Yorks 1654.

49   Countess of Huntingdon's Connexion Registers

The old registers were deposited with the Registrar-General and are now in the Public Record Office. The earliest known registers are: Berks 1816, Cambs 1787, Cheshire 1819, Cornwall 1800, Cumberland 1789, Derby 1787, Dorset 1822, Essex 1784, Glos 1790, Hants 1784, Hereford 1814, Herts 1806, Kent 1776, Lancs 1789, Lincs 1799, London 1783, Norfolk 1752, Oxford 1790, Somerset 1788, Sussex 1781. Warks 1796, Worcs 1784.

50 Hospital Registers

The registers of the Chelsea, Greenwich, Foundling and British Lying-In Hospitals were deposited with the Registrar-General and are now at the Public Record Office. Those for Chelsea and Greenwich are dealt with more fully under the section dealing with Army and Navy Records.

51 Huguenot Registers and Records

Archive enquiries should be sent to the Huguenot Society, c/o Barclays Bank, Pall Mall, S.W.1. The Society has published volumes listing naturalisations and aliens in this country from 1509-1800; further naturalisations are in the HMSO publication Index to Local and Personal Acts 1801-1947.

The old registers were deposited with the Registrar-General and are now in the Public Record Office. The Huguenot Society has published most of them.

52 Inghamite Registers

The old registers were deposited with the Registrar-General. The earliest known registers are:
London 1753, Notts 1804, Westmorland 1754 and Yorks 1753.

53 Irvingite Registers

The old registers were deposited with the Registrar-General. The oldest known registers are:
Cambs 1834, London 1829, Shrops 1835, Surrey 1833.

54 Jewish Registers and Records

The old Jewish registers were not deposited with the Registrar-General.

Registers 1687-1837 are kept at the Bevis Marks Synagogue, E.C.3. Wills and Administrations in the records of the PCC (qv) are detailed in a publication called Anglo-Jewish Notabilities published by the Jewish Historical Society of England.

Researchers should also enquire with the Anglo-Jewish Association, Woburn House, Upper Woburn Place, W.C.1., and the Jewish Museum at the same address. The archives of the United Synagogue were catalogued in 1930 by C. Roth.

55 Methodist Registers and Records

Because Methodism at one time split into so many branches records may be more easily located after initial enquiries with the circuit minister. The central repository for Methodist records is the Methodist Archives and Research Centre, Epworth House, City Road, E.C.1.

The old registers were deposited with the Registrar-General and are now at the Public Record Office. The earliest known registers are:

	Wesleyan	Primitive	New Connexion
Beds	1798		
Berks	1796	1831	
Bucks	1792	1832	
Cambs	1796	1824	
Cheshire	1793	1811	1798
Cornwall	1794	1832	1834
Cumberland	1806	1825	
Derby	1794	1821	
Devon	1787		
Dorset	1796		
Durham	1797	1823	1811
Essex	1793		
Glos	1799		
Hants	1799	1833	
Hereford	1805	1828	
Herts	1825		
Hunts	1797		
Kent	1796		
Lancs	1784	1824	1794
Leics	1795	1820	
Lincs	1801	1825	1827
London	1779	1806	1820
Middlesex	1807		
Norfolk	1795	1822	1835
Northants	1801	1824	
Northumb.	1788	1823	1798
Notts	1787	1827	1787
Oxford	1812	1835	
Rutland	1816		
Shrops	1796	1822	1829
Somerset	1780	1813	
Staffs	1795	1819	1789
Suffolk	1800	1832	
Surrey	1817		
Sussex	1795		
Warks	1802	1831	
Westmorland	1797		
Wilts	1795	1829	
Worcs	1788	1833	1829
Yorks	1753	1822	1779

The Calvinist Methodists also deposited their registers with the Registrar-General. Their earliest known registers are:

Cheshire 1805, Glos 1762, Kent 1828, Lancs 1803, London 1738, Shropshire 1821, Somerset 1775, Sussex 1825, Warks 1796.

56 Moravian Registers

The old registers were deposited with the Registrar-General and are now in the Public Record Office. The earliest known registers are:

Beds 1743, Cheshire 1784, Derby 1746, Devon 1785, Glos 1757, Hereford 1784, Hunts 1823, Lancs 1786, · London 1741, Northants 1796, Somerset 1755, Wilts 1748, Yorks 1742.

57 New Jerusalemite Registers

The old registers were deposited with the Registrar-General and are now at the Public Record Office. The earliest known registers are: Derby 1817, Essex 1813, Lancs 1803, Leics 1828, London 1816, Warks 1791, Yorks 1781.

58 Prison Registers

The registers for the Fleet and King's Bench Prisons are at the Public Record Office. The Fleet records of baptisms and marriages are from 1674 to 1756.

59 Quaker Records and Registers

The central repository for Quaker records is at the Society of Friends, Friends House, Euston Road, N.W.1. The old registers were deposited with the Registrar-General after 1837 and are now at the Public Record Office, but a digested index of over 500,000 names was made and may be consulted at Friends' House.

60 Presbyterian Registers

The old registers were deposited with the Registrar-General and are now at the Public Record Office. The earliest known registers are:

Berks 1723, Cheshire 1676, Cumberland 1745, Derby 1698, Devon 1672, Dorset 1720, Durham 1688, Essex 1796, Glos 1740, Hants 1676, Herts 1729, Hunts 1820, Kent 1710, Lancs 1644, Leics 1706, Lincs 1707, London 1705, Middlesex 1727, Norfolk 1691, Northants 1820, Northumberland 1752, Notts 1690, Oxford 1789, Shropshire 1692, Somerset 1694, Staffs 1726, Suffolk 1689, Sussex 1789, Warks 1695, Westmorland 1687, Wilts 1687, Worcs 1722, Yorks 1650.

61   Swedenborgian Registers

The old registers were deposited with the Registrar-General and are now in the Public Record Office. The earliest known registers are:

Lancs 1828, London 1787, Norfolk 1819, Northumberland 1808, Somerset 1830, Wilts 1834.

62 Unitarian Registers

The old registers were deposited with the Registrar-General and are now in the Public Record Office. The earliest known registers are:

Lancs 1762, Staffs 1788, Yorks 1817.

63 Dr Williams' Library

Registers of some Presbyterian, Congregational and Baptist chapels within 12 miles of London were formerly kept at this theological library in Gordon Square, W.C.1. They are now at the Public Record Office and cover the period 1742 to 1837.

Part Four — County and Quarter Sessions Records

64 General

From Tudor times until 1889 the Quarter Sessions Records, generally housed now in County Record Offices, form the basis of much local history research. Their records cover crime, land, licensing, the militia, county rates, roads and bridges, various taxes, some aspects of religious adherence, the treatment of the poor and insane, Friendly Societies, banks, and a multitude of other subjects. Some counties have records dated even before the Tudor period.

Since the 14th century the Justices of the Peace in each county have met four times a year at Easter, Midsummer, Michaelmas and Epiphany. Nominally the records were in the charge of the 'Custos Rotulorum' who, certainly from the 18th century, was normally also the Lord Lieutenant of the county. In practice the records were kept by the Clerk of the Peace, a professional lawyer.

The Custos Rotulorum was a private gentleman, usually a lord. The Lord Lieutenant who assumed his responsibility, was first seen in Tudor times and was a Crown appointment. He was known at that time merely as a Lieutenant. His prime function was to see to the military strength of the county.

Sessions records were kept on rolls and a great many of these have now been calendared or printed in some way. Mr F.G. Emmison's booklet 'County Records' published by the Historical Association, gives a list of what principal records are kept by the various County Record Offices and information as to which are catalogued. Many offices publish their own detailed guide to what they have available.

The   Local   Government   Act

1888 transferred most of the non-judicial functions of Quarter Sessions to the newly created county councils.

The principal types of records contained in Quarter Sessions and county collections are listed below.

65 Accounts

Up to Tudor times money for the upkeep of bridges and some roads was raised by special levies, although by the time of the County Rates Act 1739 funds were being raised on a more regular basis. Two Acts in 1601 enabled counties to levy a rate for the relief of maimed soldiers and mariners. Accounts become more frequent after the 1739 Act when the Justices had to appoint a County Treasurer who presented his figures at each Quarter Sessions. His accounts cover administrative expenses, rates, judicial expenses, upkeep of roads, buildings and bridges etc.

66 Aliens, Returns of

As from 1792 an alien arriving in this country was obliged to register with the Justices of the Peace giving his name, address, rank and occupation. In addition, house-holders who received aliens had to give notice to the parish who forwarded returns to the Clerk of the Peace.

67 Association Rolls

The Act of Association 1696 required a person holding public office to sign a declaration which was a 'Solemn Association for the better preservation of his Majesty's royal person and government'. This was lodged with the Clerk of the Peace.

68 Badgers, Kidders and other traders

From 1552 to 1772 this type of small trader as well as drovers, had to be licensed by Quarter Sessions. Their names and those of their sureties, sometimes with other details, were registered.

69 Barges

Barges and other inland waterway craft were registered by the Clerk of the Peace from 1795 to 1871.

70 Bailiffs

The names of those bailiffs present at Quarter Sessions are recorded in the rolls.

71 Bastardy Returns

The Poor Law Amendment Act 1844 empowered mothers of illegitimate children to apply to the Justices in petty sessions for a maintenance order against the father. These applications were sent in the form of annual returns to the Clerk of the Peace.

72 Charities

From 1786 the Clerk of the Peace had to send returns of charities to Parliament, receive their accounts, and register their objects, trustees etc. An Act in 1812 required details of donations based on income from land to be registered with the Clerk of the Peace.

73 Corn Rents

Corn rents is the name given to the variable payments made when tithes were commuted. The payments were reviewed every seven years and adjusted to match the average market price of corn prevailing. These payments occurred after the Tithe Commutation Act 1836 where the fixing of the rent could have gone to arbitrators. The arbitrators report may have been lodged with the Clerk of the Peace.

74 Dissenters' Meeting Houses

From 1688 Dissenters' Meeting

cluded the address, type of meeting and the person certifying it.

75 Elections
From 1762 those electing knights of the shire had to possess freehold property yielding 40s or more a year. County records might include duplicate Land Tax assessments or certificates confirming annuities.

76 Enclosure Awards
Enclosure records since the early part of the 18th century may be with the County Record Office or else with the Public Record Office or church authorities. Generally a copy of an award, sometimes with a map and details of the people and land involved, was lodged with the Clerk of the Peace.

77 Freemasons
The Seditious Societies Act 1799 exempted Freemasons' Lodges provided that each lodge submitted a list of members to each Quarter Sessions, together with their addresses and occupations. These records are quite often incomplete.

78 Friendly Societies
From 1793 registers of Friendly Societies were kept with details of their meeting places and rules. These records normally would have been transferred to the Registrar of Friendly Societies after 1846.

79 Game Duty
From 1784 to 1807 all persons qualified to kill or sell game, including the manorial gamekeepers, registered with the Clerk of the Peace who issued a certificate for which they paid a fee.

80 Gaol Delivery
Registers were kept of all prisoners delivered from gaol to stand trial at Quarter Sessions. These records include the indictments, the jurors sworn and the verdicts

reached.

81 Hearth Tax
The details of this tax are dealt with more fully in C130.
Returns of hearth tax were lodged with the Clerk of the Peace from 1662 to 1688.

82 High Constables
The High Constables of Hundreds attending Quarter Sessions were listed in the Sessions Rolls.

83 Highways
Until 1835 the upkeep of roads had been generally the responsibility of the parishes or else the Turnpike Trusts. In 1835 an Act empowered Quarter Sessions to unite parishes into larger units for this purpose and to appoint a district surveyor. Some records may exist of Quarter Session involvement in this matter but county responsibility was not significant until 1894.

84 Insolvent Debtors
Under Acts of 1670 and 1677 a debtor in gaol could petition a Justice of the Peace for a discharge if his estate was worth less than £10 and his creditors raised no objection. These petitions and any related correspondence were filed by the Clerk of the Peace.

85 Jurors
It was the duty of parish constables from 1696 to make an annual return to the Clerk of the Peace of men between 21 and 70 qualified, by ownership of land worth £10 per year, to serve as jurors at Quarter Sessions. The property qualification was established in 1285 and was varied in Acts of 1604 and 1691. In 1730 leaseholders of property worth £20 per year were also included.
In 1825 jury service was limited to men aged between 21 and 60 who owned property worth £10 per year, leased property worth £20 per year

or rented property worth £30 per year.

Lists of jurors, mostly minor freeholders, are found in the Sessions Rolls.

86 Justices
The names of those Justices present are recorded in the Sessions Rolls.

87 Juvenile Offenders
Under an Act of 1847 monthly returns of juvenile offenders were compiled with details of punishments.

88 Land Tax
A Land Tax was imposed from 1692 to 1831, and was made perpetual in 1797. Between 1780 and 1831 returns were sent to the Clerk of the Peace for the Quarter Sessions. They consist of lists of houses and their owners and occupiers, and the tax paid. Returns were made every spring.

89 Licences
Licences were issued to badgers, kidders, carriers, other petty traders and drovers.

Licences were also issued to Slaughter Houses (after 1786), Lying-in Hospitals (after 1773), butchers (in the 17th century), printing presses (after 1799), racecourses (after 1879), game-keepers (after 1710), victuallers, innkeepers, houses in which music and dancing could take place, and Literary and Scientific Societies.

90 Literary and Scientific Societies
After the Seditious Societies Act 1799, Literary and Scientific Societies were required to obtain a licence to hold meetings. An Act of 1843 exempted these societies from rates if they provided a certificate from the Barrister for Friendly Societies. A copy of their rules was deposited with the Clerk of the Peace.

91 Lunacy
From 1815 returns of pauper lunatics were sent to the Clerk of the Peace. In 1832 private asylums were licensed and inspected by the Justices.

92 Militia Returns
The Lord Lieutenant made an annual return to Quarter Sessions giving the names of commissioned officers and stating the numbers of non-commissioned officers and other ranks.

After an Act of 1854 the provision of storehouses for the militia was paid for out of the county rate.

93 Oaths of Allegiance
The Act of 1722 made it necessary for all persons in England over 18 to swear an oath of allegiance to the Crown at Quarter Sessions.

94 Order Books
These were the minute books of the Court.

95 Oyer and Terminer
A commission of Oyer and Terminer ('hear and determine') was appointed to inquire into the more serious offences such as murder, treason, insurrection, coining etc. The records were kept by the Clerk of the Peace.

96 Petitions
Petitions from individuals or parish representatives were heard by Quarter Sessions and kept by the Clerk of the Peace.

97 Petty Sessions
Petty Sessions were meetings of local justices, held since Tudor times. Some records were kept and these would have been kept by the Clerk of the Peace.

98 Plantation Indentures
The Justices of the Peace were

responsible, after 1682, for issuing indentures to those volunteering to work on the American and West Indies plantations. These records were kept by the Clerk of the Peace.

99 Police
The County Police Act 1839 enabled counties to establish paid police forces. Some counties did so soon afterwards but many didn't until as late as 1856.

100 Poll Books
These list those who voted at Parliamentary elections in the county. They are therefore quite full lists of the property owning class in the late 18th and 19th centuries.

101 Poor Rate Returns
The parishes sent to the Clerk of the Peace their poor rate returns. This enabled the Clerk to fix the county rate.

102 Printing Presses
The Seditious Societies Act 1799 directed that printing presses be licensed by the Justices. The records give the names, addresses and owners. This applied until 1869.

103 Prisons
Records of the administration of prisons would occur up to 1877 when they were still the responsibility of the counties. The documents should have been transferred to the national archives since, but some may still remain at County Record Offices.

104 Prisoners
Lists of prisoners in gaols and houses of correction, with details of their offences and sentences, may be found.

105 Process Registers
These contain lists of indictments, defendants and their parishes, the verdicts and sentences.

106 Public Undertakings
Many plans for public undertakings were deposited with the Clerk of the Peace. Turnpike trusts, canal companies, railways, tramways, docks, electricity and gas companies, water boards etc., are all represented in the records.

107 Recognizances
The Clerk of the Peace kept bonds which secured the appearance of defendants, prosecutors or witnesses at Quarter Sessions.

108 Recusants
An Act of 1657 directed that people should swear an oath abjuring the papacy. Those not doing so were presented at Quarter Sessions.

109 Removal orders for paupers
Where the legal place of settlement for a pauper was in dispute between parishes the matter could be referred to Quarter Sessions which would issue a removal order in accordance with their verdict. Copies of these would be kept by the Clerk of the Peace.

110 Sacrament Certificates
As from 1673 all persons holding civil or military office had to produce a certificate signed by a minister, churchwardens and two witnesses, that he had received the Sacrament of the Lord's Supper. These were sent to Quarter Sessions within six months of taking office.

111 Savings Banks
After 1817 banks deposited their rules, names of trustees and officers with the Clerk of the Peace. An Act of 1828 directed that banks obtain approval from the Justices.

112 Sessions Books
These contain the rough minutes kept in court by the Clerk of the

Peace. They contain details of those present, the indictments, verdicts and sentences.

113 Slaughter Houses
After 1786 owners of slaughterhouses had to obtain a licence from the Justices. They had to produce a certificate from the minister and churchwardens approving of the application.

114 Transportation
The Clerk of the Peace issued Transportation orders and arranged contracts for the convicts' transport.

115 Victuallers and Alehouse Keepers
The Alehouse Act 1552 directed that alehouse keepers be licensed by the Justices.

In 1729 the annual Brewster Sessions began at which Justices would license retailers.

116 Tyburn Ticket
This was a colloquial name for a certificate granted by the Clerk of the Peace to a person successfully prosecuting a felon. The document exempted the person from holding a parish office and was highly valued and saleable.

117 Weights and Measures
Reports from Inspectors of Weights and Measures were lodged with the Clerk of the Peace.

Part Five — Civil Records

118 Apprenticeship Records
In 1710 a stamp duty was imposed on apprenticeship indentures. The records of this tax are in a series of Apprenticeship Books at the Public Record Office and cover the period of the tax up to 1811.

Their records detail the apprentice's name and residence, the father (up till 1750) and the name and trade of the master.

The Society of Genealogists has copied a great many of these records and has many original books.

119 Bills of Mortality
Parish clerks issued weekly statements of the number dead and the causes. This custom prevailed from the 16th century until 1837, although the Guildhall Library has some for up to 1852.

120 Boards of Guardians
Records of the Boards of Guardians appointed by the Poor Law Amendment Act 1834 would normally be with the local or county record office. The Boards were abolished in 1929.

121 Commissioners of Sewers
Many towns had special bodies which controlled sewers, water supplies, walls and embankments. The City of London, for example, have records dating from the 17th century.

122 Estate Papers
Estate Papers consist of a wide variety of material, including plans and surveys, copies of leases, records of rentals etc., and can be invaluable in tracing the occupation of land. Unfortunately their preservation has been haphazard and their whereabouts sometimes difficult to trace. A great many have been deposited with local and county record offices.

The National Register of Archives, Quality House, Quality Court, Chancery Lane, W.C.2 lists collections of Estate Papers and research should begin there.

123 Freemen's Rolls
Corporate towns kept records of their freemen and guild members.

124 Highway Boards

The 1862 Highway Act empowered Quarter Sessions to set up Highway Boards to administer highways for a combination of parishes. The Boards were abolished in 1894 and their records placed in the county record offices.

125 Land Registration

Apart from in the counties of Middlesex and Yorkshire land registration is a comparatively recent requirement. A useful series of books is the official 'Return of Owners of Land' published in 1873-76, arranged on a county basis. The older land registration records of Middlesex and Yorkshire are found in the county record offices.

In Scotland land registration has existed since the early 17th century. The public records include the Return of Heirs or, fully, 'Rettours of Services and Heirs', which gives details of land inheritance from 1500 to 1700. There is also a Register of Deeds 1554-1667.

In Ireland land registration has been effective since 1708. Records are kept by the Secretary, The Registry of Deeds, The Four Courts, Dublin.

126 Lieutenancy Records

The Lord Lieutenant was a crown appointment and his importance dates from 1662. He was in control of the county militia until the 19th century and the records are mainly of use in this connection.

127 Local Directories

From the middle of the 18th century until the 1930's local directories provide information on residents, trades, churches, gentry, public services and other facets of local history. Most local authorities have collections of these. There is a Guide to the National and Provincial Directories of England and Wales (excluding London) before 1856 by Jane Norton. Also there is The London Directories 1677-1856 by C.W.F. Goss.

128 Manorial Records

These would contain records of Courts Baron and Courts Leet and other miscellaneous documents such as terriers rentals, title deeds etc. Latin was used in Court Rolls until 1732. Generally they would be in the care of the local or county archivist. The National Register of Archives, Quality House, Quality Court, Chancery Lane, W.C.2 keeps a register of manorial records in public and private hands.

129 Paving Boards

In the 19th century many Paving Boards were set up to commence and maintain the paving of streets within particular areas. Their records would normally be with the local authority.

130 School Records

Many grammar schools have kept admission registers, and the Colleges of Oxford and Cambridge have very good records. The latter are dealt with by J. Foster's Alumni Oxonienses 1500-1886 (8 volumes), and J.A. Venn's Alumni Cantabrigiensis in 10 volumes. There is also the 'Registers of the Universities, Colleges and Schools of Great Britain and Ireland' by P.M. Jacobs.

Records may be either at the school or with the county record office.

131 Settlement Certificates

The 1697 Settlement Act debarred strangers from entering a parish unless they provided a Settlement Certificate showing that they would be taken back by their home parish if they became in need of poor relief. These Certificates, where they now exist, would be with the local or county record offices.

132 Tithe Records

The Tithe Commutation Act

1836 allowed tithes to be commuted to a rent-charge based on the prevailing price of corn. A large-scale map was drawn showing each piece of land involved, and the names of the owners and occupiers were listed. Three copies of these surveys were made. One was sent to the Public Record Office, the second to the Diocesan Registry and the third to the parish authority. The central agency responsible for keeping details of existing tithe records is the Historical Manuscripts Commission, Quality House, Quality Court, Chancery Lane, W.C.2.

133 Title Deeds

In 'Title Deeds' by A.A. Dibben (1971) a Title Deed is defined as a 'legal document dealing with ownership or occupation of real estate. This comprises tangible properties (technically called corporeal hereditaments) such as lands and buildings, and intangible rights (incorporeal hereditaments) such as an advowson, a rent-charge, and a right of way or common'.

These records may be found mostly in private hands, collections of estate papers, and county or local record offices.

134 Vestry Minutes

Vestries were the forerunners of local councils. Their records are generally held by the succeeding local authority.

Wills

135 General

Before 1858 Wills, with few exceptions, were proved in ecclesiastical courts. The custom was that Wills were proved in the ecclesiastical probate court covering the area in which the testator's property lay. If property fell under two jurisdictions then a higher court would have to grant probate.

In order to trace a will quickly

the researcher would need to know not only when the testator died but in which diocese his property lay. Lewis's Topographical Dictionary 1840-47 and the Topographical Dictionary of Wales (1833), give details of the diocese in which each parish lay.

On presentation of the Will the Court when satisfied, would pass a Probate Act, endorse the Will, and give a copy to the Executors. Letters of Administration were issued on application in cases of intestacy and the recipient(s) had to sign a bond to administer faithfully the estate.

The overriding authority in matters of probate up to 1858 was the Prerogative Court of Canterbury (P.C.C.), whose records begin in 1383.

The Court of Probate Act 1857 set up a Principal Probate Registry at Somerset House in 1858 and the country was divided into District Registries subordinate to the Principal Registry.

After the Married Women's Property Act 1882 married women (as distinct from widows) were able to dispose of property by will.

136 Style of Will

An old Will would almost certainly be in Latin, begin with a prayer for the testator's soul, and commit his body to the graveyard.

137 Jurisdiction

Normally a Will was proved in the Court of an Archdeacon, or else in a Diocesan Court. A simplified county list of appropriate courts is included below, but there were many exceptions to the usual procedure and the researcher is urged to refer to the only adequate publication, Wills and Their Whereabouts by Anthony J. Camp (1963), for a more detailed guide.

If a testator's property lay in two archdeaconries but within one diocese the diocesan court would prove the will. The same principle would prevail where property lay in two dioceses but within one ecclesiastical province, in which case the Prerogative Court of Canterbury (PCC) or the Prerogative Court of York (PCY) would be the appropriate probate court. Finally, where property was divided over two Provinces the PCC would have the overriding authority.

The PCC did, in fact, also prove wills in circumstances where a lower court would have been sufficient. It also had jurisdiction over the wills of people who died at sea or abroad.

A significant departure from the procedure above was in cases where property lay within the jurisdiction of what is known as a Peculiar, or Testamentary Peculiar — an area in which the parish minister or, sometimes, the manorial authority had the right to grant probate. These Peculiars are listed in the book Wills and Their Whereabouts mentioned above.

138 Probate Courts
A simplified list of probate jurisdictions up to 1858.

Anglesey
Archdeaconry of Anglesey
Diocese of Bangor
Province of Canterbury up to 1920

Beds
Archdeaconry of Bedford
Diocese of Lincoln up to 1837
Diocese of Ely up to 1914
Province of Canterbury

Berks
Archdeaconry of Berkshire
Diocese of Salisbury up to 1836
Diocese of Oxford since
Province of Canterbury

Brecon
Archdeaconry of Brecon
Diocese of St Davids up to 1923 .
Province of Canterbury up to 1920

Bucks
Archdeaconry of Buckingham
Diocese of Lincoln up to 1845
Diocese of Oxford since
Province of Canterbury

Caernarvonshire
Archdeaconries of Merioneth and Bangor
Diocese of Bangor
Province of Canterbury up to 1920

Cambs
Archdeaconry of Cambridge
Diocese of Ely
Province of Canterbury

Cardiganshire
Archdeaconry of Cardigan
Diocese of St Davids
Province of Canterbury up to 1920

Carmarthenshire
Archdeaconry of Carmarthen
Diocese of St Davids
Province of Canterbury up to 1920

Cheshire
Archdeaconry of Chester
Diocese of Lichfield up to 1541
Diocese of Chester since
Province of Canterbury up to 1541
Province of York since 1541

Cornwall
Archdeaconry of Cornwall
Diocese of Exeter up to 1876
Province of Canterbury

Cumberland
Archdeaconry of Cumberland
Diocese of Carlisle
Province of York

Denbigh
Archdeaconry of St Asaph
Diocese of St Asaph
Province of Canterbury up to 1920

Derby
Archdeaconry of Derby
Diocese of Lichfield up to 1884
Province of Canterbury

Devon
Archdeaconries of Barnstaple,
Exeter and Totnes
Diocese of Exeter
Province of Canterbury

Dorset
Archdeaconry of Dorset
Diocese of Salisbury up to 1542
Diocese of Bristol up to 1836
Diocese of Salisbury since
Province of Canterbury

Durham
Archdeaconry of Durham
Diocese of Durham
Province of York

Essex
Archdeaconries of Essex,
Colchester and Middlesex.
Diocese of London up to 1846
Diocese of Rochester up to 1877
Province of Canterbury

Flintshire
Archdeaconry of St Asaph
Diocese of St Asaph
Province of Canterbury up to 1920

Glamorgan
Archdeaconry of Llandaff
Diocese of Llandaff
Province of Canterbury up to 1920

Gloucestershire
Archdeaconry of Gloucester
Diocese of Worcester up to 1541
Diocese of Gloucester up to 1836
Diocese of Gloucester and Bristol
since

Archdeaconry of Hereford
Diocese of Gloucester up to 1836
Diocese of Gloucester and Bristol
since

City of Bristol
Diocese of Bristol up to 1836
Diocese of Gloucester and Bristol
since
All Province of Canterbury

Hants
Archdeaconry of Winchester
Diocese of Winchester
Later divided into Diocese of Guild-
ford and Diocese of Portsmouth
Province of Canterbury

Hereford
Archdeaconry of Hereford
Diocese of Hereford
Province of Canterbury

Herts
Deanery of Braugham in the Arch-
deaconry of Middlesex
Diocese of London up to 1845
Diocese of Rochester up to 1877

Archdeaconry of St Albans
Diocese of Lincoln up to 1845
Diocese of Rochester up to 1877

Archdeaconry of Huntingdon
Diocese of Ely up to 1845
Diocese of Rochester up to 1877
Province of Canterbury

Hunts
Archdeaconry of Huntingdon
Diocese of Lincoln up to 1837
Diocese of Ely since
Province of Canterbury

Isle of Man
Diocese of Sodor and Man
Province of York

Kent
Archdeaconry of Canterbury
Diocese of Canterbury

Archdeaconry of Maidstone
Diocese of Canterbury
Parts to Diocese of Maidstone after
1845

Archdeaconry of Rochester
Diocese of Rochester
Parts to Diocese of Maidstone after
1845
Province of Canterbury

Lancs
Archdeaconry of Richmond
Diocese of York up to 1541

Diocese of Chester since
Province of York

Archdeaconry of Chester
Diocese of Lichfield up to 1541
Diocese of Chester since
Province of Canterbury up to 1541
Province of York since

Leics
Archdeaconry of Leicester
Diocese of Lincoln up to 1837
Diocese of Peterborough up to 1926
Province of Canterbury

Lincs
Archdeaconries of Lincoln and
Stow
Diocese of Lincoln
Province of Canterbury

London
Archdeaconry of City of London
Diocese of London

Archdeaconry of City of West-
minster
Diocese of London up to 1540
Diocese of Westminster

Archdeaconry of Middlesex
Diocese of London
Province of Canterbury

Middlesex
Archdeaconry of Middlesex
Diocese of London
Province of Canterbury

Merioneth
Archdeaconry of Merioneth
Diocese of Bangor
Province of Canterbury up to 1920

Archdeaconry of St Asaph
Diocese of St Asaph
Province of Canterbury up to 1920

Monmouth
Archdeaconry of Monmouth
Diocese of Llandaff
Province of Canterbury up to 1920

Montgomeryshire
Archdeaconry of St Asaph
Diocese of St Asaph

Province of Canterbury up to 1920

Diocese of Merioneth
Diocese of Bangor
Province of Canterbury up to 1920

Norfolk
Archdeaconries of Norfolk and
Norwich
Diocese of Norwich
Province of Canterbury

Northants
Archdeaconry of Northampton
Diocese of Lincoln up to 1541
Diocese of Peterborough since
Province of Canterbury

Northumberland
Archdeaconry of Northumberland
Diocese of Durham up to 1882
Province of York

Notts
Archdeaconry of Nottingham
Diocese of York up to 1839
Diocese of Lincoln up to 1884
Province of York up to 1839
Province of Canterbury up to 1934

Peculiar of Southwell
Diocese of York up to 1839
Diocese of Lincoln up to 1884
Province of York up to 1839
Province of Canterbury up to 1934

Oxon
Archdeaconry of Oxford
Diocese of Lincoln up to 1546
Diocese of Oxford since
Province of Canterbury

Pembrokeshire
Archdeaconry of St Davids
Diocese of St Davids
Province of Canterbury up to 1920

Radnorshire
Archdeaconry of Brecon
Diocese of St Davids
Province of Canterbury up to 1920

Rutland
Archdeaconry of Northampton

Diocese of Lincoln up to 1541
Diocese of Peterborough up to 1876

Archdeaconry of Oakham
Diocese of Peterborough
Province of Canterbury

Shropshire
Archdeaconry of Salop (part)
Diocese of Hereford

Archdeaconry of Salop (part)
Diocese of Lichfield
Province of Canterbury

Somerset
Archdeaconries of Bath, Wells and
Taunton
Diocese of Bath and Wells
Province of Canterbury

Staffs
Archdeaconry of Stafford
Diocese of Lichfield
Province of Canterbury

Suffolk
Archdeaconries of Sudbury and
Suffolk
Diocese of Norwich
Province of Canterbury

Surrey
Archdeaconry of Surrey
Diocese of Winchester
Large number of parishes to Diocese
of London in 1846
Province of Canterbury

Sussex
Archdeaconries of Chichester and
Lewes
Diocese of Chichester
Province of Canterbury

Warwickshire
Archdeaconry of Worcester
Diocese of Worcester
Province of Canterbury

Archdeaconry of Coventry
Diocese of Lichfield up to 1836
Diocese of Worcester after
Province of Canterbury

Westmorland
Barony of Appleby
Diocese of Carlisle
Province of York

Barony of Kendal
Diocese of York up to 1541
Diocese of Chester up to 1856
Diocese of Carlisle since
Province of York

Wilts
Archdeaconries of Salisbury and
Wiltshire
Diocese of Salisbury
Province of Canterbury

Worcs
Archdeaconry of Worcester
Diocese of Worcester
Province of Canterbury

Yorks
Diocese of York
Province of York

Probate Terms

139 Administration Bond
   In cases of intestacy the recipient
of the Letters of Administration (qv)
was required to sign an Administration Bond which required him to
administer the estate faithfully.

140 Bona Notabilia
   A term meaning 'considerable
goods', but in practice an estate
valued at over £5.

141 Caveat
   A person, usually a relative or
creditor of the deceased, was able to
lodge a caveat — a warning — at the
appropriate probate court so that
the will would not be proved without his knowledge or opportunity
to state his case.

142 Court of Arches
   This was an appeal court for the
Prerogative Court of Canterbury.
See also Court of Delegates.

143 Court of Delegates
This was the court of appeal for both Provincial Courts. See also Court of Arches.

144 Curation
The guardianship of a minor under 21, and over 14 (male) and 12 (female).

145 Decree
A court judgement. If the words 'by decree' or 'int. dec.' (intercolutory decree) appear in probate records it would indicate that the will had been contested and that the court had given a judgement.

146 Holograph Will
A will in the testator's handwriting.

147 Letters of Administration
In cases of intestacy the probate court issued a grant, called Letters of Administration, to the next of kin or some other person or persons, whoever had applied, to administer the estate.

148 Letters of Administration-with-Will-annexed
In cases where the will did not specify an executor, or where the executor was unable or unwilling to act, the court granted Letters of Administration to the next of kin or some other person or persons, whoever had applied, to administer the estate.

149 Limited Probate
Probate could be granted to cover limited parts of the estate.

150 Nuncupative
A dictated will.

151 Peculiar
See Testamentary Peculiar.

152 Personalty
Personal estate, chattels, goods etc., as opposed to real estate.

153 Probate Act
This Act was passed by the ecclesiastical court when they were satisfied with the will presented.

154 Relict
A widow or widower.

155 Testamentary Peculiar
A Peculiar is a jurisdiction over probate and can cover more than one parish. It had power to grant probate only where the property fell wholly within its jurisdiction.

156 Tuition
The guardianship of minors under the age of 15 (male) and 13 (female).

157 Will and Testament
A Will disposes of real estate and the Testament was drawn up to cover personal belongings.

Probate Records

158 Prerogative Court of Canterbury (PCC)
The Wills proved in the PCC from 1383 to 1858 are in the Department of Literary Enquiry at Somerset House. The British Records Society has published a great many indexes to them. There are also manuscript calendars up to 1852 at Somerset House.

159 Prerogative Court of York
Wills proved at the PCY from 1389 to 1858 are at the Borthwick Institute of Historical Research, St Anthony Hall, York. Some indexes have been printed.

160 Lower Court Records
The probate records of the Archdeaconry or Diocese would normally be in the Diocesan Registry or the County Record Office. For further details consult Wills and Their Whereabouts by Anthony J. Camp.

161 Probate Act Books

These contain records of probates granted. They are mostly at Somerset House, the Diocesan Registry or the County Record Offices.

162 Administration Act Books

These contain records of Letters of Administration. They are mostly at Somerset House, the Diocesan Registries or the County Record Offices.

163 Principal Probate Registry

Since 1858 wills have been proved at the Principal Probate Registry at Somerset House or in subordinate District Registries. In the former case Somerset House keeps the original will and a copy. In the latter case the District Registry keeps the original, sending a copy to Somerset House. There are indexes to all wills since 1858.

164 Calendars and Indexes

The dates used in calendars and indexes are those used when the wills were proved. In earlier times this could sometimes be years after the death.

165 Scottish Wills

Wills in Scotland were 'confirmed' at commissariat courts, the earliest established one being Edinburgh (1514). The records of these courts from 1514-1823 are at Old Register House, Edinburgh 2.

In 1824 jurisdiction over wills was given to the sheriffs' courts which, generally, keep their own records, although all those for Edinburgh are still sent to Old Register House.

166 Irish Wills

Before 1858 the Prerogative Court of Armagh had jurisdiction throughout Ireland. Abstracts of its records — most original documents were destroyed in the 1922 fire in Dublin — are at the Public Record Office in Dublin. Any originals that survived are at the appropriate Public Record Office in Dublin or Belfast.

A valuable publication is the 'Index to the Prerogative Wills of Ireland 1536-1810' by Sir Arthur Vicars.

Part Six — National Records

Most of the national records detailed below are to be found at the Public Record Office. These are the classes of most use, generally, to local history researchers, but the Record Office does have, in addition, enormous collections of miscellaneous documents such as court rolls, hundred rolls, rentals and terriers.

There is an official guide to the Public Record Office together with lists of those records already in print. The printed versions might well be in stock at county record offices.

167 Association Oath Rolls

In 1696 all persons in England and Wales holding public office had to sign a pledge of loyalty to the Crown. The directive included the gentry, clergy and the Freemen of the London Livery Companies.

168 Census

The censuses from 1801 to 1831 were concerned with numbers; names were not recorded until 1841. The returns for 1801-1831 are in print.

The 1801 returns give the numbers of people in each parish, the inhabited and uninhabited houses, and roughly classifies the occupations into agriculture, manufacturing, commerce and handicrafts.

In 1811 and 1821 more accurate information was obtained on occupations.

In 1831 males over 20 years were classed in seven occupational categories: agriculture, industrial labourers, manufacturing, professional, retail trades, servants and others.

In 1841 the names of people were recorded for the first time; the ages of those over 15 were given to the lowest term of five. In addition information was given as to what part of the country a person was born in. Where they were able the householders, for the first time, filled in their own census form.

In 1851 exact ages and birthplaces were given, together with each person's marital status and relationship to the householder. The number of blind, deaf and dumb was noted and a census of church congregations and accommodation taken.

The 1861 census recorded the number of aliens and naturalised subjects.

Apart from indigenous non-whites the number of people in the British Empire was returned in 1871. This is the most recent census for which details are available to the public.

169 Chancery Records

Chancery Records date from 1199 and include Letters Patent (1201-1920) which deal with a range of subjects of interest to the local historian. They include borough charters, grants of land and privileges, presentation to benefices, alienation and appointment to offices.

The Close Rolls (1204/5 to 1903) contain grants of the Crown closed with the Great Seal. Private instructions, mainly to the officers of the Crown, were enrolled on the face of the rolls. Their main content was enclosure awards, deeds poll, quit claims, provisioning of garrisons, aids and subsidies, and pardons. The reverse sides of the membranes were used for the enrolment of deeds, conveyance of land and records of livery of seisin, charities and wills.

Charter Rolls record grants of lands, privileges and titles. They run from 1199 to 1516.

The records also contain reports of various commissions, Inquisitions ad quod damnum held to investigate if the grant of a market or fair infringed a previous right, and title deeds.

170 Domesday Book

Domesday Book consists of two volumes compiled in 1085/6, the one dealing with Essex, Norfolk and Suffolk, the other the remainder of England. Its function was not to survey the landholdings of the country, but to register all geldable (taxable) land. Therefore, not all lands or buildings are noted because some were exempt from geld.

It detailed the number of geldable units — these are identified as hides or carucates (qv), or whatever happened to be the local land measurement terminology. It assessed a holding's annual value and, so as to establish a true geld, the rise and fall of that value in the last twenty years. It noted the number of plough teams, the pasture and pannage available — in short, any details which went to make up the annual value.

The survey was compiled hundred by hundred, vill by vill, within each shire. However, in its final assembly the entries are reorganised so that they are grouped under landholders. Thus, one parish may be shown under a number of owners.

Most researchers' needs for transcription and interpretation of their area's entries will be met by the Victoria County History series. More detailed research can be helped by reference to Professor F.W. Maitland's 'Domesday Book and Beyond' and V.H. Galbraith's 'The Making of Domesday Book'.

171 Feet of Fines
These are copies of agreements made after disputes over land ownership. Some disputes were artificial and were merely intended to register officially the ownership of land. They run from 1190 to 1833.

172 Fine or Oblata Rolls
These record the fines imposed by the Crown on subjects given particular advantages, such as having wardship of an heiress — normally held by the Crown.

173 Home Office Records
The Home Office was established in 1782. Much of its archive material, now in the Public Record Office, is concerned with law and order. There are convict transportation records from 1787 to 1870, together with numerous lists of prisoners indicted at Quarter Sessions. The Home Office dealt with police as from 1829, with aliens from 1793 and with naturalisation from 1844.

174 Inquisitiones Post Mortem
On the death of one of the king's tenants-in-chief an inquest was held which established the date of his death, the age of the heir, and the lands held. These records began in the reign of Henry III and many have been calendared by the Public Record Office. An heir paid a tax called a 'relief' to enter into the lands; in the case of the heir being a minor the land reverted to the Crown until he came of age although quite often the Crown was slow to hand the holding back.

175 Pipe Rolls
These are the accounts rendered by the sheriffs to the Exchequer, including details of rent and farm and any other form of Crown revenue, together with the sheriff's expenses. They date from 1131 to 1831, and include the Liber Niger Scaccarii, (the Black Book of the Exchequer) — a survey of England compiled in 1166.

The Pipe Rolls are so called because they were rolled around a rod or pipe.

176 Pleas
The most important series of Plea Rolls for the local historian are those for the Court of Common Pleas running from 1194 to 1875, which heard disputes between subjects. Thus, the records contain title deeds, family history and details of land transfer. These are either at the Public Record Office or the British Museum.

177 Protestation 1641
In 1641 Parliament organised a protest against the possible imposition of 'an arbitrary and tyrannical government'. The returns, arranged topographically, are in the House of Lords Record Office, and some have been printed.

Those parishes whose returns are extant:are listed in the Calendar of the Manuscripts of the House of Lords Vol. 5.

178 Subsidy Rolls
This is a general name for the records of aids and subsidies to the Crown from the 13th century to 1689. Properly the 'subsidy' refers to a tax levied in the reign of Richard II at the rate of 4 shillings in the £ on land, and 2/8d on goods.

The Rolls are arranged by counties and parishes and give lists of taxpayers. Those for 1295, 1327, 1334, 1377-81 and 1524-5 are the most useful. The 1291 taxation list has been published by the Record Commissioners.

Various taxes are included — tallage, poll-tax, carucage, scutage and hidage as well as the Hearth Tax (qv). The records of this last named tax are usually more accessible at County Record Offices. The fullest

Hearth Tax return is that for Lady Day 1664.

Part Seven — Army and Navy Records

Army Records

179 Army Lists
The official Army Lists begin in 1740 although there is a gap until 1754. These record the officers, their commissions and regiments. At the Public Record Office.

180 Casualty Returns
These give the name, rank, trade, birthplace, next-of-kin and a copy of a will if available. These run from 1809-1857 and are at the Public Record Office.

181 Chaplains' Records
Chaplains of stations abroad kept registers of births, marriages and deaths. They run from 1796 to 1880 and are at St. Catherine's House, Kingsway, London WC2.

182 Chelsea Hospital
Chelsea Hospital is a residence for Army pensioners. Its registers of baptisms (1691-1812), marriages (1691-1765) and burials (1692-1856) are at the Public Record Office.

183 Courts Martial
These records run from 1684-1847 and are at the Public Record Office.

184 Description Books
These are books detailing recruits, giving their age, trade, physical features, birthplace and place of enlistment. Some are as early as 1756 but they are more common from the beginning of the 19th century. At the Public Record Office.

185 Militia Returns

Returns were made annually after 1769 by the Lord Lieutenant to Quarter Sessions, listing the names of commissioned officers and the numbers of non-commissioned officers and men. At the Public Record Office.

186 Muster Rolls
Muster Rolls are periodic roll-calls in each regiment. They begin in 1708 and contain the names of officers and men. From 1795 they can give the place of birth and age on enlistment. At the Public Record Office.

187 Pension Records
The Public Record Office has a great many records of pensions granted from 1735 onwards.

188 Regimental Registers
St. Catherine's House, Kingsway, London, W.C.2 has some regimental registers containing births, marriages and deaths from 1790-1924.

189 Registers after 1880
Up to 1880 the Chaplains at stations abroad had kept records of births, marriages and deaths. The Registration of Births, Deaths and Marriages (Army) Act 1879 came into force in 1881 and registers were thenceforth kept by the command headquarters. They are now at St. Catherine's House, Kingsway, London W.C.2.

Navy Records

190 Births and Deaths on HM Ships
Records of births and deaths on Royal Navy vessels since 1837 are at St. Catherine's House, Kingsway, London W.C.2.

191 Births and Deaths on Merchant Ships
Records of births and deaths on merchant ships are at St. Catherine's House, Kingsway, London W.C.2 for 1837-1874, and after that with the Registrar-General for Shipping and Seamen, Llandaff, Cardiff.

192 Bounty Papers

These records referring to payments made to seamen and their relatives run from 1675 to 1822. They are at the Public Record Office.

193 Description Books

These give brief physical details of each recruit together with their age and birthplace. They begin in 1790 and are at the Public Record Office.

194 Greenwich Hospital

This hospital is for navy pensioners. The registers for baptisms cover 1720-1856, for marriages 1724-1754 and for burials 1705-1857. They are at St. Catherine's House, Kingsway, London, WC2.

The records of the apprenticing of pensioners' children are at the Public Record Office as are the registers of entry and discharge of pensioners from 1704-1869.

195 Lieutenants' Passing Certificates

These run from 1691 to 1832; since 1789 the baptismal certificates are attached. At the Public Record Office.

196 Muster Rolls

These are roll-calls of ships' companies. They give the name, rank, age and birthplace. They date from 1680, are more frequent after 1696, and complete from 1740. At the Public Record Office.

197 Navy Lists

These exist from 1749 and record the names and commissions of officers. They are at the Public Record Office.

198 Pay Books

These run from 1669 and are at the Public Record Office.

199 Pension Books

These cover the period 1734-1885. In the case of widows' pensions marriage certificates are attached. They are at the Public Record Office.

200 Sea Officers Lists

The National Maritime Museum has published 'Commissioned Sea Officers of the Royal Navy 1660-1815' which deals with careers.

201 Trinity House Records

Trinity House, founded in 1529, encourages navigational skills and supervises lighthouses, buoys etc. Petitions to Trinity House for pensions run from 1780-1854. These records are at the Society of Genealogists, 37 Harrington Gardens, S.W.7.

Part Eight — Other Records

202 Clerical Records

Crockford's Clerical Directory was first issued in 1858. Before that University records would give details of clergymen.

Institution Books at the Public Record Office date from 1556 and further information would be held by Diocesan Registries.

203 Diocesan Records

Bishops deposited their records in the Diocesan Registry although some have subsequently been transferred to county record offices.

Archives include records of cathedral and church administration, landholdings and tithes, probate, Chapter Books, Visitation Books (giving details of parishes visited), Bishops' Transcripts (copies of entries in parish registers), and Marriage Licences.

In 1676 each parish priest was instructed to return to either the archbishop of either Canterbury or York a census of parishioners (numbers only) together with details of those absenting themselves from worship. These returns known as the Compton Census (after Henry

Compton, bishop of London) are among Diocesan Records where they still exist.

204 Glebe Terriers
These are surveys of church lands and benefices compiled by the incumbent or churchwardens. They would normally be with the Diocesan Registry or the County Record Office.

205 Guild Records
In the Middle Ages entry into trade guilds was restricted. The various companies, especially in London, kept records of each tradesman and apprentice, with details of birthplace, father's name etc.

Outside London the records would probably now be deposited with the local or county record office. In London the Guildhall Library holds most of those not in the custody of the Livery Companies.

206 Hansard
Cobbett's 'Parliamentary Debates' (founded 1804) was bought by Thos. Hansard in 1811. He renamed the the publication 'Hansard's Parliamentary Debates'. Although it is now an official Government record the name has been retained, except for the period 1889 to 1943 when it was omitted from the title-page.
The records may be seen in the House of Lords Library.

207 Legal Records
The Inns of Court, originating in the 14th century, have records of entrants to the legal profession. Gray's Inn, Lincoln's Inn and the Middle Temple have printed lists since 1775.

208 Medical Records
The earlier details of those in the medical profession are in the Guildhall Library amongst the records of

the Barber-Surgeons Company, an amalgamation of two guilds which took place in 1540.
The Universities, in particular at Caius College, are useful for research into medical graduates, as are the records of the Society of Apothecaries (founded 1617) at the Guildhall Library.
Other repositories may be found at the Royal College of Surgeons (founded 1800), and the Royal College of Physicians in Regent's Park (founded 1518) which can be used on application.
The Medical Register has appeared since 1858.

209 Monastic Records
Monastic Records at the Dissolution were scattered around the country and now reside in state archives, local archives and private hands.
The main class of record is the Cartularies, volumes in which the charters relating to the endowments of the religious houses have been copied. The Royal Historical Society in 1958 published 'Medieval Cartularies of Great Britain — a Short Catalogue' by G.R.C. Davis.

210 Monumental Brasses
Collections of brass rubbings are at the British Museum, the Society of Antiquaries, the Victoria and Albert Museum, the Bodleian Library and Ashmolean Museum in Oxford, and the Cambridge Museum of Archaeology and Ethnology.

211 Monumental Inscriptions
The older inscriptions are disappearing fast from churchyards due to the difficulty in maintaining old graves. The Society of Genealogists (qv) has a large library of inscriptions and, almost certainly, the local and county record offices have details of inscriptions long since vanished
The old ones are very useful for

tracing family history. Quite often they are more accurate than the parish registers, and give more details such as age, trade, cause of death and family relationships.

212 Newspapers

The newspapers published since 1801 are at the British Museum Newspaper Library at Colindale, London, N.W.9. Those before that date are at the British Museum in Bloomsbury.

There is a 'Handlist of English and Welsh Newspapers 1620-1920' published by The Times in 1920, which is arranged chronologically Arranged geographically is a 'Handlist of English Provincial Newspapers and Periodicals 1700-1760' by G.A. Cranfield.

Part Nine — Maps and Map-makers

General

213 Cartographer

The person who surveys or draws the map. He is often signified on old maps by one of the following words or abbreviations: auctore, del., delt., delineavit, descripsit.

214 Cartouche

The panel which contains the map title, dedication, key etc. It first appeared in the 16th century and was usually highly ornamented.

215 Circle

This symbol has, from the earliest British maps, been used to denote a settlement or town.

216 Contours

The present method of depicting height with contour lines did not come into general use in this country until well into the 19th century.

217 Edition

The issues and reissues printed from one state (qv) of a plate or block.

218 Enclosure Award Maps

The Enclosure Acts usually provided that one copy of the award should be left with the Clerk of the Peace for the county, and one copy deposited in the local parish chest. Some Acts contained maps and these may still be available.

219 Engraver

The name of the engraver is quite often indicated on old maps by one of the following words or abbreviations: caelavit, engr., fecit, incidente, sc., sculp., sculpsit.

220 Estate Maps

These could be of any age and might show one manor or several.

221 Geological Maps

The Ordnance Survey completed a 1" to the mile geological survey of England between 1835 and 1888. There are three kinds of geological maps:

a) Solid — describing the nature of rocks underneath the surface.

b) Drift — these describe the upper surface only.

c) Solid with Drift — a combination of the two.

222 Hachuring

A late 16th century method of hill shading on maps.

223 Impression

A single sheet from a plate or block.

224 Issue

The total number of impressions from a plate or block at any one time.

225 Ordnance Survey

The Ordnance Survey was founded in 1791. It was called at that time the Trigonometrical Survey, and its main concern was to map Great Britain at a scale of 1″ to the mile.

The Old Series. This covered 110 sheets and its publication took place between 1805 and 1873, beginning with Essex. The New Series had already begun publication before the Old Series had completed its survey. The dating of the Old Series maps must be treated with caution and the real date of survey established by research. The actual publication can be over 20 years after the survey; alternatively it may be a revise — some plates were revised on numerous occasions and there could be twenty states of the same plates.

Further Series

The New Series, the second, was begun in 1840 and took 20 years. It was published in 300 sheets. Revision began in the 1890's. The Third Edition, 360 sheets, was begun in 1901. The Fourth Edition was surveyed in ten years from 1913 and the 146 sheets began publication in 1918. The Fifth edition began publication in 1931, the Sixth after the Second World War, and the Seventh in 1952.

The largest scale provided is 50″ to the mile for some urban areas; this will eventually cover all towns with a population of 20,000 and over.

226   Ordnance Survey Historical Maps

The Ordnance Survey have so far published:

Ancient Britain

This illustrates major archaeological remains above ground from prehistory to the Norman Conquest. Scale 1″ to 10 miles.

Southern Britain in the Iron Age

This covers an area south of a line from the Isle of Man to Scarborough, and the period 1000 years before the Roman invasion. Scale 1″ to 10 miles.

Roman Britain

This shows towns, villas and other settlements, roads, industrial sites etc. Scale 1″ to 15 miles.

Monastic Britain

This illustrates all monastic houses in medieval Britain and gives other ecclesiastical information. Scale 1″ to 10 miles.

Britain in the Dark Ages

This covers the period from the Roman Conquest to Alfred. Scale 1″ to 15 miles.

Britain in the 17th Century

This shows Britain after the Civil War. Scale 1″ to 15 miles.

227 Orientation

Maps are nowadays normally printed with the north at the head of the sheet. In medieval times east was usually at the top because of its religious significance.

228 Scale

The present statute mile was established in 1593 but long after that date maps were being drawn in local scales and relying upon local mile measurements.

229 State

If alterations were made to the plate or block, the impressions from them were said to be from a different state.

230 Tithe Maps

The Tithe Commutation Act 1836 converted the payment of tithes due to the rector of the parish into an annual rent. Tithe Maps were produced, mainly in the period 1838-1854, and were drawn to a scale between 13 and 26 inches to the mile. Three copies were made.

One copy was deposited at the Tithe Redemption Commission, 33/37 Finsbury Square, London EC2 — the most likely place to research; the second copy went to the appropriate Bishop and the third went to the parish authorities. The maps were accompanied by terriers.

Ordnance Survey published a 1″ to the mile map which showed the parishes covered by the tithe surveys. Scotland and Ireland were not affected by the legislation.

231 Transport Maps

In 1675 John Ogilby published his 'Britannia', which surveyed the country as a series of road maps. The 100 plates each had 6 or 7 strip maps. Ogilby introduced the measured statute mile to maps, ignoring local interpretations of mile measurement. He did this by the use of the 'wheel dimensurator', a device which recorded distance as it was wheeled along. Ogilby's measurements were used after 1740 for erecting milestones on main roads.

Map-Makers

232 Henry Beighton

His map of Warwickshire which he had surveyed by 1725 was one of the first to be based on trigonometrical principles. It also had the distinction of being an early 1″ to the mile depiction.

233 Emanuel Bowen

In 1720 he issued 'Britannia Depicta or Ogilby Improv'd', which contained county maps and road maps. The volume consisted of 270 plates.

234 William Camden (1551-1623)

In 1607 his 'Britannia' included a set of county maps largely based on Saxton and Norden.

235 John Cary (c1754-1835)

In 1787 he issued his 'New and Correct English Atlas' which, apart from being finely engraved, drew upon the many detailed county survey maps which had been done since the 1760's at the instigation of the Royal Society of Arts. The accurate depiction of roads is a strong feature in his maps.

236 Leonard Digges

In 1571 he published 'Pantometria' in which he described his own surveying instrument, the forerunner of the theodolite.

237 Christopher Greenwood

A prominent 19th century cartographer and publisher, his ambition was to produce a complete national set of 1″ to the mile maps, and this he nearly achieved.

238 Herman Moll (1688-1745)

In 1724 Moll, a Dutchman, issued a set of county maps in 'A New Description of England and Wales'. They were derived from previous cartographers but did include new descriptions of archaeological features.

239 Robert Morden

Morden was a publisher and cartographer. He improved and updated previous county maps, inserting roads which had been missed, asking 'knowing Gentlemen in each County' to make corrections on old plans where information was wrong. He continued to use a variety of scales with the mile representing from 1830 to 2430 yards, according to the local custom.

240 John Norden (1548-1626)

Norden set out to produce maps of each county but only Middlesex and Herts were published in his lifetime and Cornwall, Essex, Hampshire, Surrey and Sussex were printed much later. He included more roads than Saxton but the detail of these must be regarded with caution. He did, however, introduce two important innovations: a grid system whereby places could be found by a combination of letter and number, and also a distance chart in a triangular form still used today in many handbooks.

241 John Ogilby (1600-1676)

Ogilby introduced road maps or coaching maps as they were later called, which divided the country into strips and placed great emphasis on the roads available to the traveller.

242 John Rocque

Rocque issued county and town maps but his main contribution was a map of the Cities of London and Westminster on a large scale in 1746, and another one, the same year, for London and the area 10 miles around.

243 Christopher Saxton (c1542-1611)

During the period 1574-1579 he published the first county maps of England and Wales — 34 in all — and these were contained in a complete volume in 1579 called 'An Atlas of England and Wales'. Many of the plates were engraved on the Continent where engraving techniques were more advanced. Each map measured 15" a 18¼" and a variety of scales were used. The maps were deficient in their road detail.

244 Charles Smith

Smith published his 'New English Atlas' in 1809. The maps are strikingly similar to those of his contemporary, John Cary.

245 John Speed (1552-1629)

Speed was not a surveyor and compiled his maps from research. His innovation was to give a map of the county town within each county map.

Part Ten — County Record Offices, Societies and Periodicals

246

The address for a local society may normally be obtained from the local central library. Some of the societies listed may no longer be functioning.

Bedfordshire
County Record Office:
Shire Hall, Bedford.

Local Societies:
Ampthill and District Arch. Society
Bedford Arch. Society
Bedfordshire Arch. Council
Bedfordshire Historical Record Soc.
Manshead Arch. Soc. of Dunstable
South Beds. Arch. Soc.

Publications:
Bedfordshire Magazine (Crescent Press, Crescent Rd., Luton)
Bedfordshire & Northamptonshire Life

Berkshire
County Record Office:
Shire Hall, Reading

Local Societies:
Berkshire Arch. Society
Maidenhead & District Arch. and Historical Soc.
Newbury and District Field Club
Wantage and District Field Club

Local History Committee:
Central Library, Reading

Publications:
Berkshire Archaeological Journal (Berkshire Arch. Soc.)

Buckinghamshire
County Record Office:
County Offices, Aylesbury

Local Societies:

Amersham Society
Beaconsfield & District Hist. Soc.
Bletchley Arch. & Historical Soc.
Buckingham Arch. Soc.
Buckinghamshire Record Soc.
Chalfont St. Peter & Gerrards Cross
    History Soc.
Chenies Village Soc.
Cholesbury-cum-St Leonards Local
    History Group
Denham Historical Soc.
High Wycombe Historical Soc.
Little Chalfont Preservation Soc.
Long Crendon Preservation Soc.
Marlow Soc.
Middle Thames Arch. and Hist. Soc.
Pitstone Local History Soc.
Wolverton & Dist. Arch. Soc.

Publications:
The Records of Buckinghamshire
    (Bucks. Arch. Soc.)
Wolverton Historical Journal
    (Wolverton Arch. Soc.)

Cambridgeshire
County Record Office:
Shire Hall, Castle Hill, Cambridge

Local Societies:
Barrington Local History and
    Conservation Soc.
Cambridge Antiquarian Soc.
Cambridge Antiquarian Records Soc.

Local History Council:
7 Hills Road, Cambridge

Publications:
Cambridge Antiquarian Society
    Proceedings
Bulletin of the Cambs. Local
    History Council

Cheshire
County Record Office:
The Castle, Chester
City Record Office:
Town Hall, Chester

Local Societies:
Bromborough Soc.
Cheshire Community Council

Chester Arch. Soc.
Chetham Soc.
Congleton History Soc.
Halton Historical Soc.
Historic Soc. of Lancs and Cheshire
Hoylake Historical Soc.
Knutsford Soc.
Lancs and Cheshire Antiquarian Soc.
Lymm and District Local Hist. Soc.
Macclesfield & District Field Club
Marple Antiquarians Soc.
Middlewich Arch. Soc.
Record Soc. of Lancs and Cheshire
Stalybridge Historical Soc.
Stockport Historical Soc.
Winsford History Soc.

Local History Council:
Watergate House,
Watergate St, Chester.

Publications:
Cheshire Local History Ctte News-
    letter
Journal of the Chester Arch. Soc.
Transactions of the Historic Soc.
    of Lancs and Cheshire
Cheshire Historian (Cheshire
    Community Council)
Chester Life (Whitehorn Press,
    Philip's Park, Manchester 11)

Cornwall
County Record Office:
County Hall, Truro

Local Societies:
Bodmin Old Cornwall Soc.
Bude, Stratton & District OCS
Callington OCS
Camborne OCS
Carnon Downs OCS
Cornwall Arch. Soc.
Devon & Cornwall Record Soc.
Federation of Old Cornwall Socs.
Fowey OCS
Hayle OCS
Helston OCS
Launceston OCS
Liskeard OCS
Looe OCS
Lostwithiel OCS
Madron OCS

Mullion OCS
Newbury OCS
Padstow OCS
Par OCS
Penryn & Falmouth OCS
Pentewan OCS
Penzance OCS
Perranzabuloe OCS
Probus OCS
Redruth OCS
St Agnes OCS
St Austell OCS
St Ives OCS
St Just & Pendeen OCS
St Laddock OCS
Saltash OCS
Truro OCS
Tywardreath OCS
Wadesbridge OCS

Local History Group:
Gwendroc, Truro

Publications:
West Cornwall Field Club
    Proceedings
Cornish Magazine (Penpol Press,
    Falmouth)
Devon and Cornwall Notes &
    Queries
Old Cornwall (Fed. of Old Cornwall
    Societies)

Cumberland
County Record Office:
The Castle, Carlisle

Local Societies:
Cumberland and Westmorland
    Antiquarian and Arch. Soc.

Publications:
Cumbria (Dalesman Publishing Co.,
    Clapham, Lancaster)
Transactions of the Cumberland &
    Westmorland Antiq. and Arch.
    Soc.

Derbyshire
County Record Office:
County Offices, Matlock

Local Societies:

Bakewell & Dist. Historical Soc.
Belper Historical Soc.
Buxton Arch. and Natural Hist. Soc.
Derbyshire Arch. Soc.
Glossop & District Hist. Soc.
Ilkeston & District Local Hist. Soc.
Peakland Arch. Soc.
Peak District Mines Hist. Soc.
Swadlincote Arch. & Hist. Soc.

Publications:
Derbyshire Miscellany (Derbyshire
    Arch. Soc.)
Derbyshire Arch. Soc. Journal
Derbyshire Countryside (Derbyshire
    Rural Community Council, St.
    Michael's Church House, Queen
    St., Derby)

Devon
County Record Office:
County Hall, Exeter

Local Societies:
Brixham Museum and History Soc.
Devon and Cornwall Record Soc.
Devon Arch. Soc.
Devonshire Association
Exeter Industrial Arch. Group
History of Exeter & Sth West
    Research Group
Modbury Local History Society
Old Plymouth Soc.
Torquay Arch. Soc.
Totnes Museum Soc.

Publications:
Devonshire Association Transac-
    tions
The Devon Historian (Standing Con-
    ference for Devon History)
Devon and Cornwall Notes &
    Queries (Manchard House,
    Tiverton, Devon)

Dorset
County Record Office:
County Hall, Dorchester

Local Societies:
Dorset Natural History and Arch.
    Soc.
Dorset Record Soc.

Gillingham Local History Soc.
North Devon Arch. Soc.
Poole (WEA) Industrial Arch.
    Group
Shaftesbury & District Hist. Soc.
Sherborne Hist. Soc.
Wimborne Hist. Soc.

Publications:
Dorset Natural History and Arch.
    Society Proceedings

Durham
County Record Office:
County Hall, Durham

Local Societies:
Architectural and Arch. Soc. of
Durham and Northumberland
Darlington Hist. Soc.
Durham County LHS
Gateshead and Dist. Local Hist. Soc.
South Shields Arch. and Hist. Soc.
Sunderland Antiquarian Soc.
Teesdale Record Soc.
Tees-side Arch. Soc.

Publications:
Bulletin of the Durham County
Local History Society
Gateshead and District Local
    History Society Bulletin
Durham and Northumberland
    Architectural and Arch. Soc.
    Transactions

Essex
County Record Office:
County Hall, Chelmsford

Local Societies:
Benfleet & Dist. Hist. Soc.
Billericay Arch. and Hist. Soc.
Braintree & Bocking Local Hist. Soc.
Brentwood & District Hist. Soc.
Chigwell Local Hist. Soc.
Colchester Arch. Group
Colchester Preservation Group
Essex Arch. Soc.
Great Bardfield Hist. Soc.
Harlow and District Antiquarian
    Soc.
Maldon Preservation Soc.

Manningtree Preservation Soc.
Romford and District Hist. Soc.
Saffron Walden Antiquarian Soc.
Saffron Walden Hist. and Arch. Soc.
Southend-on-Sea and District Hist.
    Soc.
Thaxted Preservation Soc.
Thurrock Local History Soc.
Waltham Abbey Hist. Soc.
West Essex Arch. Group
Wickford & District Arch. Soc.
Witham Arch. Research Group
Woodford & District Hist. Soc.
Writtle Society

Publications:
Panorama (Thurrock Local Hist.
    Soc.)
Transactions of the Chigwell Local
    History Soc.
Essex Journal (Essex Arch. and
    Historical Congress)
Essex Archaeological Society
    Transactions
The Essex Countryside (Letchworth
    Printers, Norton Way North,
    Letchworth, Herts)
Journal of the Benfleet and
    District Historical Soc.
Essex Archaeological News

Gloucestershire
County Record Office:
Shire Hall, Gloucester

Local Societies:
Bristol Arch. Research Group
Bristol & Gloucestershire Arch. Soc.
Bristol Industrial Arch. Soc.
Bristol Record Soc.
Cheltenham Soc.
Cirencester Arch. and Hist. Soc.
Cotteswold Naturalists Field Club
Forest of Dean Local History Soc.
Frampton Cotterell Local History
    Group
Gloucester & District Arch.
    Research Committee
Kingswood & District Hist. Soc.
Olveston Parish Hist. Soc.
Pucklechurch Local History Soc.
Society of Thornbury Folk
South Cerney Trust (Hist. Section)
Wotton-under-Edge Hist. Soc.

Local History Committee:
Community House, College Green,
Gloucester
Publications:
Journal of the Bristol Industrial
 Arch. Soc.
Local History Bulletin from the
 Gloucester Community Council
Bristol and Gloucestershire Arch.
 Soc. Transactions
Gloucestershire Countryside
 (English Counties Periodicals Ltd.
 6 Lillington Ave., Leamington
 Spa)

Greater London
County Record Offices:
County Hall, S.E.1.
Middlesex Record Office, 1 Queen
 Anne's Gate Buildings, Dart-
 mouth Street, S.W.1.
Guildhall Library, Basinghall
 Street, E.C.2.
Local Societies:
Barking Hist. Soc.
Barnes Hist. Soc.
Barnet & District Local Hist. Soc.
Beddington, Carshalton &
 Wallington Arch. Soc.
Bexley Antiquarian Soc.
Brentford & Chiswick Local Hist.
 Soc.
Camden History Society
Chingford Hist. Soc.
City of London Arch. Soc.
City of London Soc.
Clapham Antiquarian Soc.
Ealing Local History Soc.
East London History Group
Edmonton Hundred Hist. Soc.
Enfield Arch. Soc.
Fulham History Soc.
Greater London Industrial Arch.
 Soc.
Greenwich & Lewisham Antiqua-
 rian Soc.
Hammersmith Local History Group
Hampton Hill Hist. Soc.
Harpenden & District Local Hist.
 Soc.
Hatch End & Pinner Hist. Soc.
Hayes and Harlington Local History
 Soc.
Hendon & District Arch. Soc.

Holborn Society
Hornsey Historical Soc.
Hounslow and District Hist. Soc.
Islington Antiquarian & Hist. Soc.
Kensington Society
Kingston-upon-Thames Arch. Soc.
Lamorbey & Sidcup Local History
 Soc.
Lewisham Local History Soc.
London & Middlesex Arch. Soc.
London Medieval Soc.
London Record Soc.
London Society
London Topographical Soc.
Merton & Morden Hist. Soc.
Mill Hill & Hendon Hist. Soc.
Mitcham Common Preservation Soc.
Norbury Arch. Soc.
Northolt Arch. and Hist. Research
 Group
Old Chiswick Protection Soc.
Orpington Hist. Soc.
Paddington Society
Romford & Dist. Hist. Soc.
Ruislip, Northwood & Eastcote
 Local History Soc.
St Marylebone Society
St Pancras Antiquarian Soc.
Southall Local History Soc.
Southwark & Lambeth Arch. Soc.
Staines Local History Soc.
Stanmore, Edgware & Harrow Hist.
 Soc.
Sunbury & Shepperton Local Hist.
 Soc.
Surbiton & District Hist. Soc.
University of London Staff Arch.
 Soc.
Twickenham Local History Soc.
Upminster Local History Group
Uxbridge Local History & Archives
 Soc.
Walthamstow Antiquarian Soc.
Wandsworth Hist. Soc.
Wanstead Local History Soc.
Wembley History Soc.
West Drayton & District Local
 History Soc.

Local History Committee:
3 Cameron House, Highlands Rd.,
Bromley, Kent

Publications:

London Archaeologist (7 Coalecroft
    Rd., S.W.15)
Staines Local History Soc. Journal
Transactions of the London &
    Middlesex Arch. Soc.
London Topographical Record
London & Middlesex Historian
    (London & Middlesex Arch. Soc.)
London Society Journal
East London Papers (University
    House, Victoria Park, Bethnal
    Green, E.2.)
Transactions of the Greenwich &
    Lewisham Antiquarian Soc.
Camden History Society Newsletter
Camden History Review

Hampshire
County Record Office:
The Castle, Winchester
City Record Office:
Guildhall, Portsmouth
City Record Office:
Guildhall, Winchester
Civic Record Office:
Civic Centre, Winchester

Local Societies:
Aldershot Soc.
Andover Arch. Soc.
Andover Local Archives Ctte.
Basingstoke Local History Group
Farnborough Local History Soc.
Fawley Local History Group
Fordingbridge Hist. Soc.
Hampshire Field Club & Arch. Soc.
Isle of Wight Natural History &
    Arch. Soc.
Lymington Hist. Record Soc.
Milford-on-Sea Historical Record Soc.
Petersfield Society
Southampton Arch. Soc.
South East Hampshire Genealogical
    Society
South Hampshire Arch. Rescue Gp.
Wickham History Soc.
Winchester Preservation Trust

Local History Council:
Beaconsfield House, Andover Rd.,
    Winchester

Publications:
Andover Arch. Soc. Bulletin
Hampshire Field Club and Arch.
    Soc. Proceedings

Hampshire, the County Magazine
    (Down and Son Ltd, Crowe
    Archway, Ringwood, Hants)

Herefordshire
County Record Office:
Shire Hall, Hereford

Local Society:
Archenfield Arch. Group

Hertfordshire
County Record Office:
County Hall, Hertford

Local Societies:
Berkhamstead & District Local
    History Soc.
Bishop's Stortford & Dist. Local
    History Soc.
East Herts Arch. Soc.
Edmonton Hundred Hist. Soc.
Hatfield & Dist. Arch. Soc.
Hemel Hempstead History & Local
    Record Soc.
Lockleys Arch. Soc.
North Herts Arch. Soc.
Potters Bar Hist. Soc.
Rickmansworth Hist. Soc.
St Albans & Herts Arch. Soc.
Watford & District Industrial
    History Soc.
Watford and South West Herts
    Arch. Soc.

Local History Council:
Museum and Art Gallery,
Paynes Park, Hitchin

Publications:
East Hertfordshire Arch. Soc.
    Newsletter
East Hertfordshire Arch. Soc.
    Transactions
Hertfordshire Countryside Illus-
    trated (Letchworth Printers,
    Norton Way North, Letchworth)
Hertfordshire Past and Present
    (Hertfordshire Local History
    Council)

Huntingdonshire
County Record Office:
County Offices, Huntingdon

Local Societies:
Huntingdonshire Local History Soc.

Publication:
The Records of Huntingdonshire
    (Hunts Local History Society)

Kent
County Record Office:
County Hall, Maidstone

Local Societies:
Ashford Arch. Soc.
Bearsted and District Local Hist.
    Soc.
Biddenden Local History Soc.
Broadstairs and St. Peters Arch.
    Soc.
Canterbury Arch. Soc.
Chatham & District Hist. Soc.
Cranbrook & District Local History
    Soc.
Crayford Manor House Hist. &
    Arch. Soc.
Dartford Antiquarian Soc.
Edenbridge & Dist. Hist. Soc.
Faversham Arch. Research Group
Faversham Society
Fawkham & Ash Arch. Group
Fawkham & District Hist. Soc.
Gillingham & Rainham Local
    History Group
Gravesend Hist. Soc.
Hawkhurst Local History Soc.
Headcorn Local History Soc.
Herne Bay Records Soc.
Isle of Thanet Arch. & Hist. Soc.
Kent Arch. Soc.
Kent Council for Kent Arch.
Lamberhurst Local History Soc.
Lower Medway Arch. Research Gp.
Maidstone Area Arch. Group
Orpington Historical Soc.
Otford & District Hist. Soc.
Reculver Excavation Group
St Margaret's Bay Local History
    Soc.
Sandwich Hist. Soc.

Shorne Local History Group
Sittingbourne & Swale Arch.
    Research Group
Tenterden & District Local
    History Soc.
Tonbridge Hist. Soc. Arch. Gp.
West Kent Border Arch. Group
Whitstable Hist. Soc.
Wye Hist. Soc.

Local History Committee:
1 Holmesdale Terrace, Folkestone

Publications:
Cantium
Archaeologia Cantiana (Kent Arch.
    Soc.)

Lancashire
County Record Office:
Sessions House, Lancaster Rd.,
Preston

Local Societies:
Blackburn Soc. of Antiquaries
Bolton & District Arch. Soc.
Burnley & Dist. Hist. Soc.
Chetham Society
Chorley & Dist. Arch. Soc.
Colne & District Local History Soc.
Crosby & District Hist. Soc.
Eccles & Dist. History Soc.
Formby Society
Fylde Hist. Soc.
Garstang Hist. Soc.
Helmshore Local Hist. Soc.
Historic Soc. of Lancs and Cheshire
Huyton-with-Roby History Soc.
Kirkby Local History Soc.
Lancs and Cheshire Antiquarian
    Soc.
Lonsdale Hist. Soc.
Manchester Genealogical Soc.
Middleton Hist. Soc.
Nelson Hist. Soc.
Pilling and District Hist. Soc.
Prescot Hist. Soc.
Radcliffe & District Literary &
    Scientific Soc. (Arch. and Hist.
    Section)
Record Soc. of Lancs & Cheshire
Rochdale Soc. for Industrial History
Southport Local History Soc.

Warrington & District Arch. & Hist.
    Soc.
Widnes Hist. Soc.
Wigan and District Historic &
    Antiquarian Soc.

Local History Committee:
Community Council of Lancashire
Selnec House, Manchester 14

Publications:
Transactions of the Historic Soc. of
    Lancs and Cheshire
Lancashire Life (Whitehorn Press,
    Philips Park, Manchester)

Leicestershire
County Record Office:
57 New Walk, Leicester
City Record Office:
Museum and Art Gallery, Leicester

Local Societies:
Hinckley & District Field Club
Leicestershire Arch. Excavation
    Group
Leicestershire Arch. & Hist. Soc.
Loughborough & Dist. Arch. Soc.
Market Harborough Arch. & Hist.
    Soc.
University of Leicester Arch. Soc.

Local History Committee:
133 Loughborough Road, Leicester

Publications:
Leicestershire Historian (Leics.
    Local History Committee)
Leicestershire Arch. & Hist. Soc.
    Transactions

Lincolnshire
County Record Office:
County Archives Offices, The Castle,
Lincoln

Local Societies:
Coningsby & Tattershall Local
    History Society
Grantham Local History Soc.
Holton Beckering Local History Soc.
Lincoln Arch. Research Ctte.
Lincoln Record Soc.

Lincolnshire Industrial Arch. Gp.
Lincolnshire Local Hist. Soc.
Men of the Stones
Scunthorpe Museum Soc. (Local
    History and Arch. Section)
Spalding Gentlemen's Soc.
Stamford & Rutland Arch. and
    Natural History Soc.

Publications:
Lincolnshire History & Archaeology
    (Lincs. Local History Soc.)
Lincolnshire Historian (Lincs. Local
    History Soc.)
Lincolnshire Life (Roy Faiers Ltd.
    Humber House, Town Hall Sq.,
    Grimsby, Lincs)

Norfolk
County Record Office:
Central Library, Norwich

Local Societies:
Norfolk and Norwich Arch. Soc.
Norfolk Record Soc.
Norfolk Research Ctte.
Norwich Soc.

Publications:
Norfolk Archaeology (Norfolk &
    Norwich Arch. Soc.)
East Anglian Magazine (6 Colman
    St., Ipswich)
Norfolk Life (Trades and Industrial
    Press, 31 Prince of Wales Rd.,
    Norwich)

Northamptonshire
County Record Office:
Delapré Abbey, Northampton

Local Societies:
Corby Natural History & Arch. Soc.
Irthlingborough Hist. Soc.
Northamptonshire Antiquarian Soc.
Northamptonshire Industrial Arch.
    Gp.
Northamptonshire Federation of
    Arch. Societies
Northamptonshire Natural History
    Field Club
Northamptonshire Record Soc.
Peterborough Soc.
Peterborough Museum Soc.

Thrapston & District Hist. Soc.
Upper Nene Arch. Soc.
Wellingborough & District Arch.
  Soc.
Woodford Halse Hist. Soc.

Local History Committee:
Plowmans, Stoke Road, Blisworth,
Northampton

Publications:
Northamptonshire Past and Present
  (Northants Record Soc.)
Bulletin of the Northants
  Federation of Arch. Socs.

Northumberland
County Record Office:
Melton Park, North Gosforth,
Newcastle-upon-Tyne 3

Local Societies:
Allendale Local History Group
Aln and Breamish Local History Soc.
Architectural & Arch. Society of
  Durham and Northumberland
Bellingham & North Tyne Local
  History Group
Berwick-upon-Tweed Local History
  Soc.
Haltwhistle History Soc.
Hexham History Soc.
Morpeth Antiquarian Society
Newcastle-upon-Tyne Soc. of
  Antiquaries
Northumberland Local History Soc.
Rothbury & Coquetdale Hist. Soc.
Tynemouth Antiquarian & Hist. Soc.
Wooler Local History Group

Publications:
Northumberland Local History
  Society Newsletter
Durham and Northumberland
  Architectural & Archaeological
  Society Transactions
Archaeologia Aeliana (Society of
  Antiquaries of Newcastle-upon-
  Tyne)
Newcastle Life (Trade and
  Industrial Press, Pearl Buildings,
  Northumberland St., Newcastle-
  upon-Tyne)

Nottinghamshire
County Record Office:
County House, High Pavement,
Nottingham

Local Societies:
Newark Arch. and Local History
  Soc.
Old Mansfield Soc:
Ruddington & District History Soc.
The Thoroton Society
Worksop & District Arch. & Local
  History Soc.

Local History Council:
Shire Hall, High Pavement,
Nottingham

Publications:
Transactions of the Thoroton Soc.

Oxfordshire
County Record Office:
County Hall, New Road, Oxford

Local Societies:
Banbury Hist. Soc.
Bicester Local History Circle
Enstone Local History Circle
Oxford Arch. & Hist. Soc.
Oxford Historical Soc.
Oxford University Arch. Soc.
Oxfordshire Arch. Soc.
Oxfordshire Record Soc.

Local History Committee:
Oxfordshire Rural Community
Council, Hadow House,
20 Beaumont St, Oxford

Publications:
Cake and Cock Horse (Banbury
  Hist. Soc.)
Oxoniensia (Oxford Arch. and Hist.
  Soc.

Rutland
Local Societies:
Rutland Field Research Group
Rutland Local History Soc.
Stamford & Rutland Arch. and
  Natural Hist. Soc.

Shropshire
County Record Office:
New Shirehall, Abbey Foregate,
Shrewsbury

Local Societies:
Bridgnorth & District Hist. Soc.
Offa Antiquarian Soc.
Shropshire Arch. Soc.

Local History Council:
Shrewsbury Museum, Castle Gates,
Shrewsbury

Publications:
Shropshire Arch. and Natural
    History Soc. Transactions
Shropshire Magazine (Shrewsbury
    Chronicle, Castle Foregate,
    Shrewsbury)

Somerset
County Record Office:
Obridge Road, Taunton

Local Societies:
Axbridge Caving Group & Arch.
    Soc.
Banwell Soc. of Arch.
Bath and Camerton Arch. Soc.
Bridgwater & District Arch. Soc.
Burnham-on-Sea Arch. & Natural
    History Soc.
Clevedon & District Arch. Soc.
Exmoor Society
Frome Soc. for Local Study
Glastonbury Antiquarian Soc.
North Somerset Arch. Research Gp.
Portishead Preservation Soc.
Somerset Arch. Soc.
Somerset Record Soc.
Wells Natural History and Arch. Soc.
Yeovil Arch. and Local History Soc.

Publications:
The Exmoor Review (Exmoor Soc.)
Somersetshire Archaeological &
    Natural History Society
    Proceedings
Notes and Queries for Somerset and
    Dorset (T.J. Hunt, Orchard End,
    Cheddon Road, Taunton)

Staffordshire
County Record Office:
County Buildings, Eastgate Street,
    Stafford

Local Societies:
Bilston Hist. Soc.
Burton-on-Trent Natural History
    and Arch. Soc.
Cheadle and District Hist. Soc.
Keele & Newcastle Arch. Soc.
Kinver Hist. Soc.
Lichfield and South Staffordshire
    Arch. and Hist. Soc.
Newcastle-under-Lyme Antiquarian
    Soc.
North Staffs Arch. Soc.
Old Nortonian Soc.
Old Stafford Soc.
Pattingham Local Hist. Soc.
South Staffs Arch & Hist. Soc.
Stafford Hist. and Civic Soc.
Staffordshire Record Soc.
Stoke-on-Trent Museum Arch. Soc.

Local History Council:
Pendrell Hall, College of Residential
Adult Education, Codsall Wood,
Wolverhampton

Publications:
Stafford Historical and Civic
    Society Transactions
Lichfield Arch. and Hist. Soc.
    Transactions

Suffolk
County Record Offices:
Bury St Edmunds and West Suffolk
Record Office, 8 Angel Hill, Bury
St Edmunds

Ipswich and East Suffolk Record
Office, County Hall, Ipswich

Local Societies:
Beccles and District Hist. Soc.
Framlingham & Dist. Local History
    & Preservation Soc.
Southwold Arch & Natural History
    Soc.
Suffolk Institute of Arch.
Suffolk Records Soc.

Local History Council:
County Hall, Ipswich

Publications:
Suffolk Review (Suffolk Local
    History Council)
Suffolk Institute of Arch.
    Proceedings
East Anglian Magazine (6 Colman
    St., Ipswich)

Surrey
County Record Office:
County Hall, Kingston-upon-
    Thames

Local Societies:
Beddington, Carshalton &
    Wallington Arch. Soc.
Bourne Society
Esher District Local Hist. Soc.
Farnham Museum Soc.
Horley Local History Association
Leatherhead & District Local
    History Soc.
Nonsuch & Ewell Antiquarian Soc.
Oxted & District Hist. Soc.
Sanderstead Preservation Soc.
Surrey Arch. Soc.
Surrey Record Soc.
Walton & Weybridge Local History
    Soc.

Local History Council:
2 Jenner Road, Guildford

Publications:
Bourne Society Bulletin
Bourne Society Local History
    Records
Journal of the Farnham Museum
    Soc.
Esher District Local History Soc.
    News-sheets
Nonsuch & Ewell Antiquarian Soc.
    Bulletin
Proceedings of the Leatherhead &
    District Local History Soc.
Surrey Archaeological Collections
    (Surrey Arch. Soc.)

Sussex
County Record Offices:

West Sussex Record Office, County
Hall, Chichester

East Sussex Record Office, Pelham
House, Lewes

Local Societies:
Battle & District Hist. Soc.
Brighton and Hove Arch. Soc.
Cuckfield Society
Ditchling Preservation Soc.
Eastbourne Natural History & Arch.
    Soc.
Hailsham Hist. Soc.
Hastings & St. Leonards Museum
    Association
Hawkhurst Local History Soc.
Horsham Museum Soc.
Lewes Arch. Group
Littlehampton Natural Science &
    Arch. Soc.
Northiam & District Hist. & Literary
    Soc.
Old Hastings Preservation Soc.
Old Patcham Preservation Soc.
Robertsbridge & District Arch. Soc.
Rottingdean Preservation Soc.
Rye Museum Association
Steyning Soc.
Sussex Arch. Soc.
Sussex Industrial Arch. Study Gp.
Sussex Record Soc.
Worthing Arch. Soc.

Publications:
Sussex Industrial History (Sussex
    Industrial Arch. Study Group)
Sussex Arch. Collections (Sussex
    Arch. Soc.)
Sussex Notes and Queries (Sussex
    Arch. Soc.)

Warwickshire
County Record Office:
Cape street, Warwick

Local Societies:
Alcester Civic Soc.
Atherstone Arch. Soc.
Birmingham & Warwickshire Arch.
    Soc.
Coventry & Dist. Arch. Soc.

Kenilworth Hist. Soc.
Rugby Arch. Soc.
Warwickshire Local History Soc.

Publications:
Warwickshire History (Warks Local
    History Soc.)
Warwickshire and Worcs and
    Birmingham Illustrated (English
    Counties Periodicals, 6 Lillington
    Ave, Leamington Spa, Warks)

Westmorland
Local Society:
Cumberland and Westmorland
Antiquarian and Arch. Soc.

Publications:
Cumberland and Westmorland
    Antiquarian and Arch. Soc.
    Transactions
Cumbria (Dalesman Publishing Co.,
    Clapham, Lancaster)

Wiltshire
County Record Office:
County Hall, Trowbridge

Local Societies:
Bourne Valley Hist. & Records Soc.
Cricklade Hist. Soc.
Melksham & District Hist. Assoc.
Salisbury & District Preservation
    Trust
Salisbury & Sth. Wilts Industrial
    Arch. Soc.
Swindon Public Libraries Arch. Soc.
Wiltshire Arch. & Natural History
    Group
Wiltshire Record Soc.

Publication:
Wilts Arch. and Natural History
    Society Magazine

Worcestershire
County Record Office:
Shire Hall, Worcester

Local Societies:
Alvechurch Hist. Soc.
Bordesley Soc.
Bromyard Local History Soc.

Hagley Hist. and Field Society
Kidderminster & Dist. Arch. & Hist.
    Soc.
Oldbury Hist. Soc.
Stourbridge Hist. & Arch. Soc.
Vale of Evesham Hist. Soc.
Worcestershire Arch. Soc.
Worcestershire Hist. Soc.

Publications:
Worcs. Arch. Soc. Transactions
Warwickshire, Worcs and
    Birmingham Illustrated (English
    Counties Periodicals, 6 Lillington
    Ave., Leamington Spa, Warks)

Yorkshire
County Record Offices:
East Riding: County Record Office,
County Hall, Beverley.

West Riding: Archives Department,
Sheepscar Branch Library, Leeds 7

North Riding: County Hall,
Northallerton

Local Societies:
Aireborough & Horsforth Museum
    Soc.
Barnsley Arch. Soc.
Batley Museum Soc.
Bradford Hist. and Antiquarian Soc.
Brompton Local History Group
Cleveland & Tees-side Local History
    Soc.
Cottingham Local History Soc.
East Riding Antiquarian Soc.
East Riding Arch. Soc.
East Yorkshire Local History Soc.
Forest of Galtres Soc.
Fylingdales Local History Group
Georgian Soc. for East Yorkshire
Goathland Local History Soc.
Halifax Antiquarian Soc.
Harrogate Group of Yorks Arch.
    Socs.
Hebden Bridge Literary & Scientific
    Soc. (Local History Section)
Helmsley & Area Group of Yorks
    Arch. Socs.
Historical Handsworth Group
Huddersfield & District Arch. Soc.

Hunmanby Local History Soc.
Hunter Arch. Soc.
Morton Hist. Soc.
Otley Arch. & Hist. Soc.
Pontefract & Dist. Arch. Soc.
Ripon Civic Soc.
Scarborough & Dist. Arch. Soc.
Sheffield Council for the Conservation of Sheffield Antiquities
Stannington Local History Group
The Thoresby Society (Leeds)
Wakefield Arch. Research Group
Wakefield Hist. Soc.
Wetherby & Dist. Hist. Soc.
Wheldrake Local History Soc.
Yorkshire Arch. Soc.
Yorkshire Architectural and York Arch. Soc.

Publications:
Cleveland and Tees-side Local History Soc. Bulletin
Miscellany of the Thoresby Society
Pontefract and District Arch. Soc. Annual Journal
The Hunter Arch. Soc. Transactions
The Yorkshire Arch. Journal (Yorks Arch. Soc.)
The Bradford Antiquary (Bradford Hist. & Antiquarian Soc.)
The Dalesman (Dalesman Publishing Co., Clapham, Lancaster)
Halifax Antiquarian Soc. Transactions
Yorkshire Life Illustrated (Whitehorn Press, Philip's Park, Manchester 11)

Wales
Record Offices:
National Library of Wales, Aberystwyth
Anglesey: County Record Office, Shire Hall, Llangefni
Caernarvon: County Record Office, Caernarvon
Carmarthen: County Record Office, County Hall, Carmarthen
Flintshire: County Record Office, The Old Rectory, Hawarden, Deeside
Glamorgan: County Record Office, County Hall, Cathays Park, Cardiff
Merioneth: County Record Office, County Offices, Dolgellan
Monmouthshire: County Record Office, County Hall, Newport
Pembroke: County Record Office, County Offices, Haverfordwest

Local Societies:
Abergavenny Arch. Group
Abergele Field Club
Abertillery & District Museum and Bosworth Soc.
Anglesey Antiq. Soc. & Field Club
Barry and Vale Arch. Group
Blaenavon LHS,
Brecknock Soc.
Bridgend Dist. LHS
Caerleon LHS
Caernarvonshire Hist. Soc.
Caerphilly LHS
Cambrian Arch. Ass.
Cardiff Arch. Soc.
Cardiganshire Antiq. Soc.
Carmarthenshire Antiq. Soc.
Carmarthenshire Community Council
Chepstow Soc.
Cynon Valley Hist. Soc.
Denbighshire Hist. Soc.
Dyserth Field Club
Ebbw Vale LHS
Flintshire Hist. Soc.
Gelligaer Hist. Soc.
Glamorgan Hist. Soc.
Glyncorrwy, Cymer and Afan Hist. Soc.
Gower Soc.
Llandudno, Colwyn Bay and District Field Club
Llantwit Major LHS
Maesteg Hist. and Record Soc.
Merioneth Hist. and Record Soc.
Merthry Tydfil Hist. Soc.
Monmouth Antiquarian Soc.
Monmouthshire & Caerleon Antiq. Assoc.
Monmouthshire LH Council
Mynyddislwyn and Bedwellty LHS
Neath Antiq. Soc.
Pembrokeshire LHS
Pembrokeshire Record Soc.

Penarth District LHS
Pontnewydd LHS
Pontypool and District Soc.
Pontypridd and Dist. Hist. Soc.
Port Talbot Hist. Soc.
Powys-land Club
Radnorshire Soc.
Raglan LHS
Rhondda Soc.
Risca–Oxford House Ind. Arch. Soc.
Ruabon and Dist. Field Club
South East Glamorgan Ind. Arch.
   Soc.
South West Wales Ind. Arch. Soc.
Tredegar LHS
Usk LHS

Publications:
Carmarthenshire Historian (Carmarthenshire Local History Ctte.)
Presenting Monmouthshire (Monmouthshire Local History Council)
Transactions of the Caernarvonshire Hist. Soc.
Ceredigion: Journal of the Cardiganshire Antiquarian Soc.
Caernarvonshire Record Office Bulletin
Pembrokeshire Historian (Pembroke Community Council)
Carmarthenshire Antiquary
Transactions of the Port Talbot Hist. Soc.
Journal of the Flintshire Arch. Soc.
Monmouthshire Antiquary (Monm. and Caerlean Antiq. Assoc.)
Archaeologia Cambrensis (Cambrian Arch. Assoc.)
Chester and North Wales Arch. and Hist. Society Journal
Denbighshire Historical Soc. Transactions
Glamorgan Local History Soc. Transactions
The Montgomeryshire Collections (The Powys-land Club)
Radnorshire Soc. Transactions

Scotland
   There are no County Record Offices in Scotland; records are kept by the towns themselves. The Scottish Record Office is at H.M. General Register House, Edinburgh 2.

Local Societies:
Abertay Hist. Soc.
Ayrshire Arch. & Natural History Soc.
Banffshire Soc.
Breadalbane Arch. Soc.
Cowal Arch Soc.
Cumbernauld & Dist. Hist. Soc.
Dumfriesshire & Galloway Natural History and Antiquarians Soc.
East Lothian Antiquarian and Field Naturalists Soc.
Edinburgh University Arch. Soc.
Eskdale & Liddersdale Arch. Soc.
Falkirk Arch. & Natural Hist. Soc.
Forfar & Dist. Hist. Soc.
Glasgow Arch. Soc.
Hawick Arch. Soc.
Inverness Scientific Soc. and Field Club
Kintyre Antiquarian Soc.
Kirkcaldy Antiquarian Soc.
Kirkintilloch & Dist. Soc. of Antiquaries
Lorn Arch. Soc.
Mid-Argyll Natural History & Antiquarian Soc.
Mull Field Club
Orkney Record & Antiquarian Soc.
Scottish History Soc.
Scottish Record Soc.
Selkirkshire Antiquarian Soc.
Society of Antiquaries of Scotland
Stirling Field & Arch. Soc.
West Lothian County Hist. Soc.
Wigtownshire Antiquarian & Natural History Soc.

Publications:
The Celtic Voice (Graham Bros. 5, The Street, Didmarton, Badminton, Glos.)
Scotland's Magazine (6 Castle Terr. Edinburgh)
The Scots Magazine (7 Bank St., Dundee, Angus)
Scottish Studies (University of Edinburgh, School of Scottish Studies)
Hawick Arch. Soc. Transactions

The Kist (The Natural History and Antiquarian Soc. of Mid Argyll)

Part Eleven — National Societies and Periodicals

247 Archaeology
BRITISH ARCHAEOLOGICAL ASSOCIATION, British Museum, W.C.1.

COUNCIL FOR BRITISH ARCHAEOLOGY, 8 St Andrew's Place, N.W.1.

COUNCIL FOR BRITISH ARCHAEOLOGY (SCOTTISH REGIONAL GROUP) National Museum of Antiquities, Queen St., Edinburgh 2

DESERTED MEDIEVAL VILLAGE RESEARCH GROUP, 67 Gloucester Crescent, N.W.1.

FIELD STUDIES COUNCIL, 9 Devereux Court, Strand, W.C.2.

HISTORICAL METALLURGY GROUP, Dept. of Metallurgy, University of Newcastle-upon-Tyne.

INSTITUTE OF ARCHAEOLOGY, 31 Gordon Square, W.C.1.

RESCUE, 25A, The Tything, Worcester.

ROYAL ARCHAEOLOGICAL INSTITUTE, 9 Somerset Road, New Barnet, Herts.

SOCIETY OF MEDIEVAL ARCHAEOLOGY, British Museum, W.C.1.

SOCIETY FOR POST-MEDIEVAL ARCHAEOLOGY, 3 Headingly Lane, Leeds 6.

Publications:
The Archaeological Journal (Royal Archaeological Institute of Great Britain and Ireland, c/o London Museum).
Medieval Archaeology (Soc. for Medieval Archaeology)
Current Archaeology, (9 Nassington Road, N.W.3.)
CBA Calendar of Excavations (CBA, 8 St Andrew's Place, N.W.1.)
AGO — The New Archaeological Magazine (Archaeological Centre, 50, Braidley Road, Bournemouth)

248 Army and Navy
ARMS AND ARMOUR SOCIETY 40 Great James St, W.C.1.

COMMITTEE FOR NAUTICAL ARCHAEOLOGY, c/o Institute of Archaeology, 31-34 Gordon Square, W.C.1.

LIVERPOOL NAUTICAL RESEARCH SOCIETY, 28 Alexandra Drive, Liverpool 17

MILITARY HISTORY SOCIETY Centre Block, Duke of Yorks Headquarters, S.W.3.

NATIONAL MARITIME MUSEUM, Greenwich, S.E.10.

NAVY RECORDS SOCIETY, c/o Royal Naval College, S.E.10.

SOCIETY FOR ARMY HISTORICAL RESEARCH, Library, War Office, S.W.1.

SOCIETY FOR NAUTICAL RESEARCH, National Maritime Museum, S.E.10.

249 Folklore and Dialect
ENGLISH FOLK DANCE AND SONG SOCIETY, Cecil Sharp House, 2 Regent's Park Road, N.W.1.

FOLK-LORE SOCIETY, c/o University College, Gower St. W.C.1.

GYPSY-LORE SOCIETY, The Library, The University of Liverpool

HONOURABLE SOCIETY OF CYMMRODORION, 118 Newgate St, E.C.1.

LAKELAND DIALECT SOCIETY 8 Barras Close, Morton Park, Carlisle

SOCIETY FOR FOLK LIFE STUDIES, National Museum, Queen St, Edinburgh

YORKSHIRE DIALECT SOCIETY East View, Warren Lane, Eldwick, Bingley, Yorks

Publication:
Folklore (the Folklore Society)

250 Genealogy and Heraldry
BATH HERALDIC SOCIETY, 102 Sydney Place, Bath, Somerset

COLLEGE OF ARMS, Queen Victoria Street, E.C.3.

HARLEIAN SOCIETY, Church Cottage, Thames Ditton, Surrey

HERALDRY SOCIETY, 59 Gordon Sq, W.C.1.

INSTITUTE OF HERALDIC & GENEALOGICAL STUDIES, Northgate, Canterbury

LANCASHIRE PARISH REGISTER SOCIETY, The John Rylands Library, Manchester 3

LORD LYON KING OF ARMS, H.M. Register House, Edinburgh

MANCHESTER GENEALOGICAL SOCIETY, Norwood, 685 Burnage Lane, Manchester 19

HERALDRY SOCIETY, Maj. J. Waring, Combined Stats/Record Centre F.E.

SCOTS ANCESTRY RESEARCH COUNCIL, North Saint David St, Edinburgh

SCOTTISH GENEALOGICAL SOCIETY, 16 Charlotte Square, Edinburgh 2

SOCIETY OF GENEALOGISTS, 37 Harrington Gardens, S.W.7

STAFFORDSHIRE PARISH REGISTERS SOCIETY, 22 Somerford Place, Willenhall, Staffs

YORKSHIRE ARCHAEOLOGICAL SOCIETY: PARISH REGISTER SECTION, 10 Park Place, Leeds 1.

Publications:
The Genealogist Magazine (Soc. of Genealogists)
The Scottish Genealogist (Scottish Genealogist Soc.)
The Genealogical Quarterly (Research Publishing, 52 Lincoln's Inn, W.C.2.)
The Armorial (Gayre & Nigg, 1 Darnaway St, Edinburgh 3)
The Coat of Arms (The Heraldry Society, Swalcliffe, Banbury, Oxon)
Heraldry Gazette (The Heraldry Society, Swalcliffe, Banbury, Oxon.)

251 Learned Societies and Institutions
BRITISH RECORD SOCIETY, Dept of History, University of Keele, Staffs

BRITISH RECORDS ASSOCIATION, The Charterhouse, London, E.C.1.

EARLY ENGLISH TEXT SOCIE-

TY, 40 Walton Crescent, Oxford

ENGLISH PLACE-NAME SOCIE-
TY, School of English Studies,
University of Nottingham

HISTORICAL ASSOCIATION, 59a
Kennington Park Road, S.E.11

HISTORICAL MANUSCRIPTS
COMMISSION, Quality House,
Quality Court, Chancery Lane,
W.C.2.

INSTITUTE OF HISTORICAL RE-
SEARCH, University of London,
Senate House, W.C.1.

MONUMENTAL BRASS SOCIETY,
The Elms, 90 High St, Newport
Pagnell, Bucks

MUSEUMS ASSOCIATION, 87
Charlotte St, W.1.

THE NAMES SOCIETY, 57 Chess-
ington Way, West Wickham, Kent

PIPE ROLL SOCIETY, Public
Record Office, W.C.2.

PREHISTORIC SOCIETY, c/o Sub-
Dept. of Prehistory and Roman Britain, British Museum, W.C.1.

ROYAL ANTHROPOLOGICAL
INSTITUTE OF GREAT BRITAIN
AND IRELAND, 21 Bedford
Square, W.C.1.

ROYAL COMMISSION ON HIS-
TORICAL MONUMENTS, Fielden
House, Great College St, S.W.1.

ROYAL COMMISSION ON HIS-
TORICAL MONUMENTS (Wales),
Edleston House, Queens Rd,
Aberystwyth

ROYAL GEOGRAPHICAL SOCIE-
TY, 1 Kensington Gore, S.W.7.

ROYAL HISTORICAL SOCIETY,

University College, Gower St, W.C.1.

SOCIETY FOR THE PROMOTION
OF ROMAN STUDIES, 31 Gordon
Square

SOCIETY OF ANTIQUARIES OF
LONDON, Burlington House,
Piccadilly, W.1.

SOCIETY OF ARCHIVISTS, County Record Office, County Hall,
Hertford

SURTEES SOCIETY, County Record Office, County Hall, Durham.
(Publishes documents relating to the
north of England and the Province
of York)

VIKING SOCIETY FOR NORTH-
ERN RESEARCH, University
College, Gower St, W.C.1.

Publications:
Midland History (twice yearly)
University of Birmingham. Publi-
shed by Phillimore & Co.

Scottish Historical Review
Aberdeen University Press for the
Company of Scottish History Ltd.

English Historical Review
Longman Group, 33 Montgomery
St, Edinburgh

252 Preservation
ANCIENT MONUMENTS SOCIE-
TY, 12 Edwardes Square, W.8.

CENTRAL COUNCIL FOR THE
CARE OF CHURCHES, 83 London
Wall, E.C.2.

COUNCIL FOR THE PROTECT-
ION OF RURAL ENGLAND, 4
Hobart Place, S.W.1.

COUNCIL FOR THE PROTECT-
ION OF RURAL WALES, Meifod,
Montgomeryshire

GEORGIAN GROUP, 2 Chester St.
S.W.1.

HISTORIC CHURCHES PRESER-
VATION TRUST, Fulham Palace,
S.W.6.

NATIONAL MONUMENTS RE-
CORD, Fielden House, 10 Great
College St, S.W.1.

NATIONAL TRUST FOR PLACES
OF HISTORIC INTEREST OR
NATURAL BEAUTY, 42 Queen
Anne's Gate, S.W.1.

REDUNDANT CHURCHES FUND,
St. Andrew-by-the-Wardrobe, Queen
Victoria St, E.C.4.

SOCIETY FOR THE PROTECTION
OF ANCIENT BUILDINGS, 55
Great Ormond St, W.C.1.

VICTORIAN SOCIETY, 55 Gt
Ormond St, W.C.1.

253 Religion
BAPTIST HISTORICAL SOCIETY,
Baptist Church House, 4 Southamp-
ton Row, W.C.1.

CANTERBURY AND YORK SO-
CIETY, 79 Whitwell Way, Coton,
Cambridge. (Publication of Bishops'
Registers)

CATHOLIC RECORD SOCIETY,
48 Lowndes Square, S.W.1.

CHURCH COMMISSIONERS,
1 Millbank, S.W.1.

CONGREGATIONAL HISTORI-
CAL SOCIETY (See United Reformed Church)

ENGLISH CHURCH HISTORY
SOCIETY, 68 Irby Road, Heswall,
Cheshire

FRIENDS HISTORICAL SOCIETY,
Friends House, Euston Road, N.W.1.

HUGUENOT SOCIETY OF LON-
DON, c/o The Huguenot Library,
University College, Gower St, W.C.1.

JEWISH HISTORICAL SOCIETY,
University College, Gower St,W.C.1.

LAMBETH PALACE LIBRARY,
S.E.1.

METHODIST ARCHIVES AND
RESEARCH CENTRE, 25-35 City
Road, E.C.1.

PRESBYTERIAN HISTORICAL
SOCIETY, 86 Tavistock Place, W.C.1.

STRICT BAPTIST HISTORICAL
SOCIETY, 26 Denmark Street, Bedford

UNITARIAN HISTORICAL SO-
CIETY, Unitarian College, Victoria
Park, Manchester 14

UNITED REFORMED CHURCH
HISTORICAL SOCIETY, 86 Tavistock Square, W.C.1.

WESLEY HISTORICAL SOCIETY,
94 Albany Road, Redruth, Cornwall

WESLEYAN REFORM UNION,
Church House, 123 Queen Street,
Sheffield.

254 Trade and Social History
BRITISH AGRICULTURAL HIS-
TORY SOCIETY, c/o Museum of
English Rural Life, The University
of Reading, Whiteknights Park,
Reading

BRITISH SOCIETY FOR THE HIS-
TORY OF MEDICINE, Wellcome
Historical Medical Library, Well-
come Building, Euston Road, N.W.1.

BRITISH THEATRE MUSEUM
ASSOCIATION, Leighton House,
12 Holland Park Road, W.14

BUSINESS ARCHIVES COUNCIL, 63 Queen Victoria St, E.C.4.

CAMBRIDGE UNIVERSITY HISTORY OF MEDICINE SOCIETY, 4 Sylvester Rd, Cambridge

COSTUME SOCIETY, c/o Dept. of Textiles, Victoria and Albert Museum, S.W.7.

ECONOMIC HISTORY SOCIETY, London School of Economics, Aldwych, W.C.2.

FURNITURE HISTORY SOCIETY, c/o Dept. of Furniture and Woodwork, Victoria and Albert Museum, S.W.7.

GARDEN HISTORY SOCIETY, 15 St. Margarets Close, Berkhamsted, Herts

MUSEUM OF ENGLISH RURAL LIFE, University of Reading, Whiteknights Park, Reading

NATIONAL COUNCIL OF SOCIAL SERVICE, 26 Bedford Square, W.C.1.

NATIONAL FEDERATION OF WOMEN'S INSTITUTES, 39 Eccleston Street, S.W.1.

NATIONAL UNION OF TOWNSWOMEN'S GUILDS, 2 Cromwell Place, S.W.7.

POSTAL HISTORY SOCIETY, June Cottage, North St, Petworth, Sussex

PRINTING HISTORICAL SOCIETY, St. Bride Institute, Bride Lane, E.C.4.

ROYAL SOCIETY OF MEDICINE, (History of Medicine Section), 1 Wimpole St, W.1.

SOCIETY FOR THE STUDY OF LABOUR HISTORY, 14 Brent Way, N.3.

SOCIETY FOR THEATRE RESEARCH, 103 Ralph Court, Queensway, W.2.

North West Regional Group: 12 Neale Rd, Chorlton-cum-Hardy, Manchester 21

SOCIETY OF APOTHECARIES OF LONDON: FACULTY OF THE HISTORY OF MEDICINE AND PHARMACY, Wellcome Historical Medical Library, Wellcome Building, Euston Rd, N.W.1.

VETERINARY HISTORY SOCIETY, 32 Belgrave Square, S.W.1.

YORKSHIRE POSTAL HISTORY SOCIETY, 114 Birleymoor Rd., Sheffield

Publications:
Garden History Society Journal
Journal of the Costume Society
Economic History Review
Journal of Economic History
Business Archives (Business Archives Council)
Agricultural History
Agricultural History Review (Museum of English Rural Life)
The Village (National Council of Social Service)
The Local Historian (NCSS)

255 Transport
BRITISH RAILWAYS BOARD (HISTORICAL RECORDS OFFICE) 66 Porchester Rd, W.2.

BRITISH RAILWAYS BOARD (HISTORICAL RECORDS OFFICE) 23 Waterloo Place, Edinburgh

NEWCOMEN SOCIETY, Science Museum, S.W.7.

OMNIBUS SOCIETY, 1039 Streatham Hill, S.W.2.

RAILWAY AND CANAL HISTORICAL SOCIETY, 38 Station Rd, Wylde Green, Sutton Coldfield, Warks.

Part Twelve

256 Specialist Libraries

The following is a list of some of the specialist Libraries of interest to local history researchers. Main libraries such as the British Museum, Bodleian and Public Record Offices have been excluded. County Record Offices are dealt with in detail in Part 10.

Agricultural History
Wye College (University of London) Library, Wye, Ashford, Kent.
Available to the public.

Reading University Library, Whiteknights, Reading.
Available by arrangement.

Archaeology
Society of Antiquaries of Newcastle-upon-Tyne Library, Black Gate, Newcastle-upon-Tyne
Available to researchers.

Worcester Cathedral Library
Available by arrangement.

University of London, Institute of Archaeology Library, 31/34 Gordon Square, London W.C.1.
Not available to the public.

Society of Antiquaries of London Burlington House, Piccadilly, London.
Available if introduced by Fellow.

Architecture
Architectural Association, 34/36 Bedford Square, W.C.1.
Not available to the public.

Royal Institute of British Architects, 66 Portland Place, W.1.
Available to the public.

Army and Navy History
Imperial War Museum Library, Lambeth Road, S.E.1.
(Army since 1912)
Available to the public.

University of East Anglia Library, University Plain, Norwich.
Available by arrangement.

Royal United Services Institutions Library, Whitehall, S.W.1.
Available to the public.

Army Central Library, 433 Holloway Road, N.7.
Available by arrangement.

Scottish United Services Museum Library, Edinburgh Castle.
Available by arrangement.

Royal Engineers Corps Library, Institution of Engineers, Chatham.
Available by arrangement.

Camberley College Staff Library, Staff College, Camberley, Surrey.
Assistance given to researchers.

National Maritime Museum Library, Romney Road, S.E.10.
Available by arrangement.

Britannia Royal Naval College Library, Dartmouth, Devon.
Available to the public.

Downing College Library, Cambridge.
Available by arrangement.

Brass Rubbings
Society of Antiquaries of London,

Burlington House, Piccadilly.
Available by introduction by a
Fellow.

Coins
British Numismatic Society Library,
Warburg Institute, Woburn Sq.,
W.C.1.
Available by arrangement.

Company Histories
University of Bristol,
Queens Road, Bristol.
Available by arrangement.

Chartered Institute of Secretaries,
16 Park Crescent, W.1.
Not available to the public.

Educational History
University Archives, The Old
Schools, Cambridge.
Available by arrangement.

National Institute of Adult Education, 35 Queen Anne St, W.1.
Not available to the public.

University of London Library,
Senate House.
Available by arrangement.

University of Hull, Institute of Edu-
cation Library, Cottingham Road,
Hull.
Available by arrangement.

University of Leeds, Institute of
Education, The University, Leeds.
Available by arrangement.

University of Leicester, School of
Education Library, 21 University
Road, Leicester.
Available to the public.

University of Sheffield, Institute of
Education Library, 387 Glossop
Road, Sheffield.
Available to the public.

Folk-lore and Folk-life
Welsh Folk Museum Library,
St Fagans, Cardiff.
Available by arrangement.

National Library of Wales,
Aberystwyth.
Available to the public.

Folk-lore Society Library, University
College Library, Gower St, W.C.1.
Available by arrangement.

Genealogy
Society of Antiquaries of London,
Burlington House, Piccadilly,
London.
Available by introduction by a
Fellow.

Society of Genealogists,
37 Harrington Gardens, S.W.7.
Available to the public on a fee-basis.

Heraldry
Society of Antiquaries of London,
Burlington House, Piccadilly,
London.
Available by introduction by a
Fellow.

Inner Temple Library,
Temple, London.
Available by arrangement.

Legal History
House of Commons Library.
Not available when House is sitting.

Middle Temple Library,
Middle Temple Lane, E.C.4.
Available by arrangement.

Inner Temple Library,
Temple, E.C.4.
Available by arrangement.

House of Lords Library.
Available by arrangement.

Squire Law Library, The Old
Schools, Cambridge.
Available by arrangement.

Grays Inn Library, South Square,
Grays Inn, W.C.1.
Available by arrangement.

Lincolns Inn Library, Holborn.
Available by arrangement.

Local Government History
Greater London Council Members
Library, County Hall, S.E.1.
Available to the public.

British Library of Political and
Economic Science, Houghton St,
W.C.2.
Available to the public.

Maps
Ordnance Survey Library, Romsey
Road, Maybush, Southampton.
Available to students.

Royal Geographical Society,
Kensington Gore, S.W.7.
Available to the public on a fee basis.

National Library of Wales,
Aberystwyth.
Available to the public.

University of Leeds.
Not normally available to the public.

Royal Scottish Geographical Society
Library, 10 Randolph Crescent,
Edinburgh 3.
Available to the public.

Warden and Fellows Library,
Winchester College, Winchester.
Available by arrangement.
(English Road Books)

Medical History
Wellcome Institute of the History of
Medicine Library,
183 Euston Road, N.W.1.
Available by arrangement.

Newspapers
British Museum Newspaper Library,
Colindale, N.W.9.
Available to the public.

Paleography
University of London Library,
Senate House, Malet St, W.C.1.
Available by arrangement.

Parliamentary History
House of Commons Library.
Not available while House is sitting.

House of Lords Library.
Available by arrangement.

Photographs
Radio Times Hulton Library,
35 Marylebone High Street, W.1.
Available to the public.

Politics/Franchise/Trade Unionism
Bishopsgate Institute Library,
Bishopsgate, E.C.1.
Available to the public.

British Library of Political and
Economic Science, Houghton St,
W.C.2.
Available by arrangement.

Fawcett Library, 27 Wilfred St,
S.W.1.
(Suffragettes)
Available to the public.

Labour Party Library, Transport
House, Smith Square, S.W.1.
Not available to the public.

National Liberal Club, Gladstone
Library, Whitehall Place, S.W.1.
Available by arrangement.

Police History
Scottish Police College Library,
Tulliallan Castle, Kincardine, Alloa.
Available to the public.

Post Office History
Post Office Library, Postal Headquarters, St Martins-le-Grand, E.C.1.
Not available to the public.

Printing History
St Bride Library, E.C.4.
Available by arrangement.

London College of Printing,
Elephant and Castle, S.E.1.
Available by arrangement.

Prison History
H.M. Prison Staff College Library,
Love Lane, Wakefield.
Not available to the public.

University of Warwick Library,
Coventry.
Available by arrangement.

Religious History
Lambeth Palace Library, London.
Available by arrangement.

Hartley Victoria Methodist College
Library, Alexandra Road Sth,
Manchester.
Available by arrangement.

Westminster Abbey Library, The
Cloisters, Westminster Abbey.
Available by arrangement.

Sion College Library, Victoria
Embankment, E.C.4.
(Anglican History)
Available to the public.

International Training College,
Denmark Hill, S.E.5.
(Salvation Army History)
Not available to the public.

Dr. Williams' Library, 14 Gordon
Square, W.C.1.
(Non-conformist History)
Available to the public.

Selwyn College Library, Cambridge.
(19th century church history)
Available by arrangement.

Catholic Central Library, 47 Francis
Street, S.W.1.
Available to the public.

Worcester Cathedral Library.
Available by arrangement.

Wells Cathedral Library.

Available by arrangement

Truro Cathedral Library.
Not available to the public.

Rochester Cathedral Library.
Available by arrangement.

Ripon Cathedral Library.
Available by arrangement.

St Paul's Cathedral Library.
Available by arrangement.

Lincoln Cathedral Library,
Correspondence to 3 Vicars Court,
Lincoln.
Available by arrangement.

Hereford Cathedral Library,
The Cathedral, Hereford.
Available by arrangement.

Exeter Cathedral Library, Bishops
Palace, Exeter.
Available to the public.

Durham Cathedral Library,
The College, Durham.
Available by arrangement.

Chelmsford Cathedral Library.
Available to the public.

National Library of Wales,
Aberystwyth.
Available to the public.

Huguenot Library, University
College, Gower St, W.C.1.
Not usually available to the public.

Corpus Christi College Library,
Cambridge.
(Jewish History)
Available to the public.

Bishop Phillpotts Library, Quay St,
Truro.
(Methodist History)
Available to the public.

Wesley College Library, Henbury

Road, Bristol.
Available by arrangement.

Manchester College Library, Oxford.
(Non-conformist history)
Available by arrangement.

New College Library, London
(Puritan history)

Woodbroke College Library,
1049 Bristol Road, Selly Oak,
Birmingham
(Quaker history)
Not available to the public.

Society of Friends Library,
Euston Road, N.W.1.
(Quaker history)
Available to the public.

Unitarian College, The McLachlan
Library, Victoria Park, Manchester.
Available by arrangement.

Taxation
H.M. Customs and Excise Library,
King's Beam House, Mark Lane
E.C.3.
Available by arrangement.

Topography and Local History
Greater London Council Members
Library, County Hall, S.E.1.
(London and Middlesex)
Available to the public.

University College of North Wales
Library, Bangor
(Welsh history)
Available to the public.

North Devon Athenaeum Library,
The Square, Barnstaple, Devon.
(West country)

Yorkshire Archaeological Society
Library, Claremont, Clarendon Rd,
Leeds.
Available to the public.

University of Leicester Library
University Rd, Leicester.

(English and Welsh topography)
Available by arrangement.

Leicestershire Archaeological and
Historical Society Library,
The Guildhall, Guildhall Lane,
Leicester.
Available to the public.

Thoresby Society Library, Clare-
mont, 23 Clarendon Rd, Leeds 2.
(Yorkshire, especially Leeds, area)
Available to the public.

Athenaeum Library, Church Alley,
Liverpool.
Available by arrangement.

University of Liverpool Library,
P.O. Box 123, Liverpool.
Available to the public.

Bishopsgate Institute Library,
230 Bishopsgate, E.C.1.
(London and Middlesex)
Available to the public.

Port of London Authority Library,
P.O. Box 242, Trinity Square, E.C.3.
Not available to the public.

John Ryland's Library, Deansgate
Manchester.
Available by arrangement.

Norfolk and Norwich (Subscription)
Library, Guildhall Hill, Norwich.

Shrewsbury School Library, The
Schools, Shrewsbury.
Available by arrangement.

University of Southampton Library,
Southampton.
Available to the public.

William Salt Library, Eastgate Street,
Stafford.
Available to the public.

Transport History
Montagu Motor Museum, Road
Transport Reference Library, Beau-

lieu, Brockenhurst, Hants.
Available to the public.

Aberdeen University Library,
King's College, Aberdeen.
(Railways)
Available by arrangement.

National Liberal Club, Gladstone
Library, Whitehall Place, S.W.1.
(Railways)
Available by arrangement.

University of Leicester Library,
University Rd, Leicester.
Available to students.

Institute of Transport Library,
80 Portland Place, W.1.
Available to the public.

Part Thirteen — The Calendar

257 New Style

The present style of measuring
time, devised by Gregory XIII, was
not introduced into the United
Kingdom until 1752. In that year
September 3rd was reckoned to be
September 14th and dating carried
on from that date.

Until 1752 March 25th was the
civil and legal New Year's Day.

258 The main Saints Days and Fixed Feasts

All Saints	1 Nov
St Andrew	30 Nov
St Bartholomew	24 Aug
Candlemas	2 Feb
Christmas	25 Dec
St David	1 Mar
Epiphany	6 Jan
St George	23 Apr
Gule of August	1 Aug
St James	25 Jul
St John Baptist	29 Aug
St John Evangelist	27 Dec
Lady Day	25 Mar
Lammas Day	1 Aug
St Luke	18 Oct
St Mark	25 Apr
St Martin	11 Nov
St Matthew	21 Sept
Michaelmas	29 Sept
St Patrick	17 Mar
St Paul	30 Jun
St Thomas	21 Dec
St Thomas à Becket	29 Dec

Part Fourteen

259 Regnal Years

On many documents the date is
indicated by the year of the sovereign's reign. For example, 34 Henry
II would mean 1187-88, the year
beginning on 19th December 1187
and ending on the 18th December
1188. The following is a list of regnal years up to the end of the reign
of Edward VII.

William I
25 Dec to 24 Dec

1	1066-67	8	1073-74	15	1080-81
2	1067-68	9	1074-75	16	1081-82
3	1068-69	10	1075-76	17	1082-83
4	1069-70	11	1076-77	18	1083-84
5	1070-71	12	1077-78	19	1084-85
6	1071-72	13	1078-79	20	1085-86
7	1072-73	14	1079-80	21	1086 to
					9 Sept 1087

William II
26 Sept to 25 Sept

1	1087-88	6	1092-93	11	1097-98
2	1088-89	7	1093-94	12	1098-99
3	1089-90	8	1094-95	13	1099 to
4	1090-91	9	1095-96		2 Aug
5	1091-92	10	1096-97		1100

Henry I
5 Aug to 4 Aug

1	1100-01	13	1112-13	25	1124-25
2	1101-02	14	1113-14	26	1125-26
3	1102-03	15	1114-15	27	1126-27
4	1103-04	16	1115-16	28	1127-28

```
5  1104-05 17 1116-17 29 1128-29        9  31 May 1207 to 14 May 1208
6  1105-06 18 1117-18 30 1129-30       10  15 May 1208 to  6 May 1209
7  1106-07 19 1118-19 31 1130-31       11   7 May 1209 to 26 May 1210
8  1107-08 20 1119-20 32 1131-32       12  27 May 1210 to 11 May 1211
9  1108-09 21 1120-21 33 1132-33       13  12 May 1211 to  2 May 1212
10 1109-10 22 1121-22 34 1133-34       14   3 May 1212 to 22 May 1213
11 1110-11 23 1122-23 35 1134-35       15  23 May 1213 to  7 May 1214
12 1111-12 24 1123-24 36 1135-to       16   8 May 1214 to 27 May 1215
                         1 Dec         17  28 May 1215 to 18 May 1216
                         1135          18  19 May 1216 to 19 Oct 1216
```

Stephen   **Henry III**
26 Dec to 25 Dec   28 Oct to 27 Oct

```
1 1135-36 8  1142-43 15 1149-50        1  1216-17 20 1235-36 39 1254-55
2 1136-37 9  1143-44 16 1150-51        2  1217-18 21 1236-37 40 1255-56
3 1137-38 10 1144-45 17 1151-52        3  1218-19 22 1237-38 41 1256-57
4 1138-39 11 1145-46 18 1152-53        4  1219-20 23 1238-39 42 1257-58
5 1139-40 12 1146-47 19 1153 to        5  1220-21 24 1239-40 43 1258-59
6 1140-41 13 1147-48       25 Oct      6  1221-22 25 1240-41 44 1259-60
7 1141-42 14 1148-49       1154        7  1222-23 26 1241-42 45 1260-61
                                       8  1223-24 27 1242-43 46 1261-62
```
                                       9 1224-25 28 1243-44 47 1262-63
Henry II   10 1225-26 29 1244-45 48 1263-64
19 Dec to 18 Dec   11 1226-27 30 1245-46 49 1264-65
```
1  1154-55 13 1166-67 25 1178-79       12 1227-28 31 1246-47 50 1265-66
2  1155-56 14 1167-68 26 1179-80       13 1228-29 32 1247-48 51 1266-67
3  1156-57 15 1168-69 27 1180-81       14 1229-30 33 1248-49 52 1267-68
4  1157-58 16 1169-70 28 1181-82       15 1230-31 34 1249-50 53 1268-69
5  1158-59 17 1170-71 29 1182-83       16 1231-32 35 1250-51 54 1269-70
6  1159-60 18 1171-72 30 1183-84       17 1232-33 36 1251-52 55 1270-71
7  1160-61 19 1172-73 31 1184-85       18 1233-34 37 1252-53 56 1271-72
8  1161-62 20 1173-74 32 1185-86       19 1234-35 38 1253-54 57 1272 to
9  1162-63 21 1174-75 33 1186-87                                16 Nov
10 1163-64 22 1175-76 34 1187-88                                1272
11 1164-65 23 1176-77 35 1188-89
12 1165-66 24 1177-78    to 6 July
                           1189
```

                                       Edward I
                                       20 Nov to 19 Nov
Richard I   ```
3 Sep to 2 Sep   1 1272-73 13 1284-85 25 1296-97
```                                     2  1273-74 14 1285-86 26 1297-98
1 1189-90 5 1193-94 9  1197-98         3  1274-75 15 1286-87 27 1298-99
2 1190-91 6 1194-95 10 1198 to         4  1275-76 16 1287-88 28 1299-00
3 1191-92 7 1195-96    6 Apr           5  1276-77 17 1288-89 29 1300-01
4 1192-93 8 1196-97    1199            6  1277-78 18 1289-90 30 1301-02
```                                     7  1278-79 19 1290-91 31 1302-03
                                       8  1279-80 20 1291-92 32 1303-04
**John**                               9  1280-81 21 1292-93 33 1304-05
```                                     10 1281-82 22 1293-94 34 1305-06
1 27 May 1199 to 17 May 1200           11 1282-83 23 1294-95 35 1306 to
2 18 May 1200 to  2 May 1201           12 1283-84 24 1295-96    7 July
3  3 May 1201 to 22 May 1202                                     1307
4 23 May 1202 to 14 May 1203           ```
5 15 May 1203 to  2 June 1204
6  3 June 1204 to 18 May 1205          **Edward II**
7 19 May 1205 to 10 May 1206           8 July to 7 July
8 11 May 1206 to 30 May 1207
```

```
1  1307-08  8  1314-15  15  1321-22
2  1308-09  9  1315-16  16  1322-23
3  1309-10  10 1316-17  17  1323-24
4  1310-11  11 1317-18  18  1324-25
5  1311-12  12 1318-19  19  1325-26
6  1312-13  13 1319-20  20  1326 to
7  1313-14  14 1320-21      20 Jan
                            1327
```

Edward III
25 Jan to 24 Jan
```
1  1327-28  18 1344-45  35  1361-62
2  1328-29  19 1345-46  36  1362-63
3  1329-30  20 1346-47  37  1363-64
4  1330-31  21 1347-48  38  1364-65
5  1331-32  22 1348-49  39  1365-66
6  1332-33  23 1349-50  40  1366-67
7  1333-34  24 1350-51  41  1367-68
8  1334-35  25 1351-52  42  1368-69
9  1335-36  26 1352-53  43  1369-70
10 1336-37  27 1353-54  44  1370-71
11 1337-38  28 1354-55  45  1371-72
12 1338-39  29 1355-56  46  1372-73
13 1339-40  30 1356-57  47  1373-74
14 1340-41  31 1357-58  48  1374-75
15 1341-42  32 1358-59  49  1375-76
16 1342-43  33 1359-60  50  1376-77
17 1343-44  34 1360-61  51  1377 to
                            21 June
                            1377
```

Richard II
22 June to 21 June
```
1  1377-78  9  1385-86  17  1393-94
2  1378-79  10 1386-87  18  1394-95
3  1379-80  11 1387-88  19  1395-96
4  1380-81  12 1388-89  20  1396-97
5  1381-82  13 1389-90  21  1397-98
6  1382-83  14 1390-91  22  1398-99
7  1383-84  15 1391-92  23  1399 to
8  1384-85  16 1392-93      29 Sept
                            1399
```

Henry IV
30 Sept to 29 Sept
```
1  1399-00  7  1405-06  13  1411-12
2  1400-01  8  1406-07  14  1412 to
3  1401-02  9  1407-08      20 Mar
4  1402-03  10 1408-09      1413
5  1403-04  11 1409-10
6  1404-05  12 1410-11
```

Henry V
21 Mar to 20 Mar
```
1  1413-14  5  1417-18  9   1421-22
2  1414-15  6  1418-19  10  1422 to
3  1415-16  7  1419-20      31 Aug
4  1416-17  8  1420-21      1422
```

Henry VI
1 Sept to 31 Aug
```
1  1422-23  14 1435-36  27  1448-49
2  1423-24  15 1436-37  28  1449-50
3  1424-25  16 1437-38  29  1450-51
4  1425-26  17 1438-39  30  1451-52
5  1426-27  18 1439-40  31  1452-53
6  1427-28  19 1440-41  32  1453-54
7  1428-29  20 1441-42  33  1454-55
8  1429-30  21 1442-43  34  1455-56
9  1430-31  22 1443-44  35  1456-57
10 1431-32  23 1444-45  36  1457-58
11 1432-33  24 1445-46  37  1458-59
12 1433-34  25 1446-47  38  1459-60
13 1434-35  26 1447-48  39  1460 to
                            5 Mar
                            1461
```

Edward IV
4 Mar to 3 Mar
```
1  1461-62  9  1469-70  17  1477-78
2  1462-63  10 1470-71  18  1478-79
3  1463-64  11 1471-72  19  1479-80
4  1464-65  12 1472-73  20  1480-81
5  1465-66  13 1473-74  21  1481-82
6  1466-67  14 1474-75  22  1482-83
7  1467-68  15 1475-76  23  1483-84
8  1468-69  16 1476-77      9 Apr
                            1483
```

Edward V
```
1  9 Apr 1483 to
   25 June 1483
```

Richard III
26 June to 25 June
```
1  1483-84  2  1484-85  3  1485 to
                           22 Aug
                           1485
```

Henry VII
22 Aug to 21 Aug
```
1  1485-86  9  1493-94  17  1501-02
2  1486-87  10 1494-95  18  1502-03
3  1487-88  11 1495-96  19  1503-04
4  1488-89  12 1496-97  20  1504-05
5  1489-90  13 1497-98  21  1505-06
```

6 1490-91 14 1498-99 22 1506-07
7 1491-92 15 1499-00 23 1507-08
8 1492-93 16 1500-01 24 1508 to
                              21 Apr
                              1509

Henry VIII
22 Apr to 21 Apr
1 1509-10 14 1522-23 27 1535-36
2 1510-11 15 1523-24 28 1536-37
3 1511-12 16 1524-25 29 1537-38
4 1512-13 17 1525-26 30 1538-39
5 1513-14 18 1526-27 31 1539-40
6 1514-15 19 1527-28 32 1540-41
7 1515-16 20 1528-29 33 1541-42
8 1516-17 21 1529-30 34 1542-43
9 1517-18 22 1530-31 35 1543-44
10 1518-19 23 1531-32 36 1544-45
11 1519-20 24 1532-33 37 1545-46
12 1520-21 25 1533-34 38 1546 to
13 1521-22 26 1534-35   28 Jan
                            1547

Edward VI
28 Jan to 27 Jan
1 1547-48 4 1550-51 7 1553 to
2 1548-49 5 1551-52   6 July
3 1549-50 6 1552-53   1553

Mary
1 6 July 1553 to
   5 July 1554
2 6 July 1554 to
   24 July 1554

Philip and Mary
1 & 2 25 July 1554 to 5 July 1555
1 & 3 6 July 1555 to 24 July 1555
2 & 3 25 July 1555 to 5 July 1556
2 & 4 6 July 1556 to 24 July 1556
3 & 4 25 July 1556 to 5 July 1557
3 & 5 6 July 1557 to 24 July 1557
4 & 5 25 July 1557 to 5 July 1558
4 & 6 6 July 1558 to 24 July 1558
5 & 6 25 July 1558 to 17 Nov 1558

Elizabeth
17 Nov to 16 Nov
1 1558-59 16 1573-74 31 1588-89
2 1559-60 17 1574-75 32 1589-90
3 1560-61 18 1575-76 33 1590-91
4 1561-62 19 1576-77 34 1591-92

5 1562-63 20 1577-78 35 1592-93
6 1563-64 21 1578-79 36 1593-94
7 1564-65 22 1579-80 37 1594-95
8 1565-66 23 1580-81 38 1595-96
9 1566-67 24 1581-82 39 1596-97
10 1567-68 25 1582-83 40 1597-98
11 1568-69 26 1583-84 41 1598-99
12 1569-70 27 1584-85 42 1599-00
13 1570-71 28 1585-86 43 1600-01
14 1571-72 29 1586-87 44 1601-02
15 1572-73 30 1587-88 45 1602 to
                          24 Mar
                          1603

James I
24 Mar to 23 Mar
1 1603-04 9 1611-12 17 1619-20
2 1604-05 10 1612-13 18 1620-21
3 1605-06 11 1613-14 19 1621-22
4 1606-07 12 1614-15 20 1622-23
5 1607-08 13 1615-16 21 1623-24
6 1608-09 14 1616-17 22 1624-25
7 1609-10 15 1617-18 23 1625 to
8 1610-11 16 1618-19   27 Mar
                        1625

Charles I
27 Mar to 26 Mar
1 1625-26 9 1633-34 17 1641-42
2 1626-27 10 1634-35 18 1642-43
3 1627-28 11 1635-36 19 1643-44
4 1628-29 12 1636-37 20 1644-45
5 1629-30 13 1637-38 21 1645-46
6 1630-31 14 1638-39 22 1646-47
7 1631-32 15 1639-40 23 1647-48
8 1632-33 16 1640-41 24 1648 to
                       30 Jan
                       1649

Commonwealth
Ordinary dating was used.

Charles II
  His regnal years were calculated
from the death of his father.
29 May to 29 Jan
12 1660-61

30 Jan to 29 Jan
13 1661-62 21 1669-70 29 1677-78
14 1662-63 22 1670-71 30 1678-79
15 1663-64 23 1671-72 31 1679-80
16 1664-65 24 1672-73 32 1680-81

17 1665-66 25 1673-74 33 1681-82
18 1666-67 26 1674-75 34 1682-83
19 1667-68 27 1675-76 35 1683-84
20 1668-69 28 1676-77 36 1684-85
                      37 1685 to
                         6 Feb
                         1685

James II
6 Feb to 5 Feb
1 1685-86 3 1687-88 4 1688 to
2 1686-87   11 Dec
                    1688

William and Mary
13 Feb to 12 Feb
1 1689-90 3 1691-92 5 1693-94
2 1690-91 4 1692-93 6 1694 to
                    28 Dec
                    1694

William III
28 Dec to 27 Dec
7 1694-95 10 1697-98 13 1700-01
8 1695-96 11 1698-99 14 1701 to
9 1696-97 12 1699-00   8 Mar
                       1702

Anne
8 Mar to 7 Mar
1 1702-03 6 1707-08 11 1712-13
2 1703-04 7 1708-09 12 1713-14
3 1704-05 8 1709-10 13 1714 to
4 1705-06 9 1710-11 1 Aug
5 1706-07 10 1711-12 1714

George I
1 Aug to 31 July
1 1714-15 6 1719-20 11 1724-25
2 1715-16 7 1720-21 12 1725-26
3 1716-17 8 1721-22 13 1726 to
4 1717-18 9 1722-23   11 Jun
5 1718-19 10 1723-24   1727

George II
11 June to 10 June
1 1727-28 13 1739-40 25 1751-52
2 1728-29 14 1740-41 11 Jun to
3 1729-30 15 1741-42 21 Jun
4 1730-31 16 1742-43 26 1752-53
5 1731-32 17 1743-44 22 Jun to
6 1732-33 18 1744-45 21 Jun
7 1733-34 19 1745-46 27 1753-54
8 1734-35 20 1746-47 28 1754-55
9 1735-36 21 1747-48 29 1755-56
10 1736-37 22 1748-49 30 1756-57
11 1737-38 23 1749-50 31 1757-58
12 1738-39 24 1750-51 32 1758-59
                      33 1759-60
                      34 1760 to
                         25 Oct
                         1760

George III
25 Oct to 24 Oct
1 1760-61 23 1782-83 45 1804-05
2 1761-62 24 1783-84 46 1805-06
3 1762-63 25 1784-85 47 1806-07
4 1763-64 26 1785-86 48 1807-08
5 1764-65 27 1786-87 49 1808-09
6 1765-66 28 1787-88 50 1809-10
7 1766-67 29 1788-89 51 1810-11
8 1767-68 30 1789-90 Regency
9 1768-69 31 1790-91 began
10 1769-70 32 1791-92 6 Feb 1811
11 1770-71 33 1792-93 52 1811-12
12 1771-72 34 1793-94 53 1812-13
13 1772-73 35 1794-95 54 1813-14
14 1773-74 36 1795-96 55 1814-15
15 1774-75 37 1796-97 56 1815-16
16 1775-76 38 1797-98 57 1816-17
17 1776-77 39 1798-99 58 1817-18
18 1777-78 40 1799-00 59 1818-19
19 1778-79 41 1800-01 60 1819 to
20 1779-80 42 1801-02   24 Jun
21 1780-81 43 1802-03   1820
22 1781-82 44 1803-04

George IV
29 Jan to 28 Jan
1 1820-21 5 1824-25 9 1828-29
2 1821-22 6 1825-26 10 1829-30
3 1822-23 7 1826-27 11 1830 to
4 1823-24 8 1827-28   26 Jun
                      1830

William IV
26 June to 25 June
1 1830-31 4 1833-34 7 1836 to
2 1831-32 5 1834-35   20 June
3 1832-33 6 1835-36   1837

Victoria
20 June to 19 June
1 1837-38 23 1859-60 45 1881-82
2 1838-39 24 1860-61 46 1882-83

3	1839-40	25	1861-62	47	1883-84
4	1840-41	26	1862-63	48	1884-85
5	1841-42	27	1863-64	49	1885-86
6	1842-43	28	1864-65	50	1886-87
7	1843-44	29	1865-66	51	1887-88
8	1844-45	30	1866-67	52	1888-89
9	1845-46	31	1867-68	53	1889-90
10	1846-47	32	1868-69	54	1890-91
11	1847-48	33	1869-70	55	1891-92
12	1848-49	34	1870-71	56	1892-93
13	1849-50	35	1871-72	57	1893-94
14	1850-51	36	1872-73	58	1894-95
15	1851-52	37	1873-74	59	1895-96
16	1852-53	38	1874-75	60	1896-97
17	1853-54	39	1875-76	61	1897-98
18	1854-55	40	1876-77	62	1898-99
19	1855-56	41	1877-78	63	1899-00
20	1856-57	42	1878-79	64	1900 to
21	1857-58	43	1879-80		22 Jan
22	1858-59	44	1880-81		1901

Edward VII
22 Jan to 21 Jan

1	1901-02	5	1905-06	9	1909-10
2	1902-03	6	1906-07	10	1910 to
3	1903-04	7	1907-08		6 May
4	1904-05	8	1908-09		1910

Part Fifteen — Latin

Latin was used extensively in legal, manorial and ecclesiastical records until the early 1730's. Those researchers whose knowledge of Latin is weak or non-existent are advised to use Eileen Gooder's 'Latin for Local History' (Longmans). This aims to give a student a reading knowledge of medieval Latin and contains, as well as an excellent word list, many examples of the word structure of documents.

260 Latin Word List
A quick reference to words commonly found in, mainly, local records follows:

a, ab, abs- from, away from, by

abra — maidservant
ac, atque — and
accipio (3) — to take, receive
acra — an acre or strip of land
ad — to, at, towards
advocantia — advowson
agillarius — hayward
agricola — farmer, husbandman
alieno (1) to alienatc land
aliquis — someone, anyone, some-
    thing, anything
alumnus — tanner
amercio — (1) to fine, amerce
amicus — friend
amitto (3) — to surrender, lose
ancilla — maidservant
annus — year
antea — formerly
antedictus — aforesaid
appello (1) to call, accuse, name,
    appeal
apothecarius — apothecary, shop-
    keeper
apud — near, by, at, to
architector — thatcher
area — hearth
armentarious — herdsman
armiger — esquire
aro (1) — to plough
aromatarius — grocer
arrento (1) -- to rent
assuro (1) — to convey land
aula — room, house
auster — the south
autem — however, but
autumpnus — autumn
averium — cattle
avus — grandfather

bacallarius — bachelor
balius — bailiff
baro — tenant-in-chief, baron
bedellus — beadle
beneficium — feudal estate;
    ecclesiastical benefice
bercarius — shepherd
bersarius — forester
bertona — demesne farm
bibliopegus — bookbinder
bladarius — corn chandler
bordarius — bordar, tenant
borialis — north
bosca — a wood

boscarius — woodman
bostio — cattle-driver
bovaria — bovate
brasiator — brewer
burgagium — land held by burgage
    tenure
burgus — town, borough
burriarius — dairyman

calcarius — spurrier
calcarius — shoemaker
camera — room, home, treasury
campus — field
capella — chapel
capellanus — chaplain
capio (3) — to take, seize, arrest,
    rent, to hold an eccles. court
capitalis — chief
carbo — coal
carecarius — carter
carnarius — butcher
carnifex — butcher
carpentarius — carpenter
carruca — carucate, plough
carta — charter, deed, map
catallum — cattle
catellarius — pedlar
caupona — inn
cauponarius — inn-holder
cellarius — cellarman
cementarium — mason
censeo (2) — to tax
centum — one hundred
cervisia — beer
chirurgus — surgeon
cimiterium — cemetery
cippus — gravestone
civis — citizen
civitas — city, diocesan city
clamo (1) — to claim
clausura — enclosure
clausuro — (1) to enclose
clericus — clerk
clericus parochialis — parish clerk
climax — stile
cognomen — name
comes — earl
comitatus — county, earldom
commune — common land
concedo (3) — to grant, allow
condono (1) — to pardon, grant
conductio — meeting
conjugata — married woman

conjuges — married couple
conjuncti fuere — they were married
constabularius — constable
consuetudo — custom, customary
    service, due or payment
contractio — marriage
coquina — kitchen
coram — in the presence of
coronarius — coroner
corpus — body
cotarius — cottager
cotura — piece of land
crofta — croft
croppa — crop
cuius — whose, which, what
culter — farmer
cultellarius — cutler
cum — with
cum — (conj. with verbs)
    when, since, though, whereas
curia — court-yard
curtilagium — curtilage, yard
custodia — wardship of minors;
    tenure of land
custuma — customary payment
custumarius — customary tenant

daia, deia — dairymaid, dairyman
datum — given
de — of, from, concerning
de cetero — henceforth
de post facto — afterwards
de presenti — at present
de prope — near
decanus — deacon
decem — ten
decenna — tithing
decennarius — tithing-man
decessus — demise, lease
decima — tithe, tenth
defensor — defendant
defunctus — deceased
deinde — then, next
dexter — right (direction)
dico (3) to say, declare
dictus — the said, aforesaid
dies — day
dies dominica — Sunday
dies Iovis — Thursday
dies Lune — Monday
dies Martis — Tuesday
dies Mercurii — Wednesday
dies Solis — Sunday

dies Veneris — Friday
dispensator — steward
divisa — boundary
do (1) — to give, grant
doarium — dowry
doliarius — cooper
domanicum — demesne land
domina — lady, mistress
dominus — lord, master, sir
domus — house, room
donarium — gift, grant
dotarium — widow's dower
duo — two
duodecim — twelve

e, ex — from, out of
ecclesia — church
edificium — building
edificio (1) — to build
ego — I, I myself
eius, ejus — of his, her, it, this
ephippiarius — saddler
episcopus — bishop
equus — horse
ergo — therefore, consequently
escaeta — escheat
essonia — essoin
est — it is
estoverium — estover
et — and
etiam — also, even
ex — from, out of
ex nunc — from now, hereafter
ex quo — since, inasmuch as
ex tunc — thereafter
executor — executor, administrator

faber, fabri — smith
faber aererium — coppersmith
faber cupri — coppersmith
faber ferrarius — blacksmith
faber horologicum — clockmaker
faber lignarium — carpenter
fabrica — church-fabric
fabrifer — blacksmith
facere homagium — to pay homage
famulus — male servant
femina — woman, wife
fenum — hay
feodarius — feudal tenant
feodum — fee, fief
feoffo (1) — to enfeoff
ferrator — smith

ferrifaber — blacksmith
festum — feast, wedding, festival
filia — daughter
filiastor — son-in-law, stepson
filius — son
firma — farm, rent
firmarius — farmer
focus — hearth
forum — market
fossatum — ditch-digging service
fossatus — ditch
frater — brother
frumentarius — corn-dealer
fuit — he was, she was, it was
furnarius — baker

gablum — tax, rent
garcio — boy, servant
gardianus — churchwarden
geldum — geld, tax
gener — son-in-law, grandson-in-law
generosa — lady
generosus — gentleman
gersuma — customary payment, fine
granarium — granary
grangia — barn, grange
grava — grove

habeo (2) — to have
haia — hedge
heiwardus — hayward
herbagium — pasture, the right to
    pasture
hereditamentum — hereditament
heres, heredis — heir, heiress
hic, hec, hoc — this
hida — a hide of land
hidagium — hidage
hiemalis — winter
hinc — hence
homagium — homage
homo — man
hospes — tenant
hospitator — innkeeper
hostellarius — innkeeper
hostillarius — ostler
hue usque — always of this place
huius, hujus — of this man, woman,
    thing, place
hundredum — hundred (area of
    administration)

ib, ibid, ibidem — in the same place
ibi — there
id est — that is
idem — the same
ideo — therefore
ignoti — illegitimate
ignoti parentis — of unknown
   parents
immobilia — real estate
in — in, on, into, at
in capite — in chief
in principali — in chief
incipientis — beginning
incipio (3) — to begin
incumbens — incumbent
incola — inhabitant
infra — below, within
ingenuus — freeman, yeoman
initiatus — baptised
inter — between, among
ipse, ipsa, ipsum — himself, herself,
   itself
is, ea, id — he, she, it, this, that
iste, ista, istud — this
item — the same, also, likewise

jurator — juror
juvenis — young
juxta — near, beside

lana — wool
lanatus — buried in wool
laniator — butcher
lanius — butcher
lapidarius — stonemason
largus — wide
latum — width
lectus — bed
leta — leet
lex, legis — law
liber — free
liber — book
liber baro — lord
liber rusticus — free person
liberi — freeman
lignarius — carpenter
locus — place
longus — long

magnus — large, senior
majores — ancestors
major, majoris — mayor
mandatum — order

manerium — manor
mansum — dwelling-house
manus — hand
manus mortua — mortmain
marito (1) — to marry
mariti — married couple
marlaria — marl-pit
martia — wife
mater — mother
medietas — half, moiety
mensa — table
mensis — month
messarius — hayward
messuagium — messuage, house
meta — boundary stone
mille — a thousand
minister — reeve, bailiff, minor
   official
miseracio — amercement
mola — mill
molandarius — miller
monachus — monk
monialis — nun
more novo — in the new style of
   dates
more vetere — in the old style of
   dates
mors, mortis — death
mortuarium — mortuary payment

natalis, nativitas — birth
nativus — villein
natus — born
nauta — sailor
nec — and not, nor
nec. . .nec — neither. . .nor
necnon — also
nemus — a wood
nepos, nepus — grandchild, nephew
neptis — granddaughter, niece
nihil — nothing
nomen, nominis — name or title
non — not
nondum — not yet
nos, nostrum — we
noster, nostra, nostrum — our
nothus — bastard
nunc — now
nuncius — beadle
nundinatio — market
nuntius — messenger
nuper — formerly
nupt fuerant — were married

nurus — daughter-in-law

obiit — he died
obiit sine prole — died without issue
oblatio, oblationis — offering
obolus — half-penny
obstetrix — midwife
occidens — the west
occupator — the occupier
octo — eight
oeconomus — churchwarden
officina — outbuilding
oppidum — city, town
opus — work
ordium — barley
oriens — the east

pacatio — payment
pagina — deed, page
pagus — village
panicius — baker
panis — bread
pannagium — right of pannage
parca — park, enclosure
parens — parent, grandparent
paries — wall
parmentarius — tailor
parochia — parish
parochius — parish priest
pars — part
parvus, parva, parvum — small
Pascha — Easter Sunday
Pascha floridam — Palm Sunday
passium — frequently
pateat — let it be known
pater — father
pater familias — householder
patria — district, county
per — through, by
per sic quod — on condition that
perambulatio — perambulating the
     bounds
perpetualiter — forever, perpetually
persona — parson or parsonage
personatus — parsonage
pertica — a perch (measurement)
petra — stone (building material)
piscator — fisherman
piscenarius — fishmonger
piscis — fish
pistor — baker
pistorium — bakehouse
placea — residence, open place

plaustrum — wagon, cart
plebanus — rural dean
plebeius - villein, layman
plegagium — pledge
pone — beside, behind
populus — people
porcaria — pigsty
porcarius — swineherd
porcus — pig
porta — gate
possideo (2) — to possess, occupy
post — after, behind, according to
postea — hereafter, thereafter
postac — hereafter, henceforth
prata, pratum — meadow
pre — before
prebenda — prebend
precaria — boon-work
predictus — aforesaid
prefatus — aforesaid
prefectus — reeve
presbyter — priest
presens — present
principalis — in chief, chief
priores — ancestors
pro nunc — for or at the present
pro perpetuito — forever
proficium — profit
prohibeo (2) — to forbid
proles — descendant
prope — near
propinquarius — relation
puella — girl
puer — boy

quando — when
quare — wherefore
quarta — quart, farthing
quarterius — quarter
quattuor — four
que — and
questus — acquired property
qui, quae, quod — who, which,
     what
quia — because, whereas
quietus — receipt
quinque — five
quo — wherefore, whither
quod — because
quoniam — since, whereas
quoque — also

rata — share, proportion
real — real (estate)
recordum — record
rector — rector
redditus — rent
reddo (3) — to surrender, return,
    hand over
redemptio — fine
regalis — royal
regnum — kingdom, reign
regratator — regrater
relevamentum — feudal due
relicta — widow
relictus — widower, remaining
rex — king
roda — rod (measure)
rotarius — wheelwright
rotulus — roll, record

sacerdos — priest
sal — salt
sartum — forest clearing
scotum — scot, tax
scutagium — scutage
secretarius — clerk
secta — body of court
sed — but
sedile — pew, chair, bench
seisina — seisin
seiso (1) — to seize, take possession
    of
selio — selion, open field strip
semita — footpath
senescallus — steward, seneschal
septem — seven
septentrio — the north
serjantia — land held in serjeanty
servicium — villein tenure
serviens — servant; tenant holding
    land by military service
servus — servant, villein
set — but
sex — six
shira — shire
si — if, whether
sic — thus, thus so
silva — a wood
sine — without
sinister — left (direction)
situs, sita — situated
soca — soc
socmannus — soc tenant
solarium — upper-room

solidus — shilling
solum — ground, earth, land
soror — sister; nun
sponsa — wife
sponsus — husband
stabularius — ostler
stagnum — pond
stapula — staple
stallum — market-stall
strata — street
strata alta — highway
strata regia — king's highway
sub — under, below
successio — descendants
suggestum — pulpit
sum — to be
super — above, upon
supra — above, beyond, before
sus — pig
sutor — cobbler

taberna — inn
tastator — ale-taster
tempus — time, period
tenementum — feudal holding
tenura — tenure; feudal holding
terra — land, strip, tenement
terrarium — terrier
terrenus — tenant
testamentum — will, testament, pro-
    bate
testis — a witness
tignarius — carpenter
tipulator — tippler
tofta — toft, house area
tonsor — barber
trado (3) — to demise, hand over
tres — three
tum — then
tunc — then
turba — turf

ubi — where, when
ultimo — recently
um — the late
unde — whence, wherefore
undecim — eleven
unus — one
urbs — city
ut — as, that, in order that
ut assitur — as it is asserted
uxor — wife
uxoratus — married man
uxoratus — married

vacca — cow
vaccaria — pasture for cattle
vaccarius — cowherd
vacuus — vacant
vagabundus — vagabond
vevodus — widower
via — road, way
via publica — public highway
via regis — kings highway
viaticus — tramp
vicarius — vicar
vicecomes — sheriff, reeve
viciatus — bastard
vicinum — vicinity
vicus — village

vidua — widow
viduus — widower
viginit — twenty
villa — vill, towns
villanus — villein
villenagium — land held by villein tenure
vir — man; husband
virga — virgate, yardland
vitellarius — victualler

wainagium — ploughteam
wapentachium — wapentake
wastum — waste-land

261 Christian Names in Latin

NOMINATIVE	GENITIVE	ABLATIVE	ENGLISH
Adam	Ade	Ada	Adam
Adamus	Adami	Adamo	Adam
Aegidius	Aegidii	Aegidio	Giles
Agnes	Agnetis	Agnete	Agnes
Alanus	Alani	Alano	Alan
Alberedus	Alberedi	Alberedo	Alfred
Alexander	Alexandri	Alexandro	Alexander
Alianora	Alianorae	Alionora	Eleanor
Aloysius	Aloysii	Aloysio	Lewis
Aluredus	Aluredi	Aluredo	Alfred
Andreas	Andreae	Andrea	Andrew
Andreus	Andrei	Andreo	Andrew
Anthonius	Anthonii	Anthonio	Anthony
Araldus	Araldi	Araldo	Harold
Arcturus	Arcturi	Arcturo	Arthur
Artorius	Artorii	Artorio	Arthur
Archibaldus	Archibaldi	Archibaldo	Archibald
Bartholomaeus	Bartholomaei	Bartholomaeo	Bartholomew
Basilius	Basilii	Basilio	Basil
Brianus	Briani	Briano	Brian
Brigitta	Brigittae	Brigitta	Bridget
Carolus	Caroli	Carolo	Charles
Christophorus	Christophori	Christopho	Christopher
Cudbertus	Cudberti	Cudberto	Cuthbert
Cuthbertus	Cuthberti	Cuthberto	Cuthbert
Danielus	Danieli	Danielo	Daniel
Davidus	Davidi	Davido	David
Dionysius	Dionysii	Dionysio	Dennis
Dunechanus	Dunechani	Dunechano	Duncan

NOMINATIVE	GENITIVE	ABLATIVE	ENGLISH
Duvenaldus	Duvenaldi	Duvenaldo	Donald
Eadmundus	Eadmundi	Eadmundo	Edmund
Eadwardus	Eadwardi	Eadwardo	Edward
Edmundus	Edmundi	Edmundo	Edmund
Edwardus	Edwardi	Edwardo	Edward
Egidius	Egidii	Egidio	Giles
Elfredus	Elfredi	Elfredo	Alfred
Emelina	Emelinae	Emelina	Emily
Erniscus	Ernisii	Ernisio	Ernest
Eustachius	Eustachii	Eustachio	Eustace
Eva	Evae	Eva	Eve
Francicus	Francici	Francico	Francis
Fridericus	Friderici	Friderico	Frederick
Galfridus	Galfridi	Galfrido	Geoffrey
Galterus	Galteri	Galtero	Walter
Georgius	Georgii	Georgio	George
Gerardus	Gerardi	Gerardo	Gerard
Gilebertus	Gileberti	Gileberto	Gilbert
Godefridus	Godefridi	Godefrido	Godfrey
Grahamus	Grahami	Grahamo	Graham
Gregorius	Gregorii	Gregorio	Gregory
Gualterus	Gualteri	Gualtero	Walter
Guido	Guidonis	Guidone	Guy
Guilielmus	Guilelmi	Guilielmo	William
Haraldus	Haraldi	Haraldo	Harold
Henricus	Henrici	Henrico	Henry
Hieremias	Hieremiae	Hieremia	Jeremiah
Hilarius	Hilarii	Hilario	Hilary
Hugo	Hugonis	Hugone	Hugh
Humfredus	Humfredi	Humfredo	Humphrey
Jacobus	Jacobi	Jacobo	Jacob
Joceus	Jocei	Joceio	Joyce
Johanna	Johannae	Johanna	Jane, Joan
Johannes	Johanni	Johanno	John
Jonathas	Jonathae	Jonatha	Jonathan
Judas	Judae	Juda	Jude
Justinus	Justini	Justino	Justin
Laetitia	Laetitiae	Laetitia	Lettice
Laurentius	Laurenti	Laurentio	Lawrence
Leonellus	Leonelli	Leonello	Lionel
Levelinus	Levelini	Levelino	Llewellyn
Lionhardus	Lionhardi	Lionhardo	Leonard
Lorentius	Lorenti	Lorento	Lawrence
Ludovicus	Ludovici	Ludovico	Lewis
Luolinus	Luolini	Luolino	Llewellyn

NOMINATIVE	GENITIVE	ABLATIVE	ENGLISH
Marcus	Marci	Marco	Mark
Margeria	Margeriae	Margeria	Margery
Marta	Martae	Marta	Martha
Mathaeus	Mathaei	Mathaeo	Matthew
Matildis	Matildae	Matilda	Mathilda
Meuricius	Meuricii	Meuricio	Maurice
Michaelis	Michaelis	Michaeli	Michael
Natalis	Natalis	Natali	Noel
Nicolaus	Nicolai	Nicolao	Nicholas
Normannus	Normanni	Normanno	Norman
Oenus	Oeni	Oeno	Owen
Oliverus	Oliveri	Olivero	Oliver
Omfreidus	Omfreidi	Omfreido	Humphrey
Owinus	Owini	Owino	Owen
Petrus	Petri	Petro	Peter
Prodentia	Prudentiae	Prudentia	Prudence
Radulfus	Radulfi	Radulfo	Ralph
Randolphus	Randolphi	Randolpho	Randolph
Reginaldus	Reginaldi	Reginaldo	Reginald
Richardus	Richardi	Richardo	Richard
Robertus	Roberti	Roberto	Robert
Rogerus	Rogeri	Rogero	Roger
Rohelendus	Rohelendi	Rohelendo	Roland
Salomon	Salomonis	Salomoni	Solomon
Samuel	Samuelis	Samuele	Samuel
Sibella	Sibellae	Sibelia	Sybil
Sidneus	Sidnei	Sidneo	Sidney
Stephanus	Stephani	Stephano	Stephen
Symon	Symonis	Symone	Simon
Tedbaldus	Tedbaldi	Tedbaldo	Theobald
Theobaldus	Theobaldi	Theobaldo	Theobald
Thomas	Thomae	Thoma	Thomas
Timotheus	Timothei	Timotheo	Timothy
Tobias	Tobiae	Tobia	Tobias
Umfridus	Umfridi	Umfrido	Humphrey
Villefredus	Villefredi	Villefredo	Wilfrid
Vincentius	Vincenti	Vincento	Vincent
Wilhelmus	Wilhelmi	Wilhelmo	William

SECTION E

ARCHAEOLOGY

Part 1 — Terms

Part 2 — Archaeological methods

Part 3 — Artefacts

Part 4 — Industrial Archaeology — Windmills and Watermills

Part One — Terms

1 Agger
The raised platform of a Roman road. Main roads could be between 30 and 84 feet wide and the Agger from a few inches to 2 feet thick. The Agger can be easily distinguished running beneath grass fields. Usually on each side were flat spaces or tracks called berms (qv), and on the outside of these, ditches for drainage.

2 Arras Culture
A culture named after the east Yorkshire village where extensive burial remains have been found. About 400BC the area was settled by a people who were probably part of the Parisi tribe from Gaul. Their method of burial was distinctive: their chiefs, either male or female, were buried in small barrows, with a cart presumably acting as a hearse, and their weapons and horse. Another concentration of their burials has been found at Driffield.

3 Aylesford Culture
This culture is found in Essex, Herts and north Kent and stems from Iron Age Belgic tribes from France.

Their burial method is distinctive in that the dead were cremated in pear-shaped urns mounted on pedestals and buried in flat graves.

4 Barrow
A mound of earth or chalk covering a burial. The main types are long and round and these are themselves divided into categories.

Long Barrows were common in the Neolithic Age, being graves for a tribe or family. They were usually 100 to 300 feet long and 30 to 100 feet wide, normally wider at the east. They were mounds of earth or chalk.

A Bank Barrow is a type of long barrow and is distinguished by its considerable length. The Maiden Castle example is a third of a mile long.

Round Barrows dating from the Bronze Age, are the most common in Britain. The main varieties are as follows:

Bell Barrows, shaped like a flattened bell, have a deep ditch around them, sometimes with an embankment round the ditch. The barrow itself is separated from the ditch by a flat area called a berm (qv).

Bowl Barrows are the most numerous of the varieties, obtaining their name from their upturned bowl shape. Their size ranges from 15 to over 100 feet wide, and up to 20 feet high. Some have a ditch around the mound.

Disc Barrows are mounds much flatter than either bell or bowl barrows, sometimes hardly visible. Usually they have ditches around them. Of this type saucer barrows have a slightly raised mound surrounded by a ditch and an embankment, and pond barrows which have a depression instead of a mound, surrounded by an embankment. Other types of discs include platform barrows which have a low, flat platform surrounded by a ditch, and ring barrows which have no raised mound at all but are simply burial areas covered over and surrounded by a ditch and embankment.

5 Baulk
A strip of land left between trenches during excavation. This not only provides a pathway for the excavators but also helps to show the stratigraphy of the site.

6 Beaker People
A culture named after the shape of its pottery. The people came, about 2000BC, from Holland and Germany, introducing the use of copper and thereby ending the Neolithic Age in this country and beginning the Bronze Age. They introduced also the method of burying the dead singly instead of communally under round barrows, usually with weapons. Some buried their dead in a crouching, womb-like position. They also expanded the building of henge monuments. They were itinerant farmers and traders, as well as settlers, and their influence is widespread in the country.

7 Bell Barrow
See Barrow

8 Bell Pit
A hole from which clay has been taken to use for iron-making. It is narrower at the top than at the bottom.

9 Berm
A flat area surrounding a barrow mound or a raised structure of any kind such as a fort or road.

10 Boundary Banks
The late Bronze Age or Early Iron Age earthen banks may be boundaries or defences. To make a bank a ditch was excavated. If the ditch appears on different sides of the bank depending on what was easier with the slope of the land, it would indicate that the bank was a boundary. If the bank is always on the higher side of the ditch, regardless of the slope of the land, it would probably mean that it was used for defensive purposes as well.

11 Bowl Barrow
See Barrow.

12 Broch
An Early Iron Age fortified farm in Caithness, Orkneys and Shetlands. It consisted of a round tower, 45-70 feet in diameter, with inner and outer stone walls between which the people lived. In the area inside the inner walls the cattle were kept.

13 Cairn/Carn
A pile of stones, especially in Scotland, used to mark a grave or event, or else to serve as a landmark.

14 Capstone
A stone slab used to roof a gallery or passage in a tomb.

15 Causeway

A path over earthworks and other defensive features leading to a fortified area.

16 Celtic Cross
The head of this cross has a distinctive wheel design; its shape is derived from a monogram of the first two letters of the Greek spelling of the word Christ. Also called Cornish Cross.

17 Celtic Field
Common throughout the country before the Saxons introduced strip-farming, especially in upland soils where the terrain did not permit of large, open fields. On sloping land they were usually cross-ploughed. Celtic Fields were square-shaped and usually half to 1 acre.

18 Chevaux de Frise
A defensive arrangement of closely set stakes.

19 Cist
An Early Bronze Age burial-chamber dug into rock or, in some cases, into tree trunks. It could also be a pit lined with stone slabs.

20 Contour Fort
A fort built on a hill-top and which had defensive ramparts following the contours of the hill.

21 Cornish Cross
See Celtic Cross.

22 Cove
In henge monuments, three large standing stones in a U-shape.

23 Cromlech
A Welsh term for a megalithic tomb.

24 Crop Marks
These are best seen by aerial photography. The foundations of walls produce a lighter colour in the vegetation above. Conversely vege-

tation above a ditch or pit can have a richer colour.

25 Crucifixion Chamber
A tomb in the shape of a cross.

26 Cup and Ring Marks
Cup-shaped hollows found on Bronze Age burial chambers, passage graves etc.

27 Currency Bar
Before the advent of coinage, currency bars could be used. They were lengths of iron, 30-35" long, with handles, and were shaped like swords.

28 Cursus
These consist of parallel banks of earthworks with ditches outside, sometimes running for long distances, and usually in connection with henges and long barrows. Their purpose is unknown but the main theories are that they were used for ritual processions or races.

29 Danish Forts
Normally these were in a D-shape, with a curved defensive fence or ditch, and a river forming the straight side.

30 Deer Roast
A horseshoe-shaped group of stones with an open end facing a stream. It was used for cooking.

31 Deserted Villages
These are most common in those areas affected by the enclosures of the 15th and 16th centuries when arable fields were turned into sheep runs, with a consequent lack of need for farm workers.

32 Dewponds
Shallow, rain-collecting basins, which were lined with clay and straw with flints on top. Some are pre-historic though most are comparatively modern.

33 Disc Barrows
See **Barrow**.

34 Dolmen
The stone chamber of a barrow.

35 Duns
Scottish Iron Age stone forts, usually circular or oval, with very thick drystone walls.

36 Faience
Imported glass beads and adornments. These appeared in Britain from 1550BC. They were usually coloured blue with copper salts.

37 Fogous
Iron Age underground storage chambers particularly found in Cornwall. Also known as Souterrains.

38 Gallery Graves
Long stone passages in Neolithic long barrows. They were sometimes divided transversely by stone slabs which formed the passage into sections, or else had small chambers on either side of the passage. The funeral rites were conducted in a widened area just outside the entrance. The graves were filled working from the back.

39 Hallstatt Culture
An Early Iron Age culture (550-300BC), named after a village near Salzburg, which introduced iron implements into Britain.

40 Hammerponds
Found in the Weald, these were formed in the Iron Age by damming valleys and providing water power sufficient to work a hammer that crushed iron ore.

41 Henge
Late Neolithic and Early Bronze Age circles of stone or wooden uprights, with a ditch and bank around them. Class I Henges have one entrance, Class II have two entrances facing each other.

42 Hill Figures
These were cut into chalk or limestone hills and originated in the Iron Age. Generally they depicted horses or gods and, later, crosses. The best known one is at Uffington, Berks.

43 Hypocaust
An underground chamber beneath the floor of a Roman house. Heat from a furnace was distributed into hollow tiles in the rooms above.

44 Kitchen-midden
An ancient rubbish heap in which are found bones etc. and sometimes implements. Also called shell-mound.

45 La Tène Culture
The second of the iron-using cultures in Britain, named after a village near Lake Neuchatel in Switzerland. Its influence in Britain is usually dated from 300 to 150BC.

46 Lynchets
As earth on the Celtic Fields (qv) was tilled it tended to slip down to the bottom of the field, forming banks called Lynchets.

47 Marl-pits
An 18th and 19th century method of fertilising was to spread marl — chalky earth — on the fields. This left marl-pits, a common feature of the English landscape.

48 Megaliths
Large blocks of stone.

49 Monoliths
Large standing stones either in ritual formations or standing alone.

50 Mortuary Enclosures
Neolithic storage places for bodies until the number was sufficient to warrant the construction of a barrow.

51 Mortuary house
A small dwelling for the dead, built under a barrow, and serving as a tomb.

52 Motte
A mound with a flattened top on which a Norman fort stood.

53 Passage Grave
A Neolithic mound, with a circular or rectangular burial chamber beneath, reached by a long passage from the outside.

54 Plateau Fort
A fort on a lowland area.

55 Platform and Pond Barrows
See **Barrow.**

56 Post Hole
A hole which once held an upright for a building. Even though the timber itself might have disappeared the difference in soil between that of the filled-in hole and that surrounding it will help to give the plan of the building.

57 Rath
A circular enclosure surrounded by an earthen wall used as a defensive and residential area; the older raths are Late Bronze Age.

58 Revetment
A wall or fence built to prevent a landslip.

59 Ridgeways
Tracks which anciently led from hillfort to hillfort, such as the Jurassic Ridge from Dorset to Lincolnshire and the Icknield Way in the Chilterns.

60 Ring Barrows
61 Saucer Barrows
See **Barrow.**

62 Shell Mound
See **Kitchen-midden.**

63 Sherd/Shard
Fragment of pottery.

64 Souterrains
See **Fogous.**

65 Treasure Trove
The law is complex in this matter but the main principles are as follows in England and Wales:
a) Gold and silver that has been hidden with the intention of recovery later can be claimed by the Crown. With archaeological finds the investigation has to establish the intention of the last owner when the hoard was hidden.
b) Goods which seem to have been abandoned become the property of the finder.
c) Items which have been 'lost' have to be declared when found; the finder can be accused of larceny otherwise. They are declared to the coroner, usually via the police. A common decision on archaeological finds is that the items belong to the owner of the land on which they were found.
d) When a hoard is found and declared straightaway, the Crown, if it retains it will pay the finder the full market value. Items it doesn't retain will be returned to the finder or the owner of the land.
In Scotland all treasure trove is claimed by the Crown which, in this case, doesn't have to prove that the intention was to recover the hoard.

66 Tump
A Barrow.

67 Tumulus
A Barrow.

68 Vitrified Fort
A type of fort where the stone rubble walls had been fused together by intensive heat. They date from approximately the 1st century AD in east and south-west Scotland.

69 Welwyn-type Burial

A Late Iron Age method of burial, named after a discovery in Welwyn, Herts, in which the dead were cremated and their remains placed in urns. These vessels were then placed, sometimes in circular pattern, in a flat grave without a mound. The dead were buried with possessions.

70 Wessex Culture

Early Bronze Age culture in southern England. In Wessex I stage (c 1650-1550BC) the dead were inhumed under bowl, bell and disc barrows, but in Wessex II (1550-1400BC) burials the dead were usually cremated.

71 Wheelhouse

Iron Age house in Scotland. It was circular with partitions projecting like the spokes of a wheel.

72 Windmill Hill Culture

The first Neolithic culture in Britain, generally dated from c3000 BC. It is named after a site near Avebury where there was a causewayed camp. They were farmers from northern France, Germany and the Low Countries.

Part Two

73 Archaeological Periods

The generally accepted dating of the archaeological periods is as follows:

	From	To
Lower to Middle Paleolithic	—	50000BC
Upper Paleolithic	50000	12000BC
Mesolithic	12000	3000BC
Neolithic	3000	1800BC
Early Bronze Age (Beaker)	2000	1400BC
Middle Bronze Age	1400	1000BC
Later Bronze Age	1000	550BC
Iron Age A (Hallstatt)	550	300BC
Iron Age B (La Tène)	300	150BC
Iron Age C (Belgae)	150	43AD
Roman	43	c410AD

Part Three — Archaeological Methods

74 Aerial Photography

This is used to get an overall picture of an area and by the interpretation of shadows and the colouring of vegetation to obtain, without excavation, an indication of what lies underneath.

To obtain shadow patterns photography should take place when the angle of the sun is low. Slightly raised earthworks or field boundaries, not easy to trace on the ground, cast shadows. Cropmarks occur when vegetation colour is changed by foundations or ditches underneath. Above ditches crops will appear richer and grow higher. Above foundations, roads etc., crops will be lighter and stunted. Cropmarks are best photographed after a period of dry weather.

Photography will identify, after ploughing, patterns of different soil, such as chalk from hidden burial mounds.

75 Archaeomagnetism

When clay is baked the magnetic field contained in the iron oxide is preserved. It is possible when burnt clay is found, for example in undisturbed pottery kilns, to compare the magnetic field of the burnt clay with that of clay surrounding it which has a constantly changing magnetic field. The comparison will date the burnt clay.

76 Bosing

One of the simplest methods of detection. It consists of striking the ground with a weighted stick and interpreting the sound it makes. Generally, undisturbed ground gives a dead sound and previously disturbed ground, (which never regains its consistency), gives a dull thump. This method is most useful in areas with chalk or rocks underneath.

77 Dendochronology

The dating of wood by measuring tree rings and their thickness. This method, used principally in dating boats, medieval buildings etc., requires considerable expertise and research into rainfall patterns.

78 Electrical Resistivity

Different soils have contrasting powers of conducting electricity due to their moisture. The method is to probe an area with a measuring instrument and to interpret any patterns of resistance that occur.

79 Fluorine Measurement

Fluorine, from water, is found in bones and teeth. The longer they have been left in soil the more fluorine they contain.

80 Geochronology

A general term for the dating methods based on the earth's physical history, such as Radio-carbon, dendochronology etc.

81 Probing

This method involves inserting a thin metal rod into the ground to search for walls, foundations, ditches etc.

82 Quadrant System

A method whereby a round barrow is quartered to show sections across it.

83 Radio-carbon Dating

Vegetation absorbs carbon from the atmosphere and this is transferred to man or animal when the vegetation is eaten. After death the residual radioactive carbon left in bones decays at a rate of a half approximately every 5570 years.

Part Four — Artefacts

84 Adze

A Neolithic axe, with the heavy blade set at right-angles to the haft. Used for trimming and smoothing timbers, hollowing out canoes etc.

85 Arrowhead

The tip of an arrow, made from bone, stone or metal. Generally all that remains of early arrows as the shaft has disintegrated.

86 Awl

A sharp piece of bone, metal or flint used for piercing holes.

87 Burin

A flint tool with a cutting edge on one corner. Also called Graver.

88 Clay Pipes

Elizabethan pipes are similar to the American Indian shape with thin bowls and without a spur underneath. Seventeenth century pipes have spurs and the bowl might slope forward. For identification see the collection in the London Museum.

89 Graver

See Burin.

90 Halberd

A weapon with a pointed blade at right-angles to the haft.

91 Incense Cups

A name applied to cups placed next to food vessels in Middle Bronze Age burials. They do not, however, appear to have been used for incense.

92 Microliths
Very small, mesolithic flint tools or arrow heads.

93 Querns
Implements used for crushing grain. Rotary querns consisted of one stone rotating on another. Saddle querns had an upper stone rubbing on a lower, saddle-shaped, stone.

94 Tranchet
An implement with a chisel-type edge.

Part Four — Watermills and Windmills

95 Watermills
Watermills were used in England as early as Roman times. There developed two main kinds:

96 Undershot wheel
This kind was well established at the time of the Norman Conquest. It consisted of a vertically mounted wheel with flat blades around its circumference. The wheel was turned by the flow of water underneath the wheel striking the blades.

Mills were usually situated on an artificial water-course, called a leat, which diverted water from a river and then returned it by means of a tail-race. This method enabled the miller to cut off the water supply when he wished.

97 Overshot wheel
This variation, developed in the Middle Ages, consisted of a vertically mounted wheel with troughs around its circumference. Water was fed into it near the top of the wheel, filling the nearest troughs, their weight moving the wheel round. This was the most popular type of wheel in hilly country where streams had good falls. A more sophisticated version was called a breast-shot wheel which used water more economically.

98 Tide Mills
These were situated on estuaries and could have either undershot or breast-shot wheels. They conserved water at high-tide, expending it gradually before the next tide. These mills could be used at the most for two 6-hour spells in each 24-hours, and the hours of employment were onerous because of the change of high tides.

Windmills

99 Post Mills
The earliest record of a windmill in England is of that at Bury St Edmunds in 1191. The earliest types were fixed structures usable only when the wind was blowing in the right direction. In the Middle Ages the Post Mill developed. This consisted of a timber body, containing the machinery and carrying the sails, mounted on an upright oak main-post. The body of the mill could be moved, by the use of a tail-beam, round to face the wind.

The oldest surviving mill of this kind is at Bourn in Cambridgeshire, erected in 1636.

By the 18th century an automatic fantail had been developed which turned the timber framework by wind power. Mounted on the structure was a vaned fantail which caught the wind and by a system of gears and spindles turned the wheels at the foot of the mill ladder which then went along a track round the mill.

The bottom part of the main-post was often covered by a round-house superstructure.

It was common for the mill to be set upon an artificial mound.

100 Tower Mills

Tower Mills were developed in the mid 17th century. They have a brick tower containing the machinery, on top of which is a movable top or cap. Only the cap moves to face the wind. These mills also adopted the automatic fantail described under Post Mills above.

Most of the country's surviving mills are of this variety, partly due to the use of stronger materials in their structure.

101 Smock Mills

These mills, with a movable cap similar to that of a tower mill, developed in the mid 17th century.

They were popular in areas where brick and masonry were hard to get, and were tapered wooden structures, usually weatherboarded, often octagonal.

They derived their name from their resemblance to a miller's flared smock.

102   Sails

Usually four sails were preferred. Each sail consisted of an open-latticed framework on which the miller rigged canvas.

In 1772 the 'spring-sail' was invented, a system of louvres which were opened and closed by a lever at the outer end of each sail. The adjustments were done manually. In 1807 the 'patent-sail' allowed this to be worked by a rod which ran down to the grindstones.

SECTION F

EDUCATION

Part 1 — Legislation

Part 2 — Types of Schools

Part 3 — Foundations of Schools and Universities

Part One — Legislation

1 **1829 Catholic Emancipation Act**
This Act removed discrimination against Roman Catholic teachers and schools.

2 **1844 Poor Law**
The Poor Law Commissioners were empowered to appoint a schoolmaster for workhouse children, and later District Schools were developed so that children could be educated outside the workhouse.

3 **1857 Industrial Schools Act**
This enabled magistrates to send children found begging or else needing care and protection from criminal company, to industrial schools to learn a trade.

4 **1870 Education Act (Forsters)**
This major Act provided that England should be divided into districts and that elementary schools be set up in areas where school provision was insufficient. Boards were set up to manage these districts. These were the first local authority-run schools and were supplementary, at that stage, to the voluntary, privately endowed schools. They were secular and undenominational but an amendment to the Statute allow-ed school boards to provide religious instruction if they wished.

5 **1876**
Legislation this year established the principle that all children should receive elementary education. It also imposed further restrictions on employment of children. It established school attendance committees where no school boards existed.

6 **1880 Education Act**
School attendance up to the age of 10 was made compulsory. At that age a child could obtain a certificate and leave but if he had registered too few attendances he had to stay on until 13.

7 **1889 Education Act**
County Councils were empowered to levy a 1d rate for technical education. The Board of Education was set up.

8 **1891**
Elementary education was made free.

9 **1902 Education Act (Balfour's)**
County Council education authorities were set up and superseded the School Boards, and given power to provide secondary education. Generally the secondary

schools provided were not co-educational and carried on the existing public school system of grammar schools for boys and high schools for girls.

10 1918

The school-leaving age was raised to 14.

11 1944 Education Act

Fees in state secondary schools were abolished.

Primary education was re-organised into infant and junior, and secondary into modern, grammar and technical.

The school-leaving age was raised to 15.

Part Two — Types of Schools

12 Adult School Movement

Based on the Society of Friends, and now called the National Adult School Union, it provided undenominational but basically religious schools in the 19th century.

13 Board Schools

These were established after the 1870 Education Act and were the first local authority-run schools. The country was divided into school-board districts; the boards were empowered to build new schools in areas of poor provision or else to absorb existing schools. The schools were secular and undenominational. In 1902 the Board Schools became Council Schools.

14 British Schools

In 1808 followers of Joseph Lancaster, a Quaker, formed the Royal Lancasterian Society to carry out his educational ideas. The Society altered its name in 1810 to the British and Foreign School Society once Lancaster, an indifferent manager of finance, had cut himself off from the organisation.

Lancaster did not introduce the monitorial system into education, though often credited with its innovation. It is possible that he was unaware of previous experiments in this field. However, he did popularise it and the results were evident in elementary education until comparatively recent times.

The system allowed for tuition of masses of children by other partially educated children, with a minimum of paid staff. It therefore recommended itself by its cheapness and for a long time the system, widely used by other types of school, enabled successive governments to escape expenditure which full teaching personnel at schools would have entailed.

Lancaster's schools were competitive; pupils moved backwards and forwards in the rows of desks according to their achievements.

In 1834 Parliament made a grant of £24,000 to elementary schools which was shared between the British and the National (qv) schools.

By 1851 there were 1500 British Schools in the country, drawing their main support from Nonconformist familes.

15 Cathedral and Monastic Schools

The earliest schools were those attached to cathedrals and monasteries. The first one appears to have been at Canterbury in the early 7th century — King's School is the present-day successor to that establishment.

16 Chantry Schools

Chantry schools developed in medieval times. It was a common practice for a wealthy person to endow a church in his will so that a chantry might be founded and in which priests might pray for his soul. A chantry priest would also teach at the church school.

Most of the schools were grammar schools but there were some with primary sections. They were mostly suppressed after legislation in 1547.

17 Circulating Schools

In the 18th century educational facilities in Wales were rare, partly due to the fact of a sparse and widely scattered population. In the late 17th century the Rev. Thomas Gouge had founded a society in order to instruct poor Welsh children in English and he travelled throughout Wales teaching.

In 1730 the Rev. Griffith Jones of Llandowror in Carmarthenshire founded what was to be known as a Circulating School. The instruction was carried out by itinerant teachers who stayed in localities for 3 to 6 months. The schools were for adults as well as children and Welsh rather than English was used. It is stated that in 1777 there were 6456 such schools. After 1779 when the Griffith Jones estate was disputed and held in Chancery the schools ceased to function.

18 Common Day Schools

These were private, low fee, elementary schools for poor children.

19 Dame Schools

Elementary schools run by women, the usual fee being 3d or 4d per week. Very common up to the 1870 Education Act.

20 District Schools

These provided, from the mid 19th century, education for children in workhouses but in separate buildings. They dwindled in importance after the 1870 Education Act and with the decline of the workhouse system.

21 Factory Schools

An Act of 1833 made attendance at school a condition of employment for juveniles, and in 10 years approximately 40% of children in the manufacturing areas were attending factory schools. This sort of work had already been pioneered by employers like Robert Owen and David Dale.

22 Grammar Schools

The Saxon origin of Grammar Schools lay in ecclesiastical establishments in which candidates for the priesthood learnt Latin.

In medieval times the schools were established by private benefactors — quite often beginning as chantry schools (qv) — ecclesiastical bodies and trade guilds.

In the 17th century the distinction between 'boarding' grammar schools and 'day-schools' became prominent. At first no fees were charged as costs were covered by endowments, but gradually fee-paying pupils became common.

The curriculum until the 19th century was still largely classical, a state governed by the foundations' terms. The Grammar Schools Act 1840 empowered governors to add new subjects to the range.

Under the Education Act 1904 some Grammar Schools — the least prosperous — were absorbed into the state system, the pupils remaining a mixture of fee-paying and free, but with the schools partly maintained by the state. The Education Act 1944 abolished fees in maintained schools.

23 Junior Schools

These were established after the 1918 Education Act but were not prevalent until after 1926. They taught children aged from 7 to 11 whereas the earlier elementary schools had catered for children from 7 to 14.

24 National Schools

The National Society for the Education of the Poor in the Principles of the Established Church was formed in 1811 and took over most of the schools already established by the SPCK (qv). By 1851 it controlled over 17000 schools but the 1870 Education Act, setting up Board Schools, led to its decline.

25 Public Schools

The term 'Public Schools' is now generally accepted as denoting about 200 independent schools, mainly in the south of England.

Many of them derive from the old Grammar Schools — especially those which boarded scholars. About a third of today's public schools are grammar schools founded between the 14th and 17th centuries. They became 'public' by virtue of their ability to attract pupils outside their own locality.

In 1868 the Public Schools Act required each school to draw up a constitution and laid down conditions for the appointment of governors.

26 Ragged Schools

Ragged schools developed from the work of John Pounds, a cobbler in Portsmouth. As from 1818 he provided a school for children entirely free for the very poorest children. In 1844 Lord Shaftesbury helped to organise an official union of Ragged Schools. By 1869 there were about 200 Ragged Schools as well as Sunday schools and night schools.

27 SPCK

The Society for the Propagation of Christian Knowledge was founded in 1698. Its educational activities provided schools for the industrial poor and by 1750 there were at least 1500 schools in existence. They set the pattern for 19th century education, insisting on subordination, frugality and gratitude. The schools were supported by voluntary subscription. They declined in importance in the first half of the 19th century and many of their buildings were taken over by the National Schools (qv).

28 Sunday Schools

The first Sunday School appears to have been in Catterick, Yorkshire, in 1763, but the man who made the movement successful was Robert Raikes who founded a school in Gloucester in 1780. He engaged four women to teach and charged a penny a week.

In 1785, with the movement growing in popularity, a society was formed for the Establishment and Support of Sunday Schools throughout the Kingdom of Great Britain. The Sunday School Union was founded in 1803 to improve such schools in the London area.

29 WEA

The Association to Promote the Higher Education of Working Men, as it was first called, was founded in 1903 by Albert Mansbridge, the first branch being at Reading in 1904. The name was changed to the Workers' Educational Association in 1905.

30 Workhouse Schools

Education for pauper children was either non-existent or primitive in workhouses. The 1844 Poor Law allowed the Poor Law Commissioners to appoint schoolmasters.

Part Three — Schools & Universities

31

The following are the foundation dates of some prominent schools:

Beds
Bedford	pre Norman Conquest
Bedford Modern	1566

Berks	
Abingdon pre Norman Conquest	
Blue Coat (Reading)	1646
(now Sonning)	
Reading	c1125

Bucks	
Aylesbury Grammar	1598
Dr Challoner's Grammar,	
Amersham	1620
Eton	1440
Royal Grammar, High	
Wycombe	c1548
Royal Latin, Buckingham	1540
Sir William Borlase's, Marlow	1624

Cambs	
Kings, Ely	1541
Perse, Cambridge	1615

Cheshire	
Kings, Chester	1541
Stockport Grammar	1487
Birkenhead	1860
Kings, Macclesfield	1502

Cornwall	
Truro Grammar	16th cent

Cumberland	
St Bees	1583

Derbyshire	
Ashbourne Grammar	1586
Repton	1557
Wirksworth Grammar	1584

Devon	
All Hallows, Lyme Regis	1524
Ashburton Grammar	1314
Blundell's, Tiverton	1604
Exeter	1633

Dorset	
Sherborne	c 9th cent

Essex	
Brentwood	1557
Chelmsford	16th cent
Chigwell Grammar	1629
Davenant	1680
Felstead	1584
Saffron Walden	by 1314

Bancroft's, Woodford Green	1737

Glos	
Badminton	1852
Bristol Grammar	1532
Cheltenham	1841
Cheltenham Ladies College	1853
Gloucester Grammar	12th cent
Red Maids', Bristol	1634

Hants	
Portsmouth Grammar	1732
Winchester	1394

Hereford	
Lady Margaret Hawkins	
Grammar	1625
Lucton	1708
Hereford Cathedral	1381

Herts	
Berkhamsted	1541
Christ's Hospital School	
(originally founded in London;	
to Hertford 1695)	1552
Haberdashers Askes	1690
to Herts 1961	
Richard Hale, Hertford	1617
St Albans	c 948
Stevenage Grammar	1558
Watford Grammar	1704
Aldenham	1597

Hunts	
Kimbolton	1600

Kent	
Kings, Canterbury	c 600
Sevenoaks	1418
Tonbridge	1553
St Edmunds, Canterbury	1749
St Olaves, Orpington	1749
Sutton Valence, Maidstone	1576
Kings, Rochester	604
Maidstone Grammar	by 1450

Lancs	
Bolton Grammar	1524
Burnley Grammar	by 1532
Manchester Grammar	1515
Queen Elizabeth, Blackburn.	
Refounded	1567
Stonyhurst College	1794

Queen Elizabeth, Wakefield	
Refounded	1591
Hulme Grammar	1611
Bury Grammar	1600

Leicestershire

Appleby Parva	1697
Old Grammar School, Market	
Harborough	1614
Loughborough Grammar	1496

Lincs

Bourne Free	1768
Stamford	1532

London (GLC Area)

Dulwich	1619
St Pauls Refounded	1510
Westminster	by 1339
Harrow	1571
Highgate	1565
Merchant Taylors'	1561
Mill Hill	1807
North London Collegiate	1850
Trinity, Croydon	1596
Whitgift, Croydon	1596
Alleyns	1619
Battersea Grammar	1700
City of London	1442
Kingston Grammar	1561
Latymer Upper	1624
Emanuel	1594

Norfolk

Gresham's, Holt	1555
Norwich	c1240

Northants

Oundle	1556
Wellingborough	1595

Northumberland

Morpeth	16th cent
Shafto Trust, Haydon Bridge	1685
Royal Grammar, Newcastle	1525
Dame Allan's, Newcastle	1705

Notts

Newark High School for Girls	1623
Nottingham High School	1573

Oxford

Magdalen College School	1478

Rutland

Oakham	1584
Uppingham	1584

Shropshire

Bridgnorth Grammar	by 1503
Ludlow	by 1553
Shrewsbury	1552

Somerset

King's College, Taunton	1522
King's, Bruton	1519
Taunton	1847
King Edward's, Bath	1552
Kingswood	1748

Staffs

Abbotshulme, Uttoxeter	1889
Wolverhampton Grammar	1512

Suffolk

Bungay	16th cent
Debenham	mid 17th cent
Ipswich	1400

Surrey

Charterhouse (London)	1611
(Godalming)	1872

Sussex

Lancing	1849
Roedean	1885

Warwickshire

Bablake, Coventry	1344
Bayleys	1733
King Edward's, Birmingham	1552
Rugby	1567
Stratford-upon-Avon	
Grammar	1426
Queen Mary's Grammar School,	
Walsall	1554
King Henry VIII, Coventry	1545

Westmorland

Windermere	16th cent

Wiltshire

Marlborough	1843

Worcestershire

Bromsgrove	1553

Dudley Grammar	1562	Clare	1326
Hartlebury	by 1558	Corpus Christi	1352
King's, Worcester	1541	Downing	1800
Sebright, Wolverley	1618	Emmanuel	1584
Royal Grammar, Worcester	1290	Fitzwilliam	1869
King Edward VI Grammar	1552	Gonville & Caius	1348
Malvern College	1865	Jesus	1496
		King's	1441

Yorkshire

Archbishop Holgate's		Magdalen	1542
Grammar, York	1547	Pembroke	1347
Bradford Grammar	1548	Peterhouse	1284
Bootham, York	1823	Queen's	1448
Leeds Grammar	1552	St Catherine's	1473
St Peter's, York	7th cent	St John's	1511
Sedburgh	1527	Selwyn	1882
Ampleforth	1802	Sidney Sussex	1596
Giggleswick	1512	Trinity	1546
		Trinity Hall	1350

32 Universities

The foundation dates of the Oxford and Cambridge colleges are as follows:

Other Universities

The foundation dates of other principal Universities are as follows:

Oxford

Balliol	1263
Brasenose	1509
Christ Church	1546
Corpus Christi	1517
Exeter	1314
Hertford	1740
Jesus	1571
Keble	1868
Lincoln	1427
Magdalen	1458
Mansfield	1886
Merton	1264
New	1379
Oriel	1326
Pembroke	1624
Queens	1340
St Catherine's	1962
St Edmund Hall	1278
St John's	1555
St Peter's	1929
Trinity	1554
University	1249
Wadham	1612
Worcester	1714

Cambridge

Christ's	1505
Churchill	1960

Aberdeen	1494
Belfast	1908
Birmingham	1900
Bristol	1909
Dublin (Trinity)	1591
Durham	1832
East Anglia	1963
Edinburgh	1582
Exeter	1955
Glasgow	1451
Hull	1927-54
Keele	1949-62
Kent	1965
Lancaster	1964
Leeds	1904
Leicester	1918-57
Liverpool	1881-1903
London (University College)	1826
London (King's)	1829
London (School of Economics)	1895
Manchester	1851-80
Newcastle	1834-1963
Nottingham	1881-1938
Reading	1892-1926
St Andrews	1411
Sheffield	1897-1905
Southampton	1862-1952
Sussex	1961

| Wales | 1893 |
| York | 1963 |

SECTION G

SOCIAL WELFARE

Part 1 — The Treatment of the Poor

Part 2 — Hospitals

Part 3 — Charities and Philanthropic Societies

Part 4 — Miscellaneous

Part 5 — Municipal Housing

Part One — The Treatment of the Poor

1 1388
Vagrancy was strictly controlled. If a parish could not maintain an impotent beggar out of its own resources he was sent back to his birthplace. Vagrants capable of working were severely dealt with.

2 1391 Statute of Mortmain
When a benefice was appropriated some of its revenues were reserved for the poor in the parish.

3 1494
Vagrants capable of work were subjected to very severe penalties, ranging from whipping, loss of ears to hanging.

4 1530/1
Vagrants incapable of working had to obtain a licence from the magistrates to beg within a specified area.

5 1535/6
The parish was made responsible for the care of the impotent poor. Private alms were forbidden, with the penalty of a fine of ten times the amount given, but the priest and churchwardens were to procure charitable donations on Sundays.

6 1563 Poor Law
This enacted that 'two able persons or more shall be appointed gatherers and collectors of the charitable alms of all the residue of people inhabiting in the parish'. Quite often the collectors would be the churchwardens and the Act gave them limited powers to compel generosity as well as encouraging it.

7 1572
Magistrates were to deal with inhabitants who refused to give alms. Licences for begging were abandoned and a fine of £1 was imposed for private almsgiving. The office of Overseer of the Poor was created.

He or they were appointed by the Vestry and approved by the Justices of the Peace. They supervised endowments and other charitable funds, collected any fines allotted to the relief of the poor, and later assessed inhabitants for a poor rate.

8 1597/8

A poor rate was allowed. Relief was divided into 'indoor' for those maintained in poorhouses, and 'outdoor' — for those still in their own homes. The Act enabled the Overseers to erect a poorhouse at the Ratepayers' expense. As far as possible pauper children were to be apprenticed. The Overseers were to provide work for paupers and to keep a stock of raw materials for that purpose.

9 1601 Poor Law

This Act was the basis for Poor Law administration for two centuries. It was a temporary measure made permanent in 1640.

Under its provisions in each parish the churchwardens and a few other substantial landholders were made, each year, Overseers of the Poor. Paupers were to be maintained and set to work, the funds provided by taxes on the inhabitants and holders of lands or those receiving tithes or fines in the parish. Houses of Correction were to be built and vagrants committed to them, and the Overseers were to erect poorhouses for the incapacitated poor.

10 1662 Act of Settlement

A stranger staying in a parish could be removed by the Overseer of the Poor if he had no prospect of work within 40 days, or if he did not rent property worth £10 per year. A stranger staying temporarily, for harvesting for example, had to bring a certificate from his home parish guaranteeing to take him back. After 40 days a stranger could claim that he was then settled and if need arose could become a charge on the poor rate. Persistent vagrants could be punished by transportation.

11 1691

A register of parishioners in receipt of poor relief was to be kept.

12 1697 Settlement Act

Strangers were allowed to enter a parish provided that they possessed a Settlement Certificate showing thay they would be taken back by their old parish if they became in need of poor relief.

Paupers and their families were to wear a capital P on their clothing. The punishment for disobeying this instruction could be loss of relief, imprisonment, hard labour or whipping.

13 1722/3

Parishes were encouraged to build or rent workhouses and allowed to contract out their maintenance and supervision. A parish too small to support a workhouse was allowed a union with another to make a building viable.

The children of vagrants could be apprenticed against the will of the parents, and bastard children did not receive a Settlement Certificate in the parish of their birth. A person sheltering a vagrant could be fined up to £2.

14 1782 Gilbert's Act

This attempted to humanise the administration of workhouses. Independent inspectors were appointed, orphan children were boarded out elsewhere, children under seven were not separated from their parents. Paupers were not sent to workhouses more than ten miles from their own parish. The requirement to wear a pauper's badge was abandoned if they could prove to be of good character. The union of parishes and the provision of more economic workhouses was given new stimulus.

15 1795 Speenhamland System

The Berkshire justices, meeting at Speenhamland at a time when there was much poverty due to high prices and low wages, devised a system which supplemented wages from the poor rates, based upon the current price of bread. This system, widely used in southern and eastern England, is said to have encouraged employers to underpay in the knowledge that their employees would receive additional benefit from the parish. Other effects of the system were an increase in the number of people applying for relief, the abandonment of holdings in areas where the poor rate was high, and a general demoralisation of the recipients.

16 1808 Care of Lunatics

An Act empowered the Justices in Quarter Sessions to order the building of a county asylum for lunatics.

17 1815 Care of Lunatics

An Act instructed parish overseers to send lists of pauper lunatics to the Clerk of the Peace who eventually laid them before the Quarter Sessions.

18 1834 Poor Law Amendment Act

By this Act outdoor relief was almost entirely abolished and people unable to support themselves were accepted into workhouses after being subjected to the 'workhouse test'. Employers were obliged to pay a 'living wage' and workhouses were made as unpleasant as possible so as to encourage inmates to go out and find work.

The Act established three central Poor Law Commissioners and under them independently financed Guardians of the Poor were elected locally. Parishes were encouraged to combine into unions to provide workhouses.

19 1929 Local Government Act

The Boards of Guardians were abolished and their functions transferred to county councils and county boroughs.

20 1930 Poor Law Act

It was ruled that only the aged and infirm could apply for workhouse care and that outdoor relief could be given if necessary. Local councils were to care for orphans.

Part Two — Hospitals

21 Hospitals

The foundation dates for some of the major hospitals are as follows:

Bath General	1738
Belgrave Hospital for Children	1866
Bethel (Norwich)	1713
Bethlem, London (as a priory)	1247
Brompton Hospital for Diseases of the Chest	c1842
Central London Hospital for the Throat	1874
Charing Cross Hospital (originally the West London Infirmary)	1818
City of London Maternity	1750
Devon and Exeter	1753
Durham, Newcastle-on-Tyne and Northumberland Infirmary	c1745
East London Hospital for Children	1868
Elizabeth Garrett Anderson (originally the New Hospital for Women)	1872
Exeter Eye	1806
Foundling	1739
Free Cancer Hospital, Fulham	1851
French Protestant	c1708
General Lying-in	1765
Gloucester Infirmary	1745
Grosvenor Hospital for Women	1866
Guys	1726
Hereford General Infirmary	1776
Hospital for Diseases of the Throat	1863
Hospital for Sick Children, Gt Ormond Street	1852
House of Recovery, Grays Inn Road	1802

Hull Royal Infirmary	1784
Kensington Children's Hospital	1840
King's College	1839
Leeds Hospital for Women	1853
Leeds Infirmary	1767
Leicester Infirmary	1771
Lincoln County	1769
Liverpool Infirmary for Children	1857
Liverpool Royal Infirmary	1745
Liverpool Royal Lunatic Asylum	1792
London Hospital	1740
London Fever	1802
London Homeopathic	1849
London Lock	1746
London Skin	1887
London Smallpox	1850
Magdalen	1758
Manchester Fever	1796
Manchester Hospital for Children	1829
Manchester Royal Infirmary	1752
Manchester Royal Lunatic Asylum	1766
Metropolitan Ear, Nose and Throat	1838
Middlesex	1745
Middlesex County	1746
Moorfields	1805
National Dental Hospital	1861
National Hospital for Diseases of the Heart	1857
National Hospital for Paralysis and Epilepsy	1859
National Temperance	1873
Nottingham General	1782
Poplar Hospital for Accidents	1855
Queen Charlotte's	1739
Queen's Hospital for Children	1867
Radcliffe Infirmary, Oxford	1770
Royal Dental	1858
Royal Ear	1816
Royal Eye	1857
Royal Free	1828
Royal Hospital for Diseases of the Chest	1814
Royal Hospital for Incurables	1854
Royal National Orthopaedic	1838
Royal Northern	c1856
Royal Sea Bathing Hospital, Margate	1796

Royal Westminster Opthalmic	1816
Royal Waterloo Hospital for Children and Women	1816
St Bartholomew's	c1123
St Bartholomew's, Dover	c1141
St George's, London	1734
St John's, Oxford	c1180
Refounded	1233
St John's, Canterbury	c1084
St Leonard's, York (originally St Peter's)	c 937
St Luke's, London	1751
St Mark's Hospital for Cancer	1835
St Peter's York (see St Leonard's)	
St Peter's, Bristol	1696
St Peter's Hospital for Stone, London	1860
St Thomas'	mid 12th cent
Samaritan Free Hospital for Women	1847
Sheffield Royal Infirmary	1832
Shrewsbury Infirmary	1745
Taunton and Somerset	c1810
University College	1833
Victoria Park Hospital for Diseases of the Heart and Lungs	1848
Wakefield	1787
Westminster	1720
Westminster Lying-in	1765
Worcester Royal Infirmary	1746
York County	1740
York Lunatic Asylum	1777

A comprehensive list of medieval hospitals, arranged under counties, is contained in Rotha Mary Clay's book 'The Medieval Hospitals of England' (1909).

Part Three — Charities and Philanthropic Societies

22 Charities and Philanthropic Societies

The foundation dates of some of the more important charities or philanthropic societies are as follows:

Anti-Slavery Society   1823
Association for Promoting the
    General Welfare of the
    Blind   1856
Association for the Relief of
    the Manufacturing and
    Labouring Poor   1811
Baptist Missionary Society   1793
Barnados Home   1867
British & Foreign Bible
    Society   1804
British & Foreign School
    Society   1814
Church Building Society   1818
Church Missionary Society   c1800
City Parochial Foundation   1891
Commons Preservation
    Society   1865
Destitute Children's Dinner
    Society   1864
East End Dwellings Company   1884
Edinburgh Society for
    Improving the Condition of
    the Poor   1867
Four Per Cent Industrial
    Dwellings Company   1886
Guinness Trust   1889
Home Teaching Society for
    the Blind   1855
Leeds Society for the Erection
    of Improved Dwellings   c1860
Liverpool Central Relief
    Society   1863
Liverpool Night Asylum for
    the Houseless   1830
Liverpool School for the
    Indigent Blind   1790
London Missionary Society   1795
London Society for the Pre-
    vention of Cruelty to
    Children (later the National
    Society)   1884

London Society for Teaching
    the Blind to Read   1839
Marine Society   1756
Metropolitan Association for
    Improving the Dwellings of
    the Industrious Classes   1841
National Society for Pro-
    moting Education   1809
National Society for the Pre-
    vention of Cruelty to
    Children (see London

    Society)
National Trust   1895
Peabody Dwellings   1864
Philanthropic Society (for
    children)   1788
Ragged School Union   1844
Relief of the Infant Poor
    (London)   1769
Royal National Lifeboat
    Institution   1824
Royal Society for the Pre-
    vention of Cruelty to
    Animals   1824
St Giles in the Fields School
    for the Indigent Blind   c1800
Society for Bettering the
    Condition of the Poor   c1800
Society for Improving the
    Condition of the Labouring
    Classes   c1844
Society for Promoting
    Christian Knowledge   1699
Society for the Propagation of
    the Gospel in Foreign Parts 1701
Society for the Relief of
    Distress   1860
Sunday School Society   1785
Thatched House Society (for
    aid to people in debtors'
    prisons)   1773

Part 4 — Miscellaneous

23 Almshouses

Also called Bedehouses or Spital Houses. Originally charitable institutions which provided care and hospitality for the poor, sick or pilgrims. Many were discontinued at the Reformation in 1547. In 1853 charity commissioners were appointed to control abuses in almshouses and gradually most establishments came under the control of the appropriate local authority.

24 Badgers

A term derived from the 1697 Settlement Act under which paupers were obliged to wear a capital 'P' on their clothing. The term was later used loosely for pedlars and chapmen.

25 Bairman/Bareman
A pauper.

26 Bastardy
In 1575/6 an Act allowed Justices to imprison the parents of an illegitimate child, and in 1609/10, to send the mother to prison unless she could give securities for good behaviour. Generally the child would be given the same Settlement rights as its mother (see 1697 Settlement Act) but in the case of the father being from another parish the child and mother would be settled in the father's parish if they could be persuaded to marry.

An Act of 1732/3 obliged the mother to declare that she was pregnant with an illegitimate child and to state the name of the father.

With the rise of illegitimacy in the 18th century the parish officers either obliged the parents to marry, thereby saving court expenses but risking the whole family becoming a charge on the poor rate, or else obtained a sum of money — a Bond of Indemnification — from the father, in lump sum or spread over a period to pay for the child's upkeep.

27 Beadhouse/Bedehouse
Almshouse, later workhouse.

28 Bond of Indemnification
A term which referred to the sum of money obtained from a putative father, (see Bastardy), to pay for the upkeep of his child, or else an indemnity given by relatives or friends of potential paupers who might gain a Settlement in the parish. Quite often employers were obliged to pay a Bond when taking on servants for twelve months who, by virtue of their employment, gained a Settlement.

29 Cess
A sum of money given to the poor from the parish funds.

30 Collectioner
A pauper in receipt of relief from the parish funds.

31 Dole
The distribution of money or provisions to the poor.

32 Hundred House
In East Anglia large areas such as Hundreds (qv) formed themselves into Unions to erect and maintain workhouses.

33 Leatherhouse
A London term for a poorhouse.

34 Removal
Describes the removal of a pauper to the parish in which he had a Settlement

35 Second Poor
Poor people not in receipt of parish relief.

36 Union
A combination of parishes, allowed by various Poor Laws, to erect and maintain a workhouse.

Part Five — Municipal Housing

37 1851 Labouring Classes Lodging Houses Act
This Act enabled local authorities to appoint commissioners to borrow money for the erection or purchase of lodging houses for the working-classes. The Act was totally ignored.

38 1875 Artisans and Labourers Dwellings Improvement Act
This Act gave local authorities power to buy up slum property for

demolition or improvement with compulsory purchase powers. It was rarely adopted.

39 Housing Act 1890

This Act helped local authorities to clear slums in large clearance areas as well as smaller ones. It provided for the building of working-class housing with a public subsidy. The national subsidy was adjusted in further acts of 1923 and 1924.

SECTION H

LAW AND ORDER

Part 1 — The Development of the Police

Part 2 — Prisons

Part 3 — Judicial Authorities

Part 4 — Judicial Officials

Part 5 — General

Part One — The Development of the Police

1 1285 Statute of Winchester

This Statute rationalised the previous primitive system of policing and reaffirmed the obligations of a locality to keep its own law and order. In the towns it introduced the system of Watch and Ward. Watch was the term for the night duty of constables and Ward referred to their duties during the daytime. Up to sixteen men were to guard the walls through the night and place any wrongdoers in the hands of the parish constable the next day.

The Statute also introduced the system of Hue and Cry in which a person wishing to make an arrest could call on the rest of the manor or parish to join him in pursuit. Everyone was obliged to join the Hue and, literally, cry aloud to attract other people's attention. Anyone starting a Hue and Cry without good cause was punished. The system still has a modern application in the obligation of the public to assist the police in arresting a suspect.

The third major innovation of this Statute was the establishment of the Assize of Arms. Each man between 15 and 60 had to keep weapons or effects with which to help keep the peace. The higher a person's rank, the more expensive the equipment he had to keep. The high constables in each Hundred inspected the arms twice a year.

2 Parish Constable

Throughout the post–Norman period the unpaid parish constable, or petty constable, was emerging as the local peace keeper. His duties and powers are noted under B105.

3 Justices of the Peace

An Act of 1327 laid down that in each county someone be appointed to keep the peace. The Justices of the Peace Act 1361 recognised them as justices as well as increasing their numbers considerably. Usually the Justice would be a lord of the manor or other large landowner; he derived his authority from the Crown.

4 Local Acts from 1750

From this date many towns promoted their own Acts to obtain

power to levy a local rate for policing. In some areas where the manorial organisation was still strong the powers of the manor constable could conflict with those of the town constable.

5 Metropolitan Police Act 1829

This Act set up one police force for the metropolitan area, excluding the City. It was under the authority of the Home Secretary.

6 Lighting and Watching Act 1833

This Act permitted any town with over 5000 population to appoint paid watchmen.

7 Municipal Corporations Act 1835

Each of the 178 boroughs was required to appoint a watch committee which, in its turn, appointed constables. The committee was to include not more than one third of the town council plus the mayor.

8 County Police Act 1839

This was a permissive measure which enabled the Justices to set up a paid county police force. An Act the following year authorised the amalgamation of borough and county forces where it was thought desirable. Later, the County and Borough Police Act 1856 required the Justices to set up a force for any parts of the county still not covered.

9 County Police Forces

The approximate dates for the formation of the county police forces are as follows:

Anglesey	1856/7
Bedfordshire	1840
Berkshire	1856/7
Breconshire	1856/7
Buckinghamshire	1856/7
Caernarvonshire	1856/7
Cambridgeshire	1851
Cardiganshire	1844
Carmarthenshire	1856/7
Cheshire	1856/7
Cornwall	1856/7
Cumberland	1840
Denbighshire	1840
Derbyshire	1856/7
Devon	1856/7
Dorset	1856/7
Durham	1839
Essex	1839
Flintshire	1856/7
Glamorgan	1841
Gloucestershire	1839
Hampshire	1839
Herefordshire	1841
Hertfordshire	1841
Huntingdonshire	1856/7
Isle of Ely	1841
Kent	1856/7
Lancashire	1839
Leicestershire	1839
Lincolnshire	1856/7
Merionethshire	1856/7
Monmouthshire	1856/7
Montgomeryshire	1840
Norfolk	1840
Northamptonshire	1840
Northumberland	1856/7
Nottinghamshire	1840
Oxfordshire	1856/7
Pembrokeshire	1856/7
Radnor	1856/7
Rutland	1849
Shropshire	1840
Somerset	1856/7
Staffordshire	1840
Suffolk (East)	1840
Suffolk (West)	1856/7
Surrey	1851
Sussex (East)	1840
Sussex (West)	1856/7
Warwickshire	1840
Westmorland	1856/7
Wiltshire	1839
Worcestershire	1839
Yorkshire (East)	1856/7
Yorkshire (North)	1856/7
Yorkshire (West)	1856/7

10 Local Government Act 1888

This Act abolished police forces run by boroughs with less than 10,000 population.

11 Police Act 1946

This Act abolished 45 non-county police forces and the watch committees in those boroughs lost their police powers. The Brecon, Radnor and Montgomeryshire county forces were amalgamated.

12 Police in Scotland

An Act of 1857 established county forces on the same lines as the English 1856 Act. An Act of 1946 rationalised the system.

Part Two — Prisons

13 General

It should be remembered that up to the 19th century prisons were not primarily intended for punishment or the protection of society, because most offences were punishable by death or transportation. They were used to detain debtors until their obligations had been settled or else to hold prisoners on state charges, but their main function was to keep the prisoners until they were brought to trial or else before sentence was carried out.

Prisons were, at first, contained in castles or large houses and only gradually were special buildings erected. The list below gives approximate dates of when prisons, whether castle, purpose-built or private, were in existence.

14 Early Prisons

Bedfordshire: Bedford 1165
Berkshire: Faringdon 1238 Wallingford 1241, Windsor 1260
Buckinghamshire: Aylesbury 1165, High Wycombe 13th century
Cambridgeshire: Cambridge 1165
Cheshire: Chester 1237
Cornwall: Bodmin 19th century, Helston 1184, Launceston 1186
Cumberland: Cockermouth 1394
Derby: Bakewell 1286
Devon: Exeter 1296
Dorset: Dorchester 1305
Durham: Durham 1237   Sadberge 1303
Essex: Colchester 1274   Newport 1177 Rayleigh 1254
Gloucestershire: Bristol 1240 Gloucester 1184, Tewkesbury 1273
Hampshire: Portsmouth 1278 Southampton 1182, Winchester 1250
Herefordshire: Hereford 1300
Hertfordshire: St Albans 1220
Huntingdonshire: Huntingdon 1171
Kent: Canterbury 1165 Faversham 1254, Maidstone 1279, Rochester 1165
Lancs: Kirkham 1296, Lancaster 1196, Manchester 1187, Preston 1200
Leics: Leicester 1208, Rothley 1165
Lincs: Lincoln 1254, Grimsby 1260
London: Bridewell 1829, Fleet 1290 Holloway 1851, Marshalsea 11th century, Newgate 1200, Millbank 1821, Pentonville 1842, Wandsworth 1851

Norfolk: Great Yarmouth 1213, Kings Lynn 1212, Norwich 1165
Northants: Northampton , Peterborough 1275, Buckingham 1213
Northumberland: Newcastle
Notts: Nottingham 1177
Oxfordshire: Oxford 1231
Rutland: Oakham 1253
Shropshire: Bridgnorth 1234, Shrewsbury 1221
Somerset: Bath 1275, Ilchester 1166 Taunton 1243
Staffs: Newcastle-under-Lyme 1198 Stafford 1185
Suffolk: Ipswich 1163, Orford 1244
Surrey: Dorking 1279, Guildford 1207, Kingston-upon-Thames 1220, Reigate 1279
Sussex: Chichester 1197, Lewes 1487 Steyning 1477, Winchelsea 1200
Warwickshire: Kenilworth 1185, Kineton 1165, Warwick 1200
Westmorland: Appleby 1227
Wiltshire: Malmesbury 1166, Salis-

bury 1166, Westbury 1460, Wilton 1249
Worcestershire: Worcester 1216
Yorkshire: Hull 1299, Tickhill 1165
York 1165

General Terms

15 Bridewell
Although later the name of a London prison, it was generally used to denote a county gaol.

16 Cage/Cagge
A village lock-up.

17 House of Correction
A county gaol.

18 Lob's Pounds
See Round House.

19 Marshalsea Money
Parishes were obliged, via a county rate, to contribute money for the relief of the poor prisoners in the King's Bench and Marshalsea Prisons.

20 Pledgehouse
A prison where debtors were kept.

21 Rogue Money
Parishes were obliged to contribute up to 8d a week for the relief of poor prisoners in the county gaol. This was collected by the parish constable. See also Marshalsea Money.

22 Round House
A village lock-up, usually with no windows, and with the light coming in from a domed roof. It was also called a Blind House, Cage or Lob's Pound.

23 Toll Booth
Apart from its use as a market court building, it was also used as a town gaol.

Part Three — Judicial Authorities

24 Hundred Courts
Hundred Courts appeared in the 10th century. A Hundred was an area of administration between shire and parish (see B 39). The courts were essentially folkmoots, presided over by the hundred bailiff and met, at least in Saxon times, monthly. The comparison with Shire Courts (qv) which by an ordinance of King Edgar met only twice a year, indicates the greater importance of Hundred Courts at this period.

Their use was diminished in Norman times as the legal system, based on the county as an administrative area, became more formalised under the control of the crown, whereas the Hundred Courts had tended to become the private courts of the chief landowners.

25 Sheriff's Tourn
Twice a year, within a month after Easter and Michaelmas, the sheriff presided at a special session of the hundred court (qv). The main purpose was to review the Frankpledge (qv) arrangements and to see that the tithings were up to strength. It also dealt with minor criminal cases but the more serious offences were dealt with by the Justices in Eyre (qv).

After the Assize of Clarendon 1166 the sheriff also had the power to oversee the View of Frankpledge at manor courts which were the private jurisdiction of the lords of the manors, but this power was difficult to impose.

The effective power of the Sheriff's Tourn came to an end in 1461 when the cases formerly presided over by the sheriff were transferred to the Justices of the Peace in Quarter Sessions.

The Tourn was officially abolished in 1887.

26 Shire/County Courts

Shire Courts in Saxon and early Norman times were basically folk-courts, consisting of the freemen of the county and presided over by an ealdorman. They were inclined to come under the influence of a local magnate.

They met twice a year and dealt with criminal as well as civil cases, the suitors being also the judges. Local knowledge was of great importance, defendants being found guilty by reputation rather than by evidence and innocence was established by compurgation — the system by which a defendant called enough witnesses of sufficient stature to swear that they thought him not guilty.

The Normans established the sheriff — their crown officer — in charge of these courts and gradually the courts became a part of the royal justice and the king's administration.

Until 1072 bishops also sat in the courts assisting the ealdorman or sheriff but they were removed when separate ecclesiastical courts were established.

As from 1166 Justices in Eyre (qv) sat in the county courts dealing with the more important cases with the sheriff as a subordinate. Additional restrictions were placed on the sheriff when in 1194 coroners were first appointed, responsible for keeping the pleas of the crown between visits of justices.

The Shire Courts declined in importance as from the 13th century with the rise of the Justices of the Peace sitting at Quarter Sessions.

The body of the county court acted as that responsible for electing knights of the shire to sit in Parliament.

By the 18th century the County Courts had almost ceased to exist but they were revived by the County Courts Act 1846, mainly for disputes involving land, with magistrates in place of sheriffs.

27 Honorial Courts

An Honor was the collection of estates owned by a tenant-in-chief of the crown. The properties could be scattered over a large area.

The Normans allowed these lords to hold their own courts which dealt mainly with land disputes. These courts were not an important factor in the Norman legal system and were themselves overshadowed by the king's own honor-court at which tenants-in-chief were bound to attend and at which appeals from the local honor courts could be heard.

28 Possessory Assizes

A collective name for three Assizes — Novel Disseisin, Mort d'Ancestor, and Darrein Presentment. These are described below.

29 Assize of Novel Disseisin

Novel Disseisin means 'recent dispossession.' Under a procedure, begun in 1166, a tenant unjustly ejected from possession of a holding was able to obtain a writ instructing the sheriff to summon an Assize of Novel Disseisin. Twelve jurors from their local knowledge of the situation would pronounce on the matter. Alternatively the freeholder might obtain a writ on behalf of his tenant.

Originally the action could only be brought in instances of recent dispossession but gradually the assizes dealt with cases which involved far longer periods of time. The procedure came, in time, to be used mainly for fictional court cases to establish title. It was officially abolished in 1833.

30 Assize of Mort d'Ancestor

This Assize, established by the Assize of Northampton 1176, was concerned with cases where the plaintiff claimed dispossession of property that was his by inheritance.

The plaintiff obtained a writ which called on the sheriff to summon a jury which could pronounce on the matter from its local knowledge.

Cases of this nature arose most frequently where lords had repossessed on the death of a tenant.

The procedure was formally abolished in 1833.

31 Assize of Darrein Presentment

This Assize, established in the reign of Henry II, was concerned with the dispossession of advowsons (qv). The plaintiff was able to obtain a writ which called on the sheriff to summon a jury which would pronounce on whether the plaintiff had the right to present to a benefice or not.

The Assize was formally abolished in 1833.

32 Justices on Eyre

As from 1166, and possibly earlier, the king's justices were sent on circuits (eyres) around the counties, to sit in each shire court for a short period. The term eyre is derived from the Latin itinere (on journey). Their responsibilities included an audit of the royal revenues in the county, the hearing of the crown pleas which the coroner detailed for them, and the inspection of the general administration of the county.

Their main contribution was that they supplied a standard form of justice whereas, in the shire courts, justice was administered with local variations. Usually the Justices appeared at the shire courts every seven years and this presented great difficulty in providing justice as plaintiffs, defendants or witnesses might well be missing or dead long before the court sat.

Though much used in the 13th century the system lapsed in the 14th century as speedier judicial authorities became established.

33 Kings Bench

The King's Bench court ran parallel with the Court of Common Pleas as from the 12th century, but was the senior court. It dealt with criminal and civil cases, especially those in which the king had a special interest. Though based in London with the Exchequer it travelled with the king and was the king's court in which he sometimes sat. After 1400 it rarely left London.

In 1873 its jurisdiction was assigned to the Queens Bench Division of the High Court of Justice.

34 Court of Common Pleas

A court, otherwise known as the Court of Common Bench, which developed from the 12th century and which was a subdivision of king's court. The Court, unlike the King's Bench (qv), remained in London and, indeed, the Magna Carta stipulated that it should. Its jurisdiction was confined to civil cases between subject and subject.

35 Commission of Gaol Delivery

Indicted prisoners were held in gaols awaiting trial. Itinerant judges were commissioned by the crown to try the prisoners and deliver them — set them free — if they were not guilty.

A Commission of Gaol Delivery was able to deal with offences committed outside the county covered by the Commission.

36 Commission of Oyer and Terminer

A Commission to 'hear and determine' cases on indictments at the assizes, dealing with treasons, murders and other misdemeanours.

The Commission dealt only with offences committed within the county in question.

The system of commissioning judges was less cumbersome than the Justices on Eyre (qv).

37 Grand Assize

An Assize which developed from the 12th century. Where a tenant had to defend his right to land a sheriff was issued with a writ of peace. He nominated four knights of the shire who elected twelve other knights. Their findings were conveyed to the Justices on Eyre.

The Assizes were formally abolished in 1833.

38 Quarter Sessions

The meetings of the county justices held four times a year.

Their origin stems from 1361 when the keepers of the peace were transformed into Justices and empowered to determine cases as well as to bring them. From 1363, by statute, they began to meet four times a year.

In the 15th century the Justices, with Parliamentary support, were rivalling the power of the sheriffs; in 1461 all indictments normally heard at the Sheriff's Tourn (qv) were transferred to Quarter Sessions.

The courts had no power to deal with civil cases but were able to hear cases of murder, riot, theft, assault poaching etc. They could not deal with treason and forgery.

After 1531 the Justices, through Quarter Sessions, dealt with the administration of the Poor Law and in 1601 appointed the Overseers of the Poor.

The Sessions were usually attended by the High Sheriff or his deputy, the coroner, high and petty constables and the Clerk of the Peace who was a legal adviser to the justices.

As from the 1780's it was common to have a chairman on a regular basis and some business was delegated to committees.

The Municipal Corporations Act 1835 enabled over 100 boroughs to hold their own Borough Sessions.

39 Manor Courts

The Court Baron and Court Leet are dealt with under B21 and B22.

Part Four — Judicial Officials

40 Clerk of the Peace

Clerks of the Peace were definitely established by 1380 and perhaps earlier. Their function was to keep the records of the Quarter Sessions and to frame presentments and indictments. They had to have legal training so that they could assist the Justices in the interpretation and custom of the law.

In some places the post became almost hereditary and, in many cases, delegated to a legal attorney. The office carried fees.

41 Coroners

Coroners were first appointed in 1194. Their main responsibility was to keep the pleas of the Crown. In effect this meant recording accusations and preliminary proceedings so that the details would be available for the next visit of the Justices on Eyre. They also listed any rights due to the king. By the 13th century they were also responsible for holding inquests in cases of sudden death.

Four coroners were elected by each county court. In Wales there was one coroner to each commote.

Their appointment was transferred to the new county councils by the Local Government Act 1888. Their present duties mainly concern inquest on sudden death, shipwrecks and treasure trove.

42 Justices of the Peace

Keepers of the Peace were appointed in each county in 1277 and 1287. An Act of 1327 appoints Keepers of the Peace but this sanctioned an existing situation. Their function was to keep the peace and instigate proceedings against suspects. In 1361 the Keepers became, by law, Justices, and were enabled to determine cases at quarterly sessions.

In the 14th century there were four or five Justices to a county; an Act of 1388 allowed for six, and another in 1390 for eight. By 1565 there were thirty or forty for each county.

In 1461 the indictments previously heard at the Sheriff's Tourn (qv) were transferred to Quarter Sessions. Already in 1368 the Justices had been made responsible for the enforcement of wage regulations and gradually their civil responsibilities increase. They enforced laws against the Roman Catholics, licensed hawkers and brewers, administered the employment of the poor etc. The matters which came before Quarter Sessions are dealt with in greater detail under D 64-117.

Matters of civil administration were transferred to the new county councils in 1888.

Until fairly recent times Justices tended to be the leading landowners in a county and the automatic selections of the Lord Lieutenant. The Justices Qualification Act 1744 laid down that each Justice had to have an estate of freehold, copyhold or customary tenure of the yearly value of £100. Property qualification was abolished by the Justices of the Peace Act 1906.

Part Five — General

43 Abjuration of the Realm
From Anglo-Saxon times criminals could seek sanctuary in churches and churchyards. After 40 days the criminal could, in the presence of the crown's representative, confess to the crime, swear to abjure the realm and submit to banishment.

He would travel to a named port, wearing sackcloth, and take the first available ship. His only hope of return lay in a king's pardon. By 1623, when it was abolished the right to sanctuary had been considerably diminished.

44 Affeerors
Jurors sworn to fix the amount of an amercement or fine.

45 Amercement
Convicted offenders were 'in the king's mercy' and were liable to a monetary penalty — an amercement.

46 Approver
A criminal turned informer who, to achieve a pardon, was required to fight five battles under the customs laid down for Trial by Battle (qv). He was hanged if he lost. The practice had largely disappeared by the 15th century.

47 Assize
Royal declarations were called Assizes, and so were judicial proceedings such as the Possessory Assizes. In addition, decisions reached by an assembly were sometimes said to be assized — most commonly in the case of assized rents.

48 Attainder
In medieval times offenders sentenced to death or banishment were subject to attaint — they forfeited their lands and possessions and their heirs were disinherited.

49 Benefit of Clergy
This was a privilege granted to the Clergy allowing them to be discharged from a temporal court and be tried by an ecclesiastical court. This was extended eventually to all those who could read and could therefore become clerks, and in 1706 it was extended to all those who couldn't read. By the 18th century most serious offences were

capital ones and the only way the legal system could ameliorate the severity of the law was to help offenders plead Benefit of Clergy — in the ecclesiastical courts the sentences were less severe.

It was abolished in 1827.

50 Capias
A warrant for arrest.

51 Compurgation
The system by which the accused might call on twelve others (oath helpers) who would swear that they believed him innocent. The value of their oaths depended on their wergilds (qv). Also called Wager of Law.

52 Deodand
An object, whether animal or inanimate, which contributed to the death of someone who had reached the age of discretion, was believed to share the guilt of his death. The object or its value was forfeited to the crown which applied it for charitable purposes. Deodands were formally abolished in 1846.

53 Distress
Originally applied to the taking of possessions, generally livestock, in return for an alleged breach of service obligations. In modern times a landlord takes out a distress warrant to seize goods in lieu of rent.

54 Doom
The judgement of a court in Old English times.

55 Ducking Stool
A seat at the end of a plank overhanging a pond, to which people were tied and then ducked in the water. The most usual recipients of this punishment were scolds and dishonest tradesmen.

56 Duelling
Duelling was prohibited and treated as a criminal offence in 1818.

The last duel appears to have occurred in Camden Town, London, in 1843.

57 Faitours
Villains.

58 Forfang
A reward for recovering stolen property.

59 Forfeiture
Offenders sentenced to death or banishment quite often forfeited their possessions and lands. Possessions of those convicted of high treason went to the crown, lands of other offenders went to the crown for one year and then reverted to the lord of the manor.

60 Hidegild
A fine paid in lieu of flogging.

61 Inganenthief
The right of a lord of a manor to try and punish a thief caught in the manor.

62 Inns of Chancery
Formerly collegiate houses for younger law students before admittance to the Inns of Court. The Inns of Chancery consisted of Barnard's, Clement's, Clifford's, Furnival's, Lyon's, New, Staple's, Strand, Symonds, and Thavie's Inn.

63 Inns of Court
Collegiate houses which have the exclusive privilege of conferring the rank of barrister-at-law. There are four Inns — Lincoln's Inn, Middle Temple, Inner Temple and Gray's Inn.

64 Jurors
A property qualification for jurors was first established in 1285. An Act of 1692 laid down that a juror should possess freehold, copyhold or life tenure land worth at least £10 per year. In 1730 lease-

holders of land worth £20 per year were included.

Lists of eligible jurors were compiled by constables after 1696 and presented to Quarter Sessions.

The Jury Act of 1825 limited jury service to those between 21 and 60 who possessed freehold property worth £10 per year, or leasehold property worth £20 a year, or who were householders of houses worth £30 a year. Lists of eligible jurors were sent to the Clerk of the Peace.

65 Kinbote
A fine paid to the family of a murdered person.

66 Mainprise
A writ to the sheriff instructing him to collect sureties for a defendant's appearance. The sureties were collected from mainpernors.

67 Murder Fine
In Norman and Danish times it was incumbent upon the Hundred in which a man had been murdered to prove that he was English, and not Norman or Danish. To prove Englishry or Englescherie meant that the Hundred escaped a collective fine.

68 Oath Helpers
Defendants, in medieval times, could present witnesses — oath helpers — who would swear that they believed him innocent. The value of an oath depended on the witness's wergild (qv).

69 Outfangenethief
The right of a lord of the manor to pursue a thief outside the manor boundary and bring him back to his own court for trial.

70 Outlawry
An absconded prisoner accused of a criminal charge could be declared an outlaw after being summoned without response at 4 consecutive courts. He forfeited his land to the crown for a year, and thereafter to the lord. He could be killed on sight.

The punishment was formally abolished in 1879.

71 Presentment
The report of a jury concerning an offence brought to its notice, or the report of the homage at a manor court concerning alienations.

72 Quit Claim
A release and disclaimer of all rights, interest and potential legal actions from a grantor to a grantee.

73 Replevin
An action to recover property, usually livestock, which had been distrained in lieu of alleged non-performance of services to the lord, or non-payment of rent.

74 Sanctuary
A fugitive criminal had the right, from Anglo-Saxon times, to take refuge in a church or churchyard. After 40 days he could confess, be fore the crown's representative, abjure the realm and submit to banishment, rather than face trial.

It was decided in 1486 that Sanctuary should not protect persons charged with treason. Henry VIII further reduced Sanctuary areas and designated eight cities where refuge might be sought: Derby, Lancaster, Manchester, Northampton, Norwich, Wells, Westminster and York.

Sanctuary for criminals was abolished in 1623 and for civil offences in 1697 and 1723.

75 Stocks
A short spell in the village stocks was a normal reward for blasphemy, drunkenness, breaking the Sabbath etc. An Act of 1405 stated that stocks should be provided in every town and village. The practice had

lapsed by the 1830's.

76 Trial by Battle
A method of settling a legal dispute in Saxon and early Norman times. The accuser and the accused would do battle on the assumption that God would protect the person in the right. In civil cases substitutes — 'champions' — were allowed. The last Battle appears to have been waged in 1817 and the procedure was made illegal in 1819.

77 Trial by Ordeal
A method of testing innocence or guilt in criminal cases on the assumption that God would protect the innocent.

In Ordeal by fire, allowed to freemen, the accused had to carry a heated iron 9ft during mass; his hand was then bandaged and he was declared innocent if there were no scars after three days.

In Ordeal by water, the accused was lowered, bound, into cold water. If he sank he was innocent, if guilty he floated, for the water rejected him.

In 1215 clergy were forbidden to officiate at Trials by Ordeal and the custom died out soon afterwards.

78 True Bill
A bill of indictment was presented to the grand jury who, having heard the evidence, endorsed it as a 'true bill' if they considered a prima facie case had been made.

79 Wager of Law
See Compurgation.

80 Wergild
In effect, the monetary value of a man's life in Anglo-Saxon times. Each class in the community was assigned a Wergild, and if one of its members was murdered this was the amount payable by the murderer or his family to the family of the deceased.

A coerl's Wergild was 2000s, a gesith or thane was valued at 1200s. The Wergild for a serf was paid to his master.

81 Witchcraft
Under Acts of 1541 and 1603 Witchcraft was punishable by death, and the last execution took place in 1716. The Witchcraft Act 1735 repealed the death penalty.

SECTION J

PUBLIC UTILITIES AND SERVICES

Part 1 — Fire

Part 2 — Post Office

Part 3 — Water

Part 4 — Cemeteries

Part 5 — Gas

Part 6 — Electricity

Part 7 — Public Libraries

Part One — Fire Brigades

1 General

The first organised fire-fighting groups were those employed by the individual fire insurance companies. Each company maintained its own liveried staff and dealt with fires only in premises insured by them.

The earlier engines appear to be those in 1707 (Hand-in-Hand), 1716 (Sun Fire Office) and 1720 (Westminster Fire Office).

In London joint efforts were begun in 1791 between the Phoenix, Sun Fire Office and the Royal Exchange Assurance Company, and in 1826, together with the London Assurance formed one brigade. In 1865 by Act of Parliament, a Metropolitan Fire Brigade was established, paid for by the government, county, and insurance companies. This was retitled the London Fire Brigade in 1904.

It was normal for a company firemark to be fixed to the wall of the insured building and many of these still exist. The earlier ones were made of lead, the later ones of copper and iron. The policy number is engraved on the plaque.

2 Fire Insurance Brigades

The foundation dates of some of the earlier companies which had brigades are as follows:

Aberdeen	1825
Albert	1864
Albion	1805
Alliance	1824
Amicable Contributionship (Hand-in-Hand)	1696
Anchor	1849
Anchor (Norwich)	1808
Athenaeum	1852
Atlas	1808
Aylsham New Association	c1820
Bath Fire	1767
Bath Sun	1776
Beacon	1821
Berks and Glos	1824
Birmingham District	1834
Birmingham Fire Office	1805
Bon Accord	1845
Bristol Crown Fire Office	1718
Bristol Fire Office	1769
Bristol Union	1814
Bristol Universal	1774
Britannia	1868

British Commercial	1820	London Assurance	1720
British Crown	1907	London Fire Insurance Co.	1879
British Dominions	1897	London and Lancashire	1862
British Fire	1799	London and Provincial	1888
British Fire Insurance	1908	Manchester Fire Office	1771
British Fire Office	1799	Manchester Fire Assurance	1824
British and Irish United	1804	Middlesex	1874
Caledonian	1805	National	1878
Central London	1899	National Reliance	1898
Church of England	1840	National Union Fire Office,	
Commercial Union	1861	Bedford	1894
Company of London Insurers		Newcastle-upon-Tyne	1783
(Sun Fire Office)	1710	New Fire Office (Phoenix)	1782
County Fire Office		Newport Association	c1811
Dundee	1782	North British	1809
Eagle	1807	North British & Mercantile	1862
Eastern Counties	1890	Northern Assurance	1836
Economic of Kent	1824	Norwich General	1792
Empress	1895	Norwich Union Fire Ins.	1797
Equitable	1873	Notts. and Derbyshire	1835
Essex and Suffolk	1802	Palatine	1886
Etna	1866	Palladium	1824
Exchange House Fire Office	1708	Patriotic	1824
Farmers	1840	Phenix	1680
Fife	c1800	Phoenix (New Fire Office)	1782
Friendly Society	1683	Property	1898
Friendly Society of		Property Fire	1887
Edinburgh	1720	Protector Fire Ins. Co.	1825
General Accident	1885	Queens Ins. Co. (Liverpool)	1857
General Fire and Life	1837	Reading	1822
Glasgow	1805	Reliance	1881
Globe	1803	Royal	1845
Great Britain Fire	1871	Royal Exchange Assurance	1720
Guardian	1821	Royal Farmers	1843
Hand-in-Hand	1696	Salamander	1822
Hants, Sussex and Dorset	1803	Salop	1780
Hercules	1809	Saint Patrick	1824
Herts, Cambs and Country	1824	Scottish Commercial	1865
Hibernian	1771	Scottish Union	1824
Hope	1807	Sea	1875
Imperial	1803	Sheaf of Arrows	1683
Insurance Co. of Scotland	1821	Sheffield	1808
Kent Fire Insurance Co.	1802	Shropshire and North Wales	1837
King	1901	South British	1872
Lancashire	1825	South of England	1841
Leeds	1777	Star	1845
Leeds and Yorkshire	1824	State Assurance	1891
Leicestershire	1834	Suffolk and General Country	1799
Licensed Victuallers	1836	Sun Fire Office (Company of	
Licences & General	1890	London Insurers)	1710
Lion	1879	Surrey and Sussex	1825
Liverpool and London	1846	Union	1714
Liverpool and London Globe	1836	United British	1915

Western Fire	1863	Sanquhar Sub. (Dumfries) c1800	
West of England	1807	Donaghmore Sub., Dungannon	
West of Scotland	1886	c1834	
Westminster Fire Office	1717	Edderton Sub., Dinwall, probably	
Worcester	1790	1843	
York and London	1834	Shipton-under-Wychwood, Oxford,	
York and North of England	c1834	c1845	
Yorkshire	1824	Kings Worthy, Winchester 1845	

Records of the Westminster Fire Office are with the Westminster City Libraries.

Records of the London Assurance and the Hand-in-Hand Companies are at the Guildhall Library.

Other towns which had Fire Insurance Brigades include: Aberdeen, Andover, Baldock Bath, Bradford, Burnley, Bury St Edmunds, Cambridge, Canterbury, Chatham, Chelmsford, Chester, Coventry, Crayford, Darlington, Dartford, Edinburgh, Exeter, Gateshead, Grimsby, Hereford, Kidderminster, Loughborough, Ludlow, Maidstone, Middlesbrough, Oxford, Ramsey, Rochester, Swansea, Whitchurch and Wootton-under-Edge.

Wormshill, Sittingbourne 1847
Dennington, Woodbridge, c1847
Banbury Head Post Office, 1849
Guyhirn, Wisbech, 1854
Penshurst, Tonbridge, 1861
Stoke Climsland, possibly 1839
Pottersbury, Towcester c1866
Darlington Head Post Office 1865
Edinburgh General 1866
Caergeiliog, Holyhead 1894, possibly 1840

Part Two — The Post Office

3 General

From about 1784 mail was carried by mail-coach. In 1830 it was first carried on the Liverpool-Manchester railway. At this stage letters were charged by weight and distance. In 1840 the Penny Post began and fifteen years later the first pillar boxes were erected in London. Post cards were introduced in 1870, and postal orders in 1881.

4 Old Post Offices

The Post Office Magazine in 1966 held a competition to find the oldest post office in continuous use. The following were noted in the results:

Part Three — Water

5 The suppliers of water have traditionally been a mixture of private companies and local authority undertakings, each usually established by Act of Parliament.

The earliest charters enabling boroughs to have piped water appear to be for Southampton (1420), Hull (1447), Bath (1500) and Gloucester (1542). Generally speaking, however, springs and wells supplied the needs of many towns until well into the 19th century.

A Royal Commission sitting in 1843/5 reported on the unsatisfactory and unhygienic nature of water supplies in populous areas. At that time water mains could only be laid in the main streets. The Public Health Act 1848 enabled a local authority to provide a water supply.

In rural districts the position was more complicated as the total rateable value of many areas was not adequate to finance expenditure on water supply. The Public Health (Water) Act 1878 stipulated that no new house should be built in rural areas unless it was within reasonable distance of water supply.

In London the Metropolis Water Act 1852 laid down new standards of hygiene, specifying that all reservoirs within 5 miles of St Pauls should be covered.

In 1871 the Board of Trade appointed a water examiner.

Part Four — Cemeteries

6 Burial Acts 1852 and 1853

Before the passing of these Acts most people were buried in church graveyards. By the middle of the 19th century, especially in those parishes whose populations had grown with the industrial revolution, the churchyard over-crowding was a serious health risk.

Burial Acts were passed in 1852 for London, and in 1853 for the rest of the country, enabling local authorities to administer their own cemeteries. Vestries elected Burial Boards to manage them.

7 Local Government Act 1894

The duties of the Burial Boards were transferred to District Councils and Parish Councils.

Part Five — Gas

8 General

Until the development of statutory regional boards gas supply was usually the responsibility of limited companies or municipal undertakings. The first company established was the Chartered Gas Light and Coke Co. (later commonly known without the word Chartered), in Westminster, which began in

1812. It was given a charter by Parliament and its area was restricted to London, Southwark, Westminster and adjacent areas. Its success stimulated the formation of other companies in London and elsewhere, each requiring permission from Parliament which laid down the areas they might serve.

By 1815 it was estimated that there were 4000 gas lights in London, and by 1819, 51,000. In 1822 there were seven gasworks in London and it was quite normal for there to be three or four gas companies supplying the same street, each with their main pipes underneath the pavement.

By 1819 there was gas lighting in a great many towns including Bath, Birmingham, Brighton, Bristol, Cheltenham, Chester, Edinburgh, Exeter, Glasgow, Kidderminster, Leeds, Liverpool, Macclesfield, Manchester, Nottingham, Preston and Sheffield.

The Gasworks Clauses Act 1847 consolidated legislation regarding construction, profits etc. By the middle of the century competition, particularly in London, was cutthroat with the companies making small profits. An agreement was reached between the major companies to parcel out London so that each area was served by one company to avoid duplication and to enable a higher charge for gas to be levied. This arrangement was approved by the Metropolis Gas Act 1860, which also imposed standards of illumination.

9 Gas Companies

A list of some gas companies follows:

Berks

Ascot and District Gas and Electric
  Co. 1883
Bracknell Gasworks c1862
Hungerford Gas Co.
Lambourn Gas, Coal & Coke Co.

Maidenhead Gas Light & Coke Co. 1835

Windsor Royal Gas Light & Coke Co. 1827

Bucks
Amersham Gas Light & Coke Co. 1851
Beaconsfield Gas Co. 1865
Burnham United Gas Light & Coke Co. 1863
Great Marlow Gas Co. 1845
High Wycombe Gas Light & Coke Co. 1848
Slough Gas & Coke Co. 1848

Devon
Torquay & Paignton Gas Co.

Essex
Barking Gas Co. 1837
Billericay Gas Co. 1892
Brentwood Gas Co. 1834
Chigwell, Loughton & Woodford Gas Co. 1863
Grays & Tilbury Gas Co. 1853
Ilford Gas Co. 1839
Ingatestone & Freyerning Gas Co. 1858
Laindon Gas and Water Co. 1896
Leigh-on-Sea Rural District Undertaking 1899
Rochford Gas Co. 1847
Romford Gas Co. 1847
Shoeburyness Gas Co. 1870
Shoeburyness RD Undertaking 1879
Southend-on-Sea District Gas Co. 1854
South Essex Gas Light & Coke Co. 1852
Stanford-le-Hope Gas Co. 1905

Glos
Cirencester Gas Co.
Fairford Gas Co.
Tewkesbury & Wichcombe Gas Co.

London
Aldgate Gas Light & Coke Co. 1815
British Gaslight Co. 1825
Chartered Gas Light & Coke Co. 1812

City of London Gas Light & Coke Co. 1816
Commercial Gas Co. 1847
County and General Consumers Co. (Lea Bridge) 1856
East London Gas Light & Coke Co. 1831
Equitable Gas Co. 1842
Gas Light and Coke Co. 1812
Great Central Gas Consumers Co. 1849
Imperial Gas Light & Coke Co. 1820
Independent Gaslight and Coke Co. 1829
Lea Bridge District Gas Co. 1868
London Gas Co. 1843
London Gaslight & Coke Co. 1833
North Woolwich Undertaking 1850
Phoenix Gaslight & Coke Co. 1824
Portable Gas Co. 1821
Ratcliff Gas Light & Coke Co. 1823
South Metropolitan Gaslight & Coke Co. 1842
Victoria Docks Gas Co. 1858
Walthamstow Gas and Coke Co. 1854
Western (Cannel) Gas Light & Coke Co. 1845
West Ham Gas Co. 1845
West London Junction Gas Co. 1865
West Suburban Gaslight & Coke Co. 1905
Whitechapel Road Gas Light & Coke Co. 1821

Middlesex
Brentford Gas Co. 1821
Great Stanmore Gas Co. 1858
Harrow Gas Co. 1872
Hornsey Gas Co. 1857
North Middlesex Gas Co. 1862
Pinner Gas Co. 1868
Staines & Egham District Gas Co. 1833
Sunbury Gas Consumers Co. 1861
Uxbridge Gas Co. 1841

Oxon
Bampton Gas Co.

Surrey
Chertsey Gas Co. 1852

County and General Consumers Co.
  (Chertsey) 1858
Richmond Gas Co. 1847

Warks
Birmingham Municipal Gas Undertaking 1874

Wilts
Salisbury Gas Co.
Swindon Gaslight & Coke Co.
Swindon New Gas Co.
Swindon United Gas Co.
Marlborough Gas Co.

Worcs
Pershore Gas Co.

Scotland
Arbroath Gaslight Co. by 1834
Kilmarnock Gaslight Co. by 1826

Part Six — Electricity

10 Generally the provision of electrical supply has been in the hands
of the local authorities. The Electric
Lighting Act 1882 was the basis of
future legislation and enabled local
authorities to purchase any private
companies after 21 years of opera-
tion.

Part Seven — Public Libraries

11 Public Libraries Act 1850
This empowered boroughs with a
population of over 10,000 to provide public libraries. However, provision required a consent of two-
thirds of the ratepayers in an assembled meeting, and limited expenditure to ½d per £1 rate. More important, it gave the authorities no power
to buy books — only to lend those
donated to them.

Warrington and Salford had already opened libraries in 1848 and
1849 using the Museums Act as their
basis.

12 Public Libraries Act 1854
This extended the provisions of
the 1850 Act to Scotland.

13 Public Libraries Act 1855
This Act increased the permitted
expenditure to 1d in the £1 rate.

14 Public Libraries Act 1892
This was the most important
early Libraries Act. It enabled all
local government units, except
counties, to become library authorities but it was not until 1919 that
more than 1d in the £1 rate could
be spent. It was found that some of
the authorities set up by the 1892
Act were spending only £10 a year
on purchasing books.

15 Public Libraries Act 1919
Limits on library expenditure
were removed. County councils
could become library authorities
and serve rural districts. Further
impetus was provided by the Carne-
gie United Kingdom Trust and the
Passmore Edwards foundation.

SECTION K

TRANSPORT

Part 1 — Roads

Part 2 — Railways

Part 3 — Canals

Part 4 — Road Transport

Part One — Roads

Legislation

1 1285 Statute of Winchester

This affirmed the manorial responsibility for upkeep of the king's highway and, by implication, charged the constable to supervise the work.

2 1530 Repair of Bridges

A county rate was allowed to repair those bridges, outside towns, which were not the responsibility of an authority or person.

3 1555 Highway Act

This transferred responsibility for the upkeep of the king's highway from the manors to the parishes. Each parishioner owning a ploughland in tillage, or keeping a draught or plough, was liable to give, for four days a year, a cart. In addition, each able-bodied householder or tenant was required to give four days labour a year (increased in 1691 to six). It was possible to commute this statute labour by payment, or else by providing a substitute person.

It was provided that a surveyor or surveyors should be appointed by each parish, and originally this selection was made by the churchwardens, constable and some parishioners in Easter week. In 1662 this task had to be done by people approved by the majority of parishioners. By 1691 however, this power had diminished; the parish officers merely supplied a suitable list to the justices who then made the appointment.

The office of surveyor was not popular and was often commuted. In some manors he was appointed simply by being in the house next on the row.

4 Turnpike Roads

In the 18th century thousands of special Acts of Parliament established trusts which were given the right to collect a toll in exchange for providing and maintaining a road. A General Turnpike Act was passed in 1773 to speed up the Parliamentary process.

5 1835 Highway Act

This Act abolished statutory labour and empowered the levy of a highway rate. It provided for the unification of parishes into a highway district and allowed the payment of a district surveyor.

6 1862 Highway Act
This Act empowered the justices to compulsorily unite parishes into highway districts when they thought necessary.

7 1888 Local Government Act
The responsibility for main roads was transferred to the newly established county councils.

8 1894 Local Government Act
Roads other than main ones were now made the responsibility of local councils.

Terms

9 Borstal
A southern term for a path up a steep hill.

10 Bridle Path
A path suitable for horses and pedestrians but not for vehicles, which, legally, are barred. Legislation has tended to make the pedestrian's right to use a bridle path stronger than on a footpath. Also known as Halter-Path, Sheergate, Sheerway, Wapple and Wobble.

11 Causey/Causeway
A pavement or raised footpath.

12 Chare
An alley; a term found in northern England, Midlands and Glos.

13 Chase
In this sense, a road leading to a field or farmhouse; a green lane.

14 Chimin
A legal term for a road.

15 Drang/Dring/Drong
A passage between two walls or hedges.

16 Drift/Drove Roads
Ancient roads which were not subject to toll, and used mainly for long-distance herding of cattle to fairs. Their importance was greatest from the 16th century to the advent of the railways. Generally they were not kept in repair by any authority.

17 Enclosure Roads
Prior to the period of large-scale enclosure of land, roads and paths followed the erratic contours of the small-holdings. Enclosure entailed the making of new roads through the enlarged holdings. Usually these are straight and have wide strips of grass on either side. The enclosure awards laid down that the distance from hedge to hedge should be 40ft; this allowed for vehicles to go on the grass verges if the road were impassable.

18 Farrow
A road.

19 Footpaths
The National Parks and Access to the Countryside Act 1949 defines a footpath as 'a highway over which the public has a right of way on foot only'.
Maps showing footpaths have to be available for the public at County Council offices.   Footpaths are shown (to distinguish them from Bridle Paths) as lines of red dots. County Councils, generally on the recommendation of rural district councils, are able to close footpaths, but the extinguishment order has to be confirmed by the Secretary of State for the Environment or the Secretary of State for Wales. Footpaths may be diverted if this leads to a more efficient land use. If the termination point of the path is a road this may be altered, but otherwise the termination point must remain the same.
Liability for maintenance is sometimes unknown but parish councils are empowered to do the work. It is an offence to block a path with a gate and a walker has the right to

follow the line of the path through crops if necessary.

20 Ford
In some places meant a road.

21 Fordraught
A path between two farms.

22 Gate
Middle English word for road.

23 Gatrum
A Lincolnshire term for a rough path between two fields.

24 Gennell
A north country term for a narrow passage between houses.

25 Green Lane
Sometimes synonymous with a Driftway (qv). As its name implies it is grassed and was probably a road to market. It was a right of way.

26 Halter Path
See Bridle Path.

27 Hollow Way
A sunken road. Also known as Howegait.

28 Howegait
See Hollow Way.

29 Leet
A meeting point of roads. Also known as Releet.

30 List Road
A Kent term for a Green Lane (qv).

31 Load/Loan/Lode
A lane, sometimes across a marshy area.

32 Loke
An East Anglian term for a lane, sometimes a private one.

33 Marchway

A boundary road.

34 Mear/Meer Path
A path between two holdings.

35 Port Way
A path leading to a market town which normally would have had a gateway.

36 Raik/Rake
A cattle path.

37 Releet
See Leet.

38 Ridding
A green lane (qv) through a wood.

39 Ridgeway
A path along a ridge of land, chosen because it would dry quicker than other paths.

40 Roman Roads
Roman roads connected the main garrison towns and were essential for the quick movement of troops and supplies. In addition there was a substantial network of subsidiary roads, much of it still being discovered.

The most authoritative book on the subject is 'Roman Roads in Britain' by Ivan Margary. A reasonably up-to-date survey of known Roman roads is contained in the Ordnance Survey Map of Roman Britain.

The roads are generally straight in stretches between prominent points; at these they might well change direction.

The raised, cambered platform of the roads — the agger — was bounded by a kerb and a V-shaped ditch on either side, the latter serving as drainage. The platform had a bed of large stones in an excavated ditch, smaller, bonded stones on top and a surface of gravel, flints etc. The main roads could be as much as 80ft wide, the smaller ones generally about 21ft between ditches.

41 Saltways
   Found in salt-boiling areas like Cheshire and Worcestershire, they lead from brine-pits where salt was boiled.

42 Sheergate/Sheerway
   See **Bridle Path**.

43 Signposts/Direction Stones
   Legislation in 1697 required posts and stones at crossroads but this injunction was often neglected. Similarly the General Turnpike Acts of the 18th century laid down that posts or stones should be provided at turnpike crossroads. Mileposts were already provided, quite often erected to the distances shown on Ogilby's maps rather than the other way round.

44 Smoot
   A north country term for a passage between two houses.

45 Tenantry Road
   A Sussex term derived from the open-field farming system. It was a road about 8ft wide dividing different holdings in the fields.

46 Tewer
   A Midlands term for an alley or narrow lane.

47 Turnpike Roads
   The first Act establishing a Turnpike road was in 1663 but the period 1750 to 1770 saw the most expansion, with individual Acts of Parliament for each road, which empowered local trusts or companies to charge a toll in exchange for the right to build and maintain a road. A General Turnpike Act was passed in 1773 to speed up the Parliamentary process. In 1888 the county councils assumed responsibility for most of these roads and the trusts were wound up.
   A toll house was built, usually projecting on to the road, in which the toll collector (pikeman) lived. A normal toll would be a farthing for a head of cattle and 6d for a carriage horse. Local cart traffic and that to church or to a funeral was exempt from toll.

48 Twissell/Twitchell
   A narrow footpath between hedges; a path that forks.

49 Wapple
   See **Bridle Path**.

50 Went
   A narrow land.

51 Wobble Road
   See **Bridle Path**.

52 Wynd
   An alley or court.

Part Two — Railways

53 The following is a list of most of the railway lines built in England, Wales and Scotland, together with their dates of incorporation and opening where known, and also further details of their later history.

	Inc.	Open	Other Information
Abbotsbury	1877	1885	1896 to GWR
Aberdare	1845	1846	1847 to Taff Vale
Aberdare Valley	1855	1856	1864 to Vale of Neath
Aberystwith & Welsh Coast	1861	1863	1865 to Cambrian
Abingdon	1855	1856	1904 to GWR
Alcester	1872	1876	1878 to GWR and Stratford-upon-Avon
Alexandra (Newport) Dock	1865		1882 name change to Alexandra (Newport and South Wales) Dock and Railway
Alexandra (Newport & Sth. Wales) Dock and Railway	1882		1897 merged with Pontypridd, Caerphilly & Newport
Anglesey Central	1863	1867	1876 to LNWR
Ashover Light	1919	1925	1950 closed
Aylesbury & Buckingham	1860	1968	1890 to Metropolitan
Ayr and Wigtownshire	1887		1892 to G & SWR
Bala and Dolgelly	1862	1868	1877 to GWR
Bala and Festiniog	1873	1882	1910 to GWR
Banbury and Cheltenham	1873	1881	1897 to GWR
Bangor & Caernarvon	1851	1852	1852 to Chester & Holyhead
Barnoldswick	1867	1871	1899 to Midland
Barnstaple & Illfracombe	1870	1874	1890 to LSWR
Barry	1884	1888	1922 to GWR
Bedford	1845	1846	1845 to London & Birmingham
Bedford & Cambridge	1860	1862	1865 to LNWR
Bedford & Northampton	1865	1872	1885 to Midland
Berkshire & Hampshire	1845	1847	1846 to GWR
Berkshire & Hampshire Extension	1859	1862	1882 to GWR
Birkenhead			1859 name change from Birkenhead, Lancs and Cheshire. 1860 to LNWR
Birkenhead, Lancs and Cheshire	1846	1850	1859 name change to Birkenhead
Birmingham & Derby Jc	1836	1839	1844 to Midland
Birmingham & Gloucester	1836	1840	1846 to Midland
Birmingham & Henley-in-Arden	1873	1894	1900 to GWR
Birmingham, North Warwickshire & Stratford-upon-Avon	1894	1907	1900 to GWR

	Inc.	Open	Other Information
Birmingham & Oxford Jc	1846	1852	1848 to GWR
Birmingham West Suburban	1871	1876	1875 to Midland
Birmingham, Wolverhampton & Dudley	1846	1854	1848 to GWR
Birmingham, Wolverhampton & Stour Valley	1846	1852	1847 to LNWR
Bishops Castle	1861	1865	1935 closed
Bishops Stortford, Dunmow & Braintree	1861		1865 to GER
Bishops Waltham	1862	1863	1932 closed
Blackburn	1857		Amalgam of Blackburn, Darwen & Bolton, and Blackburn, Clitheroe & North Western. 1858 amalgamated with Lancs & Yorks, and the East Lancs
Blackburn, Clitheroe & North Western			1857 to Blackburn
Blackburn, Darwen & Bolton			1857 to Blackburn
Blackpool & Lytham	1861	1863	1871 to Preston & Wyre
Blythe & Tyne	1852		1874 to NER
Bolton and Leigh	1825	1828	1845 to Grand Junction
Bolton and Preston	1837		1843 to North Union
Bourne & Essendine	1857		1864 to GNR
Bourton-on-Water	1860	1862	1874 to GWR
Bradford & Thornton	1871	1878	to GNR
Bradford, Eccleshill & Idle	1866		1871 to GNR
Brecon & Merthyr Tydfil Junction	1859	1863	1922 to GWR
Bridgewater	1882	1890	1923 to LSWR
Bridport	1855	1857	1901 to GWR
Brighton and Dyke	1877	1887	1938 closed
Bristol & Exeter	1836	1841	1876 to GWR
Bristol & Gloucester	1828	1835	1846 to Midland
Bristol & North Somerset	1863	1873	1884 to GWR
Bristol & Portishead Piers	1863	1867	1884 to GWR
Bristol and South Wales	1857	1863	1868 to GWR
Bristol Port	1862	1865	1890 to Midland and GWR
Briton Ferry Dock & Railway	1851	1861	1873 to GWR
Bromley Direct	1874	1878	1879 to SER
Brynmawr & Blaenavon	1866	1869	1869 to LNWR
Brynmawr & Western Valleys	1899	1906	1902 to LNWR and GWR
Buckfastleigh, Totnes & South Devon	1864	1872	1897 to GWR
Buckingham & Brackley Junction	1846		1847 to Buckinghamshire
Buckinghamshire	1847		Amalgam. of Buckingham & Brackley Jc, and Oxford & Bletchley Jc. 1847 to LNWR
Buckley	1860		1923 to Great Central

	Inc.	Open	Other Information
Bullo Pill	1809	1812	1826 to Forest of Dean
Burry Port & Gwendreath			
Valley	1865	1869	1922 to GWR
Bute Docks	1886		1897 name change to Cardiff
Caernarvon & Llanberis	1864	1869	
Caernarvonshire	1862	1867	
Caledonian	1845		Amalgam. of Scottish North Eastern, Scottish Central, Wisham & Coltness, Garnick & Glasgow, Glasgow, Kilmarnock & Ayr, Glasgow & Greenock, Perth & Methuen and others
Calne	1860	1863	1892 to GWR
Cambrian	1864		Amalgam. of Oswestry & Newtown, Oswestry, Ellesmere & Whitchurch, Llanidloes & Newtown, Newtown & Machynlleth, and Aberystwith & Welsh Coast. 1922 to GWR
Cannock Chase	1860		1863 to LNWR
Cannock Mineral			1855 name change from the Derbys, Staffs and Worcs Jc. 1869 to LNWR
Canterbury & Whitstable	1827	1830	1844 to SER
Cardiff		1911	1897 name change from Bute Docks
Cardiff & Ogmore Valley	1873	1876	1876 to Llynvi & Ogmore
Cardiff, Penarth & Barry Jc.	1885	1887	1889 to Taff Vale
Cardiff & Silloth Bay	1855	1856	1880 to North British
Carmarthen & Cardigan	1854	1860	1881 to GWR
Caterham	1854	1856	1859 to SER
Central London	1891	1900	
Central Wales	1859	1862	1868 to LNWR
Central Wales & Carmarthen Junction	1873		1873 name change from Swansea and Carmarthen
Central Wales Extension	1860	1866	1868 to LNWR
Chard & Taunton	1861	1866	1863 to Bristol & Exeter
Cheddar Valley & Yatton	1864	1869	1865 to Bristol & Exeter
Cheltenham & Gt. Western Union	1836	1841	1843 to GWR
Cheshire Midland	1860	1862	1865 to Cheshire Lines Committee

	Inc.	Open	Other Information
Chester & Birkenhead	1837	1840	1847 to Birkenhead, Lancs & Cheshire Junction
Chester & Crewe	1837	1840	1840 to Grand Junction
Chester & Midland	1844	1846	1856 to LNWR
Chesterfield & Brampton	1870	1873	1871 to Midland
City & South London	1884	1890	previously known as London & Southwark Subway
Cleobury Mortimer & Ditton Priors Light	1901	1908	1922 to GWR
Cockermouth & Workington	1845	1847	1866 to LNWR
Coleford	1872	1883	1884 to GWR
Coleford, Monmouth, Usk & Pontypool	1853	1856	1887 to GWR
Colne Valley & Galstead	1856	1859	1923 to LNER
Conway & Llanrwst	1860	1863	1867 to LNWR
Cornwall	1846	1859	1889 to GWR
Cornwall Minerals	1873		1896 to GWR
Corris	1858	1883	1930 to GWR
Corwen & Bala	1862	1866	1896 to GWR
Cowbridge	1862	1865	1889 to Taff Vale
Cowbridge & Aberthaw	1889	1892	1895 to Taff Vale
Cowes & Newport	1859	1862	1887 to Isle of Wight Central. 1923 to SR
Cromford & High Peak	1825	1831	1862 to LNWR
Culm Valley Light	1873	1876	1880 to GWR
Dare Valley	1863	1866	1889 to Taff Valley
Dartmouth & Torbay	1857	1859	1862 to South Devon
Deeside	1846/ 1852	1853	1875 to Great North of Scotland
Denbigh, Ruthin & Corwen	1860	1862	1879 to LNWR
Derbyshire, Staffordshire, & Worcestershire Junction	1847	1859	1855 name changed to Cannock Mineral
Devon & Somerset	1864	1871	1901 to GWR
Didcot, Newbury & South-ampton	1873	1882	1923 to GWR
Dore & Chinley	1884	1893	1888 to Midland
Dorset Central	1856	1860	1862 to Somerset & Dorset
Dover & Deal	1874	1881	Jointly vested in LCDR and SER
Duffryn, Llynvi & Porcawl	1825	1829	1847 to Llynvi Valley
Dulas Valley Mineral	1862		1863 name change to Neath & Brecon
Dunstable	1845	1848	1845 to London & Birmingham
Dursley & Midland Junction	1855	1856	1861 to Midland

	Inc.	Open	Other Information
Easingwold Light	1887	1891	Was not nationalised. Passenger service withdrawn 1948
East & West India Docks & Birmingham Junction	1846	1850	1853 name change to North London
East and West Junction	1864	1871	
East Anglian	1848	1848	Amalgam. of Lynn & Ely, Lynn & Dereham, and Ely & Huntingdon. 1852 to Eastern Counties
East Cornwall Mineral	1869	1872	1891 to Plymouth, Devonport & Sth Western Jc. Previously known as the Callington & Calstock
East Gloucestershire	1862	1873	1890 to GWR
East Kent Light	1911	1916	1948 closed to passengers
East London	1865	1869	1892 to LBSCR, Metropolitan and Metropolitan-District
East Somerset	1856	1858	1874 to GWR
East Usk	1885	1898	1892 to GWR
Eastern & Midlands	1882		Amalgamation of Lynn & Fakenham, Gt Yarmouth & Stalham Light, and Yarmouth Union. 1893 to Midland & Gt Northern Joint Committee
Eastern Union	1844	1846	1867 took in Ipswich & Bury
Edinburgh & Dalkeith	1826		1845 to North British
Edinburgh & Glasgow	1838	1842	
Edinburgh & Northern	1844	1847	
Edinburgh, Leith & Granton	1836	1848	1847 to Edinburgh, Perth & Dundee
Edinburgh, Perth & Dundee	1847	1847/ 1848	1862 to North British
Ely & Clydach Valleys	1873	1878	1880 to GWR
Ely & Huntingdon	1845		1848 to East Anglian
Ely & St Ives	1864		1876 to GER
Ely Valley	1857	1860	1903 to GWR
Ely Valley Extension	1863	1865	1865 to Ogmore Valley
Epsom & Leatherhead	1856	1859	
Erewash Valley	1845	1847	1845 to Midland
Evesham & Redditch	1863	1866	1882 to Midland
Exeter	1883	1903	1923 to GWR
Exeter & Crediton	1845	1877	1886 to GER
Exeter Valley	1874	1885	1875 to Bristol & Exeter
Faringdon	1860	1864	1886 to GWR

	Inc.	Open	Other Information
Felixstowe Ry & Dock	1875	1877	1886 to GER
Festiniog & Blaenau	1868		1910 to GWR
Findhorn	1859	1862	
Fleetwood, Preston & West Riding Junction	1846	1850	1867 to LNWR and L&YR
Forcett	1865		1873 to NER
Forest of Dean	1826		1847 to South Wales
Forest of Dean Central	1856	1868	1923 to GWR
Forth Bridge	1873	1890	1882 to Midland
Freshwater, Yarmouth & Newport	1873	1889	
Furness & Midland	1863	1867	1863 to Midland and Furness Rys jointly
Glasgow & Milngavie Jc	1861		1876 to North British
Glasgow & Sth Western	1850		Previously the Glasgow, Paisley, Kilmarnock & Ayr
Glasgow, Bothwell, Hamilton & Coatbridge	1874	1878	1878 to North British
Gloucester & Cheltenham	1809	1811	1837 to Birmingham & Gloucester
Gloucester & Dean Forest	1846	1851	1871 to GWR
Golden Valley	1876	1881	1899 to GWR
Grand Junction	1833	1837	1846 to LNWR
Gravesend	1881	1883	1883 to LCDNR 1953 closed
Great Marlow	1868	1873	1897 to GWR
Great North of Scotland	1849		
Great Western	1835	1838	
Great Western & Brentford	1855	1859	1871 to GWR
Great Western & Uxbridge	1846	1856	1847 to GWR
Great Yarmouth & Stalham Light	1876	1877	1882 to Eastern & Midlands
Gwendreath Valleys	1866	1871	1923 to GWR
Halesowen & Bromsgrove Branch	1865	1883	1876 name change to Halesowen. 1872 jointly worked by Midland and Gt Western
Hampstead Junction	1853	1860	1867 to LNWR
Harrow & Stanmore	1886	1890	1899 to LNWR
Hay	1811	1816	1860 parts to Hereford, Hay & Brecon
Helston	1880	1887	1898 to GWR
Hemel Hempstead	1863	1877	1886 to Midland
Henley-in-Arden & Gt Western Junction	1873		1884 name change to Birmingham & Henley-in-Arden
Hereford, Hay & Brecon	1859	1863	1874 to Midland

	Inc.	Open	Other Information
Hereford, Ross & Gloucester	1851	1853	1862 to GWR
Hertford & Welwyn Junction	1854	1858	1855 merged with Dunstable & Welwyn Jc to form Hertford, Luton & Dunstable
Hertford, Luton & Dunstable	1855		Formed from merger of Hertford & Welwyn Jc, and Dunstable & Welwyn Jc
Highland	1865		Amalgam. of the Inverness & Aberdeen Jc, and the Inverness & Perth Jc. Later took in Ross-shire, Sutherland & Caithness, and Golspie & Helmsday
Huddersfield & Manchester Ry and Canal	1845	1847	1847 to LNWR
Hull & Barnsley	1905		1922 to NER
Hull & Selby	1836		1846 to York & Nth Midland
Hunstanton & West Norfolk Jc	1874		Amalgam. of Lynn & Hunstanton and the West Norfolk Jc. 1890 to GER
Inverness & Aberdeen	1856		1865 to Highland
Inverness & Nairn	1854	1855	1861 merged with Inverness and Aberdeen
Inverness & Perth	1861		1865 to Highland
Inverness & Ross-shire	1860	1863	1862 to Inverness & Aberdeen
Isle of Wight Central	1887		Amalgam. of Cowes & Newport, Isle of Wight (Newport Jc), and the Ryde & Newport
Keighley & North Valley	1862	1867	1881 to Midland
Keith & Portessie	1882	1884	
Kendal & Windermere	1845	1846	1857 to Lancaster & Carlisle 1879 to LNWR
Kent Coast	1857		1871 to LCDR
Lambourne Valley	1883	1898	1905 to GWR
Lampeter, Aberayron & New Quay Light	1906	1911	1922 to GWR
Lanarkshire & Ayrshire		1888	1884 name changed from Barrmill & Kilwinning
Lancashire & Yorkshire		1854	An amalgam. of several Lancs and Yorks lines
Lancashire Union	1864	1869	1883 to LNWR
Lancaster & Carlisle	1844	1846	1859 to LNWR
Lancaster & Preston Junction	1837	1840	1849 to Lancaster &

	Inc.	Open	Other Information
			Carlisle
Lauder Light	1882	1901	
Launceston & Sth Devon	1862	1865	1869 to Sth Devon
Lee-on-Solent	1892	1894	1931 closed to passengers
Leeds & Bradford	1844	1846	1851 to Midland
Leeds, Dewsbury & Man-			
chester	1845	1848	1847 to LNWR
Leicester & Swannington	1830	1832	1846 to Midland
Leominster & Bromyard	1874	1884	1888 to GWR
Leominster & Kingston	1854	1857	1898 to GWR
Leven	1852	1854	1861 to Leven & East of Fife
Leven & East of Fife	1861		Amalgam. of Leven and the East of Fife. 1877 to NBR
Liskeard & Caradon	1843	1846	1909 to GWR
Liskeard & Looe	1825	1879	1923 to GWR
Liverpool & Manchester	1826	1830	1845 to Grand Junction
Liverpool Central Station	1864	1874	1865 to Cheshire Lines Ctte
Liverpool, St Helens & Suth Lancs			1893 name change from St Helens & Wigan Jc.
Liverpool, Southport & Preston Junction	1884	1847	
Llanelly & Mynydd-Mawr	1875	1883	1923 to GWR
Llanelly Ry & Dock	1828	1833	1889 to GWR
Llangollen & Corwen	1860	1865	1896 to GWR
Llanidloes & Newtown	1853	1859	1864 to Cambrian
Llantrisant & Taff Vale Jc.	1861	1863	1889 to Taff Vale
Llynvi & Ogmore	1866	1883	Amalgam. of Llynvi Valley, Ogmore Valley, and the Cardiff & Ogmore Valley
Llynvi Valley	1846	1861	1866 to Llynvi & Ogmore
London & Birmingham	1833	1837	1846 to LNWR
London & Croydon Districts		1839	to LBSCR
London, Brighton, Sth Coast			Amalgam. of London & Croydon and London & Brighton 1923 to SR
London, North Western	1846		Amalgam. of London & Birmingham, North British & Gt North of Scotland, Colne Valley & Halstead, East & West Yorks Union, Mid-Suffolk Light and others
London, Tilbury & Southend	1862	1854	1912 to Midland
Lostwithiel & Fowey	1862	1869	1877 to Cornwall Minerals
Louth & East Coast	1872	1877	
Ludlow & Clee Hill	1861	1864	1892 to LNWR and GWR

	Inc.	Open	Other Information
Lydney & Lidbrooke	1809	1813	1810 name change to Severn & Wye Ry and Canal. 1879 to Severn & Wye and Severn Bridge Ry
Lynn & Dereham		1846	to East Anglian
Lynn & Ely		1846	to East Anglian
Lynn & Fakenham	1876	1879	1882 to Eastern & Midlands
Lynn & Sutton Bridge	1861	1865	1866 to Midland & Eastern
Maidens & Dunure Light		1906	Closed 1930. Reopened 1932 Closed 1933
Maidstone & Ashford	1880	1884	1883 to LCDR
Malmesbury	1872	1877	1880 to GWR
Manchester & Milford	1860	1866	1911 to GWR
Manchester & Stockport	1866	1875	1869 to Midland
Manchester, Buxton, Matlock & Midlands	1846	1848	1871 to Midland
Manchester, Sheffield & Lincs	1849		Amalgam. of Sheffield, Ashton-under-Lyne & Manchester, Grimsby & Sheffield Jc, Sheffield & Lincs, Sheffield & Lincs Extension, Manchester & Lincoln Union
Manchester Sth District	1873	1880	1877 to Midland
Manchester Sth Jc & Altrincham	1845	1849	1849 to LNWR and MS and LR
Mansfield	1910	1913	to GCR
Mansfield & Prinxton	1817	1819	(horse drawn); 1849 loco. 1848 to Midland
Marlborough	1861	1864	1896 to GWR
Marlborough & Grafton	1896	1898	1899 to Midland & Sth Western Junction
Marple New Mills & Hayfield Junction	1860	1865	
Maryport & Carlisle	1837	1840	
Mawddwy	1865	1865	1923 to GWR
Merthyr, Tredegar & Abergavenny	1859	1862	1862 to LNWR
Mid Hants	1861		1881 to LSWR
Midland	1844		Amalgam. of Midland Counties, North Midland, and Birmingham & Derby Jc, and other smaller lines
Midland & Sth Western Jc	1884		Amalgam. of Swindon, Marlborough and Andover, and Swindon & Cheltenham Extension

	Inc.	Open	Other Information
			1923 to GWR
Midland and Eastern	1866		Amalgam. of Lynn & Sutton Bridge, andSpalding & Bourne
			1883 to Eastern & Midlands
Midland Counties	1836	1839	1844 to Midland
Mid Wales	1859	1864	1904 to Cambrian
Milford	1856	1863	1896 to GWR
Minehead	1871	1874	1897 to GWR
Mitchelson Road & Forest of Dean Junction	1871	1885	1880 to GWR
Mold	1847	1849	1849 to Chester & Holyhead
Mold & Denbigh	1861	1869	
Monkland	1848		Amalgam. of Monkland & Kirkintilloch, the Ballochney, and the Slamannon. To NBR
Monmouthshire	1792	1798	Canal at first. 1880 to GWR
Morayshire	1846	1852	1880 to Gt North of Scotland
Morecambe Ry & Harbour	1846	1848	1871 to Midland
Moreton Hampstead & Sth Devon	1862	1866	1872 to Sth Devon
Much Wenlock & Severn	1859	1862	1896 to GWR
Nantlle	1825	1828	1867 to Caernarvonshire
Nantwich & Market Drayton	1861	1867	1897 to GWR
Narbeth & Maenclochog	1872	1876	1881 amalgamated with Nth Pembroke & Fishguard
Neath & Brecon	1863	1864	1869 to Swansea Vale & Neath & Brecon Jc.
Nerquis			1866 to LNWR
Newent	1873	1885	1892 to GWR
Newmarket & Bury Ext.	1846	1848	
Newport, Abergavenny & Hereford	1846	1854	1860 to West Midland
Newport Pagnell	1863	1867	1875 to LNWR
Newquay & Cornwall Jc.	1864	1874	1884 to Cornwall Minerals
Newtown & Machynlleth	1857	1863	1864 to Cambrian
Norfolk	1845		Amalgam. of the Yarmouth & Norwich, and the Norwich & Brandon
Norfolk & Suffolk Joint	1898	1898	
North and Sth Western Jc	1851	1853	1871 to LNWR, Midland and North London. 1921 to LMS
North British	1844		Eventually included 50 lines
North Cornwall	1882	1886	

	Inc.	Open	Other Information
North Devon & Cornwall Light		1925	
North Eastern	1854		Amalgam. of many lines
North Lindsey Light	1900	1906	
North London		1850	1853 name change from East & West India Docks & Birmingham. 1909 to LNWR. 1921 to LMS
North Midland	1836	1840	1844 to Midland
North Pembrokeshire & Fishguard	1884		name change from Rose-bush & Fishguard. 1898 to GWR
North Staffs	1847		Amalgam. of several lines
North Wales Mineral	1844	1846	1846 to Shrewsbury & Chester
North Western	1846	1849	1871 to Midland
Norwich and Spalding	1853	1858	1877 to Midland & Eastern
Nottingham Suburban	1886	1889	
Nuneaton & Hinckley	1859	1862	1860 name change to Sth Leics. 1867 to LNWR
Ogmore Valley	1863	1865	1865 to Llynvi & Ogmore
Oldbury	1873	1884	1894 to GWR
Oldham, Ashton-under-Lyne & Guide Bridge	1857	1861	1862 to LNWR and Manchester & Lincs
Oswestry & Newtown	1855	1860	1864 to Cambrian
Oswestry, Ellesmere & Whitchurch	1861	1864	1864 to Cambrian
Otley & Ilkley	1861	1865	
Oxford	1843	1844	1844 to GWR
Oxford & Bletchley Jc	1846	1850	1847 to Buckinghamshire
Oxford & Rugby	1845	1850	1846 to GWR
Oxford, Worcs & Wolverhampton	1845	1850	1860 to West Midland
Pembroke & Tenby	1859	1863	1897 to GWR
Penarth Extension	1876	1878	1923 to GWR
Penarth Harbour, Dock & Railway	1856	1859	1922 to GWR
Peterborough, Wisbech & Sutton	1863	1866	1883 to Eastern & Midlands
Pontypool, Caerleon & Newport	1865	1874	1876 to GWR
Pontypridd, Caerphilly & Newport	1878	1884	1897 to Alexandra (Newport & Sth Wales) Dock & Railway
Port Talbot Ry & Docks	1894	1897	1922 to GWR
Portpatrick	1857	1861	1885 to Portpatrick & Wigtownshire Jt Ctte

	Inc.	Open	Other Information
Portpatrick & Wigtownshire Jt Ctte			1885 amalgam. of Portpatrick and Wigtownshire. 1885 to Midland
Preston & Longridge	1836	1840	1856 to Fleetwood, Preston & West Riding Jc
Preston & Wigan	1831	1838	1834 to North Union
Preston & Eyre	1835	1840	1847 to Lancs & Yorks and LNWR
Princetown	1878	1883	1922 to GWR
Ramsey	1861	1863	1875 vested in GER
Ramsey & Somersham Jc	1875	1889	1897 to GER and GNR
Ravenglass & Eskdale	1873	1875	
Redditch	1858	1859	1874 to Midland
Rhondda & Swansea Bay	1882	1885	1922 to GWR
Rhondda Valley & Hirwain	1867	1878	1889 to Taff Vale
Rhymney	1854	1858	1922 to GWR
Rosebush & Fishguard	1878	1895	1884 name change to Pembrokeshire & Fishguard
Ross & Ledbury	1873	1885	1892 to GWR
Ross & Monmouth	1865	1873	1922 to GWR
Rugby & Leamington	1846	1851	1846 to London & Birmingham
Rumney	1825	1836	1863 to Brecon & Merthyr Tydfil Jc
Rye & Camber		1895	
St George's Harbour & Ry	1853	1858	1861 to LNWR
St Helens & Runcorn Gap	1830	1833	1845 to St Helens Canal & Ry
St Helens Canal & Ry	1845		1864 to LNWR
Scottish Central	1845	1848	1865 to Caledonian
Scottish Midland Junction	1848	1855	
Severn & Wye			See Lydney & Lidbrooke
Severn & Wye & Severn Bridge	1879		1894 to Midland and GWR
Severn Bridge	1872	1879	1879 to Severn & Rye & Severn Bridge
Severn Valley	1853	1862	1870 to GWR
Sheffield & Rotherham	1838	1838	1845 to Midland
Shrewsbury & Birmingham	1846	1849	1854 to GWR
Shrewsbury & Chester	1846		1854 to GWR
Shrewsbury & Hereford	1846	1852	1862 to LNWR, GWR and West Midland. 1870 to GWR and LNWR jointly
Shrewsbury, Oswestry & Chester Junction	1845	1848	1846 to Shrewsbury & Chester
Sirhowy	1802	1805	Opened as Tramroad. 1860 name change to S. Railway. 1876 to LNWR

	Inc.	Open	Other Information
Solway Junction	1864	1869	
Somerset & Dorset	1862		Amalgam. of Somerset Central and Dorset Central. 1875 to Midland & LNWR. 1923 to SR and LMS
Somerset Central	1852	1854	1862 to Somerset & Dorset
South Devon	1844	1846	1878 to GWR
South Devon & Tavistock	1854	1859	1865 to South Devon
South Leicestershire	1860		Previously called the Nuneaton & Hinckley. 1867 to LNWR
South Staffordshire	1846	1847	Amalgam. of Sth Staffs Jc and Trent Valley, Midland and Grand Junction 1867 to LNWR
South Staffordshire Jc	1846		1846 to Sth Staffs
South Wales	1845	1850	1863 to GWR
South Wales Mineral	1853	1860	1923 to GWR
Southern	1923		
Southport & Cheshire Lines Extension	1881	1884	1881 to Cheshire Lines Ctte
Southsea		1885	To LBSCR and LSWR
Spalding & Bourne	1862	1866	1866 to Midland & Eastern
Staines & West Drayton	1873	1884	1900 to GWR
Stockport & Woodley Jc	1860	1863	1865 to Cheshire Lines Ctte
Stockport Timperley & Altrincham Junction	1861	1866	1865 to Cheshire Lines Ctte
Stocksbridge	1874	1876	
Stockton & Darlington	1821		1863 to NER
Stonehouse & Nailsworth	1863	1867	1878 to Midland
Stourbridge	1860	1863	1870 to GWR
Stratford & Moreton	1821	1826	1845 to Oxford, Worcs & Wolverhampton
Stratford-upon-Avon	1857	1860	1883 to GWR
Stratford-upon-Avon, Towcester & Midland Junction	1879	1882	
Swansea & Carmarthen	1865		1873 name change to Central Wales and Carmarthen Jc
Swansea & Mumbles		1806	Closed 1960
Swansea & Neath	1861	1863	1863 to Vale of Neath
Swansea Vale & Neath & Brecon Jc	1864	1875	1869 to Neath & Brecon 1922 to GWR
Swansea Valley	1847		1855 to Swansea Vale
Swindon & Highworth	1875	1883	1882 to GWR
Swindon & Cheltenham Extension	1881	1883	1884 to Midland & Sth Western Jc

	Inc.	Open	Other Information
Swindon, Marlborough & Andover	1873	1881	1884 to Midland & Sth Western Jc
Taff Vale	1836	1840	1922 to GWR
Tanat Valley Light	1898	1904	1921 to Cambrian
Teign Valley	1863	1882	1923 to GWR
Tenbury	1859	1861	1869 to LNWR and GWR
Tenbury & Bewdley	1860	1864	1869 to GWR
Tewkesbury & Malvern	1860	1862	1876 to Midland
Tiverton & Nth Devon	1875	1884	1894 to GWR
Torbay & Brixham	1864	1868	1882 to GWR
Tottenham & Forest Gate	1890	1894	1914 to Midland
Tottenham & Hampstead Jc	1862	1868	1902 to Midland, and Gt Eastern
Treferig Valley	1879	1883	1889 to Taff Vale
Trent Valley	1845	1847	1846 to London & Birmingham, Grand Junction, and Manchester & Birmingham
Trent Valley Midland & Grand Junction	1846		1846 to Sth Staffs
Vale of Clwyd	1856	1858	1867 to LNWR
Vale of Glamorgan	1889	1897	1922 to GWR
Vale of Llangollen	1859	1861	1896 to GWR
Vale of Neath	1846	1851	1863 to Swansea & Neath
Vale of Rheidol	1897	1902	1913 to Cambrian
Vale of Towy	1854	1858	1889 to GWR
Van		1871	1923 to GWR
Wakefield, Pontefract & Goole	1845	1848	Later to Lancs and Yorks
Wallingford & Wallington	1864	1866	1872 to GWR
Warrington & Altrincham Jc	1851	1853	1853 to Warrington & Stockport. 1859 to LNWR and St Helens
Warrington & Newton	1829	1831	1836 to Grand Junction
Warrington & Stockport			See Warrington & Altrincham Jc
Warwick & Leamington Union	1842	1844	1843 to London & Birmingham
Watford & Rickmansworth	1860	1862	1881 to LNWR
Watlington & Princes Risborough	1869	1872	1883 to GWR
Watton & Swaffham	1869	1875	1880 to GER
Wellington & Drayton	1862	1867	1864 to GWR
Wellington & Severn Jc	1853	1857	1892 to GWR
Welshpool & Llanfair Light	1899	1903	1923 to GWR
Wenlock	1861	1864	1896 to GWR
West Cheshire	1861	1869	1865 to Cheshire Lines Ctte
West Cornwall	1846	1852	1878 to GWR

	Inc.	Open	Other Information
West Lancs	1871	1878	1897 to Lancs and Yorks
West London Extension	1859	1863	Jointly held by LNWR, GWR, LSWR and LBSCR
West Somerset	1857	1862	1922 to GWR
Weston, Clevedon & Portishead Light	1885	1897	
Weymouth & Portland	1862	1865	
Whitby, Redcar & Middlesbrough Union	1866	1883	1889 to NER
Whitechapel & Bow	1897	1902	1897 to London, Tilbury & Southend. 1912 to Midland
Whitehaven, Cleator & Egremont	1854	1856	1877 to LNWR. 1878 to LNWR and Furness
Whitehaven & Furness Jc	1845	1849	1866 to Furness
Whitehaven Jc	1844	1847	1866 to LNWR
Widnes	1873	1877	1875 to Sheffield & Midland Joint
Whitland & Cardigan	1869	1873	1890 to GWR
Wigtownshire	1872	1875	1885 to Portpatrick & Wigtownshire Jt Ctte
Wiltshire, Somerset & Weymouth	1845	1848	1851 to GWR
Witney	1859	1861	1890 to GWR
Wolverhampton & Walsall	1865	1872	1876 to Midland
Wolverhampton, Walsall & Midland Jc	1872	1879	1874 to Midland
Woodstock	1886	1890	1897 to GWR
Worcester & Hereford	1853	1859	1860 to West Midland
Worcester, Bromyard & Leominster	1861	1874	1888 to GWR
Wrexham & Ellesmere	1885	1895	1922 to GWR
Wrexham & Mineral	1861	1862	1871 to GWR
Wrington Vale Light	1897	1901	Closed 1931
Wycombe	1846	1854	1867 to GWR
Wye Valley	1866	1876	1905 to GWR
Yarmouth & North Norfolk	1876	1877	1882 to Eastern & Midlands
Yarmouth Union	1880	1882	1882 to Eastern & Midlands
Yorkshire Dales	1897	1902	Later to Midland

Part Three — Canals

54 The following are dates of completions of some of the main canals. In a number of cases small stretches of a canal were opened and then the rest over a number of years. Where appropriate the dates of the first and last completion dates are given.

Aberdare	1812
Aberdeenshire	1805
Andover	1794
Ashby-de-la-Zouch	1804
Ashton-under-Lyne	1792/6
Barnsley	1799
Basingstoke	1796
Birmingham & Fazeley	1790
Birmingham & Liverpool	1835
Birmingham & Warwick	1844
Bradford	1774
Brecknock & Abergavenny	1812
Bridgewater's (Duke of)	1761
Bridgewater & Taunton	1827/41
Bude	1823
Burnturk	c1800
Caledonian	1822
Campbeltown	1794
Carlingwark	1765/80
Carlisle	1823
Chard	1842
Chelmer & Blackwater	1796
Chester	1779
Chesterfield	1776/7
Coombe Hill	1796
Coventry	1790
Crinan	1801
Cromford	1794
Croydon	1809
Dearne & Dove	1804
Derby	1796
Donnington Wood	1765/8
Droitwich	1777
Droitwich Junction	1853
Dudley	from 1779
Edinburgh & Glasgow	1822/3
Ellesmere	from 1795
Erewash	1779
Exeter	c1565
Fletchers	c1791

Forth & Clyde	1790
Fossdyke	Roman
Glamorganshire	1798
Glasgow, Paisley & Johnstone	1811
Glastonbury	1833
Gloucester & Berkeley	1822
Grand Junction	1799-1822
Grand Surrey	1810/26
Grand Union	1814
Grand Western	1812
Grantham	1797
Grosvenor	1824
Hackney (Devon)	1843
Hereford Union	1830
Huddersfield Broad	1811
Huddersfield Narrow	1798
Isle of Dogs	1805
Kennet & Avon	1798-1810
Kensington	1828
Ketley	1788
Kilbagie	c1780
Lancaster	1819/26
Leeds & Liverpool	from 1781
Leicester Navigation	1794
Liskeard & Looe	1828/31
Louth	c1765
Macclesfield	1831
Manchester, Bolton & Bury	1808
Manchester & Salford	1839
Manchester Ship	1894
Monkland	from 1793
Montgomeryshire	1797
Montgomeryshire (West)	1821
Newcastle-under-Lyme	c1800
Newdigate	1795
Newport Pagnell	1817
North Wilts	1819
Nottingham	1794-1842
Nutbrook	1795
Oakham	c1803
Oxford	1790
Par	1847
Peak Forest	1800
Portsmouth & Arundel	1823/31
Ravenhead	c1773
Regent's	1820
Rochdale	from 1794
St Columb	1777/9
Sankey Brook	from 1759
Sheffield	1819
Shrewsbury	1796
Shropshire Union	1792
Somerset Coal	1805/11

Staffs & Worcs	1772
Stourbridge	1779
Stourbridge Extension	1840
Stover	1792
Stratford-upon-Avon	1816
Stroudwater	1778/9
Tavistock	1817
Tennant	1790
Thames & Medway	1824
Thames & Severn	1789
Torrington	1827
Trent & Mersey	from 1777
Ulverston	1796
Walsall	c1798
Warwick & Birmingham	1800
Warwick & Napton	1800
Wey & Arun	1816
Wilts & Berks	1803/19
Woodeaves	c1802
Worcester & Birmingham	1815
Wyrley & Easington	from 1795

Part Four — Trams, Buses and Cars

55 Tramways

The first trams, horse-drawn, were introduced c1860. The earliest public undertaking was that of Liverpool in 1865.

In London the first tramway ran between Marble Arch and Porchester Terrace in 1861. By 1870 there were three companies — the North Metropolitan, London Tramways and London Street Tramways.

The Tramways Act 1870 enabled local authorities to run tramways but the tendency was for the local authority to establish them and to lease them to private companies.

56 Buses

In 1829 Schilliber ran his horse-drawn omnibus between Paddington and the Bank. A year later 39 buses were running in London.

The 1832 Stage Carriage Act permitted buses to ply for hire within the hackney-cab's metropolitan area.

Birmingham had regular horse-bus services in 1834, and the London General Omnibus Company was established in 1859 although it had previously traded as the Compagnie Generale des Omnibus de Londres.

The first motor-bus service, in 1898, was in Edinburgh. They were introduced in that year also in Clacton, Falkirk, Llandudno, Mablethorpe, Mansfield and Torquay. London followed in 1899 under the auspices of the Motor Traction Company which went out of business the next year.

The first rural bus service was from Newport Pagnell to Olney in 1898.

57 Motor-Cars

The first cars with internal combustion engines were introduced in the 1880's. The Red Flag Act passed in 1865 to control steam vehicles, and which restricted speeds to 4mph in towns, was repealed in 1896.

SECTION L

RELIGION

Part 1 — Church of England Administration

Part 2 — Religious Sects

Part 3 — Miscellaneous Terms

Part One — Church of England Administration

1 General

The Church of England is organised into two Provinces — Canterbury and York. The Province of Canterbury, the senior of the two, covers the midland and southern counties and, until 1920, Wales. York administers the remaining English counties. The Province of Wales (which includes Monmouthshire) was created in 1920.

Each Province is divided into Dioceses each in the charge of a bishop. A Diocese is divided into Archdeaconries each in the charge of an Archdeacon. Rural deaneries are sub-divisions of Archdeaconries with ecclesiastical parishes beneath them. Large parishes can be sub-divided into chapelries — areas served by dependent chapels.

Administrative Bodies

2 Chapter

A Chapter consists of the full members of a religious house. At one time it could have substantial secular jurisdiction over tenants occupying Chapter lands.

3 Consistory Court

The bishop's court.

4 Court of Augmentations

Created in 1535 to administer lands, possessions and revenues of the dissolved religious houses. It was abolished in 1554 and its functions transferred to the Exchequer.

5 Court of Arches

The Court of the Province of Canterbury.

6 Court of Chancery

The Court of the Province of York.

7 Donative

A parish wholly or partly exempt from the jurisdiction of the diocesan bishop.

8 Ecclesiastical Courts

Ecclesiastical courts exercised jurisdiction over clergy, laity and matters of heresy, interpreting canon law. The archdeacon's court was the lowest rank with right of appeal to a consistory or bishop's court. Above these were the provincial courts — the Court of Arches for Canterbury and the Court of Chancery for York.

9 Peculiar

A parish or church exempt from the jurisdiction of the Ordinary or Bishop in whose diocese it lies.

Church of England Officials

10 Archdeacon
A bishop's deputy, with jurisdiction over the incumbents.

11 Curate
Although in its full sense meaning a minister in charge of souls, the term is normally used to denote an assistant to a vicar or rector. A Perpetual Curate is sometimes synonymous with a vicar.

12 Dean
An official who presides over a cathedral Chapter.

13 Incumbent
A rector, parson, vicar or minister, and sometimes a perpetual curate.

14 Ordinary
An ecclesiastical superior — archbishop, bishop or archdeacon.

15 Parson
In the strictest sense, a rector, rather than a vicar.

16 Rector
The person in receipt of the great or rectorial tithes. He may be either a parson or a lay impropriator. At times the rector might also be in receipt of the small or vicarial tithes as well.

17 Rural Dean
A bishop's deputy but inferior to an Archdeacon.

18 Surrogate
A clergyman or other person appointed by the bishop as his deputy to grant licences for marriage without banns.

19 Vicar
In cases where the tithes of a parish had been appropriated by a monastic house and, later, a lay person, a deputy was appointed to fulfil the tasks of a rector. He was given the small or vicarial tithes for his maintenance.

Part Two — Religious Sects

20 Anabaptists
This sect appeared in Saxony early in the 16th century. It repudiated infant baptism and converts were rebaptised in adult life, a practice that led to the sect's name. The followers also taught equality and the common ownership of goods. There is evidence of suppression of Anabaptists refugees from the continent in 1534 and further persecution in the reign of Elizabeth.

21 Baptists
The Baptists were founded by John Smyth, a refugee from England, in Amsterdam in 1609. They believed in baptism for believers only, and then by total immersion; thus they repudiated infant baptism. Thomas Helwys, Smyth's disciple, established the 'General' Baptists at a church in Newgate. The 'Particular' Baptists began in Southwark in 1633. The 'General' Baptists believed in general redemption for believers; 'Particular' Baptists with Calvinist leanings, believed in redemption only for particular believers.

Baptists were persecuted during the reign of Charles II but this was stopped after the Toleration Act 1689. Towards the end of the 18th century the 'General' Baptists divided. The New Connection was formed in 1770 while the Old Connection became Unitarians. The Baptist Union in 1813 promoted closer co-operation between the various parts of the sect and in 1891 the 'Particular' Baptists and the New Connection merged.

22 Barrowists

A congregationalist sect in Elizabeth I's reign, founded by Henry Barrow. He was executed in 1593, the year that the Conventicle Act punished non-churchgoers with death or exile. Many Barrowists that year went to Holland and New England.

23 Brownists

A congregationalist sect named after Robert Browne who established a group in Norwich c1580. It rejected Episcopacy and Presbyterianism and any form of state association with religion. Browne himself, however, eventually accepted Church of England ordination in 1591 and was a rector in Northants until his death.

24   Catholic Apostolic Church

A group, founded in 1826, formed around H. Drummond, though soon under the influence of Edward Irving a Scottish revivalist minister. They believed in a 'Second Coming' and appointed Apostles in preparation for the event. Their central church was in Gordon Square, London, but other groups existed in Cambs, Shropshire and Surrey.

25 Congregationalists

A sect, sometimes synonymous with Brownists (qv), which believed in the autonomy of the local congregation and an absence of state intervention in religion. They were sometimes known as Independents and, in the 19th century, many became Unitarians. Their existence was allowed by the Toleration Act 1689. The sect played a leading role in the establishment of London University.

26 Free Church of England

A small Protestant sect which was formed in 1843 after dispute with the Church of England.

27 Free Church of Scotland

Formed in 1843 when about a third of the Church of Scotland divided from it. In 1900 it joined with the United Presbyterian Church to form the United Free Church.

28 Huguenots

The first Huguenot immigrants came in the reigns of Henry VIII and Edward VI with concentrations of settlements in London, the Cinque Ports, Norwich and Bristol. The Revocation of the Edict of Nantes in 1685 caused at least another 40,000 French Huguenots to settle in England, many of whom went to the west country and London.

29 Independents

See Congregationalists.

30 Irvingites

See Catholic Apostolic Church.

31 Jews

It is likely that Jews first settled in England during the reign of William the Conqueror. Henry I gave them a charter of protection. The largest settlements were in Bristol, Canterbury, Gloucester, Lincoln, London, Northampton, Norwich and York. The Jews were expelled in 1290 and admitted again by Cromwell.

32   Methodists

John Wesley formed a Society, in 1740, which is the ancestor of today's Methodist church. The various secessions from the main body include the Methodist New Connexion (1797), the Primitive Methodist Connexion (1811), the Bible Christians (1815), the Protestant Methodists (1828) and the United Methodist Free Church (1857). The Bible Christians, the Methodist New Connexion and the United Methodist Free Church combined in 1907 to form the United Methodist Church, and this in turn joined the Wesleyans and the Primitives in 1932. Still separate are the Wesleyan Reform Union, and the Independent Methodists (mainly confined to Lancashire).

33 Pilgrim Fathers

The Pilgrim Fathers sailed from Holland and Plymouth in 1620 and founded a colony at Plymouth in Massachusetts.

34 Plymouth Brethren

A Calvinist sect formed in Plymouth in 1830.

35   Quakers

A sect founded by George Fox. There were meetings of Friends as early as the 1650's although the movement was consolidated in the 1660's despite the Conventicle Acts.

36 Unitarians

A Congregationalist sect tracing their origins to the Presbyterianism of the 17th century. In 1928 the General Assembly of Unitarians and Free Christian Churches was formed.

37 United Free Church of Scotland

Formed in 1900 upon the merger of the Free Church of Scotland and the United Presbyterian Church. In 1929 it joined with the Church of Scotland.

Part Three — Miscellaneous Terms

38 Advowson

The right of presenting a clergyman to a benefice. A Collative Advowson is when the right to present is held by the bishop who also appoints. A Presentative Advowson occurs when the right of presenting is held by some other person, usually lay. Normally the bishop could not. refuse the choice.

Lay Advowsons are known since the 8th century. In 1933 parochial councils were allowed to purchase advowsons except where they were. the gift of the crown or bishop. Since 1924 a lay advowson may not be sold after two vacancies have occurred.

39 Advowson Appendant

An advowson annexed to an estate or manor.

40 Advowson In Gross

An Advowson belonging to a person.

41 Benefice

A clerical appointment with specified duties and maintained by particular revenues (temporalities).

42 Benefit of Clergy

From the Middle Ages until its abolition in 1827, clergy could claim exemption from trial by a secular court.

43 Bierbalk

A churchyard path.

44 Canons

Ecclesiastical laws.

45 Chantry

It was common in the Middle Ages for a wealthy person to endow, on his death, the establishment of a chapel within a church in which priests could sing masses for his soul. Its establishment required the Crown's consent and the ordinary's approval. In 1547 nearly 2400 chantries and guild chapels were suppressed.

46 Church Ale

A feast to commemorate the dedication of a church at which ale was sold in aid of funds for church expenses.

47 Church House

The old equivalent of a parish hall, normally adjoining the church or churchyard. Some date from the early 16th century.

48 Collation

The institution of a clergyman to a benefice which the bishop has in his own gift, or in cases where a

Presentative Advowson (see Advowson) has lapsed after six months.

49 Constitutions
Regulations adopted by a Provincial synod.

50 Impropriation
The annexation of a benefice by a lay person or corporate body.

51 Litten
A churchyard or burial ground.

52 Prebend
A stipend granted to a member of a cathedral chapter for his support. It would normally consist of the revenues of one of the manors in the cathedral estates. The term can apply to both the benefice and its holder.

53 Presentation
The nomination of a clergyman to a benefice by the holder of the advowson (qv), to the bishop.

54 Recusants
Those who declined to attend their parish church. The term, after 1570, normally referred to Roman Catholics.

55 Royal Peculiar
A benefice, usually a royal chapel, where the crown has the right to nominate the clergyman.

56 Temporalities
Secular sources of income for a religious house, such as buildings and lands.

57 Wake
Originally an all-night vigil prior to a holy day, but later the term used to denote the feast and celebration on the day itself.

SECTION M

THE LOCAL MILITIA

1 The Fyrd

In Anglo-Saxon times military service was connected with ownership of land. The military force was called the Fyrd and the obligation to serve, the fyrd-bote — one of the three duties of the thegns under the Trinoda Necessitas (qv).

Alfred divided the Fyrd into two parts, one under arms, one resting, alternating with each other. As a permanent force the king would have a group of experienced thegns and their retainers.

It was unusual for a county Fyrd to fight outside its own boundaries.

2 Knight Service

In 1070 William I introduced a system, now called Knight's Service, whereby he negotiated with his tenants-in-chief for a number of knights to be equipped and available for duty. In peacetime the amount of service was normally 40 days a year.

3 Assize of Arms 1181

In 1181 Henry II issued an Assize of Arms which set down the weapons and equipment required of each knight, freeman and burgess. The sheriff was responsible for raising the levy and justices were sent round to the shires to enforce the Assize. It was provided that juries from towns and hundreds should make the assessments of military obligation. By the 13th century the unfree were liable for military service as well.

4 Scutage

By the reign of Henry I it was established that knights could excuse themselves from military service and pay instead shield money — scutage. This money was used to hire mercenaries. The tenant-in-chief would recoup the scutage from his tenants. Scutage was last levied in 1327.

5 Commissions of Array

The king exercised control by appointing Commissions of Array which compiled the Muster Rolls that showed the men available for service in each shire.

6 The Tudor Militia

In Tudor times the Lord Lieutenant was the nominal head of the county militia, delegating his responsibilities to deputy lieutenants. Locally the parish constable was responsible for raising the levy. The county force was called the posse comitatus. Able-bodied men between 16 and 60 were liable to serve.

A number of enactments reorganised the militia in Tudor times. The first set forth the provision of equipment. The community was divided into 10 classes ranging from those who were required to keep a coat of armour, a helmet and a longbow, to those who had to provide 16 horses, 80 suits of light armour, 40 pikes, 30 long bows and other items of equipment.

Trained bands were established but these were not sent on service abroad.

General musters — formal inspections of county forces — were held at least every three years and more frequently in disturbed times. These musters were held on two days with an interval between each day so that defects found on the first day could be remedied by the second.

SECTION N

ARCHITECTURE

Part 1 — General Architectural Terms

Part 2 — Church Architecture

Part 3 — Castle Architecture

Part 4 — Building Materials

Part One — General Architectural Terms

1 Abacus
The slab on the top of a classical column separating it from the entablature.

2 Abutment
Part of a pier or wall which supports an arch, by taking the lateral thrust of the arch.

3 Acanthus
A representation of leaves found in the capitals (qv) of the Corinthian and Composite Orders (qv).

4 Angel Beam
Hammer Beams (qv) were sometimes carved at the ends with a representation of an angel or human being.

5 Architrave
The entablature on a classical order — that part above the actual column — is divided into three parts. The lowest part is the architrave which rests on the slab (abacus) at the top of the column.

6 Atrium
The entrance hall in a Roman house.

7 Baluster
A pillar supporting a handrail, normally slender at the top and thicker at the bottom.

8 Balustrade
A row of balusters (qv) usually employed on terraces, balconies etc, supporting a coping.

9 Barge Board
A board covering the rafters of a roof which overlap the walls of the house.

10 Bartizan
A battlemented turret overhanging a tower.

11 Bas-Relief
An abbreviation of Basso-relievo, where the figures of a carving project from the wall to less than half their true proportions.

12 Belvedere
A turret projecting from the roof of a house designed to provide extensive views.

13 Boss
An ornamental projection placed

at the intersection of ceiling ribs.

14 Bracket
An ornamental projection from a wall which supports a statue etc.

15 Cantilever
A beam with support only at one end, mainly used to hold balconies etc.

16 Capital
The carved or moulded head of a column. See **Classical Orders**.

17 Cartouche
A stone tablet carved in the shape of a scroll of paper, bearing an inscription.

18 Caryatid
A column in the form of a female figure. The most famous example is the Erectheum in Athens.

19 Classical Orders
In Classical architecture an Order is an entire column consisting of base, shaft, capital and entablature. There are three principal kinds — Doric, Ionic and Corinthian — which are Greek in origin, and Composite and Tuscan which were Roman developments of the Greek originals.

Doric, Ionic and Corinthian are shown in the illustrations. The Composite order uses the ram's horns volutes of the Ionic and the acanthus leaves of the Corinthian. The Tuscan Order is a larger version of the Doric.

Corinthian

20 Clerestory
An upper storey or wall near the root of a high building or church with a row of windows, rising above the roofs of adjoining buildings.

21 Cloister
A covered way round a quadrangle, especially in a monastery or college.

22 Coffering
Recessed panelling in ceilings etc. mainly for decoration, but quite often it was a method used to reduce the weight of the panels.

23 Collar-beam roof
A horizontal beam connecting the mid-points of the sloping rafters of a pitched roof.

24 Colonnade
A series of columns.

25 Column
A round pillar. It includes the base, shaft and capital and other named features which, in Classical architecture, have precise proportions.

26 Console
A bracket or corbel, usually decorated, in Classical architecture.

27 Coping
The sloped capping, either brick or stone, on the top of a wall. It

Doric

Ionic

allows rain water to run off.

28 Corbel
A bracket, or projecting beam, supporting a weight. It can sometimes be carved in the shape of a raven.

29 Cornice
A horizontal moulding at the top of a column beneath the frieze, or else an ornamental moulding at the top of a wall immediately beneath the ceiling.

30 Cove
A concave moulding at the junction of ceiling and wall.

31 Crocket
A carving representing leaves to be found on spires and pinnacles of Gothic architecture.

32 Crucks
Pairs of curved timbers, each pair from a single tree, which hold up the ridge-beam of the roof in a timber-frame house.

33 Cupola
A dome covering a square, circular or polygonal base.

34 Cusps
The projecting points in a Gothic arch which separate the foils.

35 Dado
a) The cube forming the body of a pedestal between the base and the cornice.
b) The lower part of a wall when coloured differently from that above.

36 Diapered
A diamond-shaped pattern on a wall, carved or painted. The term is applied also to brickwork using different coloured bricks to give a diamond pattern.

37 Dormer
A window in an upper floor projecting through the roof. It was named by being normally a window in a bedroom.

38 Dovecote
Free-standing dovecotes were introduced from Normandy and were the prerogative of the lord of the manor. Tenants, usually, were forbidden to have them. Doves at that time were an important source of winter meat and their droppings were used for manure.

39 Dressed Stone
Smoothly finished stonework.

40 Drum Columns
The cylindrical sections of a stone column.

41 Entablature
The superstructure above a row of columns. It is divided into architrave, frieze and cornice.

42 Entasis
A device originally used by the Greeks to correct the optical illusion of columns appearing to curve inwards. The columns were made thicker at the top than at the base to correct this.

43 Fan Vault
Vaulting used mainly in Late Perpendicular architecture in which the ribs have the same equal curve giving an effect like the bones of a fan.

44 Fillet
A narrow flat band between mouldings.

45 Finial
An ornamental feature at the head of pinnacles, canopies etc. in Gothic architecture.

46 Fluting

Semi-circular channels cut into the shafts of columns in Classical architecture.

47 Foils
The inside arcs between the cusps of a window.

48 Frieze
The centre section of an entablature (qv) in Classical architecture between the architrave and cornice. In the Ionic, Corinthian and Composite orders it is usually ornamented, in the Doric order it has slight projections and in the Tuscan order it is plain.

49 Gable
The triangular upper part of a wall immediately beneath a ridged roof.

50 Garderobe
The privy in a castle or medieval house. Usually at the end of a Z-shaped passage, it was built into the thickness of a wall with a shaft underneath.

51 Gargoyle
An ornamented spout projecting from gutters for carrying rain water away from the wall. It is usually carved in the form of a human's, demon's or animal's mouth.

52 Gazebo
A tower or turret overlooking a garden view; a belvedere.

53 Hammer Beams
Beams supported by brackets, in pairs, which project at right-angles from the walls.They eliminated the the need for a tie beam.

54 Herringbone
A style in walls etc. in which the masonry, bricks or timber blocks are laid diagonally and give a zigzag pattern.

55 Ingle Nook
A seat built into a wall next to the fireplace.

56 Keystone
A wedge-shaped stone positioned centrally at the head of an arch.

57 King Post
A post standing on the tie beam and reaching up to the roof ridge.

58 Lintel
A horizontal piece of timber, stone or steel, placed over a doorway or window, supporting the wall above.

59 Loggia
A covered verandah open on one or more sides.

60 Long Houses
Early forms of thatched houses for the peasants, which provided accommodation for the family at one end and the cattle at the other, separated by a screen.

61 Long and Short Work
Mainly seen on stuccoed buildings, corner stones alternately laid horizontal and upright.

62 Mansard
A roof which has two slopes, the lower one steeper than the upper.

63 Masons' Marks
Itinerant stone masons cut their signatures or symbols on pieces of worked stone.

64 Moulding
Ornamental projections of carvings on walls and ceilings. There are many kinds such as billet, cable, chevron, cove, hood, plain and roll.

65 Mullion
A vertical division of stone, wood or metal, separating the lights of a window.

66 Newel Post
The central post, sometimes extending to the roof, to which the steps of a winding staircase are set.

67 Oculus
A round window.

68 Oriel
Originally part of a room set aside for prayer, quite often overlooking the oratory below, from which the lord and his family could follow the service below. The term then came to be applied to any projecting part of a room, and then to a projecting window supported by corbels.

69 Pantile
An S-shaped roof tile with one curve larger than the other.

70 Parapet
A low wall, in earlier times for defensive purposes, on the roof of a building, but later used at the edge of balconies in a decorative manner.

71 Pargetting
Ornamental plasterwork, more especially on a timber-framed house.

72 Parlour
A room originally set aside in a house or convent for talking.

73 Pebble-dash
A result obtained by embedding small pebbles to surface rendering while it is still wet. Sometimes called rough-cast.

74 Pediment
In Classical architecture, the triangular feature above the portico.

75 Pele/Peel Tower
A small fortress, generally found in northern England, built as defence against border raids.

76 Pier
A vertical support, especially that for a bridge.

77 Pilaster
In Classical architecture, a flat rectangular pillar projecting but not usually detached from a wall; a decorative feature.

78 Pinnacle
In Gothic architecture, a pointed turret terminating a buttress or tower.

79 Plinth
The square projecting base of a column.

80 Portico
A range of columns supporting a roof, forming the entrance to a building.

81 Quatrefoil
In Gothic architecture an opening in tracery, in the shape of four leaves.

82 Quoin
The external angles of a building; the external corner stones of a building.

83 Revet
Face with masonry.

84 Rib
A projecting band on a ceiling.

85 Rose Window
In Gothic architecture, a circular window with tracery resembling the petals of a rose. Alternatively called a wheel-window.

86 Rotunda
A domed circular building.

87 Rustication
Masonry joints made conspicuous by chiselling grooves or channels.

88 Saddle-backed roof

A pitched roof or tower.

89 Scagliola
Plaster painted to resemble marble.

90 Shaft
The main part of a column between base and capital.

91 Shingle
A flat, wooden tile used in churches, particularly in south-east England.

92 Solar
A quiet room in the upper storey, usually in the sunniest place. Used as a study.

93 Stanchion
A vertical bar or strut.

94 String Course
A projecting ornamental band running round the face of a building.

95 Tessellated Pavement
Pavement made from small pieces of stone, marble, brick etc.

96 Tie Beam
A horizontal beam between the ends of two rafters.

97 Tile Hanging
The surfacing of outer walls with overhanging tiles pegged on to the timber frame. Especially popular in Elizabethan architecture.

98 Tracery
Ornamental stonework — mullions and transoms — in the upper part of Gothic windows.

99 Transom
A horizontal bar in a window separating panes of glass.

100 Tympanum
The triangular space between a lintel and an arch.

101 Vault
An arched roof or ceiling.

102 Vise
A spiral staircase with the steps inset into a newel post (qv).

103 Voussoirs
The wedge-shaped stones forming an arch.

104 Wheel Window
See **Rose Window.**

Part Two — Church Architecture

105 Aisle
A division of a church running parallel to the nave and pillars. In England it is rare to find more than two in a church.

106 Altar
The raised table or platform used for the Holy Sacrament. The Council of Epone in AD 509 instructed that it should be made of stone but most stone altars were destroyed at the Reformation. Rails to protect the altar from desecration were widely introduced in early Elizabethan times.

107 Apse
A semi-circular or polygonal part of a church at the end of the choir or aisles, usually with a domed or arched roof.

108 Belfry
The tower in which the church bells are hung. It need not necessarily be part of the church building.

109 Bell Gable
Where there is no belfry (qv), for example in small churches and chapels, the bell gable is a turret at the west end

110 Bench Ends
In the 15th and 16th centuries it was a practice to carve the ends of the oak benches.

111 Brasses
Engraved brass plates fixed to tombs, generally on the floor of the church, inlaid into slabs of stone.

112 Buttress
A projecting support to a wall. In Classical architecture it was disguised as a pilaster. The Norman style included buttresses which were broad with a low projection, but the Early English style had greater projection and less breadth. These latter are familiarly known as Flying Buttresses.

113 Chancel or Choir
The eastern part of a church which includes the main altar used by the clergy and choir. It is separated from the nave by a screen or rails etc.

114 Chantry Chapel
It was common in the Middle Ages for a wealthy person to endow, on his death, the establishment of a chapel within a church in which priests could sing masses for his soul. Quite often the chapel was built over the grave of the testator.

115 Chapter House
The assembly room in which the governing body of a cathedral or monastery transact their business.

116 Chest
All churches were once obliged to possess a strong chest in which the records of the church and parish, the registers for example, could be stored under lock and key.

117 Choir
See Chancel.

118 Cressets
Metal holders for the grease or oil used for light. It is common nowadays to call the cresset stones in church (which held the metal holders), cressets.

119 Crossing
The space where nave and transept meet in a cross-shaped church under the central tower.

120 Crypt
A vault, usually found under the east end of a church. It was built beneath the holiest part of the church mainly to hold tombs and relics or else to house pilgrims.

121 Dorter/Dortour
In monasteries, a first-floor dormitory connected to the south transept by a night stairway.

122 Lairstal
A grave inside a church. Covered by a lairstone.

123 Lancet
A tall pointed arch window in a church, found in Early English architecture.

124 Ledgers
Black marble slabs laid over graves in the floor of a church, usually in the chancel. Particularly used in the 17th and 18th centuries.

125 Lychgate
Corpse-gate (lich — a corpse). A roofed gateway at the entrance to a churchyard under which bearers of the coffin passed.

126 Nave
The main body of a church from the inner door to the choir, in which the congregation assembles.

127 Oratory
A small private chapel in a church.

128 Presbytery
The part of the church east of the choir used by those who minister the services.

129 Reredos
An ornamented wall or screen at the back of the altar.

130 Rood
A crucifix; a name generally applied to the large cross at the entrance to the chancel in Roman Catholic churches.

131 Sacristy
A room in a church in which vestments, vessels etc. are stored. Often called the Vestry.

132 Slype
A covered passage from transept to chapter-house in a cathedral.

133 Transept
The short arms of a cruciform-shaped church.

134 Vestry
See Sacristy.

Part Three — Castle Architecture

135 Bailey
The space which existed between the fortified walls of a castle. It could also be called a court or ward. Depending on the distance from the outer wall to the central keep, there could be two or three such baileys.

136 Barbican
An outer tower before the gate of a castle or fortified settlement. It could serve as a watch-tower as well as being a defensive feature.

137 Bastion
A fortified projection, usually an irregular pentagon, on a wall.

138 Battlement
An indented parapet; its original purpose on castles was to provide cover and outlets for archers.

139 Curtain Wall
The wall between fortified towers.

140 Donjon
See Keep.

141 Embrasure
An opening in a battlement wall used by defenders, through which they fired weapons.

142 Garderobe
The privy. Usually at the end of a Z-shaped passage, it was built into the thickness of a wall with a shaft underneath.

143 Gatehouse
A tower over the entrance to a castle on its outside wall.

144 Keep
The chief, inner tower in a castle. Alternatively called the Donjon.

145 Machiolation
Openings in the floor of projecting parapets through which missiles were dropped.

146 Merlons
The teeth on an embattled parapet.

147 Motte and Bailey
The Normans introduced the motte-and-bailey castle. The bailey, a forecourt, was surrounded by an earth rampart. The motte was a mound, flat at the top, 20-40 feet high, upon which stood the lord's house or keep. The rest of the castle's inhabitants lived in a wooden hall in the bailey. The whole was enclosed by wooden fortifications. This type of castle was the forerunner of the medieval stone castle.

148 Portcullis

A heavy, grated gateway, a defensive feature of medieval castles. It could be raised or lowered only from the inside.

149 Ravelin

A pointed, defensive screen outside the main walls of a castle.

Part Four — Building Materials

150 Ancaster Stone

An easily cut and carved limestone quarried on Wilsford Heath in Lincolnshire. It can be of various colours but weathers to grey.

151 Ashlar

Square stones applied as facing for a wall, usually covering irregularly cut stone.

152 Bath Stone

A yellow stone quarried around Box and Corsham in Wiltshire. Easily cut.

153 Bricks

Medieval bricks varied in size and could be up to 15" long. Flemish bricks introduced in the late 13th century were thin, approximately $9\frac{3}{4}$ x $4\frac{3}{4}$ x $2\frac{1}{2}$ and common in Tudor buildings. A tax on bricks in 1780 made it economical to produce larger sizes.

154 Clipsham Stone

A honey-coloured limestone quarried at Clipsham in Rutland.

155 Clunch

Chalk generally used for internal carving work.

156 Cob

A mixture of unburnt clay and straw used for walls and domestic houses.

157 Cotswold Stone

A grey limestone quarried in the Cotswolds.

158 Gallets

Pebbles or chips of stone inserted into the pointing of walls to give more strength. Generally found in south-east England.

159 Hopton Wood Stone

A grey limestone quarried in Derbyshire. It polishes well and is used particularly for floors.

160 Ironstone

Limestone or sandstone coloured by iron oxide. It has a brown or green colour.

161 Kentish Rag

A greyish-green, sandy limestone quarried in Kent. It is very hard, resists moisture and is used extensively for facing buildings.

162 Ketton Stone

A cream limestone quarried in Rutland.

163 Moorstone

A granite found in the west of England. Used for buildings, monuments and paving.

164 Portland Stone

A limestone which turns white on exposure, found in south-west England and particularly in Dorset. It was too hard for common use until better cutting tools were made in the 17th century.

165 Purbeck Marble

A dark limestone containing fossils, mined near Swanage and used particularly for monuments.

166 Slate

The main slate quarry areas are Cornwall, Devon, Wales, Cumberland, north Lancashire, Westmorland, Argyllshire and Perthshire. Welsh slates can be green, blue, purple, red, or grey, Westmorland's are usually green, Cornwall's bluish-grey.

A tax was imposed on slates in 1831 but soon removed.

167 Stucco

A rendering of lime, gypsum or cement applied to a wall surface, or used on architectural decorations. It was used in England in the 16th century but it became most popular when the Adam brothers introduced their own patent kind — known as Adams' Cement.

168 Weldon Stone

A creamy, easily-cut stone, quarried in Northants.

SECTION O

PLACE NAMES

General

Place names are rarely what they seem. Modern spellings are quite often far removed from their original roots and even the short glossary of very common place names and elements below must be used with great caution.

The most authoritative works of reference are The Oxford Dictionary of English Place Names by Eilert Ekwall and the volumes (arranged by counties, but still incomplete) issued by the English Place Name Society.

Place names are important in local history research. They give clues to land ownership, physical features since disappeared or trades and buildings which have vanished. It is important to trace a name back through its forms to its origins although quite often local records go back no further than the 16th century.

Glossary

aber — river mouth, confluence
avon — river
barrow · hill
barton — barley or corn farm
beck — stream
bryn — hill
burgh/bury — fortified place
burn — stream
by — village
caster/chester — city; fortified place
den, dean, dene — wooded valley
dol — field, dale
dun — fort; hill
field — open land, forest clearing
garth — enclosure
gate — street, road, passage
grange — farm; grain store

haigh, hay — place surrounded by a hedge
ham — village, manor, dwelling place
hirst, hurst — hillock, copse
holm — island, usually in a river or lake
holt — copse
howe — valley, depression
ing — people   (Barking — Berica's people)
ley — wood clearing; meadow land
llan — church
magna — great
march, mark — boundary
over — bank, shore, slope, hill
parva — little
pont — bridge
sey — island
shaw — small wood
stead — place, religious place
stoke — religious place; secondary settlement
stow — (religious) place
super — on
thorp(e) — hamlet; secondary settlement
thwaite — forest, paddock, meadow
toft — homestead
ton — enclosure, village, farm
warden — enclosure
wick — premises, quite often for dairy produce
wootton — farm by a wood
worth — enclosure

SECTION P

COINS AND TOKENS

Part 1 — Coins

Part 2 — Mints

Part 3 — Numismatic Terms

Part One

Coins

Values are expressed in old currency.

1 Angel

A gold coin worth 6/8d, minted in 1464/5 and replacing the old version of the Noble (qv). Quite often the coin was pierced by a hole and used as a touch-piece to bring good health. It was discontinued in the reign of Charles II. There was also a half-angel called an Angelet.

2 Atcheson

A Scottish coin struck in the reign of James VI, worth two-thirds of an English penny.

3 Crown

A gold coin minted in 1526 and worth 4/6d. In 1551 it appeared as a silver coin and was valued at 5/-. The Crown was discontinued in Victorian times but has been revived for recent commemorative issues.

4 Dandiprat

A 16th century coin worth 1½d.

5 Doit

A copper coin worth 1d in Scotland but one-twelfth of an English penny.

6 Farthing

Until 1279 a farthing was obtained by cutting a penny into quarters. Silver farthings were issued from this date until the reign of Edward VI. Copper farthings were minted in 1672 and were eventually made of bronze. It was discontinued in 1956.

7 Florin

A gold coin minted in 1344 and worth 6 shillings. It took its name from Florence where it was first introduced. In 1849 silver florins were first minted.

8 Groat

A silver coin introduced in 1279 without much popularity. It was re-introduced in 1351 and was worth 4d and it remained until 1662. A small silver groat was later minted but discontinued in 1855. A Half-groat was introduced in 1351.

9 Guinea

A gold coin worth £1 minted in 1663. It took its name from the place where the gold came from — Guinea in West Africa, later called Gold Coast. In 1717 it was revalued at 21 shillings and discontinued in 1813.

10 Half Crown

A gold coin first introduced in the reign of Henry VIII, but later reissued by Edward VI as a silver coin.

11 Half-penny

Until 1279 a half-penny was obtained by cutting a penny in half. Silver half-pennies were issued from this date until 1672 when they were minted in copper. In 1860, in common with the penny, it was made in bronze.

12 Half Ryal

A gold coin, worth five shillings, introduced in the reign of Edward IV.

13 Helm

A quarter of a florin, first issued in 1344.

14 Leopard

A gold coin issued in 1344, worth half a florin.

15 Mark

The Mark was not a coin in England but was often used as a unit in accountancy, especially in Danelaw counties. It was a weight of metal originally valued at 128 silver pennies (10/8d), but later revalued at 13/4d.

16 Noble

A gold coin minted in 1344 and worth 6/8d (half a mark). In 1464/5 it was reissued worth 10 shillings and called a ryal, but a new Noble was also introduced called an Angel (qv).

17 Ora

This was not a coin in England but was a monetary unit in Danelaw counties. It represented 16 silver pennies.

18 Penny

First issued in the 8th century as a silver coin, probably in the reign of Aetherlbert II of Kent. It was called a denier, from the Roman silver coin the denarius. For nearly 500 years it was the only coin struck in England and remained a silver coin until 1797. The Saxon penny weighed 22½ grains, hence there were 240 pennies to a pound weight of silver. By the tenth century a long cross appeared on the reverse side so that the coin could be broken down into half-pennies and farthings.

In 1180 a new series of pennies was issued now known, from its reverse side, as the shortcross coinage. In 1247 further longcross coins were minted on which the ends of the cross reached to the edge of the coin as a deterrent against clipping.

In 1279 Edward I issued new designs and added groats, half-pennies and farthings to the coinage.

In 1797 a copper penny was introduced and weighed 1oz and in 1799 was made smaller in size. In 1860 it was reduced to its latest size and made of bronze. These Victorian coins were called 'Bun' pennies as the Queen's hair was tied in a bun. No pennies were issued in 1923-5, 1941-3, 1952 and 1954-60. Only a token supply was minted in 1933.

19 Pound

Originally a pound weight of silver from which 240 pennies could be minted. The pound was the name of a short-lived coin in the reign of Charles I. Pound notes were first issued in 1797.

20 Ryal

See Noble.

21 Sceat

A mid-7th century gold coin, particularly found in Anglo-Saxon southern settlements.

22 Shilling

A silver coin first minted in 1504 and was then called a Testoon. It had a chequered career due to its continual debasement.

23 Sixpence

A silver coin introduced in 1551. In 1947 it was made of cupro-nickel although the 'silver' coin had for some time been made of debased metal.

24 Sovereign

A gold-coin minted in 1489 and by the reign of Elizabeth I was worth 30 shillings. It was discontinued by James I in favour of the Unite (qv), but reintroduced from 1817 to 1917.

25 Testoon

See Shilling.

26 Three Farthings

A silver coin issued in 1561 and discontinued in 1562.

27 Threepenny piece

A silver coin first minted in 1551 and issued only spasmodically. It became most popular in Victorian times and in this form was discontinued in 1937 when the twelve-sided nickel-brass coin appeared.

28 Thrymsa

An Anglo-Saxon gold coin.

29 Twopenny piece

Issued in the years 1797-1799. It was very large and nicknamed 'cartwheel'; it weighed 2ozs.

30 Unite

A gold coin minted early in the 17th century, named after the union of England and Scotland. It replaced the sovereign for the time being, and was worth £1.

Part Two

31 Mints

Mints have existed at the following places:

Beds — Bedford

Berks — Reading, Wallingford

Bucks — Aylesbury, Buckingham

Cambs — Cambridge

Cheshire — Chester

Cornwall — Launceston

Derbys — Derby

Devon — Barnstaple, Exeter, Lydford, Totnes

Dorset — Dorchester, Salisbury, Sherborne, Wareham, Weymouth

Durham — Durham

Essex — Colchester, Horndon, Maldon

Glos — Berkeley, Bristol, Gloucester, Winchcombe

Hants — Southampton, Winchester

Herefordshire — Hereford

Herts — Hertford

Hunts — Huntingdon

Kent — Canterbury, Dover, Hythe, Rochester, Romney, Sandwich

Leics — Leicester

Lincs — Horncastle. Lincoln, Stamford

London — Tower of London, Durham House, Strand, London Mint Tower Hill

Norfolk — Caistor, Kings Lynn, Norwich, Thetford

Northants — Northampton, Peterborough

Northumberland — Corbridge, Newcastle-upon-Tyne

Notts — Newark, Nottingham

Oxon — Oxford

Shropshire — Shrewsbury

Somerset — Axbridge, Bath, Bridport, Bruton, Cadbury, Crewkerne, Ilchester. Langport, Taunton, Watchet

Staffs — Stafford, Tamworth

Suffolk — Bury St. Edmunds, Ipswich, Sudbury

Surrey — Guildford, Southwark

Sussex — Chichester, Hastings, Lewes, Steyning, Pevensey, Rye

Warks — Warwick

Wilts — Bedwyn, Cricklade. Malmesbury, Salisbury, Warminster, Wilton

Worcs — Pershore, Worcester

Yorks — York

Part Three   Numismatic Terms

32 AE
Applied to coins made of brass, bronze or copper.

33 Broke Money
Coins in the Middle Ages which were cut in half or quarters to make smaller denominations.

34 Clipping
The practice of cutting pieces from the coinage. At times this was punishable by death.

35 Grades of Coin
Coins are graded according to their condition. The terms used are:

Proof — specially struck coin
FDC — Fleur-de-coin. In perfect mint condition
UNC — uncirculated coin
EF — Extremely fine. Unworn but not perfect
VF — very fine; slight wear
F — fine; worn but with the image distinct
Fair — considerably worn or damaged
Mediocre
P — poor

In describing the condition of both sides of a coin the obverse (face) side is stated first. Thus EF/F means that the face is extremely fine and the reverse is fine.

36 Hoard
A large cache of coins. Probably the largest Hoard in this country has been the 20,000 coins of Edward I and Edward II found at Tutbury.

37 Jettons
Metallic or card counters, sometimes resembling coins, generally used in gambling.

38 Jugate
The overlapping of heads on a coin.

39 Legend
The wording around the coin inside the border

40 Longcross
Refers to the penny struck from 1247-1272 on which the cross extends to the edge of the coin to discourage clipping.

41 Maundy Money
Specially minted sets of silver coins, 1d, 2d, 3d and 4d pieces, distributed by the monarch on Maundy Thursday to poor people. The number of recipients is equivalent to the age of the sovereign.

42 Milled
A term now applied to the serrated edge around a coin.

43 Obverse
The face side of a coin.

44 Reverse
The reverse of the face side of a coin.

45 Shortcross
Refers to the penny struck from 1180-1247 with a short cross on the reverse which enabled the coin to be cut into halves or quarters.

46 Tealby
Refers to the first coinage of Henry II.

47 Tokens
Issued in times of monetary change or shortage and used within a locality in exchange for goods. The three main periods of their use were the mid 17th, late 18th and early 19th centuries.

SECTION Q

HERALDRY

Part 1 — General

Part 2 — Heraldic Terms

Part One

1 General

Heraldry, or more properly, Armory, began in England in the 12th century. Most probably its purpose was the identification of important individuals when they were in armour and their faces obscured. Heraldic devices were emblazoned on the linen surcoat worn over the armour (the origin of 'coat of arms'), and on the shield that was carried. In addition, but later, crests were worn on helmets.

2 College of Arms

The College of Arms, or Heralds' College, was instituted in 1483 and is empowered to make grants of arms. At its head is the Earl Marshal a hereditary title held by the Duke of Norfolk. He has thirteen principal officers: three Kings of Arms — Garter, Clarenceux and Norroy, six heralds — Chester, Lancaster, Somerset, Richmond, Windsor and York, and four pursuivants — Rouge Croix, Rouge Dragon, Portcullis and Blue Mantle.

3 Visitations

In 1529/30 the College of Arms was responsible for periodic visits to parts of the country to establish if coats of arms were being used incorrectly or without permission. The last Visitation was in the late 1680's. Many of the Visitation records have been published by the Harleian Society.

4 Components of a Coat of Arms

a) *The Shield*

A shield's right and left hand is how they are viewed by the holder, i.e. the opposite to a person looking at it. Dexter is right, Sinister is left.

A shield's main points are shown thus:

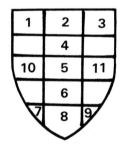

1 Dexter Chief Point
2 Middle Chief Point
3 Sinister Chief Point
4 Honour Point
5 Heart Point
6 Navel Point
7 Dexter Base Point
8 Middle Base Point
9 Sinister Base Point
10 Right Flank
11 Left Flank

A shield's area is what is known as its ground or field and whatever is blazoned upon it is said to be charged upon it.

As a general rule descriptions of a coat of arms refer to the upper part of a shield first.

b) *Divisions of a Shield*

Some common divisions of the field of a shield are as follows:

Party per fesse

Party per pale

Party per bend

Party per bend sinister

Party per chevron

Quarterly

Gyronny of eight

Party Per Saltire

Ente en point

Champagne

c) *Tinctures*

The tinctures which are used on a coat of arms may be colours, metals or furs. In black and white illustrations these are denoted by a system of dots and lines. The most common tinctures are as follows:

Colours
azure — blue (horizontal lines)
gules — red (perpendicular lines)
vert — green (diagonal lines from dexter chief to sinister base)
sable — black (horizontal and perpendicular lines crossing each other
purpure — purple (diagonal lines from sinister chief to dexter base)
sanguine — reddish/mauve (diagonal lines dexter to sinister crossing each other

Metals
or — gold (dots)
argent — silver (plain white)

Furs
ermine — white field with black spots
ermines — black field with white spots
erminois — gold field with black spots
pean — black field with gold spots
vair — argent and azure pattern in rows
counter-vair — same as vair except that figures are placed base against base, point against point
vaire — when the figures forming the vair are of more than two tinctures
potent — resembles the heads of crutches placed head to head

The term 'proper' is used when the object is depicted in its natural colour.

A field is 'counter-charged' when it is made up of two tinctures — metal and colours, with the metallic part of the charge falling upon the field colour and the coloured part of the charge falling upon the field metal.

d) *Charges*

Charges are the devices blazoned on the shield field. The most commonly used are called 'Ordinaries' and these are roughly mathematical shapes. The most common Ordinaries are:

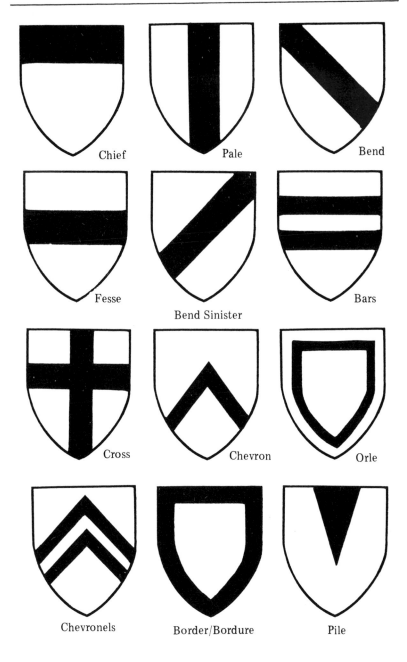

Chief

Pale

Bend

Fesse

Bend Sinister

Bars

Cross

Chevron

Orle

Chevronels

Border/Bordure

Pile

Pall

Canton

Flanches

Gyron

Mascle

Fusil

Billet

Fret

Escutcheon

Annulet

Bar

Lozenge

The most common charges other than Ordinaries are:

animals: lions, heraldic tigers, wolves, antelopes etc.
birds: notably the eagle
fish: especially the dolphin
mythical beasts: dragon, centaur, griffin etc.
the human body or head
flowers, fruit and trees
heavenly bodies
military weapons and buildings
ships

e) Supporters

This term refers to the two figures, usually animals, on either side of the shield. They are used in England only by the Crown, peers, and some orders of knighthood.

f) Crest

Above the shield usually appears a crest secured to a helmet by a wreath with lambrequin or mantling hanging down.

g) Mottoes

A family motto may appear beneath and above the shield.

5 Coats of Arms for Women

A spinster's or widow's coat of arms is charged with a lozenge (diamond shape). On marrying, her arms are placed on the sinister side and her husband's on the dexter. This is called impalement.

In cases where she is an heraldic heiress (the eldest daughter, without brothers), her arms are depicted on a small shield known as an 'inescutcheon of pretence' in the middle of her husband's arms which occupy the remainder of the shield.

6 Coats of Arms for Children

Children may quarter their shields with the paternal arms in the top dexter and bottom sinister quarter and the maternal arms in the other quarters.

Part Two

Heraldic Terms

Some of the many terms used in heraldry are as follows:

7 Achievement

Describes a coat of arms fully marshalled.

8 Annulet

A ring, a device probably derived from chain mail.

9 Argent

Silver, depicted on engravings as plain white.

10 Armed

Describes the showing of claws, horns, hoofs etc. of an animal or bird.

11 Armory

The study of coats of arms; now usually called Heraldry.

12 Augmentations

Additions to coats of arms usually granted as an honour.

13 Azure

Blue; depicted on engravings as horizontal lines.

14 Badges

Distinctive insignias worn by soldiers and retainers.

15 Bar

A device obtained from two horizontal lines across the shield.

16 Barry

Describes a shield divided by horizontal lines.

17 Bearing

A general word to describe an heraldic device.

18 Bend

A charge consisting of the area between two parallel lines drawn from top right to bottom left of a shield. A shield is divided per bend when a single line is drawn in the same direction.

19 Bend Sinister
A charge consisting of the area between two parallel lines drawn from top left to bottom right of a shield.

20 Border/Bordure
A charge which consists of a border round the edge of a shield.

21 Cadency
The distinction between various members of a family.

22 Cadet
A junior member of a family.

23 Canton
A charge consisting of a box in the top right hand part of a shield.

24 Charge
A device emblazoned on a shield face. It may be an Ordinary or a figure.

25 Checkered/Checky
Describes a shield divided into chess-board squares.

26 Chevron
A charge consisting of an inverted V-stripe. A field is divided party per chevron when it is divided by a single line in the same shape.

27 Chevronels
Small chevrons.

28 Chief
The upper part of the shield.

29 Cinquefoils
Five leaves of grass emerging from a centre point.

30 Coat of Arms
The shield, crest, mantling and helmet.

31 Couchant
Describes an animal lying down but with head up.

32 Counter-changed
Describes a field where two tinctures are used; the charges use the same two tinctures.

33 Crescent Moon
Denotes a second son.

34 Crest
An insignia fixed to the helmet by a wreath.

35 Crowned
Describes a crowned animal.

36 Dexter
Righthand side.

37 Differences
Charges which denote different branches of a family.

38 Displayed
Describes the spread wings of a bird.

39 Ermine
A fur tincture — depicted as white with black spots.

40 Ermines
A fur tincture — depicted as a black field with white spots.

41 Fesse
The area between two parallel lines drawn across the centre of the shield. A shield is divided per fesse when a single line crosses it in the same direction.

42 Fesse Point
The centre point of a shield.

43 Field

The surface of a shield or escutcheon.

44 Garb
A sheaf of wheat or corn.

45 G(u)ardant
Describes a beast full-faced or looking forward.

46 Gules
Red; depicted in engravings by perpendicular lines.

47 Gyronny
The division of the shield into triangles. The most common device is the Gyronny of Eight.

48 Hatchment
The arms of a deceased person shown on the front of his house.

49 Impalement
A shield is impaled when it is divided into two equal parts, the arms of the husband being on the right and those of the wife on the left.

50 In escutcheon
The shield of arms of an heraldic heiress placed within the arms of her husband.

51 Label
A charge with three points as a distinctive mark for an eldest son.

52 Leopards
In France these figures are leopards; in England they are royal lions.

53 Lozenge
A diamond-shape.

54 Lozengy
A term to describe a field covered with diamond-shapes.

55 Mascle
A diamond-shape charge through which the field can be seen.

56 Mullet
A rowel of a spur used to distinguish the third son.

57 Or
Gold; depicted in engravings by black dots on a white ground.

58 Ordinaries
The most commonly used charges.

59 Pale
An Ordinary (qv) consisting of the area between two perpendicular parallel lines drawn in the centre of a shield. A shield divided per pale has a single perpendicular line in the same direction.

60 Party
Divided or parted.

61 Passant
Describes a beast in a walking position.

62 Pile
A V-shaped charge drawn from the top of the shield.

63 Proper
The natural colour.

64 Purpure
Purple; depicted on engravings by diagonal lines drawn from top left to bottom right.

65 Quarterings
Partitions of a shield holding coats of arms.

66 Quarterly
Describes the division of the field into four equal parts by one horizontal and one perpendicular line.

67 Rampant
Describes an upright animal.

68 Roundel
A disc-like charge.

69 Sable
Black; depicted in engravings by horizontal and perpendicular lines crossing each other.

70 Saltire
Party per Saltire is the division of the field into four equal parts by two diagonal lines crossing each other.

71 Segreant
Describes a griffin on its hind legs and its wings back to back.

72 Sinister
Lefthand side.

73 Supporters
Figures, usually animals, on either side of the shield. Its use is restricted in coats of arms to the Crown, peers and some orders of knighthood.

74 Torteaux
Red roundels.

75 Trick
A method of quickly depicting a coat of arms using a generally recognised shorthand to describe tinctures, charges etc.

76 Vert
Green; depicted in engravings by diagonal lines from the top right to the bottom left.

SECTION R

TRADE, COMMERCE AND INDUSTRY

Part 1 — City of London Livery Companies

Part 2 — Fairs and Markets

Part 3 — Public Houses and Brewing

Part 4 — Old names for Trades and Occupations

Part 5 — Legislation on Employment and Wages

Part One — City of London Livery Companies

1 The most important London companies are or were:

Air Pilots and Air Navigators
Apothecaries
Armourers & Braziers (inc 1452)
Bakers (inc 1509)
Barber-Surgeons (Barbers inc 1462)
Basket Makers
Blacksmiths
Bowyers
Brewers (inc. 1437)
Broderers
Butchers
Carmen
Carpenters (inc. 1477)
Clockmakers
Clothworkers
Coachmakers and Coach Harness Makers
Cooks (inc. 1482)
Coopers (inc. 1501)
Cordwainers (inc. 1439)
Curriers
Cutlers
Distillers
Drapers (inc. 1488)
Dyers (inc. 1471)

Fanmakers
Farriers
Fellowship Porters
Feltmakers
Fishmongers (inc. 1433)
Fletchers
Founders
Framework Knitters
Fruiterers
Fullers (inc. 1480)
Gardeners
Girdlers
Glass Sellers
Glaziers
Glovers
Gold and Silver Wiredrawers
Goldsmiths'
Grocers (inc. 1428)
Gunmakers
Haberdashers
Horners
Innholders (inc. 1515)
Ironmongers (inc. 1463)
Joiners
Leathersellers
Loriners
Masons
Master Mariners
Mercers
Merchant Tailors
Musicians (inc. 1472)
Needlemakers
Painter-Stainers

Parish Clerks (inc. 1442)
Patternmakers
Paviors
Pewterers (inc. 1468)
Pinners
Plasterers (inc. 1501)
Playing Card Makers
Plumbers
Poulters (inc. 1504)
Saddlers
Salters
Scriveners
Shipwrights
Silk Throwsters
Skinners
Solicitors
Spectacle Makers
Stationers
Surgeons
Tallow Chandlers (inc. 1462)
Tanners
Tinplate Workers
Tilers and Bricklayers
Tobacco Pipe Makers and Tobacco
   Blenders
Turners
Upholders
Vintners (inc. 1436)
Watermen
Wax Chandler (inc. 1484)
Weavers
Wheelwrights
Woodmongers
Woolmen

Part Two — Markets and Fairs

2 General

Until the concentration of population into towns and the advent of good transport services, fairs and markets were the most important means of trading. Many are of ancient origin, pre-dating the earliest known grant or charter. Gradually, after the Norman Conquest, most were regularised by charters granted by the Crown. In the 13th century 3300 charters were granted, in the 14th century 1560. This profusion of grants enabled the Crown to obtain revenue from the local landowners and the latter to receive tolls from the tradesmen.

Fairs took place at specified dates in the year and markets on a particular day or days each week. Frequently the charter for both was granted together. In effect, the granting of a charter was the granting of revenues, rather than the right to hold a fair or market. Usually grants were made to a noble landowner, possibly as a reward for services to the Crown, or else as a form of endowment to a religious establishment.

Some of the older sites for fairs are by funeral barrows or else at junctions of old tracks or drove roads. They may also be at boundaries or on hilltops.

3 Legislation

In 1285 it was made an offence to hold fairs in churchyards although this still occurred for a considerable time afterwards.

In the reign of Henry VI it became illegal to hold fairs on Good Friday, Ascension Day, Corpus Christi, Whit-Sunday, Trinity Sunday, the Assumption of the Virgin Mary, All Saints and on any Sunday except the four at harvest time.

Fairs were opened by proclamation and sometimes by a local customary ceremony, such as the pinning up of a glove. Any merchant found selling after the end of the fair was liable to forfeit to the Crown double the value of all that he had sold.

In the reign of Edward II it became illegal to buy goods on the way to market and to resell them for a profit at the market. An offender was called a regrator or forestaller. This legislation was not totally repealed until 1844 although it had long fallen into disuse.

4 Administration

The fair or market was under the jurisdiction of the steward of the lord of the manor or, where the charter was owned by a religious establishment, the abbot. He also presided over the Pie Powder Court — so called from a corruption of 'pieds poudreux' (the 'dusty-footed'), which was empowered to dispense instant justice to what was mainly an itinerant trading community. It would settle disputes, fine regrators and any other offenders.

The Pie Powder Court met in a building called a tolbooth or tolsey, and this word survives in a number of areas as a building for local administration. The tolbooth also served as a meeting-place for merchants, who also helped to dispense justice. During the period of the fair or market the judicial powers of the local courts were suspended to give precedence to the market's court.

Local inhabitants quite often had the right to trade first and outsiders were only allowed to trade after paying a toll. These outsiders were given various names, such as stallingers, censers or chensers, intrants or customarii etc.

5 Ale-Tasters

Most localities had ale-tasters appointed by the local courts to examine ale and bread for quality and quantity. They were also called aleconners and alefounders.

6 Aulnager

A royal officer responsible for examining the size and quality of woollen cloth. Standards were first laid down in 1196 and aulnagers first appointed in the reign of Edward I to enforce them. The regulations on size were repealed in 1381 but those to do with quality not until 1699.

7 Clerk of the Market

Originally this was a post in the King's household, and was concerned with the market supply to the royal retinue, and with weights and measures. As the Court travelled he went with them and exercised authority over all markets within the Verge, that is, within 12 miles of wherever the Court was.

For a time his responsibility was enlarged to cover the country and he farmed the concession out to local landowners. An Act of 1640 restricted his power once more to the Verge, and elsewhere gave it to the local mayors, lords of the manors etc.

Normally he attended from 10 a.m. to sunset and trading commenced when he rang a bell.

8 Leather Searcher

Responsible for examining all leather being traded and to stamp it with a die or seal.

9 Overseers of the Markets

Sometimes called market-lookers, they were the mayor's representatives.

10 Ponderator

A person responsible for weighing goods at market.

11 Markets and Fairs — Charters

In 1889 the Government published a list of market and fair charters as part of a report on the existing state of market tolls and rights. The list had been prepared from a MSS volume in the Public Record Office styled 'Palmer's Index No. 93' and is believed to contain a complete list of all Letters Patent preserved in the PRO relating to Markets and Fairs in England from the reign of King John to 22 Edward IV.

The list has been rearranged in county order where counties have been noted. Where no county has been noted the entry has been put into the alphabetical list at the end of the county list.

The spelling quoted in the Report has been retained and no effort has been made to check the accuracy of the county designations.

BEDS

Dunstable F 5John
Bello Loco F 22Ed1
Weston MF 32Ed1
Shafford MF 5Ed2
Blunham MF 8Ed2
Sonyndon MF 9Ed2
Tudington MF 9Ed2
Synelesho MF 12Ed2
Merston MF 17Ed2
Luton MF 12Ed3
Jslepe MF 38Ed3
Amville M 3Hen3
Wardon MF 1Ed2

BERKSHIRE

Neubery F 17John
Wallingford F 6John
Newbery F 17John
Henton M 2Hen3
Badelking M 2 Hen3
Wallingford M 2Hen3
Badelkinge M 3Hen3
Tachcham M 2Hen3
Farendon M 2Hen3
Spencs M 2Hen3
Wanting F 1Hen3
Lamburne F 3Hen3
Shalingford F 5Hen3
Abenden F 18Ed1
Aldermanston MF 20Ed1
Catmere MF 34Ed1
Bastildene MF 2Ed2
Asshamsted MF 2Ed2
Chepin facedon M 6Ed2
Yatindon MF 12Ed2
Badele et Wykingesham 2F 38Ed3
Bokingham F 15, 16, 17Ric2
Chepinghamborne M 2F 1to21&24Hen6
Finchhamsted MF 27to39Hen6

BUCKS

Agmondesham MF 2John
Agmundesham F 2John
Eton M 5John
Teyngwyke M 31Hen3
Fenystratford F 5Hen3
Newport Paynell MF 54Hen3
Burnham MF 55Hen3
Stony Stratford F 18Ed1
Hamslappe MF 21Ed1
Hadenham MF 23Ed1
Wormhale MF 32Ed1
Bitlesden MF 8Ed2
Olney F 9Ed2
Hameldon MF 9Ed2
Brikhull MF 12Ed2
Iuyngho MF 12Ed2
Newport Paynell F 1Ed3
Stoke MF 5Ed3
Stoke Puges F 7Ed3
Hoghston MF 8Ed3
Stork MF 8Ed3
Dachett F 9Ed3
Wendover F 21Ed3

Brehull F 21Ed3
Mussenden MF 41Ed3
Burnham M 2Hen5
Muresle MF 3&4Hen5
Bruckhull parva M2F 1to21&24Hen6
Eton 2F 1to24Hen6
Horewode MF 25&26Hen6
Eton juxta Windsore M 27to39Hen6
Stoke Pogeis F 5Ed3

CAMBS

Cantbury F 2John
Cambridge F 2John
Berkham MF 10Ed1
Clopton MF 20Ed1
Kingeston MF 34Ed1
Foyton F 4Ed2
Sutton MF 5Ed2
Trumpeton F 5Ed2
Elye 2F 12Ed2
Pappeworth F 17Ed2
Everard F 17Ed2
Foxton MF 19Ed2
Shepereth F 17Ed2
Wisebech F 1Ed3
Wykes MF 5Ed3
Bassingborn MF 9Ed3
Badburgham MF 9Ed3
Abington M 9Ed3
Barington MF 9Ed3
Bassingborn 18Ed3 MF
Badburnham MF 9Ed3
Abington M 9Ed3
Barington MF 9Ed3
Bassingborn 18Ed3 MF
Badburnham M 18Ed3
Bernwell F 11/12/13Ric2
Cambridge F 1to24Hen6
Westreete MF 27to39Hen6

CHESHIRE

Bromburg MF 6Ed1
Manpas MF 9Ed1
Onere MF 9Ed1
Thorple MF 10Ed1
Aldelym MF 23Ed1
Burton MF 27Ed1
Burton in Wirehale MF 11,12,13Ric2
Knottesford MF 6Ed3

CORNWALL

Derteine M 7John
Penrin MF 43Hen3
Polrram MF 20Ed1
Naute MF 24Ed1
Mosehole MF 28Ed1
St. Brian MF 31Ed1
Ponton MF 5Ed2 .
Lawinton MF 5Ed2
Caergaule MF 5Ed2
St Germayne MF 5Ed2
Castelleterell MF 6Ed2
Boswythy MF 6Ed2
Shiriock in Crostilberne MF 8Ed2
Jnneswerk MF 13Ed2
Jnneswerk MF 9Ed3
De S. Proboin MF 14Ed2
Marghasion MF 5Ed3
Pensans MF 6Ed3
Rydreth MF 7Ed3
Columb Magna MF 7Ed3
Shepstall MF 9Ed3
Helleston MF 10Ed3
Polran MF 25,26,27Ed3
Plemute F 30Ed3
Polruan MF 5&6Ric2
Penzans MF 6&7Hen4
Talker M 6John
Fawe MF 9Ed2

CUMBERLAND

Morpeth MF 1John
Cokermue M 5Hen3
Kesewik MF 4Ed1
Derewentfelles MF 4Ed1
Bothecastre MF 7Ed1
Setone MF 8Ed1
Melmorby MF 28Ed1
Arcwret MF 35Ed1
Botill MF 21Ed3
Hayton MF 6Ed1

DERBY

Chesterfield MF 6John
Chesterfeld F 15John
Chesterfeld F 17John
Dunebruge MF 4Ed1
Sallowe MF 29Ed1
Wirkeworth MF 34Ed1
Mersham MF 4Ed2
Chavelsworth MF 2Ed3
Deneby MF 8Ed3
Monyashe MF 14Ed3
Menyassh MF 22Ed3
Tydeswell MF 15,16,17Ric2
Pleseleghe MF 13Ed1
Melborne MF 2Ed3
Salowe 11,12&13Ric2

DEVON

Axemynster M 6John
Bradenesse MF 10John
Axemynstre M 17John
Exon M 15John
Mobir M 2Hen3
Chidelamiton M 2Hen3
Chedelinton M 2Hen3
Bovey M 3Hen3
Hatherleghe MF 4Hen3
Ternemue M 4Hen3
Chiristonwe M 4Hen3
Kingesburgh M 4Hen3
Cumbermartyn F 6Hen3
Wulnberg M 5Hen3
Plimpton F 5Hen3
Cumbmartin F 6Hen3
Poplesford M 10Hen3
Seton MF 4Ed1
Ilfridecombe MF 7Ed1
Porlemuth MF 8Ed1
Herctone MF 9Ed1
Devenebr' MF 14Ed1
Leye Canonicorum MF 14Ed1
Leigge Canonicorum M 17Ed1
Chetwode F 18Ed1
Deveneber MF 18Ed1
Sydebyr MF 19Ed1
Aulescomb MF 20Ed1
Strete MF 20Ed1
Tamerton Foliet MF 21Ed1
Merwode F 22Ed1
Peynton MF 23Ed1
Beer MF 24Ed1
Zele Tony MF 27Ed1
Toppesham MF 28Ed1
Clifton sup. Dertmouth MF 31Ed1
Westhamelesworth F 31Ed1
Ermington MF 32Ed1
Bradelegh 2F 2Ed2
Stoke in Tinhide MF 3Ed2
Aspton MF 3Ed2
Chuddelegh MF 3Ed3
Clifte MF 3Ed3
Cwydyton MF 3Ed3
Thorncomb MF 6Ed2
Asphton F 7Ed2
Morlegh MF 9Ed2
Bokeland Clompton MF 11Ed2

Jppelpon MF 11Ed2
Baunton M 15Ed2
Langford MF 7Ed3
Morton MF 8Ed3
Saunford Pewell MF 9Ed3
Wylteford MF 16Ed3
Holecombe MF 17Ed3
Whittford F 20Ed3
Buckfastelegh M 25,26,27Ed3
Cokynton MF 25,26,27Ed3
Tuffeld MF 39&40 Ed3
Otery MF 1Ric2
Taunton F 21,22,23Ric2
Kingesbrig ct MF 27to39Hen6
Buckfastlegh F 27to39Hen6
Plympton F 15to22Ed4
Black Torriton M 3Hen3
Wodebir MF 14Ed1
Pilton juxta Barnstaple MF 18Ed3

DORSET

Heford M 5John
Bere M 17John
Sturminster F 2Hen3
Cerdestockes M 3Hen3
Newton M 5Hen3
Corfe MF 32Hen3
Weymuth MF 35Hen3
Hunton MF 56Hen3
Middelton MF 8Ed1
Abbottesbery M 9Ed1
Ockeford Nichell MF 10Ed1
Bemester MF 12Ed1
Nova Villa MF 14Ed1
Stapelbrig MF 18Ed1
Rym MF 26Ed1
Yateminster MF 28Ed1
Piddelton MF 29Ed1
Esthemesworth MF 32Ed1
Liditon MF 32Ed1
Blaneford F 35Ed1
Tarent Gundevill MF 1Ed2
Whitchurch MF 4Ed2
Melcombe MF 8Ed2
Ockford Stilling MF 1Ed3
Poukestoke MF 7Ed3
Acford Nicholai MF 11Ed3
Dalwode F 18Ed3
Fordington MF 29Ed3
Capel Sci. Jacobi de
Holte F 42Ed3
Shireborne MF 15,16&17Ric2
Yatesminster MF 15,16&17Ric2
Cheping Blancford F 3&4Hen5
Cherdestoke M 1to24Hen6
Cerne F 27to39Hen6
Hankchurch F 27to39Hen6
Pole Villa MF 27to39Hen6
Cernemue MF 7Ed1
Kingston Russell MF 12Ed1
Sturminster F 6Ed3
Wichampton MF 21Ed3

DURHAM

Hertipole MF 17John

ESSEX

Moreton F 9John
Turrok M 9John
Witham M 3Hen3
Hatfield M 3Hen3
Angre F 4Hen3
Rammesden M 5Hen3
Thurrok M 5Hen3
Branketre F 10Hen3
Dunningbr' MF 8Ed1
Horington F 8Ed1
Borham MF 9Ed1
Bradwell MF 11Ed1

Amllers MF 14Ed1
Borham MF 17Ed1
Aveton Giffard MF 18Ed1
Felstede MF 20Ed1
Royndon MF 21Ed1
Bures MF 21Ed1
Waldene M 23Ed1
Theydone MF 33Ed1
Godynestre MF 2Ed2
Coringham MF 10Ed2
Fobbing MF 11Ed2
Redeswell MF 12Ed2
Assendon MF 9Ed2
Bradfeld MF 13Ed2
Herewith M 13Ed2
Turrock MF 4Ed3
Eleford MF 4Ed3
Halsted MF 3Ed3
Terlinge MF 5Ed3
Lalton MF 6Ed3
Bures MF 12Ed3
Stebbing MF 12Ed3
Wodhamniferres MF 12Ed3
Renham MF 16Ed3
Burnham MF 22Ed3
Goldhanger MF 22Ed3
Hebrugg MF 28Ed3
Orste MF 29Ed3
Witham et Neuland M 3Ric2
Epping bruer' MF 11/12/13Ric2
Watham MF 11/12/13Ric2
Halsted Villas MF 5/6Ed4
Havering Villa F 5/6/7Ed4
Chelmsford M 1John
Wakering F 1John
Chelmsford F 2John
Newport F 5John
Newport F 5John

GLOUCESTER

Berkely M 1John
Wicton MF 2John
Briave M 9John
Yates M 2Hen3
Kenenerton M 2Hen3
Persor M 3Hen3
Lemenister M 2Hen3
Northleche MF 4Hen3
Neuenton F 10Hen3
Campden MF 33Hen3
Solebury MF 8Ed1
Tokynton MF 9Ed1
Pukelicherch MF 12Ed1
Frompton MF 13Ed1
Warrick MF 13Ed1
Borneston MF 21Ed1
Gloucester Burgus F 30Ed1
Alerinton MF 32Ed1
Tortworth MF 32Ed1
Newent MF 6Ed2
Dorthurst 2F 12Ed2
Payneswick MF 14Ed2
Teukesbury F 17Ed2
Dene Magna MF 2Ed3
Guyting MF 4Ed3
Stowe MF 4Ed3
Barkeley MF 4Ed3
Berkeleyernes MF 4Ed3
Thomerton MF 6Ed3
Newport juxta Berklee F 22Ed3
Tettebury F 24Ed3
Brynesfeld MF 28Ed3
Tettebury F 29Ed3
Campden F 34/35Ed3
Winterborne MF 15/16/17Ric2
Berkley F 18/19Ric2
Prestbury M 18/19Ric2
Alvaninton MF 18/19Ric2
Tewkesbery F 1to21&24Hen6
Mershefeld mag. MF 2/3/4Ed4

Brightstede F 8/9/10Ed4
Almundesbury MF 13Ed1

HANTS

Leton MF 10John
Kerton M 16John
Scanburne M 17John
Clere M 2Hen3
Mildenhall MF 4Hen3
Porcester M 4Hen3
Charuton M 8Hen3
Dogmaresfeld MF 6Ed1
Thurkeleston MF 32Ed1
Bourhunt MF 32Ed1
Middelton MF 32Ed1
Neuton MF 11Ed2
Middleton MF 12Ed2
Aulton F 14Ed2
Ev'este MF 10Ed3
Ringewode F 11Ed3
Motesfonte MF 25,26,27Ed3
Hamelhoke MF 28Ed3
Middleton MF 38Ed3
Romesey F 11,12,13Ric2
Suthwike MF 15,16,17Ric2
Suthwick MF 1to24Hen6
Tichefeld F 25&26Hen6
Havont MF 27to39Hen6
Winton Civitas MF 27to39Hen6
Basingstoke F 27to39Hen6
Berton M 5Hen3

HEREFORD

Ledbery M 3John
Cast. Godrici M 6John
Wilton M 7John
Ross M 2Hen3
Bromyard F 2Hen3
Fothoppe MF 5Hen3
Hereford F 10Hen3
Prestined MF 10Hen3
Overne MF 9Ed1
Leomonster F 9Ed1
Crukhowell MF 9Ed1
Credeley MF 13Ed1
Staundon MF 21Ed1
Flamstede MF 27Ed1
Castr' MF 27Ed1
Levenhales MF 29Ed1
Kilpeck MF 2Ed2
Wynfreton MF 12Ed2
Hatfeld MF 12Ed2
Leverhales MF 13Ed2
Levenhales MF 14Ed3
Bodenham MF 2Ric2
Maddeley MF 5&6Ric2
Lennally MF 7&8Ric2
Mokars MF 2Ed3
Kynardeste MF 31Ed3

HERTS

Ware M 1John
Bernet M 1John
Ware M 8John
Royston F 14John
Sabrichworth M 6Hen3
Chesterhunt F 41Hen3
Styvenack MF 9Ed1
Knebworth F 20Ed1
Benyngton MF 33Ed1
Kingeston MF 34Ed1
Sabrightesworth MF 35Ed1
Pokerich MF 8Ed2
Trenge MF 9Ed2
Pekeriche MF 1Ed3
Chesthunt MF 9Ed3
Watford F 9Ed3
Chesthunt M 18Ed3
Marthier MF 30Ed3

Buntingford MF 34/35Ed3
Buntingford 41Ed3
Sabrichsworth MF 25/26Hen6
Hatfield MF 5/6/7Ed4
Huche F 11Ed2

HUNTS

Sumersham M 1John
Kinebocton MF 1John
Ramesey M 2John
Wodeston MF 52Hen3
Gidding MF 31Ed1
Everton MF 35Ed1
Fenstanton MF 9Ed2
Erehethe MF 12Ed2
Keston MF 15Ed3
Fareshered MF 25/26/27Ed3
Lecton MF 7/8Ric2
Spaldiwich M2F 1to21&24Hen6
Kymbarton MF 1to21&24Hen6
Alwalton M 52Hen3
Wodeweston MF 33Ed1
Somsham Brandonferry MF 13Ed2

KENT

Northflet F 2John
Orpington M 7John
Strodes M 7John
Frikestone MF 16John
Northflete F 2John
Strode F 7John
Winchelsey F 17John
Kemesing M 3Hen3
Eisherster M 5Hen3
Sutton F 6Hen3
Burne F 10Hen3
Serres M 10Hen3
Alinton MF 8Ed1
Werehorn MF 8Ed1
Sandhuge MF 9Ed1
Shipbourne MF 13Ed1
Sole juxta
Kemsing MF 13Ed1
Grommbrig MF 13Ed1
Sandwich F 18Ed1
Farnbergh MF 18Ed1
Chelesford MF 18Ed1
Cranbrock M 18Ed1
Chileham MF 19Ed1
Impeton MF 29Ed1
Ashe MF 31Ed1
Newenham MF 31Ed1
Eseling MF 32Ed1
Waynflete MF 33Ed1
Preston juxta
Wengham MF 35Ed1
Swaffham MF 3Ed2
Wetringbury MF 4Ed2
Haukehurst MF 5Ed2
Ricolure MF 7Ed2
Wrotham MF 8Ed2
Stanstede F 9Ed2
Biyle MF 9Ed2
Chileham MF 9Ed2
Rydelingweld MF 9Ed2
Erheth MF 9Ed2
Lesnes MF 9Ed2
Tonge F 9Ed2
Ringeston F 9Ed2
Ringesdonne F 9Ed2
Westwickham MF 11Ed2
Elding MF 12Ed2
Tonebruge F 12Ed2
Balsham M 12Ed2
Shingeldwell MF 4Ed3
Smerdene MF 6Ed3
Elham F 6Ed3

Tanete MF 10Ed3
Gillingham MF 10Ed3
Smethe MF 11Ed3
Lenham F 11Ed3
Farnebergh MF 18Ed3
Folkeston M 22Ed3
Hierne MF 25/26/27Ed3
Elmestede MF 28Ed3
Lenham F 29Ed3
Apuldre MF 32Ed3
Goodmersham MF 38Ed3
Cobeham MF 41Ed3
Gouthurst MF 3Ric2
Freningham Villa 7&8Ric2
Canterbury 4F 7&8Ric2
Preston MF 9&10Ric2
Bernwell F 11/12/13Ric2
Erde MF 20Ric2
Eltham M2F 1to24Hen6
Charring 2F 1to24Hen6
Bromley MF 25/26Hen6
Holingbourn MF 25/26Henry6
Munketon M 25/26Hen6
Mepeham M 25/26Hen6
Chart M 25/26Hen6
Eythorne F 27to39Hen6
Kingesmede F 27to39Hen6
Swanneston F 27to39Hen6
Wimblingweld F 27to39Hen6
Bettesworth F 27to39Hen6
Esshatisford MF 5/6/7 Ed4
Eltham F 8/9/10Ed4
Serres M 4Hen3
Esheteford F 22Ed3
De La Zele MF 39&40Ed3
Gravesend MF 39&40Ed3
Shepey Queensburgh MF 1Ric2

LANCS

Hermitage F 1John
Normules MF 4Hen3
Waletun MF 5Hen3
Ulverston MF 8Ed1
Furneysei MF 8Ed1
Ergum MF 8Ed1
Chernock MF 12Ed1
Werington MF 13Ed1
Ormescherch MF 14Ed1
Brumley MF 22Ed1
Newton in Makerfeld MF 29Ed1
Eukeston MF 31Ed1
Lathom MF 32Ed1
Robye MF 32Ed1
Hale MF 32Ed1
Gayrstrange MF 4Ed2
Wygan MF 3Ed3
Prestcote MF 7Ed3
Netherton MF 12Ed3
Rughford MF 13Ed3
Bradewater M 7/8Ric2
Bradwater F 11/12/13Ric2
Prestcote M 27to39Hen6

LEICESTERSHIRE

Lutterworth M 16John
Northburge M 3Hen3
Luteburg MF 5Hen3
Asshby la Zouche MF 45Hen3
Donynton MF 6Ed1
Halverton MF 12Ed1
Rothelee MF 12Ed1
Halluton MF 12Ed1
Boseworth MF 13Ed1
Ceggeworth MF 18Ed1
Erverbye MF 20Ed1
Mountstorrell MF 20Ed1
Whitewick MF 21Ed1
Speldeford MF 22Ed1
Wymondham MF 32Ed1

Leicester F 1Ed2
Stapelford MF 2Ed2
Northburgh MF 12Ed2
Gonteby MF 13Ed2
Lobenham 2MF 1Ed3
Bredon F 4Ed3
Wymundwold MF 12Ed3
Glentnertell MF 22Ed3
Leicester MF 34&35Ed3
Assheby F 11,12,13,14Ed4
Leicester F 11,12,13,14Ed4
Esseby MF 3Hen3
Norburg M 4Hen3
Halyhton MF 32Ed1
Sherle MF 4Ed2

LINCOLN

Wrengel M 7John
Necton M 16John
Norton M 16John
Irenham M 16John
Tateshall M 3John
Flet M 6John
Gednay M 6John
Westrasne M 3Hen3
Rasne M 3Hen3
Torkesey M 3Hen3
Dekinges M 4Hen3
Uphaven M 4Hen3
Nauenby MF 5Hen3
Wraggeby M 5Hen3
Cueya MF 10Hen3
Welowe F 35Hen3
Saltfletby MF 52Hen3
Birton MF 8Ed1
Gosberkerk MF 9Ed1
Brunne MF 9Ed1
Sutton in Holland MF 10Ed1
Lutton MF 10Ed1
Swaneton MF 10Ed1
Wayneflett MF 10Ed1
Wrangel M 10Ed1
Teteney M 10Ed1
Alford MF 11Ed1
Multon MF 18Ed1
Surfflett MF 18Ed1
Langw'ah MF 19Ed1
Geynesborgh F 20Ed1
Saleby M 20Ed1
Grenham MF 20Ed1
Wrightebald F 21Ed1
Multon F 22Ed1
Saleby M 24Ed1
Swyneshead F 26Ed1
Tottele MF 27Ed1
Burowell M 28Ed1
Skytebrok MF 29Ed1
Marom MF 31Ed1
Estdeeping MF 32Ed1
Fillingham MF 32Ed1
Gerbethorp MF 33Ed1
Barton sup Humber MF 1Ed2
Edenham MF 1Ed2
Kirkton in Holland 2Ed2
Mumby MF 3Ed2
Stanygad MF 6Ed2
Burton Stather MF 8Ed2
Blaunkenney MF 9Ed2
Tateshale MF 9Ed2
Thoresway MF 10Ed2
Wynelefford MF 10Ed2
Wintringham MF 11Ed2
Bondeby MF 12Ed2
Thurleby juxta Brunne MF 12Ed2
Pinchebeck MF 12Ed2
Gretham MF 16Ed2
Trikingham MF 2Ed3
Agham MF 4Ed3
Knaythe MF 4Ed3

Wintringham MF 7Ed3
Wintrington MF 8Ed3
De La Lee MF 9Ed3
Pincebek M 13Ed3
Binbroke MF 24Ed3
Gosberkerk MF 15Ed3
Suthkyme F 17Ed3
Thorkesey MF 19Ed3
Repinghall MF 20Ed3
Navenby F 21Ed3
Hollandbrugge MF 30Ed3
Then MF 36Ed3
Axolm MF 5/6Ric2
Messingham MF 5/6Ric2
Bough in le Mersh Villa MF 2Hen4
Crull MF 1to21 & 24Hen6
Harlow MF 27to39Hen6
Bradle F 16John
Grymesby F 2John
Edlington MF 13Ed1
Torkesey MF 14Ed1
Spillesby MF 33Ed1
Skidbroke MF 33Ed1
Oroby MF 19Ed3
Swinderby MF 27to39Hen6

MIDDLESEX

Staines M 3Hen3
St. James, Westminster F 18Ed1
Weybridgge MF 22Ed1
Hundeslow MF 24Ed1
Westminster F 26Ed1
Enefield MF 31Ed1
Brainford MF 35Ed1
Harewe MF 8Ed2
Skrine MF 4Ed3
Pynnore MF 10Ed3

NORFOLK

Langley M 1John
Norton F 2John
Karleton F 2John
Grymeston F 2John
Wymundham MF 5John
Haneworth F 5John
Lenne F 5John
Hurtendun MF 5John
Haneworth F 5John
Walsingham MF 10Hen3
Cauntel MF 19Hen3
Snafham MF 41Hen3
Burneham MF 55Hen3
Reffham MF 5Ed1
Crikes MF 9Ed1
Stanford MF 11Ed1
Feltwell MF 11Ed1
Oxeburg MF 12Ed1
Shepedon MF 13Ed1
Oxburg F 13Ed1
Sisslaund MF 20Ed1
Lyng F 23Ed1
Lucham MF 25Ed1
Saham MF 27Ed1
Diste F 28Ed1
Upton MF 30Ed1
Halughate MF 31Ed1
HerdwikMF 32Ed1
Tacolnested MF 32Ed1
Bermingham MF 32Ed1
Ryburgh MF 33Ed1
Billingford MF 33Ed1
Kirpby MF 33Ed1
Harpele MF 35Ed1
Tacolneston MF 35Ed1
Swaffham 2F 2Ed2
Holte MF 3Ed2
Cley F 3Ed2
Attelburgh F 4Ed2
Guthereston F 4Ed2

Lenne F 9Ed2
Snyterton MF 9Ed2
Ryburgh F 11Ed2
Bermingham MF 12Ed2
Whetaer' MF 12Ed2
Lynge MF 14Ed2
Jugeworth F 15Ed2
Sheppeden M 19Ed2
Oxeburgh M 19Ed2
Madanton MF 2Ed3
Fretton MF 2Ed3
Wanborn MF 7Ed3
Massingham Magna MF 8Ed3
Nerford MF 2Ed3
Banham MF 12Ed3
Worsted MF 13Ed3
Sloley F 13Ed3
Havinglond MF 21Ed3
Wigenhall MF 21Ed3
Felbrug MF 25/26/27Ed3
Harleston M 43/44/45Ed3
Fransham MF 1Ric2
Windham M2F 1to24Hen6
Woking Villa F 27to39Hen6
Castelacre MF 8/9/10Ed4
Etherling MF 15to22Ed4
Brock MF 10Ed1
Tylney F 12Ed1
Wynebergh MF 12Ed1
Canutele F 12Ed1
Wanborne MF 14Ed2
Frenge MF 46Ed3
Castleacre 15,16&17Ric2

NORTHANTS

Wendlingbrig M 2John
Burgo F 2John
Rowol MF 5John
Kenton M 5John
Adumlinger F 9John
Trapeston M 6John
Rowell M 9John
Braclee M 2Hen3
Rawell M 4Hen3
Wardun M 4Hen3
Fyndon MF 45Hen3
Torpell MF 48Hen3
Peterburgh F 52Hen3
Undle F 52Hen3
Bricklesworth MF 53Hen3
Aldrington MF 6Ed1
Bernewell MF 6Ed1
Buckeley MF 8Ed1
Burkeby MF 9Ed1
Westhaddon MF 20Ed1
Bolewyk MF 22Ed1
Northburgh MF 23Ed1
Sibertoste MF 28Ed1
Higham MF 28Ed1
Milton MF 33Ed1
Tychmersh MF 33Ed1
Northholme juxta
Eye MF 34Ed1
Fodringey MF 2Ed2
Yardeley MF 8Ed2
Corby MF 9Ed2
Tonewstr' F 12Ed2
Heytildesham F 13Ed2
Ayngho MF 4Ed3
Flore MF 7Ed3
Northampton Villa 11Ed3
Ford Castr' MF 14Ed3
Bernwell MF 23Ed3
Buckton F 25/26/27Ed3
Weldon F 30Ed3
Coleworth MF 47/48/49/50/51Ed3
Haringworth Castr. MF 9/10Ric2
Loffwyke MF 9/10Ric2
Fodringhay M 27to39Hen6

Briggstoke Villa MF 5/6/7Ed4
Grafton Widvile MF 5/6/7Ed4

NORTHUMBERLAND

Wulloer M 1John
Felton MF 1John
Newbigging MF 5John
Roderham F 9John
Anyemue 9John
Morpathe MF 1John
Bowelton M 10Hen3
Ellesden MF 9Ed1
Morpath F 13Ed1
Wilton MF 18Ed1
Newton Werecorth MF 10Ed1
Alnewyke MF 25Ed1
Tynnemouth F 32Ed1
Bolum MF 33Ed1
Bareweford MF 33Ed1
Hantswisill in Tyndale MF 35Ed1
Torpell MF 2Ed2
Newbigging MF 3Ed2
Heyndenbridge MF 17Ed2
Werke MF 7Ed3
Ford MF 36Ed3

NOTTINGHAMSHIRE

Bolestoure M 10Hen3
Coleston basset MF 12Ed1
Wirkesope MF 24Ed1
Sutton sup. Trent MF 2Ed2
Eppreston MF 4Ed2
Retford F 7Ed2
Bingham MF 8Ed2
Cokeney MF 10Ed2
Estbrigford MF 1Ed3
Sutton super Trent MF 2Ed3
Northcarlton MF 2Ed3
Newerk MF 3Ed3
Whatton MF 12Ed3
Werkesope MF 24Ed3
Estbridggford MF 34&35Ed3
Rettford F 46Ed3
Mansfield F 1Ric2
Nottingham F 1Ric2
Newerk F 2Ric2
Luda F 2Ric2
Slafford M 2Ric2
Edenstowe F 4Ric2
Matersley MF 3&4Hen4
Sherwode M2F 10,11,12Hen4
Warsope MF 10,11,12Hen4
Mernham Chaworth MF 1to24Hen6

OXFORD

Norton F 6John
Wudstock M 6John
Wudstock M 9John
Howarowell F 16John
Edlingbury M 2Hen3
Rollendrith MF 53Hen3
Burencester F 53Hen3
Middelington MF 22Ed1
Watlington M 31Ed1
Stratton Audele MF 12Ed2
Boreford F 16Ed2
Church Hull MF 1Ed3
Drayton F 3Ed3
Dunstone F 3Ed3
Bannebury MF 3Ed3
Chepingnorton F 4Ed3
Norton F 5Ed3
Tene MF 29Ed3
Biggenhull in Burcestre MF 17Hen6
Burcester MF 1Ric2
Witteney 2F 2Hen3
Henle sup. Thames M2F 1to24Hen6
Hoggnorton MF 1to24Hen6
Eynesham MF 1to24Hen6

Chorlebury M 1to24Hen6

RUTLAND
Uppingham MF 9Ed1
Market Overton MF 9Ed2
Empingham MF 12Ed2
Belton MF 4Ed3
Belton MF 6Ed3
Berghdon MF 23Ed3
Burle Villa F 47,48,49,50& 51Ed3

SHROPSHIRE
Clune F 6John
Castle Richard MF 18John
Norton F 6John
Wemme MF 7John
Hales MF 4Hen3
Ellesmere M 5Hen3
Clebury F 10Hen3
Strettundale M 37Hen3
Welinton MF 11Ed1
Abburbury MF 12Ed1
Chastell Holegod MF 19Ed1
Cheswarthin MF 32Ed1
Whitstanton MF 34Ed1
Prez M 36Ed1
Salop Villa F 2Ed2
Suffenhale MF 9Ed2
Aderley MF 9Ed2
Chetewynde MF 13Ed2
Leye in Botewode M 13Ed2
Salop burg F 1Ed3
Lodelowe MF 2Ed3
Tressell MF 5Ed3
Stepelton MF 8Ed3
Cherthstretton MF 11Ed3
Hales Owenne MF 18Ed3
Brugenorth F 33Ed3
Whitchurch F 36Ed3
Acton Burnell MF 38Ed3
Presse MF 11,12,13Ric2
Chastell MF 18&19Ric2
Wenlock MF 5,6,7Ed4
Shuffenale M2F 11,12,13Ed4
Rushbur MF 11Ed1
Whethull MF 28Ed1
Albrighton MF 31Ed1

SOMERSET
Brigewater MF 2John
Northcury M 7John
Wiccleford M 8John
Bath and Glaston MF 16John
Brigewater M 5Hen3
Asshele MF 5Ed1
Axbrug F 7Ed1
Stratton MF 10Ed1
Rode MF 11Ed1
Glaston MF 11Ed1
Burnham F 13Ed1
Winelescumb MF 13Ed1
Heselbere MF 14Ed1
Compton juxta Dunden MF 17Ed1
Hanse M 18Ed1
Lydyed MF 19Ed1
Cherleton Camuill MF 22Ed1
Norton F 22Ed1
Kelne MF 24Ed1
Netherwere MF 26Ed1
Hacche MF 29Ed1
Coclinton MF 32Ed1
Staweye MF 32Ed1
Bradewey MF 32Ed1
Saunford Bret MF 34Ed1
Dilnton MF 34Ed1
Shipman MF 2Ed2
Yerlington MF 8Ed2
Chedesey MF 8Ed2

Thurlebere F 8Ed2
Ayshull MF 10Ed2
Ayshull MF 16Ric2
Backwell M 11Ed2
Shepton Malett MF 11Ed2
Netherpederton MF 12Ed2
Bekington MF 12Ed2
Ubbele MF 12Ed2
Somiton F 14Ed2
Corymallet MF 16Ed2
Weston MF 6Ed3
Dichesgate MF 6Ed3
Wrynton MF 6Ed3
Welles MF 8Ed3
Wedmore MF 11Ed3
Norton M 17Ed3
Norton MF 19Ed3
Kingesbrampton MF 22Ed3
Chienton MF 22Ed3
Brente F 25/26/27Ed3
Wrokeshalle MF 36Ed3
Porlock MF 39/40Ed3
Bethon 2M 43/44/45Ed3
Mulburn Villa MF 21/22/23Ric2
Mulburne Burg MF 21/22/23Ric2
Westharptre MF 2Hen5
Waltelegh F 1to21&24Hen6
Southpederton F 25/26Hen6
Castelcary MF 8/9/10Ed4
Keynesham MF 31Ed1
Berton F 9Ed3

STAFFS
Stafford F 16John
Wallesall MF 4Hen3
Kinefare M 5Hen3
Bromlegh MF 5Hen3
Aston MF 20Ed1
Draicote MF 25Ed1
Yayhale MF 28Ed1
Melewith MF 32Ed1
Swynerton MF 34Ed1
Uttohantr' MF 2Ed2
Makelston MF 3Ed2
Pencrich F 6Ed2
Palingeham MF 10Ed2
Offyle MF 1Ed3
Harlaston MF 2Ed3
Faresley MF 9Ed3
Newcastle F 10Ed3
Lichefeld MF 11Ed3
Maddeley MF 15Ed3
Pencrich MF 38Ed3
Witton F 4Ric2
Alresford F 4Ric2
Lichfeld MF 11,12,13Ric2
Heiwode MF 11,12,13Ric2
Langedon MF 11,12,13Ric2
Ruggell MF 11,12,13Ric2
Kannochbyry MF 11,12,13Ric2
Brewode MF 11,12,13Ric2
Berewick MF 11,12,13Ric2
Eccleshale MF 11,12,13Ric2
Lichfeld F 11,12,13Ric2
Draiton Besset MF 21,22,23Ric2
Faresley MF 21,22,23Ric2
Walshale MF 21,22,23Ric2
Stafford MF 13&14Hen4
Walshale MF 5Hen5
Newcastle F 1to24Hen6
Roucester MF 1to21&24Hen6
Esseleghe M 4Hen3
Lichfeld F 35Ed1

SUFFOLK
Beggler F 7John
Lawford MF 9John
Estrindham F 16John

Bunge F 1John
Wintringham M 1John
Lakingheth M 3John
Redgrave MF 4Hen3
Debeham M 5Hen3
Tuwand MF 5Hen3
Stradbrock M 10Hen3
Welle MF 8Ed1
Mendlesham MF 9Ed1
Baudressey MF 11Ed1
Britewell F 13Ed1
Grundesburg MF 13Ed1
Walcton MF 17Ed1
Levenham F 18Ed1
Thurstenston MF 18Ed1
Benhole MF 20Ed1
Ketelbergh MF 20Ed1
Noun MF 21Ed1
Carleton MF 23Ed1
Letheringham F 25Ed1
Sagam Baire MF 31Ed1
Stoke Atteneylund MF 31Ed1
Shottele MF 31Ed1
Clopton MF 32Ed1
Leistoft MF 2Ed2
Coue F 3Ed2
Stradbroke F 3Ed2
Reydon MF 4Ed2
Saxmondham MF 4Ed2
Leyston MF 6Ed2
Saham MF 7Ed2
Leysson F 9Ed2
Blyburgh MF 17Ed2
Erlestanham MF 1Ed3
Blyburg MF 4Ed3
Melford MF 4Ed3
Eston Bavent MF 4Ed3
Stowmkett MF 12Ed3
Claxston MF 14Ed3
Blyburgh MF 14Ed3
Winterton MF 19Ed3
Stowmarkett MF 21Ed3
Westhorp MF 46Ed3
Jxworth Villa MF 7/8Ric2
Bury St Edmunds F 6/7Hen4
Mildenhall MF 13/14Hen4
Wodebridge MF 25/26Hen6
Layfeld MF 11/12/13/14Ed4
Stoke MF 15to22Ed4
Lakingheth M 2John
Sutherton M 10Hen3
Muleton M 26Ed1
Houton M 35Ed1
Wodebrige MF 16Ed3
Leiston M 14Ric2

SURREY

Lamtrey MF 1John
Lambhith F 1John
Karenton F 1John
Ripele F 4Hen3
Rocham MF 27/28Hen3
Croydon MF 5Ed1
Ceres MF 10Ed1
Belchingley F 11Ed1
Ockeley MF 31Ed1
Wodington F 31Ed1
Drakehull mons. juxta
Guilford F 2Ed2
Shire MF 3Ed2
Reygate M 6Ed2
Croydon MF 8Ed2
Ledrede MF 5Ed3
Wanton MF 7Ed3
Merstham MF 12Ed3
Corby MF 20Ed3
Guilford MF 20Ed3
Haselmore MF 15/16/17Ric2
Godalming MF 15/16/17Ric2

Chidingford MF 15/16/17Ric2
Certesley F 1to24Hen6
Suthwerk F 1to24Hen6
Betesworth F 27to29Hen6
Fernham M 17John

SUSSEX

Pagham MF 5John
Cicestre F 6John
Soreham MF 6John
Shorham F 3John
Boscham M 2Hen3
Raculf M 4Hen3
Huckfeld M 4Hen3
Rokeland MF 10Hen3
Preston MF 10Hen3
Westgrensted MF 8Ed1
Arundell F 13Ed1
Cocking MF 13Ed1
Grensted MF 13Ed1
Ferrenthe MF 25Ed1
Gatinges MF 29Ed1
Wapham MF 32Ed1
Preston MF 1Ed2
Brightelmeston MF 6Ed2
Cukefeld MF 6Ed2
Dicheningh MF 6Ed2
Hurst F 6Ed2
Westmeston F 6Ed2
Porteslade F 6Ed2
Bradwater MF 6Ed2
Pageham MF 8Ed2
Estlenete F 8Ed2
Tanghemore MF 8Ed2
Slyndon MF 8Ed2
Manfeld MF 8Ed2
Lambherst MF 8Ed2
Fremefeild F 8Ed2
Watersyde MF 9Ed2
Hethfylde MF 9Ed2
Bourne MF 9Ed2
Brembre MF 10Ed2
Rokeland MF 19Ed2
Rogate MF 20Ed2
Clyne juxta Stonham MF 5Ed3
Brembre MF 6Ed3
Wrotling MF 11Ed3
Bocstape F 11Ed3
Dalinton F 11Ed3
Lindefeld MF 17Ed3
Bradwater MF 47/48/49/50/51Ed3
Ukkefeld F 2Ric2
Rogate MF 1Ric2
Bodiham MF 5/6Ric2
Estangm'ing MF 7&8Ric2
Bradewater F 11/12/13Ric2
Maghfeld MF 15,16,17Ric2
Alfrisheton MF 6&7Hen4
Rye Villa M 6&7Hen4
Clyve Villa M2F 10/11/12Hen4
Clyve MF 10/11/12Hen4
Feringe M 1to24Hen6
Horsham MF 27to39Hen6
Egeden MF 8Ed1
Pevense F 7Ed2
Rotherfeld F 12Ed2
Clivejuxta Lewes MF 19Ed3
Stratford MF 7&8Ric2
Storghton M 3F 1Hen4

WARWICK

Coleshull MF 9John
Brinkelaw M 2Hen3
Budeford M 4Hen3
Haule MF 5Hen3
Ekeshall M 5Hen3
Eton M 10Hen3

Cumpton MF 15Hen3
Warrewick F 18Ed1
Bydiford MF 19Ed1
Alecester F 21Ed1
Sutton MF 28Ed1
Filungley MF 29Ed1
Alcestr F 31Ed1
Thestrewaure MF 33Ed1
Wolseye MF 33Ed1
Newenham Parva MF 33Ed1
Kerkely MF 33Ed1
Neubolt MF 33Ed1
Paunton MF 33Ed1
Herdebergh MF 33Ed1
Walton MF 33Ed1
Weyley MF 33Ed1
Astath MF 12Ed2
Alcester F 13Ed2
Sullyhull MF 13Ed2
Napton MF 15Ed2
Snyttenfeld MF 17Ed2
Wolinge MF 19Ed2
Hullemorton MF 8Ed3
Tamworth MF 10Ed3
Tysho MF 15Ed3
Sutton in Colefeld MF 25,26,27Ed3
Jchenton MF 11,12,13Ric2
Stratford MF 14Ric2
Warwick F 1Hen5
Coventre F 1to24Hen6
Alcester MF 25&26Hen6
Kinton M 4Hen3
Stratford Sup. Avene. MF 2Ed2

WESTMORLAND

Barton MF 16John
Brugys MF 2John
Barton M 16John
Overton MF 6Ed1
Kirkeby in Kendale MF 3Ed2
Bethum MF 4Ed2
Burgh MF 4Ed3
Kerkeby MF 7Ed3
Heversham MF 8Ed3
Stavele in Kendale MF 2Ed3
Kerkeby Stephan MF 25,26,27Ed3
Morland MF 36Ed3

WILTS

Chippenham MF 6John
Hethtredbir MF 16John
Devizes F 9John
Hechtredbury M 16John
Melkesham M 3Hen3
Knoll M 3Hen3
Cardestok M 3Hen3
Rammesbery M 3Hen3
Brinford MF 4Hen3
Salisbury F 5Hen3
Wilcot M 5Hen3
Poulton MF 48Hen3
Rusleshale F 13Ed1
Cosham M 13Ed1
Westbury MF 19Ed1
Westbury MF 25Ed1
Withford MF 26Ed1
Sutton Magna MF 27Ed1
Remesbury M 28Ed1
Helm'ton F 28Ed1
Abradmere M 31Ed1
Calne MF 31Ed1
Chippenham F 4Ed2
Chipham F 6Ed2
Chippenham MF 8Ed2
Castelcomb MF 9Ed2
Colorne MF 9Ed2
Heghtredbury MF 9Ed2
Ambresbury MF 10Ed2
Littleton MF 12Ed2

Chippenham MF 13Ed2
Up Avene F 17Ed2
Hynedon F 5Ed2
Merton M 6Ed3
Grafton MF 21Ed3
Holte MF 22Ed3
Colingburn MF 25,26,27Ed3
Bradenestoke MF 34&35Ed3
Ashton MF 11,12,13Ric2
Devises F 15,16,17Ric2
Sarum F 15,16,17Ric2
Rambery F 15,16,17Ric2
Mere Villa MF 9Hen4
Mere M 9Hen4
Wilton F 2Hen5
Wilton F 3&4Hen5
Haydenbradley M 32Hen3
Ambresbury MF 53Hen3
Westharnham F 1to24Hen6
Warmester F 25&26Hen6
Colerne MF 25&26Hen6
Westbury Villa MF 27to39Hen6
Westbury MF 27to39Hen6

WORCS

Bromegrave M 1John
Norton F 2John
Carlton F 2John
Grimston F 2John
Feckenham M 37Hen3
Bloctell MF 14Ed1
Severnestoke MF 3Ed2
Bymmesgrave MF 11Ed2
Rookes MF 2Ed3
Ambreslay MF 28Ed3
Beaulien MF 47/48/49/50/51Ed3
Holt F 47/48/49/50/51Ed3
Bloklegh F 14Ric2
Aluithlechirch MF 14Ric2
Evesham MF 1to24Hen6
Beaudley MF 25/26Hen6
Lilborne M 3Hen3

YORKS

Harewod MF 10John
Bingley M 14John
Ertepocle MF 3John
B'ngell M 14John
Rodenham F 9John
Batr. F 15John
Wiltun M 2Hen3
Lith MF 4Hen3
Alingflet M 4Hen3
Fyfley M 5Hen3
Wike sup. le Hulle MF 7Ed1
Richmond F 7Ed1
Pikeringe MF 9Ed1
Handeburg MF 9Ed1
Whernelton MF 9Ed1
Whernelton MF 9Ed1
Neweton sup. Use MF 10Ed1
Brandesborton MF 14Ed1
Braithwell MF 17Ed1
Peningshalt MF 18Ed1
Tollerton MF 19Ed1
Suthcave MF 19Ed1
Pickering Esingwald F 19Ed1
Bringenhale MF 20Ed1
Cliffe MF 20Ed1
Depontefracto MF 22Ed1
Bradeford MF 22Ed1
Camsale MF 22Ed1
Slaghteborne MF 22Ed1
Almanbir MF 22Ed1
Duffeld MF 22Ed1
Baltrey M 22Ed1
Hemmygburgh MF 23Ed1
Sheffeld MF 24Ed1
Pokelington MF 27Ed1

Kornetby MF 27Ed1
Skipton in Craven MF 28Ed1
Hedon F 28Ed1
Holme MF 29Ed1
Fayeflete MF 29Ed1
Tuierington MF 31Ed1
Osgodby MF 31Ed1
Sledmere MF 31Ed1
Poklington MF 31Ed1
Synelinton MF 32Ed1
Panchale juxta Sideford MF 32Ed1
Wandesford MF 32Ed1
Louthorp MF 32Ed1
Keighlay MF 33Ed1
Swinflet MF 33Ed1
Pykehall MF 35Ed1
Worteley MF 35Ed1
Roderham MF 35Ed1
Burton in Lovesdale MF 35Ed1
Aberford MF 35Ed1
Penyngesale MF 1Ed2
Roderham MF 2Ed2
Boghes MF 3Ed2
Thomor MF 4Ed2
Appeltrewick F 4Ed2
Crauncewik MF 4Ed2
Patrington MF 4Ed2
Wighton juxta Beverlacum MF 5Ed2
Wath MF 6Ed2
Suthcave MF 7Ed2
Duffeld F 7Ed2
Warke M 7Ed2
Singlesthorn F 8Ed2
Roderham MF 9Ed2
Bland MF 10Ed2
Wendeslegh MF 11Ed2
Dryffeld Magna MF 12Ed2
Cottingham MF 12Ed2
Patheley Brig MF 13Ed2
Skeleton MF 13Ed2
Borton Constable MF 15Ed2
Topcliff sup. Swale MF 1Ed3
Massham MF 2Ed3
Bedale MF 2Ed3
Applekewike F 2Ed3
Wakefield F 5Ed3
Aldeburgh MF 6Ed3
Killum MF 8Ed3
Abreford MF 9Ed3
Kerkeby MF 9Ed3
Wherlneton MF 11Ed3
Whythyrnesse MF 12Ed3
Buttet Ram MF 17Ed3
Wilm'sley MF 20Ed3
Staynford MF 21Ed3
North Newbald MF 22Ed3
Rikhall MF 24Ed3
Sheffeld MF 24Ed3
Buttercramb MF 25/26/27Ed3
Cukewald MF 28Ed3
Riplay MF 31Ed3
Hornesse F 32Ed3
Tollerton MF 32Ed3
Duffeld MF 37Ed3
Kirkborne MF 43/44/45Ed3
Shireveton MF 1Ric2
Lekingfeld MF 5/6Ric2
Semir MF 5/6Ric2
Middleham MF 11/12/13Ric2
Masseham MF 15/16/17Ric2
Honedon F 15/16/17Ric2
Bridelington F 15/16/17Ric2
Bradeford MF 21/22/23Ric2
Estwitton MF 1Hen4
Pontefreit M2F 9Hen4
Wighton MF 27to39Hen6
Donecaster F 5/6/7Ed4
Hornsee M 41Hen3
Bradford MF 15to22Ed4

Cottingham M 1John
Doncaster F 1John
Buttrecombe MF 1John
Cottingham F 1John
Annerton F 1John
Hovedon F 1John
Fakeham F 2John
Bridlington MF 2John
Wakefield F 5John
Skipton F 5John
Gersington MF 9Ed1
Eskelby MF 28Ed1
Cokewald MF 32Ed1
Stodley MF 18Ed3

Alphabetical List of places without counties designated

Abberford MF 33Hen3
Abberford MF 35Hen3
Abiton MF 41Hen3
Acton MF 54Hen3
Acton Burnell MF 54Hen3
Adingflet MF 44Hen3
Adnere MF 28Hen3
Aete F 41Hen3
Albomonaster F 36Hen3
Albo Monasterio F 37Hen3
Albrichton MF 16Hen3
Album Monasterium F 12Hen3
Album Monaster' MF 53Hen3
Aldringham MF 18Ed1
Aldringham F 12Ed2
Alebroke M2F 51Hen3
Alfinton MF 56Hen3
Alindechurch MF 24Hen3
Almchecherch M 8Hen3
Almethchurch MF 51Hen3
Alnedale M 32Hen3
Alnemuthe MF 37Hen3
Alneton MF 49Hen3
Aloynton MF 52Hen3
Altoworth F 41Hen3
Alureton MF 36Hen3
Alverichseye MF 54Hen3
Amethull MF 26Hen3
Ammesbery M 11Hen3
Andeby MF 55Hen3
Andeford MF 37&38Hen3
Andredelegh MF 37&38Hen3
Angr F 14Hen3
Annesburton MF 41Hen3
Apeldorefeld MF 37&38Hen3
Appelby MF 51Hen3
Ardeslegh MF 9Hen3
Arnham MF 56Hen3
Ars Boys MF 11Hen3
Ashby F 56Hen3
Asheford MF 27,28Hen3
Aslaketon MF 55Hen3
Aspele MF 51Hen3
Assuvens' Civitas & Villa MF 3Ric2
Athethm MF 30Hen3
Aton MF 37Hen3
Attingham F 53Hen3
Attleburgh MF 10Hen3
Aufridecumbe MF 17Hen3
Avenemul M 9John
Averberg M 6Hen3
Axbrugge F 23Hen3
Axesbiry F 23Hen3
Ayston F 37Hen3

Bacwell MF 54Hen3
Badburnham M 18Ed3
Badelingham MF 37&38Hen3
Bagewortche MF 54Hen3
Baion' F 21Hen3
Baldoc M 1John

Baldoc F 10Hen3
Baldock M 11Hen3
Balesham MF 29Hen3
Bampton MF 25Hen3
Bampton MF 39Hen3
Bancwell F 37&38Hen3
Banuton M2F 51Hen3
Bardney M 16Hen3
Barewe MF 5John
Barewe MF 51Hen3
Barking M 10Hen3
Barnstaple MF 23Ed1
Barton MF 30Hen3
Barton super Humber F 30Hen3
Bassingburn MF 37Hen3
Baston MF 41Hen3
Baumburgh MF 44Hen3
Baunton F 42Hen3
Baunton F 52Hen3
Beaudesort MF 11Hen3
Beccles F 44Hen3
Bedall MF 35Hen3
Bekeneffeld F 2Hen5
Beknesfeld M 39Hen3
Belesale M2F 52Hen3
Belton MF 28Hen3
Belton MF 51Hen3
Belver MF 45Hen3
Berchamsted F 26Hen3
Berden F 6Hen3
Bere MF 16Hen3
Bere MF 20Hen3
Bere MF 51Hen3
Bereden F 51Hen3
Beretre F 30Hen3
Berewic M 15Hen3
Berewick MF 43Hen3
Berewod MF 43Hen3
Berghstede F 8,9,10Ed4
Berghton MF 31Hen3
Berkhamsted M 2Hen3
Berkhamsted M 3Hen3
Berking F 10Hen3
Berkweye MF 54Hen3
Berling MF 51Hen3
Bermdeset MF 43Hen3
Bernesleya MF 33Hen3
Bernewell F 12Hen3
Bernwell MF 51Hen3
Berton MF 25Hen3
Berton F 32Ed1
Bery F 51Hen3
Beteleg MF 4Hen3
Bettelegh MF 11Hen3
Bewyk M 53Hen3
Bickenoure M 2John
Bideford MF 56Hen3
Binington M 39Hen3
Bissey MF 54Hen3
Blackmore F 16Hen3
Blacktoriton F 3Hen3
Blakebergh F 28Hen3
Blandford M 2Hen3
Blockell F 8Hen3
Bloelege F 54Hen3
Bocland F 24Hen3
Bocland MF 42Hen3
Bocland Bruere MF 18Ed1
Boisars M 5Hen3
Bolynges MF 55Hen3
Bony MF 44Hen3
Bosco Arso M 36Hen3
Bosworth M 8Hen3
Boswythy MF 6Ed2
Botlesford MF 55Hen3
Botolf F 2Hen3
Bottele MF 51Hen3
Bouche MF 1to24Hen6
Boughes MF 18Ed3
Boulton MF 36Hen3

Bouy M 11Hen3
Bowes MF 26Hen3
Box MF 53Hen3
Boxgrave F 19Hen3
Brackele M 3Hen3
Braclee M 2Hen3
Brancheshey F 14Hen3
Bradenstok F 16Hen3
Bradnesse MF 23Hen3
Bradwell MF 37&38Hen3
Brampton MF 36Hen3
Brampton MF 55Hen3
Brandeslegh F 17Hen3
Brandon 11Hen3
Brandon MF 55Hen3
Brasford M 35Hen3
Brassingburgh MF 55Hen3
Braunton F 37Hen3
Brayle MF 32Hen3
Bren MF 37&38Hen3
Bretford M 11Hen3
Brickhul MF 12Hen3
Brickhull MF 41Hen3
Bridlington MF 2John
Brie M 15John
Brigenhale MF 49Hen3
Brincklaw M 24Hen3
Brinkel MF 37&38Hen3
Bristol F 1John
Bristoll F 39Hen3
Briwud M 5Hen3
Brodchembr MF 18Ed1
Brohton MF 29Hen3
Bromholm F 13Hen3
Bromholme M 9Hen3
Bromholme F 10Hen3
Bromhull F 8Hen3
Bromleg MF 11Hen3
Bromyard F 2Hen3
Brorat MF 35Hen3
Bruer MF 43Hen3
Bruges F 10Hen3
Brumesgrave M 34Hen3
Brumfield MF 54Hen3
Brumley M 7John
Brumpton MF 37Hen3
Brundall F 37&38Hen3
Brunfeld M 5John
Brunkell MF 45Hen3
Brunton M 6Hen3
Budiford M 10Ed1
Buidiford MF 37Hen3
Bulewarheth MF 3Ed2
Bumacy MF 37Hen3
Bungey M 7&8Ric2
Bunham MF 10Hen3
Bureford MF 51Hen3
Bures MF 55Hen3
Burg MF 56Hen3
Burg' super Humbr. MF 23Hen3
Burgate MF 56Hen3
Burghersh MF 3Ed2
Burghsted Mag. MF 37Hen3
Burgus M 10Hen3
Burn F 16Hen3
Burnathorp F 7Hen3
Burnham MF 37&38Hen3
Burstow MF 31Hen3
Burton in le Cley MF 56Hen3
Button M 15Hen3
Buttun M 5Hen3
Bynebroc MF 19Hen3

Calon M 11Hen3
Calweton MF 52Hen3
Cambok MF 37&38Hen3
Cambridge F 1to24Hen6
Camelford MF 44Hen3
Camelton M 13Hen3

Campden F 2Hen3
Campden F 3Hen3
Campen MF 31Hen3
Candlesby MF 15Ed3
Cannell MF 48Hen3
Cardstok M 11Hen3
Carhou F 7John
Carhoue F 56Hen3
Carleton MF 51Hen3
Cassingeland MF 35Hen3
Castelholgod M 37&38Hen3
Cateby F 33Hen3
Catesby F 33Hen3
Catteby M 31Hen3
Causton F 48Hen3
Caxton M 32Hen3
Cedder MF 37&38Hen3
Certeleg MF 5Hen3
Certesey F 33Hen3
Cestrchunt MF 26Hen3
Cestresham MF 41Hen3
Cettre MF 41Hen3
Chanebolton MF 1John
Chanunlegh MF 37&38Hen3
Chatton MF 37Hen3
Chedder M 11Hen3
Chelebir F 36Hen3
Chennevor MF 30Hen3
Cheping Taunton MF 55Hen3
Cherl MF 55Hen3
Cherl MF 35Hen3
Cherleton MF 53Hen3
Chiltham MF 10Hen3
Chipenham M 10Hen3
Chipinghamburne F 11Hen3
Chiping Lamburn F 11Hen3
Chippeham F 51Hen3
Chircheden F 36Hen3
Chitham MF 7Hen3
Chornever MF 26Hen3
Christechirch F 42Hen3
Cinhtiton F 14Hen3
Claithorp MF 37Hen3
Clare MF 35Hen3
Clarir MF 37Hen3
Clavering MF 1Ric2
Clay MF 53Hen3
Clebury F 10Hen3
Clent F 37&38Hen3
Clere F 11Hen3
Clif MF 49Hen3
Cliffe MF 20Ed1
Clifford MF 45Hen3
Clifton MF 54Hen3
Clumel F 9Hen3
Cluna F 37Hen3
Clunmor MF 14Hen3
Clyve MF 41Hen3
Codeford Magna M 37&38Hen3
Codicot M 52Hen3
Cokefeld MF 39Hen3
Cokermue M 11Hen3
Cokermuth M 6Hen3
Coldingham MF 33Ed1
Colecester F 52Hen3
Coleward MF 48Hen3
Colf Ely MF 18Ed1
Colton M 25Hen3
Congleton MF 10Ed1
Corby MF 23Hen3
Corney MF 37Hen3
Corslegh MF 16Hen3
Corslegh MF 19Hen3
Cotenham MF 49Hen3
Cotum MF 41Hen3
Couern MF 39Hen3
Coventre F 3Hen3
Coventre F 11Hen3
Coventry F 2Hen3
Coventry F 11Hen3

Cramlington MF 54Hen3
Cranden M 3Hen3
Crandun M 2Hen3
Craule MF 56Hen3
Crawcombe MF 11Hen3
Crawcombe MF 14Hen3
Crekelad F 41Hen3
Crich MF 53Hen3
Criditon MF 15Hen3
Crokeston MF 54Hen3
Crofte MF 27Ed1
Croxton MF 13Hen3
Cruchampton M 7Hen3
Crude M 37&38Hen3
Cubbelegh MF 39Hen3
Cudicote F 56Hen3
Culing F 9Hen3
Culing F 11Hen3
Culinton F 9John
Culmeton MF 42Hen3
Culminton MF 41Hen3
Cumbermere MF 49Hen3
Cumbwell F 11Hen3
Cumbwell M 16Hen3
Cuningbery M 2John
Cyrencestre F 10Hen4

Dalton in Furneis F 23Hen3
Dalton in Furneis F 30Hen3
Debeham MF 6Hen3
Debenham MF 6Hen3
Deneham MF 11Hen3
Dennlys MF 48Hen3
De Pecco M 7Hen3
Dertmuth MF 15Hen3
Devises F 7Hen3
Ditton MF 55Hen3
Docking MF 52Hen3
Dodebroke MF 41Hen3
Donynton MF 37Hen3
Dorcestr' Magna MF 51Hen3
Dorevald MF 30Hen3
Draiton MF 30Hen3
Drencheston MF 51Hen3
Dublyn F 36Hen3
Duffeld MF 53Hen3
Dundall F 14Hen3
Dunham M 2John
Dunington MF 39Hen3
Dunnawe MF 11Hen3
Dunmowe MF 37&38Hen3
Dunstable M 11Hen3
Dunster er Watchet M 7Hen3
Durecurt M 7Hen3
Durles F 7Hen3
Dymmoc MF 6Hen3

Eadwardeston M 25Hen3
Eccleshall MF 43Hen3
Edredeston MF 31Hen3
Edrethston F 30Hen3
Egeton MF 53Hen3
Egremunt MF 51Hen3
Eismanhawe F 10Hen3
Eleford MF 23Hen3
Elimested MF 37Hen3
Elkesdon M 36Hen3
Ellesford MF 37&38Hen3
Elmele MF 37&38Hen3
Elsing MF 3Ric2
Ely M 8Hen3
Emeldon MF 42Hen3
Emelesworth MF 23Hen3
Enemere Villa MF 2Hen4
Enesfeld F 37&38Hen3
Enmeley MF 37Hen3
Eppeworth MF 5&6Ric2
Epping MF 37Hen3
Ercalewe MF 51Hen3
Esingwolde M5Hen3

Esseby MF 11Hen3
Estbanes F 7Hen3
Estdeeping MF 2Ed2
Estisted F 54Hen3
Eston MF 41Hen3
Eston Boterell MF 48Hen3
Estrye F 25&26Hen6
Estwesterham M 11Hen3
Estwilton MF 35Ed1
Estwyk MF 37Hen3
Ethen M 17Hen3
Ethone F 27to39Hen6
Eton M 11Hen3
Eton F 23Hen3
Etyndon MF 42Hen3
Eversett MF 14Ed1
Eygtham MF 9Ed2
Eyton MF 35Hen3

Fakynton MF 41Hen3
Falesham MF 52Hen3
Falewest M 8Hen3
Farendon F 11Hen3
Favilla F 2John
Fecham F 28Hen3
Fekenham MF 34Hen3
Ferendon M 2Hen3
Ferendon M 3Hen3
Ferendon F 6Hen3
Finell MF 24Hen3
Fiskerton MF 54Hen3
Fleet MF 28Hen3
Fobbing MF 11Hen3
Folkland MF 48Hen3
Framton MF 25,26,27Ed3
Frampton MF 37&38Hen3
Fremingham MF 55Hen3
Freston F 48Hen3
From F 54Hen3
Fromton sup. Severne MF 4Ed2
Fukeston M 6John
Fulemere M 5John

Gannoc MF 34Hen3
Garing MF 41Hen3
Gedeney MF 11Hen3
Gerboldesham MF 56Hen3
Gernard M 23Hen3
Gerolveston F 42Hen3
Gestling F 37&38Hen3
Geynbury F 27&28Hen3
Geyton MF 37&38Hen3
Ginge Atteston MF 17Ed1
Gissing Villa MF 2Ric2
Glanfordbridge MF 20Hen3
Glaybury F 11Hen3
Glen MF 56Hen3
Gmelton F 37&38Hen3
Godalming MF 28Ed1
Gonsell MF 42Hen3
Gravenby MF 36Hen3
Graystok MF 29Hen3
Gremston MF 35Hen3
Grenested MF 31Hen3
Gresham MF 27&28Hen3
Grimston F 37&38Hen3
Gringelay MF 37Hen3
Grunham F 21Ed3
Guilford F 11Hen3
Guilford Ecclia F 9Hen3
Gyseburne MF 45Hen3

Hachetune F 11Hen3
Hadlegh M30Hen3
Haleg M 15Hen3
Hales MF 6Hen3
Halesworth M 7Hen3
Halesworth MF 21Ed1
Halfned M 8Hen3
Halvedon M 41Hen3

Hampford MF 25Hen3
Hampton MF 35Hen3
Hampton Monialium MF 53Hen3
Hanene M2F 46Hen3
Hankesbury MF 37Hen3
Hanlegh M 3Hen3
Hanlegh M 11Hen3
Harolueston F 13Hen3
Haselbere M 52Hen3
Hatfeld M 11Hen3
Havennt'r M 2John
Haylesham M 36Hen3
Hecham F 35Hen3
Hecham MF 56Hen3
Hedicrumbe MF 35Hen3
Hedon F 56Hen3
Hegtredebiry M 7Hen3
Hekeling M 5John
Heleghton M 56Hen3
Helpringham MF 44Hen3
Helton MF 56Hen3
Heltrideberye MF 11Hen3
Hemenhale MF 3Ric2
Hemenale Villa MF 3Ric2
Heminehaule M 10Hen3
Hengham F 49Hen3
Herdildesham F 7Hen3
Hereford F 6Hen3
Hereford F 11Hen3
Hereford F 25Hen3
Herewardstok M 23Hen3
Herewardstoke M 52Hen3
Herewarton MF 37&38Hen3
Herewes MF 45Hen3
Herewyke MF 37Hen3
Herlawe F 5Hen3
Hernested MF 37Hen3
Hertford F 10Hen3
Hertinge MF 55Hen3
Herton F 14Ed1
Heselbergh M 49Hen3
Heselerton M 32Ed1
Heslarton MF 53Hen3
Hetherbridberye M 11Hen3
Hethe F 45Hen3
Hextildesham MF 23Hen3
Heywode MF 36Hen3
Heywud MF 43Hen3
Hicche F 6Hen3
Hildesley M 6Hen3
Hilleland F 41Hen3
Hocham F 33Hen3
Hocham MF 51Hen3
Hocham MF 56Hen3
Hoddesdon MF 53Hen3
Hoggeston F 33Hen3
Hoggeston F 35Hen3
Hoggeston F 37&38Hen3
Holbech MF 37Hen3
Holdich M2F 10,11,12Hen4
Holecumbe MF 45Hen3
Holgod Castrum M 7Hen3
Holowstowe in Berksoure F 19Hen3
Holt F 53Hen3
Hornese M 41Hen3
Horolinston F 44Hen3
Horsham F 17Hen3
Horsley MF 51Hen3
Hoton Paynell MF 37&38Hen3
Hou MF 55Hen3
Hovingham MF 36Hen3
Hoxton M 11Hen3
Huleburge MF 53Hen3
Hull Morton MF 52Hen3
Hulmarton MF 49Hen3
Hulmo MF 36Hen3
Humersfeld F 11Hen3
Hune M 35Hen3
Huneton F 4Hen3
Hunstantane M 9Hen3

Huntingdon F 36Hen3
Huntinton MF 41Hen3
Hunyton F 42Hen3
Hurtendon MF 56Hen3
Huttockeshatre MF 36Hen3
Hydeshall.MF 29Hen3

Ichenton MF 43Hen3
Ikelington M 6Hen3
Ikkeburgh MF 41Hen3
Iklington M 6Hen3
Ilfrichcombe MF 56Hen3
Illecley MF 37Hen3
Illeya Arsa MF 44Hen3
Ilsinton MF 54Hen3
Imelac' MF 28Hen3
Incheslada M 12Hen3
Insowena F 24Hen3
Ipswich F 1John
Irby MF 21Hen3
Ivingho F 9Hen3
Iwern Courtney M2F 45Hen3
Ixnyng MF 42Hen3

Jackell F 10Hen3
Jackell F 11Hen3
Jrneham MF 36Hen3
Jvengo F 11Hen3

Kanokbirc MF 43Hen3
Karesbroke F 41Hen3
Karswell Regis MF 52Hen3
Kaus F 32Hen3
Kedwelly 2M1F 52Hen3
Kelarnny M 23Hen3
Kelmeston MF 37&38Hen3
Kemsing M 3Hen3
Kenefare MF 41Hen3
Kenelworth MF 52Hen3
Kenemerford MF 51Hen3
Kenetbiry M2F 52Hen3
Kenetorf M 23Hen3
Keninghale F 10Hen3
Keresey M 37Hen3
Kernikall F 2John
Kershall 1 John
Kershalton MF 43Hen3
Ketelberg MF 49Hen3
Kibworth M 7Hen3
Kikeham MF 14Ed1
Kilcalgan MF 26Hen3
Kildale MF 37Hen3
Kilkenny F 30Hen3
Killing M 21Ed3
Killum MF 11Hen3
Kilminton MF 41Hen3
Kinemerford MF 27,28Hen3
Kinemersford MF 52Hen3
Kineton MF 14Hen3
Kingesnede Villa F 27to39Hen6
Kings Brompton M 22Ed3
Kinton M 11Hen3
Kirkby MF 45Hen3
Kirkby in Kendal F 52Hen3
Kirkeby F 11Hen3
Kirkeby MF 30Hen3
Knokyn MF 33Hen3
Knol MF 11Hen3
Koneford F 28Ed1
Kurleton F 37&38Hen3

Lacok M 26H3
Lacok M 44H3
Ladnes F 20E1
Lakyngheth MF 3E2
Lamberton F 16H3
Lamburn F 11H3
Laneham MF 41H3
Langedon MF 43H3
Langerugg MF 56H3

Langham M 6H3
Langham M 11H3
Langworth MF 54H3
Lanstaunton M 7J
Lapfield M 10H3
La Pole MF 23H3
Latton MF 41H3
Lavendon MF 33H3
Laycok F 21H3
Ledburnworth MF 33H3
Ledbury North MF 33H3
Lednes MF 29H3
Lee MF 17E3
Leicestre F 13H3
Leke M 9J
Lemenister M 2Hen3
Lenge MF 52Hen3
Lenhall MF 11Hen3
Lenington MF 46Hen3
Lenn F 2Hen3
Lenton F 14Hen3
Leominster M 3Hen3
Lerky MF 19Hen3
Lesnes MF 41Hen3
Lesseby F 19Hen3
Levene MF 55Hen3
Lichfield MF 43Hen3
Lideford MF 54Hen3
Lidell MF 51Hen3
Lidford MF 52Hen3
Lidiford M 11Hen3
Lidum MF 51Hen3
Lilburn M 11Hen3
Lillechurch F 11Hen3
Lincoln M 7Hen3
Lindridge M 20Hen3
Lingercroft F 11Hen3
Lingerscroft F 10Hen3
Linton MF 30Hen3
Lithe MF 37&38Hen3
Lodnes F 49Hen3
Lohfloer M 23Hen3
Lokerie MF 56Hen3
Lostwithiel MF 8Hen3
Lothnwistoft M 1to24Hen6
Lotrache MF 37&38Hen3
Lucteburg MF 11Hen3
Lucteburgh MF 13Hen3
Luctebury MF 11Hen3
Luda F 2Ric2
Luffeld F 14Hen3
Luford MF 36Hen3
Lunt MF 41Hen3
Lutton MF 53Hen3
Lydham M 54Hen3
Lydney MF 53Hen3
Lyme MF 55Hen3
Lyminster M 3Hen3
Lyminton F 41Hen3
Lync elade MF 35Hen3
Lyncumbe F 32Ed1
Maddele MF 53Hen3
Magefeud MF 44Hen3
Malevill M 1John
Malmesbury M 7Hen3
Mammesbury M 36Hen3
Manchester F 6Hen3
Manchester F 11Hen3
Manesfield M 11Hen3
Marblethorp MF 37Hen3
Marlebergh F 20Hen3
Marnham Chaworth MF 41Hen3
Martek M 31Hen3
Masseham MF 35Hen3
Massingham M 49Hen3
Massingham parva MF 56Hen3
Maydenstan F 52Hen3
Maylagham M 30Hen3
Mayperly MF 51Hen3
Meanton Mag. 35Hen3

Melburne F 14Hen3
Melchburne MF 49Hen3
Meleburne MF 30Hen3
Melindresansy F 5&6Ric2
Melkesham MF 34Hen3
Melksham MF 3Hen3
Melleford MF 19Hen3
Mendelshol MF 23Hen3
Menestok MF 31Hen3
Mereworth MF 18Ed1
Merket Overton MF 51Hen3
Merlebergh F 13Hen3
Merston F 32Hen3
Merston M 44Hen3
Merton M 10Hen3
Merton M 11Hen3
Meycolithe MF 13Hen3
Meydinton M 54Hen3
Middleton F 14Hen3
Midsomer Norton F 32Hen3
Mildenhall MF 4Hen3
Millum MF 35Hen3
Modyndon F 37&38Hen3
Monte Acuto F 30Hen3
Moreton MF 55Hen3
Moreton sup. Trent M 37Hen3
Morton M 11Hen3
Morton F 12Hen3
Morton Hinmersh F 53Hen3
Mote MF 51Hen3
Mudgumer M 9Hen3
Mukbston F 37&38Hen3
Muntgaret M 9Hen3
Muntgumery F 8Hen3
Mursle MF 27&28Hen3

Nanesby M 5John
Nas F 10Hen3
Neulond F 13Hen3
Neuton MF 42Hen3
Newbigging MF 43Hen3
Newbigging F 45Hen3
Neweton in Fertelagh F 16Hen3
Newent MF 37Hen3
Newmarket F 7Hen3
Newmarket F 10Hen3
Newmarket F 11Hen3
Newport F 11Hen3
New Salisbury M 8Hen3
Niahus F 1John
Nobir F 11Hen3
Noketon F 41Hen3
Norham F 37Hen3
Normanton M 2Hen3
Northampton F 52Hen3
Northbrug M 11Hen3
Northleg MF 11Hen3
North Multon MF 54Hen3
Northwell F 41Hen3
Norton M 26Hen3
Norton F 37Hen3
Norton F 39Hen3
Novum Burgum M 16John
Nudford F 8Hen3
Nuny MF 44Hen3
Nymeton MF 43Hen3

Ocham M2F 36Hen3
Odeston MF 48Hen3
Offculum M2F 51Hen3
Okeneutone M 4Hen3
Old Sarum M 3Hen3
Omerton M 3Hen3
Ongar F 6Hen3
Orewell MF 37&38Hen3
Orlanston MF 51Hen3
Otery MF 11Hen3
Oterye MF 1Ric2
Ottele F 7Hen3
Ottele MF 23Hen3

Otteley MF 11Hen3
Otteley F 13Ed2
Ottery MF 11Hen3
Overton M 2Hen3
Overton MF 31Hen3
Owesdon MF 37&38Hen3
Oxbrug MF 33Hen3
Oxeburg MF 33Hen3
Oxney F 33Hen3

Parrok MF 53Hen3
Parrok MF 52Hen3
Paterinton M 11Hen3
Patrinton M 7Hen3
Pecco M 30Hen3
Penbrigg MF 23Hen3
Pencriz M 28Hen3
Pendrun MF 21Hen3
Penryn F 5Ed2
Perers MF 24Ed1
Pereton MF 15John
Pereton F 36Hen3
Persere M 11Hen3
Persore F 10Hen3
Persore F 11Hen3
Petresore MF 37Hen3
Petresfeld 2F 39Hen3
Petrisfeld M 45Hen3
Plimton M 7John
Plumsted M 51Hen3
Pokelington F 29Hen3
Poklinton F 56Hen3
Pollesworth MF 26Hen3
Pons Roberti MF 9Hen3
Ponte Belli MF 27/28Hen3
Popeshall MF 36Hen3
Popleford MF 37/38Hen3
Porcestr M 9Hen3
Portbury MF 22Ed3
Portesmew M 2John
Porthenesse MF 51Hen3
Pottone F 11Hen3
Poulet F 41Hen3
Precs MF 43Hen3
Prestbury MF 33Hen3
Preston F 11Hen3
Preston Canonicorum MF 37Hen3
Pritellwell MF 41Hen3
Pulrebache MF 37&38Hen3
Pulteney MF 48Hen3

Quadlod MF 39Hen3

Rachedall MF 35Hen3
Radnore F 34Ed1
Rakenford MF 19Hen3
Rammesbury MF 24Hen3
Ramsey MF 51Hen3
Rasen M 3Hen3
Ravenserot MF 35Hen3
Redcote MF 56Hen3
Redepethe MF 51Hen3
Redgrave MF 11Hen3
Relkington MF 49Hen3
Rengles F 10John
Repinghale MF 52Hen3
Resketon M2F 51Hen3
Retford F 44Hen3
Reyndon MF 41Hen3
Reynham MF 54Hen3
Ringmere MF 11Ed1
Ringwode M 10Hen3
Rippelegh MF 36Hen3
Robery M 7Hen3
Rochford MF 41Hen3
Rochford M2F 48Hen3
Rod F 37&38Hen3
Roenge MF 39Hen3
Rogate F 52Hen3

Roing M 5Hen3
Rokeby MF 39Hen3
Rokelaund MF 35Hen3
Rokingham F 7Hen3
Rokingham M 56Hen3
Romesey F 56Hen3
Ros M 2Hen3
Ros MF 25Hen3
Rothinges Alba MF 53Hen3
Rothwell MF 9Hen4
Rotour F 11Hen3
Roucester MF 11Ed1
Royston F 20Hen3
Royston F 26Hen3
Rudham F 11Hen3
Rudham F 33Hen3
Ruggwyk F 44Hen3
Rugwell MF 43Hen3
Rumford F 34Hen3
Rysing F 37&38Hen3

Sabrichewrth M 6Hen3
Sabrichworth M 7Hen3
St. Botolpham F 5John
St Edmond 2F 19Hen3
St Germaine MF 9Ed1
St Germyn M 6Hen3
St Ive F 42Hen3
St Ives M 11Hen3
St Keymno M 10Hen3
St Olavus F 10Hen3
St Osithe M 3Hen3
St Osithe M 11Hen3
Saleby M 7Hen3
Saleby F 10Hen3
Salehurst M 53Hen3
Salemanstowe F 9Hen3
Salisbury M 7Hen3
Salisbury F 10Hen3
Sallow MF 43Hen3
Salop F 51Hen3
Sandling MF 37&38Hen3
Sandyacrer MF 53Hen3
Sarum M 7Hen3
Sarum F 30Hen3
Sarum F 51Hen3
Saxmundesham MF 56Hen3
Schepton MF 44Hen3
Scheule MF 52Hen3
Scippedham MF 29Hen3
Schiringh MF 23Hen3
Sci. Edmundi F 10Hen3
Scryvelby M 43Hen3
Scrywelby MF 42Hen3
Scryrland MF 35Hen3
Sechill M2F 42Hen3
Sedburg MF 35Hen3
Selburn MF 54Hen3
Sele MF 17Hen3
Selflegh M 11Hen3
Selneleg M 10Hen3
Senebod M 9Hen3
Sepewesce F 14Hen3
Setel MF 33Hen3
Shalingford F 5John
Shapwyke MF 52Hen3
Shelve MF 45Hen3
Shepton F 52Hen3
Shereston MF 32Hen3
Sheriffhoton MF 1Ric2
Shirborn F 24Hen3
Shirburn M 7Hen3
Shirburne MF 23Hen3
Shirburne Neuton MF 54Hen3
Shireborne M 28Ed1
Shireburne MF 11Hen3
Shorestan M 25Hen3
Shorn MF 55Hen3
Shorstan F 36Hen3
Shoueldon MF 35Hen3

Shrivenham MF 41Hen3
Shuwell F 23Hen3
Siltrell MF 7Hen3
Sislaund MF 49Hen3
Skipse M 56Hen3
Skipse MF 12Ed3
Slafford M 2Ric2
Snath M 7Hen3
Snellsham M 11Hen3
Snilleby F 43Hen3
Solbir MF 11Hen3
Solbir MF 55Hen3
Southwic MF 19Hen3
Spafford M 8Hen3
Spalding M 26Hen3
Spenes M 2Hen3
Spillesby MF 39Hen3
Stafford F 29Hen3
Stafford F 45Hen3
Stakel F 37&38Hen3
Stameston MF 53Hen3
Stanes M 11Hen3
Stanes F 12Hen3
Stanes MF 35Hen3
Stanlake MF 14Hen3
Stanlegh MF 53Hen3
Sapilford MF 23Hen3
Staundon MF 41Ed3
Saunford M 14Hen3
Stayngrew MF 41Hen3
Stenington MF 56Hen3
Stepellanimton MF 37&38Hen3
Stockbrug F 5Hen3
Stokeferie MF 32Hen3
Stokeland F 53Hen3
Stokell F 8Hen3
Stoksey MF 56Hen3
Stoteden MF 28Hen3
Stow F 28Hen3
Stowa F 42Hen3
Stowe F 52Hen3
Stradbroc M 11Hen3
Stradebroc M 11Hen3
Strafford F 8Hen3
Strafford F 41Hen3
Stratford F 1John
Stratford F 24Hen3
Stratford F 54Hen3
Stratford sup. Avon F 53Hen3
Stratton F 9John
Stratton M 41Hen3
Stratton F 42Hen3
Stratton MF 51Hen3
Stret MF 41Hen3
Strete F 1John
Strethan MF 54Hen3
Strethamtoftes F 56Hen3
Sturminstre F 3Hen3
Stuturg M 16John
Styvekey MF 55Hen3
Sudwalde MF 11Hen3
Suham M 11Hen3
Sulihull MF 26Hen3
Sumcombe F 11Hen3
Sumertune MF 10Hen3
Suminster M 11Hen3
Sumoncour MF 31Hen3
Sutbrain F 11Hen3
Sutham MF 23Hen3
Sutham MF 41Hen3
Sutton F 6Hen3
Sutton MF 37&38Hen3
Sutton MF 42Hen3
Suttonger M 16John
Sutton in Holland MF 53Hen3
Sutton Resis MF 36Hen3
Swafham MF 37Hen3
Swamseye F 45Hen3
Swanesey MF 28Hen3
Swaneton F 53Hen3

Swanneston Villa F 27to39Hen6
Swanseye MF 55Hen3
Swere F 56Hen3
Sweyneston MF 39Hen3
Swinescumbe F 18Hen3
Swinestre Capella F 9Hen3
Swynecumbe F 5John
Swynesheved F 11Hen3
Sypton M 8Hen3

Tacham F 6Hen3
Tachbrok MF 43Hen3
Tacheham M 2Hen3
Tacheham M 3Hen3
Tackle MF 37&38Hen3
Tadcastre MF 55Hen3
Talacher F 32Hen3
Tamerton MF 54Hen3
Tanet Insula M 11Hen3
Tapleton M 7Hen3
Tasquinthin MF 30Hen3
Taterford MF 56Hen3
Tateshale F 3Ed2
Taushelf MF 41Hen3
Teingnemuth MF 37Hen3
Telneleg MF 11Hen3
Temetbury MF 33Hen3
Tenham MF 44Hen3
Teynton MF 54Hen3
Thaydon MF 23Hen3
Theydon MF 9Hen3
Thirning MF 48Hen3
Thorent in Tyndale M 5Hen3
Thoresweye MF 36Hen3
Thormerton F 37&38Hen3
Thornbury F 23Hen3
Thornham MF 30Hen3
Thornhill MF 10Ed2
Thornory F 30Hen3
Thurok M 11Hen3
Thurrok MF 23Hen3
Titleshall MF 51Hen3
Toke F 1John
Tonge F 56Hen3
Tonge Villa F 27to39Hen6
Topesham F 42Hen3
Toppefeud MF 36Hen3
Torkes F 11Hen3
Torkesey M 3Hen3
Totole MF 39Hen3
Touthull MF 41Hen3
Trapstone F 10Hen3
Trapston F 29Hen3
Tressell MF 35Hen3
Trigeny F 51Hen3
Trillane Magna MF 56Hen3
Tristedermot F 33Hen3
Tuddworth MF 55Hen3
Tunsted MF 44Hen3
Turboc MF 41Hen3
Tuyverton MF 42Hen3
Twenge MF 41Hen3
Tybract MF 21Hen3
Tydeswell MF 35Hen3
Typerneham M 53Hen3

Upton MF 53Hen3
Upton Escudemore MF 51Hen3

Vergrave M 3Hen3

Wadburg M 11Hen3
Wadehurst MF 37Hen3
Wahull M 6Hen3
Wahull M 26Hen3
Wakenfeud F 42Hen3
Wakering M 49Hen3
Wakerl F 48Hen3
Walden F 33Hen3
Waleford MF 11Hen3

Walesburn Parva MF 30Hen3
Waleton M 2John
Waleton MF 55Hen3
Waleton in ye Dale MF 29Ed1
Wallesford F 11Hen3
Wallesford M 25Hen3
Walpole MF 56Hen3
Walsingham MF 36Hen3
Walsingham parva M 41Hen3
Waltham MF 3Hen3
Waltham M 4Hen3
Waltham MF 11Hen3
Wamberge F 36Hen3
Wandesle MF 35Ed1
Waneting F 30Hen3
Wanteford F 15Hen3
Wardon M 11Hen3
Wardune MF 11Hen3
Ware F 37&38Hen3
Warewell F 9John
Warhull 7Hen3
Warsop MF 23Hen3
Wastonisham F 37&38Hen3
Watindune M 6John
Watlesburgh MF 56Hen3
Watlington M 36Hen3
Watre MF 36Hen3
Watton F 32Hen3
Waure MF 41Hen3
Wausingham parva F 35Hen3
Wautham 2F 37Hen3
Waybrugg MF 23Hen3
Wedmere MF 39Hen3
Wekinge M 11Hen3
Weleford M 7Hen3
Welkested MF 35Hen3
Wellburne MF 56Hen3
Welleford MF 36Hen3
Wellehagh MF 52Hen3
Welles F 31Hen3
Welpington MF 51Hen3
Welwe M 36Hen3
Wendon MF 46Hen3
Wendour M 18John
Wenge MF 39Hen3
Wenlock MF 11Hen3
Wenlok M 8Hen3
Werch M 7John
Wergrave M 2Hen3
Were M 2Hen3
Were MF 25Hen3
WereHorn MF 52Hen3
Werigge MF 33Hen3
Werk MF 12Hen3
Werk MF 25Hen3
Werk MF 36Hen3
Wermister F 37&38Hen3
Wernington MF 5Ed1
Werre M 8Hen3
Werreby M 25Hen3
Werwell F 44Hen3
Westaur M 32Ed1
Westbyre MF 36Hen3
Westerham MF 11Hen3
Westerham MF 25,26,27Ed3
Westham MF 37Hen3
Westlydford MF 44Hen3
Westmell MF 10Hen3
Westm. F 30Hen3
Weston MF 48Hen3
Weston F 55Hen3
Weston M 7Hen3
Westrasen M 3Hen3
Westrasen MF 23Hen3
Westrasin M 11Hen3
West Tillbery M 41Hen3
Weydelyngton MF 42Hen3
Weymouth MF 32Hen3
Whaddon F 31Hen3

Wherinton F 39Hen3
Wherlneton MF 53Hen3
Wherwell M 51Hen3
Whitchurch M 25Hen3
Whitchurch MF 29Hen3
Whitchurch MF 32Hen3
Whitchurch MF 35Hen3
Wichebereghe F 11Hen3
Wicombe F 23Hen3
Wigan MF 29Hen3
Wigeton MF 46Hen3
Wigorn F 2Hen3
Wigorn F 3Hen3
Wiham MF 14John
Wikes F 9Hen3
Willinton MF 28Hen3
Willum M 2Hen3
Wilton MF 9Hen3
Wilton MF 41Hen3
Wiltun M 2Hen3
Wimblingwold F 27to39Hen6
Wimborne M 3Hen3
Wimburne M 2Hen3
Winburn MF 9Hen3
Winchester F 1John
Winebergh M 5Hen3
Winesham MF 46Hen3
Winterburne St Martin MF 52Hen3
Wirmegey F 28Hen3
Wirmegey 2F4 2Hen3
Wiscum MF 32Hen3
Wiscum MF 35Hen3
Wiset MF 51Hen3
Witell F 3Hen3
Witell F 11Hen3
Witelsham M 11Hen3
Witham M 1John
Witham M 11Hen3
Withe M 11Hen3
Witinton MF 4Hen3
Witleford MF 51Hen3
Woburn MF 26Hen3
Wodstok F 34Hen3
Wokendon MF 37&38Hen3
Wokinton MF 37&38Hen3
Wollamston MF 44Hen3
Worthyn MF 54Hen3
Wotton M 3Hen3
Wragby M 6Hen3
Wraggeby M 11Hen3
Wragly M 7Hen3
Wrigge MF 33Hen3
Writlington MF 54Hen3
Wudburge M 11Hen3
Wulneberg F 5Hen3
Wulverhampton MF 42Hen3
Wutton MF 36Hen3
Wycombe F 13Hen3
Wygan M2F 42Hen3
Wyhton M 36Hen3
Wyke M 5Hen3
Wyke MF 32Hen3
Wyke MF 37Hen3
Wykes M 5John
Wykham MF 53Hen3
Wyleby MF 32Hen3
Wymburn M 3Hen3
Wyncanton M 20Hen3
Wynerdeston F 15Hen3
Wynerdeston MF 56Hen3
Wyneslawe MF 19Hen3
Wyteby F 14Hen3
Wytingham MF 51Hen3
Wytinton MF 41Hen3
Wyttney F 15Hen3

Yohyll MF 18Hen3
Ywurdeby MF 37&38Hen3

12 Markets and Fairs 1792 and 1888

In 1889 the Government published two volumes entitled 'Market Rights and Tolls' which examined the history and the existing position of fairs and markets.

The Report showed those fairs and markets noted in 1792 in Owen's 'New Book of Fairs' and gave its own research details for 1888.

The county-by-county extract below follows the Report's spelling, some of which is doubtful or changed since. Also it is apparent that a number of places have been included under the wrong county heading, but once again, the Report has been followed.

Anglesey	1792	1888
Aberfrau	F	
Amlwich	F	
Beaumaris	FM	
Bodedern		F
Llanerchymedd	FM	F
Llangefrii		F
Menai Bridge		F
Newburgh	FM	
Pentraeth	F	F
Porthathway	F	
Trefdraeth		F
Valley		F
Beds		
Ampthill	FM	FM
Bedford	FM	FM
Biggleswade	FM	FM
Dunstable	FM	FM
Elstow	F	F
Harrold	FM	F
Ichwell	F	
Leighton Buzzard	FM	F
St Leonards nr		
Bradford	F	
Luton	FM	FM
Odell	F	F
Potton	FM	FM
Shefford	F	FM
Silsoe	F	F
Toddington	FM	FM
Woburn	FM	FM

Berks	1792	1888
Abingdon	FM	FM
Aldermaston	F	
Bracknell	F	F
Chapel Row nr Reading	F	
Cookham		F
East Ilsley	F	F
East Hagburn	F	
Farringdon	F	
Finchamstead	F	
Hungerford	FM	FM
Lambourn	FM	FM
Long Cromarsh	F	
Maidenhead	FM	
Mortimer	F	F
Newbridge	F	
Newbury	FM	FM
Oakingham	FM	
Reading	FM	FM
Thatcham	F	
Stanford Dingley		F
Twyford	F	
Wallingford	FM	FM
Wadley	F	
Wantage	FM	FM
Waltham St Lawrence	F	
Windsor	FM	
Woburn		FM
Wokingham		FM
Yattenden	F	

Brecon	1792	1888
Brecon	FM	F
Builth	F	
Crickswell	FM	FM
Hay	FM	F
Llangynider		F
Talgarth	F	FM
Trecastle	F	

Bucks	1792	1888
Amersham	FM	FM
Aylesbury	FM	F
Beaconsfield	FM	F
Brill		F
Buckingham	FM	F
Burnham	F	F
Chesham	FM	FM
Colnbrook	FM	F
Eton	F	
Fenny Stratford	FM	F
Gt Marlow		F

	1792	1888
Hanslope	F	F
Iver	F	F
Ivinghoe	FM	FM
Lavenden	F	
Little Brickshill	F	F
Marlow	F	
Newport Pagnell	F	
Olney	FM	F
Princes Risboro'	FM	FM
Stony Stratford	F	FM
St Peters Chalfont	F	
Wendover	FM	F
Winslow	FM	F
Wooburn	F	F
Wycombe	F	

Cambs	1792	1888
Cambridge	FM	FM
Caxton	F	
Chatteris		F
Ely	FM	FM
Ickleton	F	
Linton	F	
Marsh	FM	FM
Newmarket		F
Roach	F	
Soham	FM	
Sturbich Fair	F	
Thorney	FM	F
Whittlesea	F	FM
Wisbech	FM	FM

Cardigan	1792	1888
Archryd		F
Cardigan	FM	FM
Capel St Silim	F	
Cappel Cannon	F	
Deheuidd	F	F
Lampeter	FM	F
Leechnyd		F
Llanarth		F
Llandyfell	F	
Llannarth	FM	
Llanwenen	F	
Llanwenog	F	
Pontrhydfendigaid		F
Rhos Fair	F	
Tulsarn	F	
Tregarron	FM	FM
Ystradmyrick	F	

Carmarthen	1792	1888
Abergwili	F	F
Ammanford		F
Capel Gwynfe		F
Carmarthen	FM	FM
Cayo	F	
Drustlwyn	F	
Fairhach	F	
Kidwelly	FM	
Lanawog	F	
Llanddang		F
Llanedy	F	
Llanelly	FM	FM
Llandebie	F	F
Llandilo-fechan		F
Llandilo-fawr		F
Llandovery	FM	FM
Llandiloe	F	
Langhorne	F	
Llangadock	F	FM
Langindairne	F	
Llangennech	F	F
Llanon	F	F
Lansadwin	F	
Llansaint		F
Lansawel	F	
Lanvichangel	F	
Lanwinie	F	
Llanybyther		F
Llanybidder	F	
Little Mountain	F	
Mothvey		F
Mwrras	F	
Myrdrim	F	
Newcastle Emlyn	FM	F
Pembrey		F
Pencdrreg		F
Pentre	FM	
Penybout	F	
Talley		FM
Three Lords	F	

Cheshire	1792	1888
Altrincham	FM	F
Astbury		F
Budworth	F	
Chester	FM	FM
Congleton	FM	FM
Frodsham	FM	F
Halton	FM	
Knutsford	FM	FM
Lymm		F
Macclesfield	FM	FM

	1792	1888
Malpas	FM	
Nantwich	FM	F
Northwich	FM	FM
Over		F
Prestbury		F
Runcorn		F
Sandbach	FM	FM
Stockport	FM	FM
Tarporley	FM	F
Winsford		FM
Woodhead		F

Cornwall	1792	1888
St Austell	FM	
Blisland		F
Bodmin	FM	FM
Bolingley	F	
Boscastle	FM	F
Boyton	F	F
Bridgend		F
St Blazey	F	
Camborne	F	FM
Camelford	F	FM
Canworthy		F
St Columb	FM	
Dubwalls		F
East Looe	FM	
Falmouth	FM	
Five Lanes		F
Fowey	FM	
St Germans	FM	
Goldfithnay	F	
Grampound	F	
Helston	F	
St Ives	FM	
Kellington	FM	
Kilhampton	F	
Lane		F
Lanreath		F
Launceston	FM	
St Lawrence	F	
Lelant	F	
Liskeard	FM	F
Londrake	F	
Lostwithiel	FM	FM
Marazion		F
Marhamchurch		F
Manhenit	F	
Marketjew	F	
Melbrooke	F	
Mitchell	F	F
Padstow	FM	FM

	1792	1888		1792	1888
Penrose		F	Maryport		F
Penryn	FM	F	Netherwasdale		F
Pensance	FM	FM	Penrith	FM	FM
Plint	F		Ravenglass	FM	F
Poundcross		F	Renwick		F
Praye Crowan		F	Rosley Hill	F	F
Probus	F		Ulpho	F	
Redruth	FM	FM	Whitehaven	FM	FM
Roche		F	Wigton	FM	FM
Saltash	F		Workington	FM	FM
St Austell		FM			
St Blaze		FM	**Derbyshire**		
St Brewad		F	Alfreton	FM	FM
St Columb Maj.		FM	Ashbourn	FM	FM
St Columb Min.		FM	Ashover	F	F
St Lawrence		F	Bakewell	FM	FM
St Merryn		F	Belper	F	FM
Stratton	F		Bolsover	F	
St Stephens	F		Buxton		F
St Tudy	F	F	Castleton		F
Stockeclimsland		F	Chapel-en-le-Frith	FM	F
Summercourt		F	Chesterfield	FM	FM
Tintagel		F	Clay Cross		FM
Tregonetha		F	Crich	F	F
Tregony	FM		Cubley	F	
Tresillian Br.	F		Darley Flash	F	
Trevena	F		Derby	FM	FM
Trew	F		Dronfield	FM	F
Trewenn	F		Duffield	F	FM
Truro	FM	FM	Glossop		FM
Wadebridge	F	FM	Hartington		F
Wainhouse Corner		F	Hayfield		F
Week St Mary	F	F	Higham	FM	F
West Looe	F		Hope	F	F
			Matlock	F	F
Cumberland			Newhaven	F	F
Abbey Holme	FM	FM	Pleasley	F	
Alston	FM	FM	Ripley	F	F
Armathwaite		F	Sawley	F	
Boonwood		F	Tideswell	FM	F
Bootle	F	F	Winster	FM	
Brampton	FM	F	Wirksworth	FM	FM
Carlisle	FM	FM			
Cockermouth	FM	F	**Devonshire**		
Croglin		F	Alphington	F	
Egremont	FM	FM	Ashburton	FM	F
Eskdale		F	Axminster	FM	FM
Hesket New Mark.		F	Bampton	FM	F
Ireby		FM	Barnstaple	F	FM
Keswick	FM	F	Bideford	FM	
Kirkoswald	F		Bishops Nympton	F	
Longtown	FM	FM	Bovey Tracey	F	

	1792	1888		1792	1888
Bow	FM		Sidmouth	F	
Bratton Clovelly		F	Silverton	F	
Brent	FM	F	South Molton	F	FM
Broadclift	F		Tavistock	FM	FM
Broadhembury	F		Teignmouth	F	
Broadworthy	F		Thaverton	F	
Buckfastleigh	F	FM	Thorncomb	FM	
Buckland	F		Tiverton	FM	FM
Chawley	F		Torrington	FM	FM
Chegford	F		Totnes	FM	FM
Chimley	F		Uffculme	FM	F
Chudleigh	FM		Underwood	F	
Chumleigh		F	Upottery	F	F
Churchingford	F	F	Wimple	F	
Columpton	FM		Witheridge	F	F
Colyford	F				
Colyton		F	**Dorset**		
Crediton	FM	FM	Abbey Milton	F	
Cullompton	FM	FM	Abbotsbury	FM	
Culmstock	F	F	Allington	F	
Dalwood	F		Bailey-ridge	F	
Dawlish		F	Beaminster	F	FM
Denbury	F		Blandford	FM	F
Dolton	F		Bridport	FM	FM
Ermington	F		Broadway	F	
Exbourn	F	F	Castleton	F	
Exeter	FM	FM	Cerne Abbey	FM	
Hartland	FM	FM	Corfe Castle	FM	F
Highhickington	F		Cranborne	FM	
Holsworthy	FM	FM	Crewkerne		F
Honiton	FM	FM	Dorchester	FM	FM
High Budleigh	F		Emmergreen	F	
Kilmington	F		Evershot	FM	F
Kingsbridge	FM	F	Farnham	F	
Lifton	F		Frampton	F	
Membury	F		Gillingham	F	FM
Modbury	FM		Hermitage	F	
Morbath	F		Holt-wood	F	
Moreton Hamstead	FM		Lambert's Castle	F	F
Newton Abbot	FM	FM	Lyme	FM	
Newton Peppleford	F		Lyme Regis		FM
North Moulton	F	F	Maiden Newton	F	F
North Tawton	F	F	Martins Town	F	F
Norton	F		Milborne	F	F
Okehampton	F	FM	Ower-mayne	F	
Otterton	F		Poole	FM	FM
Ottery St Mary	FM	FM	Painpill	F	
Plymouth	FM	FM	Piddle Town	F	
Plympton	FM	F	Portland		F
Sampford Peverell	F	F	Shaftesbury	FM	FM
Seaton	F		Sherborne	FM	FM
Sheepwash	F	F	Shroton	F	F

	1792	1888		1792	1888
Sidland	F		Chelmsford	FM	FM
Stalbridge	FM	FM	Chesterford	F	
Stockland	F		Chigwell	F	
Sturminster	FM	FM	Great Clackton	F	
Toller Down	F	F	Little Clackton	F	
Verwood		F	Coggeshal	FM	
Wareham	FM	FM	Colchester	FM	FM
Winbourne	F		Colt	F	
Woodbury Hill	FM	F	Danbury	F	
Woodland	F		Dedham	F	
Woolbridge	F	F	Dunmow	F	F
Wanford Eagle	F		Earle a Corne	F	
Yeominster		F	Elmstead	F	
			Epping	FM	FM
Durham			Fairlock	F	
Barnard Castle	FM	F	Ford Street	F	
Bishop Auckland	FM	F	Fingringhoe	F	
Cornhill	F		Foulnese Island	F	
Darlington	FM	FM	Grays	FM	
Durham	FM	FM	Gt Bardfield		F
Hartlepool	FM		Gt Hollingbury	F	
Houghton-le-Spring		F	Gt Oakley	F	
Middleton in Teesdale		FM	Gt Tey	F	
Norham	F		Gt Wakering	F	
North Shields		FM	Goldanger	F•	
Sedgfield	F		Hadleigh	F	
South Shields		FM	Hadstock	F	
Stanhope		FM	Halstead	FM	
Stockton-on-Tees	FM	FM	Harlow	F	F
Walsingham	F		Harwick	F	
Weardale		F	Hatfield Broad Oak	F	
			High Ongar	F	
Essex			Hornden	FM	
Abridge	F		Ingatstone	F	F
Althorne	F		Kelvedon	F	
Audley End	F		Kirby	F	
Bardfield	F		Lachingdon	F	
Barking	FM		Leigh	F	
Basildon	F		Malden	FM	FM
Belchamp St Pauls	F		Manuden	F	
Bentley	F		Manningtree	FM	
Billericay	FM		Messing	F	
Blackmore	F		Newport	F	
Bradwell	F		Ostend	F	
Braintree	FM	FM	Ongar	FM	
Brentwood	F	F	St Osith	F	
Brightlingsea	F		Paverel	F	
Bulmer Tye	F		Prittlewell	F	
Burnham	F		Purleigh	F	
Canewdon	F		Ramsey	FM	
Canvey Island	F		Rayleigh	FM	FM
Castle Hedingham	F		Rochford	FM	

	1792	1888		1792	1888
Rumford	FM		Sodbury	FM	
Saffron Walden		FM	Stanehouse	F	F
Salcote	F		Stow-on-the-Wold	FM	FM
Sth Benfleet	F		Stroud	FM	FM
Southminster	F		Tetbury	FM	
Stanstead	F	F	Tewkesbury	FM	FM
Stanaway	F		Thornbury	FM	FM
Stebbing	F	F	Westerleigh	F	F
Steple	F		Wickwar	FM	F
Tarling	F		Winchcomb	FM	FM
Tendering	F		Wotton-under-Edge	FM	F
Thaxted	FM	F			
Thorpe	F		**Hampshire**		
Tillingham	F		Alresford	FM	FM
Tiptree Place	F		Alton	FM	F
Tolesbury	F		Andover	FM	F
Tolleshunt Darcy	F		Appleshaw	F	F
Walden	FM		Barton	F	
Waltham Abbey	FM		Basingstoke Downs	F	
Walton	F		Basingstoke	FM	F
Wicks	F		Beaulieu	F	
Witham	FM		Bishops Waltham		F
Wivenhoe	F		Blackwater	F	F
Woodham Ferries	F		Botley	F	F
Writtle	F		Brading	F	
			Broughton	F	
Glos.			Christchurch	FM	
Barton Regis	F		Eastleon	F	
Berkeley	FM	FM	Ealing	F	F
Bisley	FM	F	Emsworth	F	
Blakeney	FM	F	Eversly	F	
Campden	FM	FM	Fareham	FM	
Cheltenham	FM	FM	Fordingbridge	F	
Chipping Sodbury		FM	Giles Hill nr Winton	F	
Cirencester	FM	FM	Gosport	FM	F
Coleford	FM	FM	Hambledon	F	
Dursley	FM	FM	Hartley Row	F	F
Fairford	F	F	Havant	F	
Frampton	F		Heckfield	F	
Gloucester	FM	FM	Kingsclear	FM	
Hampton	FM	F	Liphook	F	
Iron-Acton	F	F	Liss	F	
Lechlade	FM	FM	Lymington	FM	F
Littledean	F	F	Lyndhurst		F
Lydney	FM	FM	Magdalen Hill nr		
Marshfield	FM	F	Winton	F	
Mitchel Dean	FM		Mattingley	FM	
Moreton	FM	FM	Newton	F	
Newent	FM	FM	Odiham	FM	F
Newnham	FM	F	Overton	FM	F
Northleach	FM	FM	Petersfield	FM	FM
Painswick	FM		Portsmouth	FM	

	1792	1888		1792	1888
Post Down	F		Hertford	FM	FM
Ringwood	FM	FM	Hitchin	FM	
Rowlands Castle	F		Hoddesdon	F	
Romsey	FM	FM	Little Hadham	F	
Selborne	F		Much Hadham	F	
Southampton	FM	FM	Northall	F	
Southwick	F		Preston	F	
Stockbridge	F	F	Puckeridge	F	
Sutton	F		Purton	F	
Tangley	F		Redbourn	F	
Titchfield	F		Rickmansworth	FM	
Waltham	F		Royston	FM	FM
West Cowes	F		Sawbridgworth	FM	
Weyhill	F	F	Standon	FM	
Wherwell	F	F	Stevenage	FM	F
Whitchurch	FM		Stortford, Bishops	FM	
Wickham	F	F	Tring	F	F
Winchester	FM	FM	Ware	FM	F
Yarmouth	F		Watford	FM	
Hereford			**Hunts**		
Brampton Brian	F	F	Alconbury	F	
Bromyard	FM	FM	Earith Bridge	F	F
Dorstone	F		Godmanchester	F	FM
Eardisley		F	Huntingdon	FM	F
Hereford	FM	FM	Kimbolton	FM	FM
Huntingdon	F	F	Leighton	F	
Kingsland	F	F	St Ives	F	FM
Kington	FM	FM	St Neots	FM	F
Ledbury	FM	FM	Ramsey	FM	
Leintwardine		F	Sommersham	FM	
Leominster	FM	FM	Spaldick	F	
Longtowne nr Bishops			Stilton	FM	
Castle	F		Yaxley	F	
Orleton	F	F			
Pembridge	FM	F	**Kent**		
Ross	FM	FM	Ackhole	F	
Weobly	FM		Acris Mill	F	
Wigmore	F	FM	Alresford	F	
			Appledore	FM	
Herts			Ash	F	
St Albans	FM		Ashford	FM	FM
Albury	F		Babbington	F	
Baldock	FM	FM	Badlesmore	F	
Barnet	FM	FM	Benenden	F	F
Barkway	FM		Bethersden	F	
Bennington	F		Biddenden	F	F
Berkhamstead	FM		Billingston	F	
Braughing	F		Blackheath	F	
Buntingford	FM	F	Boughton	F	
Hatfield	FM	F	Brastead	F	
Hemel Hempstead	F	FM	Bromfield	F	

	1792	1888		1792	1888
Bromley	FM		Lidd	F	
Brompton	F		Littleburn	F	
Brookland	F		Lyminge	F	
Canterbury	FM		Maidstone	FM	FM
Chalk	F		Malling	FM	
Challock	F		Marden	F	
Charing	F		Meopham	F	
Chevering	F		Mersham	F	
Chilham	F		Milton	FM	
Chiselhurst	F		Minster	F	
Church Witfield	F		Mongham	F	
Cliff	F		Monkton	F	
Cobham	F		Newenden	F	
Cowden	F		Newnham	F	
Cranbrook	FM	FM	New Romney		F
Crayford	F		North Down	F	
Dartford	FM		Old Chaple	F	
Deal	FM		Orford	F	
Dover	FM		Orpington	F	
Dulwich	F		Ospringe	F	
Eastchurch	F		Oxted	F	
Eastling	F		Peckham	F	
East Malling	F		Pembury	F	
Eastroy	F		Penshurst	F	
Edenbridge	F		Pluckley	F	
Eltham	FM		Preston	F	
Elmstead	F		Queenborough	F	
Farnborough	F		Rochester	FM	F
Farningham	FM	FM	Rumney	FM	
Faversham	FM	FM	St Lawrence	F	
Folkestone	FM		St Peters	F	
Frittenden	F		St Margarets nr Dover	F	
Gillingham	F		St Mary Cray	F	
Goodnestone	F		Sandwich	FM	
Goudburst	FM		Sandhurst	F	F
Gravesend	FM	FM	Sarr	F	
Great Chart	F		Seale	F	
Greenstreet	F		Sellinge	F	
Groombridge	F		Sevenoaks	FM	
Hadlow	F		Shoreham	F	
Hamstreet	F		Sittingbourne	F	
Harriotsham	F		Smarden	FM	
Hawkhurst	F		Smith	F	
Hearn	F		Staple	F	
Hedcorn	F		Steiling	F	
Horsemonden	F	F	Stockbury	F	
Hythe	F		Stone	F	
Ingleham	F		Stroud	F	
Kennington	F		Tenterden	FM	
Lamberhurst	F		Tonbridge	FM	FM
Lenham	FM		Warborn	F	
Leigh	F		Waldershare	F	

	1792	1888		1792	1888
Westerham	FM		Padiham	F	
Whitstable	F		Poulton le Fylde	FM	F
Wingham	F		Prescot	FM	F
Wittersham	F		Radcliffe Bridge	F	
Woodnesborough	F		Rochdale	FM	F
Wrotham	FM		Rufford	F	
Wye	F		Scholes in Wigan		F
Woolwich	FM		Skerton		F
Yalding	F		Stalybridge		FM
			Standish	F	F
Lancashire			Todmorden		FM
Ashton-under-Lyne	F	F	Ulverston	FM	FM
Accrington		FM	Upholland	FM	F
Bartholomew	F		Warrington	FM	FM
Blackburn	FM	FM	Weeton	F	F
Bolton	FM		Westoughton		F
Bolton-le-Moors		FM	Wigan	FM	FM
Booth	F		Wray		F
Broughton	F	F			
Burnley	F	FM	**Leicester**		
Bury	FM	FM	Ashby-de-la-Zouch	FM	
Carnforth		FM	Belton	F	F
Cartmell	FM	F	Billesden	FM	F
Chipping	F	F	Bosworth	F	
Chorley	FM	F	Castle Donington		FM
Clitheroe	FM	F	Hallaton	FM	F
Colne	FM	F	Hinckley	FM	FM
Coniston		FM	Husbands Bosworth		F
Crewe		F	Kegworth	F	
Dalton in Furness	FM	FM	Leicester	FM	F
Garstang	FM	F	Loughborough	FM	FM
Gt Eccleston		F	Lutterworth	FM	FM
Harwood		FM	Market Bosworth	FM	FM
Haslingden	FM	FM	Market Harborough	FM	FM
Hawkshead	FM	F	Melton Mowbray	FM	FM
Heywood		F	Mountsorrel	FM	F
Hornby	FM	F	Waltham on the Wolds	FM	F
Inglewhite	F	F			
Kirkham	FM	F	**Lincs**		
Lancaster	FM	F	Alford	FM	FM
Leigh		FM	Barnwell	F	
Littleborough	F		Barton-upon-Humber	FM	FM
Liverpool	FM	F	Belton	F	
Longridge		F	Boston	FM	FM
Manchester	FM	FM	Bourn	FM	FM
Mossley		FM	Brigg	FM	FM
Newburgh	F	F	Caistor	FM	FM
Newchurch	F	F	Caythorpe		F
Newton-le-Willows	FM	F	Corby	FM	F
North Meots		F	Couthorpe	F	
Oldham	F	F	Crowland	FM	
Ormskirk	FM	FM	Crowle	FM	FM

	1792	1888		1792	1888
Donnington	FM	FM	Hounslow	FM	F
Epworth	FM	FM	Southgate		F
Falkingham	FM	FM	Staines	FM	FM
Fillingham	F		Uxbridge	FM	
Gainsborough	FM	FM			
Glentham		F	Monmouthshire		
Grantham	FM	FM	Abergavenny	F	FM
Grimsby	FM	F	Blackwood		F
Haxey	F		Blaenavon		FM
Heckington	F	F	Bishton		F
Holbeach	FM	FM	Caerleon	FM	FM
Horncastle	FM	FM	Castletown	F	
Kirton Lindsey	FM	F	Chepstow	FM	
Lincoln	FM	FM	Christchurch		F
Long Sutton		FM	Grosmont		F
Louth	FM	FM	Maesycwmur		F
Ludford	F		Magor	F	FM
Market Deeping	FM		Monmouth	FM	FM
Market Rasen	FM	FM	Newport	FM	FM
Massingham	F	F	Peterstone		F
Navenby	FM		Pontypool	FM	FM
Partney	F	F	Raglan		FM
Saltfleetby	F	F	Redwick		F
Scotter	F	F	Risca		F
Sleaford	FM	FM	Tredegar		F
Spalding	FM	FM	Usk	FM	FM
Spilsbury	FM	FM			
Spital		F	Norfolk		
Stainton	FM		Aldeburgh	F	
Stamford	FM	FM	Attleborough	FM	FM
Stockwith	F		Aylsham	FM	FM
Stow Green	F		Binham	F	F
Stow	F	F	Bromhall	F	
Swineshead	F		Brumhill	F	
Swinstead	F		Burnham	FM	
Tattershall	FM		Castle Acre	F	
Torksey	F		Cawston	FM	
Wainfleet	FM	FM	Clay	F	
Winteringham	F		Coltishall	F	
Winterton	F	FM	Cressingham Magna	F	
Wragby	FM	F	Cromer	FM	
Wroot		F	East Dereham	FM	
			Dereham		FM
Middlesex			Diss	FM	
Bow	F		Downham	FM	FM
Beggars Bush	F		Elmham	F	
Brentford	FM	FM	East Harling	FM	
Chiswick	F		Fakenham	F	
Edgware	FM		St Faiths	F	
Edmonton	F		Feltwell	F	
Enfield	FM	FM	Fineham	F	
Hammersmith	F		Forncett	F	

261

	1792	1888		1792	1888
Foulsham	FM	F	Upwell		F
Frettenham	F		Warron	FM	
Fring	F		Weasenham	F	
Gaywood	F		Wells		F
Gissing	F		Worstead	FM	
Gorlestone	F		Wymondham	FM	FM
Gressinghall	F		Yarmouth	FM	FM
Harleston	FM				
Harling		F	**Northants**		
Harpley	F		Boughton Green	F	F
Hempsall	F		Brackley	FM	FM
Hempton	F	FM	Brigstock	F	F
Hingham	FM		Brixworth	F	
Hitcham	F		Daventry	FM	F
Hockham	F		Fatheringay	F	F
Hockhold	F	F	Higham Ferrers	FM	F
Holt	FM		Kettering	FM	FM
Horning	F		King's Cliff	FM	F
Ingham	F		Northampton	F	F
Kenninghall	F	FM	New Inn Road	F	
Kipmash	F		Long Buckby		F
Loddon	FM		Oundle	FM	F
Lycham	F		Peterborough	FM	FM
Lynn, Kings	FM	FM	Rockingham	F	F
Magdalen Hill nr			Rowell	FM	F
Norwich	F		Thrapstone	F	FM
Martham nr Yarmouth	F		Towcester	FM	F
Massingham	F		Weldon	F	F
Mattishall	F		Wellingborough	FM	FM
Methwould	F	FM	West Haddon	F	
New Buckenham	FM		Yardley	F	
Northwalsham	FM				
Northwold	F	F	**Northumberland**		
Norwich	FM	F	Allendale Town		F
Outwell		F	Allentown	F	
Oxborough	F		Alnwick	FM	FM
Pulham St Mary			Bedford	F	
Magdalen	F		Belford		F
Reepham	FM		Billingham	FM	F
Roudham	F		Berwick	FM	FM
Scole	F		Blanchland		F
Scotto	F		Elsdon	F	
Seeching	FM		Fenton		F
Shouldham	F	F	Haltwhistle	FM	F
South Repps	F		Harbottle	FM	F
Sprowston	F		Hexham	FM	FM
Stoke	F		Morpeth	FM	F
Stoke Ferry		F	Newcastle	FM	FM
Stow Bridge	F	F	Ovingham	F	
Swaffham	FM	FM	St Ninian	F	
Thetford	FM		Stagshawkbank	F	F
Walsingham	FM	F	Stamfordham	F	F

	1792	1888		1792	1888
Warkworth	FM	F	**Shropshire**		
Weelwoodbank	F		Albrighton	F	
Whittingham	F		Battlefield	F	
Whitsunbank		F	Bishops Castle	FM	FM
Wooller	FM	FM	Bridgnorth	FM	FM
			Broseley	F	F
Notts			Church Stretton		FM
Bawtry		F	Cleobury	FM	FM
Bingham	FM	FM	Clun	F	FM
Blyth	FM	F	Elesmere	FM	
Dunholme	F		Halesowen	FM	F
Eastwood	F		Hodnett	F	
Edwinstowe		F	Ironbridge		FM
Gringley	F	F	Llanymynech	F	F
Lenton	F	F	Ludlow	FM	F
Mansfield	FM	FM	Market Drayton	FM	FM
Marnham	F	F	Minsterley		F
Newark	FM	F	Much Wenlock		FM
Nottingham	FM	FM	Newport	FM	
Ollerton	F	FM	Oswestry	FM	FM
Retford	FM	FM	Powder Batch	F	
Southwell	FM	FM	Ruiton	F	
Sutton-in-Ashfield		FM	St Kenelms	F	
Tuxford	FM	F	Shifnal	FM	FM
Warsop	F	F	Shrewsbury	FM	M
West Stockwith		F	Stretton Church	FM	
Worksop	FM	FM	Wattlesbury	F	
			Wellington	FM	FM
Oxfordshire			Wem	F	FM
Bampton	FM	F	Wenlock	FM	
Banbury	F	FM	Westbury	F	
Bicester	FM	FM	Whitchurch	FM	F
Burford	FM	FM			
Charlbury	FM	F	**Somerset**		
Chipping Norton	FM	FM	Ashbrittle	F	
Cromarsh		F	Ashcott		F
Deddington	FM	F	Ashill	F	
Dorchester	F	F	Axbridge	FM	FM
Henley	FM	FM	Backwell	F	
Heyford		F	Bagnor West	F	
Hook Norton	F		Banwell	F	
Nettlebed	F	F	Bath	FM	F
Oxford	FM	FM	Binegar	F	F
Stokenchurch	F	F	Bishops Lydcard	F	
Thame	FM	FM	Bleagon	F	
Watlington	FM		Borough Bridge		F
Wheatby	F		Brewton	FM	
Witney	FM	FM	Bridely		F
Woodcote	F	F	Bridgewater	FM	FM
Woodstock	FM	FM	Bristol	FM	F
			Broadway		F
			Bromfield	F	

	1792	1888
Bruton		F
Buckland	F	
Buckland St Mary	F	
Burnham	F	
Castle Cary	FM	FM
Chard	FM	F
Cheddar	F	F
Chisselborough	F	
Cock Hill	F	
Comb St Nicholas	F	
Congresbury	F	F
Coombe St Nicholas		F
Crewkerne	FM	FM
Crowcomb	FM	
Curry Rival	F	
Draycott		F
Dulverton	FM	
Dundry	F	
Dunster	FM	
East Brent	F	
Freshford	F	
Frome	FM	FM
Glastonbury	FM	FM
Hinton St George	F	F
Highbridge		F
Holloway	F	
Huntspill	F	
Ilminster	F	F
Ivelchester	FM	
Keynsham	FM	F
Kilminton	F	
Kingsbrumpton	F	
Langeridge	F	
Langport	FM	FM
Lansdown	F	F
Lidford-Green	F	
Limpsham	F	
Lyng		F
Mark	F	
Martock	F	F
Midsomer Norton		F
Milborne	F	F
Miles	F	
Milverton	F	
Minehead	FM	
Moorlinch	F	
Montacute	F	
North Curry	FM	
North Petherton	FM	F
Norton St Philip		F
Nunny	F	
Otterford	F	
Pawlet		F
Pensford	F	
Philips-Norton	F	
Porlock	FM	F
Portbury	F	
Priddy	F	F
Queen Camel	F	
Red Linch	F	
Road	F	
Ruishton	F	
Shepton Mallet	F	F
Snowdon	F	
Somerton	F	
South Brent	F	
South Petherton	F	F
Staverdale	F	
Stanford	F	
St Decumans	F	
Stoford		F
Stogursey	F	
Stoke-Gomer	F	
Stoke under Hamden	F	F
Stowey	F	
Sucklebridge	F	
Taunton	FM	FM
Ubley	F	
Watchet	F	
Wedmore	F	F
Wellington	FM	FM
Wellow	F	F
Wells	FM	FM
Weston-super-Mare		M
Weston Zoyland	F	F
West Pennard		F
Whit-down	F	
Williton	F	F
Winsham	F	
Wincanton	FM	FM
Wivilscombe	FM	
Wootton-Courtney	F	
Woolavington		F
Yarlington	F	F
Yeovil	FM	FM

Staffordshire

	1792	1888
Abbot's Bromley	FM	
Barton Underwood	F	
Bentley	F	
Breewood	F	
Burslem		FM
Burton-on-Trent	FM	FM
Cannock	F	FM

	1792	1888		1792	1888
Caverswall		F	Earl Soham	F	
Cellar Head		F	Eye	FM	
Cheadle	FM	FM	Felsham	F	
Eccleshall	F		Finningham	F	
Fazeley	F	FM	Framlingham	FM	
Flash		F	Framsden	F	
Gnosall		F	Glemsford	F	
Grindon		F	Gorleston	F	
Hayward Heath	F		Gt Thurlow	F	
Holy Cross	F		Hacheston	F	
Ipstones		F	Hadleigh	FM	
Kinver		F	Halesworth	FM	M
Leek	FM	FM	Handford	F	
Lichfield	FM	F	Haughley	F	
Longnor	FM	FM	Haverhill	F	
Newcastle-under-Lyme	FM	FM	Hinton	F	
Pattingham	F		Horringer	F	F
Penkridge	F	F	Hoxne	F	
Rugeley	FM	FM	Hundon	F	
Sandon	F		Ixworth	FM	
Stafford	FM	FM	Ipswich	FM	FM
Stone	FM		Kersey	F	
Tamworth	FM	FM	Lavenham	FM	F
Tean	F		Laxfield	F	
Tutbury	FM		Lindsey	F	
Uttoxeter	FM	FM	Long Melford		F
Walsall	FM	FM	Lowestoft	F	
Wednesbury	F	F	Luston		F
Wolverhampton	FM		Market Weston	F	
Wetley Rocks		F	Massingham	F	
Yoxall	F		Mattishaw	F	
			Melford	FM	
Suffolk			Mendlesham	FM	
Aldborough	F		Milden Hall	FM	
Beccles	FM	FM	Nayland	FM	
Bergholt	F		Needham	FM	
Bildestone	FM		Newmarket	FM	
Blythborough	F		Orford	FM	
Botesdale	FM		Polstead	F	
Boxford	F		Saxmundham	FM	
Boxtead	F		Snape	F	
Brandon	F		Somerliton	F	
Bricet	F		Southwold	FM	FM
Bungay	FM	FM	Stanton	F	
Bures	F		Stoke	F	
Bury St Edmunds	FM	FM	Stoke-by-Nayland		F
Cavendish		F	Stowmarket	FM	
Clare	FM		Stradbrooke	F	
Cooling	F		Stratford	F	
Debenham	FM		Sudbury	FM	
Dunwich	FM		Thrandiston	F	
Elmset	F		Thwaite	F	

	1792	1888		1792	1888
Woodbridge	FM		Beckeley	F	
Woolpit	F	F	Beeding	F	
			Billingshurst	F	
Surrey			Bines Green	F	
Bletchingly	F	F	Bodiham	F	F
Bookham	F		Bognor		F
Camberwell	F		Bolney	F	
Chertsey	FM	FM	Boreham Street	F	
Cobham	F	F	Brede	F	
Croydon	FM	F	Brightelmstone	FM	
Dorking	FM	FM	Broadwater	F	
Dulwich	F		Burwash	F	F
Egham	F		Buxted	F	
Epsom	F	FM	Catstreet	F	
Esher	F		Charley	F	
Ewell	FM	F	Chelwood	F	
Farnham	FM	FM	Chichester	FM	FM
Frogerheath	F		Clayton	F	
Godalming	FM	F	Crawley	F	F
Guildford	FM	FM	Cross-in-Hand	F	F
Ham	F		Crowborough	F	F
Haslemere	FM	FM	Cuckfield	FM	
Katherine Hill	F		Danehill	F	
Kingston	FM	FM	Dicker	F	
Knaphill		F	Ditchling	F	
Leatherhead	F		Eastbourne	FM	F
Limpsfield	F		East-Dean	F	
Lingfield	F		East Grinstead	FM	FM
Mitcham	F	F	East Hoathly		F
Mortlake	F		Egdean	F	
Peckham	F		Ewhurst	F	
Reigate	FM	F	Findon	F	F
Ripley	F	F	Fletching	F	
Southwark	F		Forest Row	F	F
Sydenham	F		Franfield	F	
Thorp	F		Garner Street	F	
Walton	F		Green	F	
Wanbro'	F		Guestling	F	
Wandsworth	F		Hafield	F	
Woking	FM		Hailsham	FM	F
			Hartfield	F	
Sussex			Hastings	FM	
Adversean	F		Haywards Heath		FM
Alfriston	F		Heathfield		F
Angmering	F		Henfield	F	
Ardingley	F		Holdly	F	
Arundel	FM	FM	Hollington	F	
Ashington	F		Hooe	F	F
Ashurst	F		Horley	F	
Balcombe	F	F	Horsebridge	F	F
Bat and Ball		F	Horsebridge Common	F	
Battle	FM	F	Horsham	FM	FM

	1792	1888		1792	1888
Horstead-kayne	F		Wellington	F	
Hurst-Green	F		Westfield	F	F
Hurstpierpoint	F		West-ham	F	
Iventon	F		West-heathley	F	
Lamberhurst	F	F	Wevilsfield	F	
Lewes	FM	F	White-smith	F	
St Leonards Forest	F		Wilmington	F	
Lindfield	F	F	Winchelsea	FM	
Longbridge	F		Wisborough		F
Loxwood		F	Withyam	F	
Maresfield	F	FM	Wood's Corner	F	
Mayfield	F	F	Worley Common	F	
Midhurst	FM	F			
Newick	F				
Newhaven	F		Warwickshire		
Northiam	F	F	Atherstone	FM	FM
Nutley	F		Alcester	F	
Old Tye Common	F		Bedworth		FM
Peasemarsh	F		Birmingham	FM	F
Pembury	F		Brailes	F	FM
Pett	F		Coleshill	FM	FM
Petworth	FM	F	Coventry	FM	FM
Pevensey	F		Dunchurch		F
Playden	F		Hampton-in-Arden		FM
Pulborough	F		Henley-in-Arden	FM	F
Racham	F		Hockley Heath		F
Rogate	F		Kenilworth	F	F
Robertsbridge	F	F	Kineton	FM	F
Rotherfield	F	F	Nuneaton	F	FM
Rudgwick	F		Rugby	FM	FM
Rushlake Green	F		Solihull	F	
Rye	FM		Southam	FM	FM
Seaford	FM		Stratford-upon-Avon	F	FM
Shoreham	FM		Studley		F
Sidley	F		Sutton	FM	
Silmiston	F		Warwick	FM	FM
Slangham	F				
Sinford	F		Westmorland		
Southbourne	F		Ambleside	FM	F
South-harting	F		Appleby	FM	F
Southwater	F		Brough	FM	F
Southwick	F		Brough Hill	F	F
St Johns Common		F	Burton-in-Kendal		F
Steyning	FM	F	Grasmere		F
Storrington	FM	F	Kendal	FM	FM
Tarring	F		Kirkby Lonsdale	FM	FM
Thakeham	F		Kirkby Stephen	FM	FM
Ticehurst	F	F	Low Borough Bridge		F
Turners Hill	F		Milnthorpe	F	F
Uckfield	F	F	Orton	FM	F
Wadhurst	F	FM	Shap	F	FM
Warnham	F		Staveley		F

	1792	1888		1792	1888
Wiltshire			Bromsgrove	FM	FM
Ambersbury	FM		Droitwich	FM	
Berwick-hill	F		Dudley	FM	FM
Bradford	FM		Eversham	FM	F
Bradford Leigh	F	F	Feckenham	F	
Bradford-on-Avon		F	Kidderminster	FM	F
Britford	F	F	King's Norton	F	
Calne	FM		Pershore	FM	FM
Castle Combe	F	F	Shipston	F	F
Chippenham	FM	F	Shipton	F	FM
Clack	F		Stourbridge	FM	FM
Collingburn-duces	F		Stourport	FM	
Corsham	F	F	Tenbury	FM	FM
Corsle-heath	F		Upton-on-Severn	FM	F
Cricklade	FM	FM	Worcester	FM	FM
Devizes	FM	FM			
Dilton-marsh	F		Yorkshire		
Downton	F	F	Aberforth	FM	
Gt Bedwin	FM	F	Addingham		F
Heytesbury	F	F	Adwalton	FM	F
Highworth	FM	FM	Aldborough	F	
Hindon	FM	F	Appletreewick	F	F
Kingsdown Box		F	Askrigg	F	FM
Laycock	F		Astwick	F	
Luggershall	F	F	Barnoldswick		F
Maiden Bradley	F		Barns-Burton	F	
Malmesbury	F		Barnsley	FM	FM
Marlborough	FM	F	Bawtry	F	F
Melksham	FM	FM	Bedal	FM	
Mere	FM	F	Benham		F
Norlease	F		Bentham	F	FM
North Bradley	F		Beverley	FM	F
Ramsbury	F	F	Bingley	F	F
St Ann's Hill (Devizes)	F		Black-Burton	F	
Salisbury	FM	FM	Bolton by Bowland	F	F
Sherstone	F		Boroughbridge	FM	F
Swindon	FM	FM	Bradfield	F	
Tan Hill		F	Bradford	FM	FM
Trowbridge	FM	FM	Bridlington	F	FM
Uphaven	F		Brighouse		F
Warminster	FM	FM	Brumpton	F	
Westbury	FM	F	Buckden		F
Whitchbury	F		Cawood	F	
Wilton	FM	F	Clapham	F	
Wootton Bassett	FM	FM	Coxwould	F	
Yarborough Castle	F	F	Cross Hills		F
			Dewsbury	F	FM
Worcestershire			Doncaster	FM	FM
Alvechurch	F	F	Easingwold	F	
Bellbroughton	F		East Wilton		F
Bewdly	FM		Egton	F	F
Blockley	F		Frodlingham	F	

	1792	1888		1792	1888
Ford Inn		F	Pontefract	FM	FM
Gargrave	F	F	Reeth	F	
Giggleswick		F	Richmond	FM	F
Gisburn	F	F	Ripley	FM	F
Grasington	F	F	Ripon	FM	FM
Grinton	F		Romald Kirk		F
Guisborough	FM	FM	Rotherham	FM	F
Halifax	FM	FM	Scarborough	FM	
Harwood	F		Seamer	F	F
Hawes	F	FM	Sedbergh	F	FM
Haworth	F	F	Selby	FM	FM
Headon	FM		Settle	FM	FM
Helmsley	FM	FM	Sheffield	FM	FM
Holmfirth	F	F	Sherburne	FM	
Hornsey	F		Silsden		F
Howden	FM	FM	Skipton	FM	FM
Huddersfield'	FM	F	Slaidburn	F	F
Hull	FM	FM	Snaith	FM	FM
Hunmanby	F	F	South Cave	F	
Ingleton	F	F	Stamford Bridge	F	F
Kettlewell	F	F	Tadcaster	FM	
Keighley	F	FM	Stokesley	FM	
Kilham	FM		Thirsk	FM	FM
Kirby-moor-side	FM		Thorne	FM	F
Kirkham	F		Tollerton	F	F
Knaresborough	FM	FM	Topcliffe	FM	F
Lee	F		Topcliff	FM	F
Leeds	FM	FM	Wakefield	FM	FM
Leighton	F		Weighton	FM	
Leyburn	F	FM	Wetherby	FM	
Little Driffield	F		Whitby		FM
Long Preston	F	FM	Whitgift	F	
Lothersdale		F	Wibsey		F
Luiton		F	Yarm	FM	F
Malham	F	F	York	FM	FM
Malton	FM	FM			
Marsden		F			
Masham	FM	FM			
Meltham		F	**Part 3 — Public Houses and**		
Middleham	FM	F	**Brewing**		
Middlesmoor		F			
Moor-kirk	F				
New Mill		F	13 General		
Northallerton	FM	F			
Northouram	F				
North Duffield	F				
Otley	FM	FM			
Pateley Bridge		F			
Patrington	FM				
Penistone	F	FM			
Pickering	FM				
Pocklington	FM	FM			

Part 3 — Public Houses and Brewing

13 General

By the 15th century there were three main types of retail outlets:

Alehouses (sometimes called tippling houses), where beer and ale were brewed and sold on the premises. Ale was the more ancient of drinks -- beer, which included hops, had been introduced from Flanders c1400.

Taverns, where wine as well as beer and ale could be sold.

Inns, which provided shelter, stabling etc., as well as food and drink.

Legislation

14 Magna Carta 1215
This laid down that there should be standard measures of wine and ale.

15 1266/7 Assize of Bread and Ale
From this date a periodic announcement by the civic authority in each locality laid down the price of bread and ale, based upon the current prices of corn and malt.

16 1495 Licensing Statute
This gave JPs the power to supervise and suppress local ale sellers.

17 1529 Ecclesiastical Brewing
Legislation suppressed ecclesiastical brewing.

18 1552 Additional Licensing powers
JPs were given additional powers to license as well as suppress — a power they have retained to present day.

19 1553 Limitation of Taverns
Legislation this year limited the number of taverns. Those towns allowed more than one were: Bristol 6, Cambridge 4, Canterbury 4, Chester 4, Colchester 3, Exeter 4, Gloucester 4, Hereford 3, Hull 4, Ipswich 3, Lincoln 3, London 40, Newcastle-upon-Tyne 4, Norwich 4, Oxford 3, Salisbury 3, Shrewsbury 3, Southampton 3, Westminster 3, Winchester 3, Worcester 3, York 9.

20 1590 Limitation of Taverns
One extra tavern was allowed (see 1553) in Brightlingsea, Bristol, Colchester, Coventry, Exeter, Greenwich, Harwich, Hull, Ipswich, Lowe-stoft, Norwich, Sandwich, Southampton and Worcester.

21 1729 Brewster Sessions
The Brewster Sessions at which JPs would license retailers, were instituted.

22 1736 Second Gin Act
One of the series of enactments to reduce the sale of gin and the social disorder it was causing. This Act required a retailer to take out a licence for £50 and pay a duty of £1 on every gallon and also restricted licences to victuallers. It was unsuccessful and the problem was overcome gradually by other legislation.

23 1828 Alehouse Act
This consolidated previous legislation and re-defined the role of the JPs.

24 1830 Beerhouse Act
This allowed a householder, assessed to the poor rate, to retail beer from his own house, on payment of 2 guineas. The purpose of this Act was to discourage the sale of spirits.

TERMS

25 Ale Silver
A fee or gift paid to the Lord Mayor of London for the privilege of selling ale in London.

26 Aletaster
The first record of the appointment of an aletaster is in the City of London in 1377. In other places he was appointed by either a manor or vestry and his duties included the proclamation of the permitted price for selling beer and ale as laid down by the Assize of Bread and Ale 1266/7, and the sampling of the quality of ale offered for sale, differentiating between the grades. When brewers wished him to call they put up an 'ale-stake' at the front of their dwelling.

27 Bede-Ales
Drinking parties at which money was raised for someone fallen on hard times.

28 The Brewers Company
The Brewers Company was incorporated in 1437.

29 Bride-Ales
On her wedding day the bride's parents provided ale for which the guests paid.

30 Brewcreech
A term found in Cumberland, Lincs, Warks, Worcs and Scotland, meaning a duty paid by brewers.

31 Brew farm
A fee for a licence to sell ale.

32 Custom pottes
A fee paid to the lord of the manor at brewing time.

33 Host house
An inn.

34 Hucksters
Street sellers of ale, usually women.

35 Hush-shop
A house illicitly selling spirits.

36 Jigger
An illegal distillery.

37 Kidley-wink
A west-country term for an illicit alehouse.

38 Shebeen
A Scottish and Irish term for a house where beer or spirits were illicitly sold, brewed or distilled.

39 The Temperance Movement
The Temperance movement originated, in England, in the 1820's from American influences. In 1831 the British and Foreign Temperance Society was formed and extended its influence over the country in a decade. In 1847 the Band of Hope, a temperance organisation for children, was founded.

In 1853 the United Kingdom Alliance, founded in Manchester, aimed to persuade politicians, national and local, into a policy of prohibition. It was an aggressive organisation and not always popular with less militant societies. The Church took up the cause in 1862 when the Church of England Total Abstinence Society was established.

Local societies were an important feature of the community at this period, closely linked with nonformist and liberal organisations.

The movement lost much of its impetus and influence after the First World War.

40 Tippler
An alehouse-keeper.

Part 4 — Old Names for Traders and Occupations

41
Ackerman — oxherd.
Ale Draper — innkeeper, publican
Backster/Baxter — baker, occasionally a female baker.
Badger — a pedlar of food.
Badger — corn dealer, miller.
Barker — tanner.
Blaxter — bleacher.
Bowyer — maker of and dealer in bows.
Brewster — brewer.
Buckler — buckle maker.
Bunter — rag and bone man.
Cadger — a carrier, pedlar of small wares.
Cafender — carpenter.
Caffler — rag and bone man.
Capper — cap maker.
Carter — wagoner, stable headman.
Cashmarie — fish pedlar.

Chambermaster — boot and shoe maker.

Chapman — pedlar, dealer in small wares.

Collier — charcoal seller.

Copeman — a dealer. In the 18th century came to mean a receiver of stolen goods.

Cordwainer — a shoemaker.

Costermonger — originally an apple seller.

Couper — dealer in cattle and horses.

Cursitor — a clerk in the Court of Chancery who drew up writs.

Dexter — dyer.

Eggler — egg dealer.

Elliman — oil man.

Farandman — itinerant merchant.

Fell monger — a dealer in hides.

Flesher — butcher.

Fletcher — maker of and dealer in bows and arrows.

Fogger — a pedlar; headman at a farm, groom, manservant.

Frobisher — an armour polisher.

Furner — baker.

Gaffman — a bailiff.

Garthman — yardman, herdsman.

Greave/Grieve — bailiff, foreman.

Hacker — maker of hoes, mattocks, etc.

Haymonger — dealer in hay.

Higgler — itinerant dealer, generally with horse and cart.

Hillier — slater, tiler of roofs.

Hind — farm labourer.

Hooker — reaper.

Jagger — itinerant fish pedlar.

Lavender — washerwoman.

Leightonward — gardener.

Litster — dyer.

Lorimer — spurmaker.

Lotseller — street-seller.

Malender — a farmer.

Navigator — a labourer digging canals, then railways etc. Now called navvy.

Neatherd — cowherd.

Pigman — crockery dealer.

Pikeman — an assistant to a miller.

Rippier — fishmonger.

Roper — rope and netmaker.

Salter — maker of and dealer in salt.

Scrivener — clerk, specialising in drawing up bonds.

Spurrier — spur-maker.

Swailer/Swealer — miller; dealer in corn.

Tasker — reaper, thresher.

Tucker — fuller.

Webster — weaver.

Whig — Scottish horse drover.

Whittawer — saddler.

Wright — a constructor.

Part 5 — Legislation on Employment and Wages

42 1349 Ordinance of Labourers

This is the first statute to regulate wages. It fixed a maximum for different kinds of work.

43 1351 Statute of Labourers

This reinforced the 1349 Ordinance and attempted to hold wages at the levels pertaining before the Black Death. There were severe penalties for infringement but even so, the shortage of labour after the plague meant that the Statute was frequently ignored.

44 1562/3 Statute of Artificers

This laid down that wages were to be assessed by Justices, and that all able-bodied men between 12 and 60 should work in the fields if required. Servants were to be hired for at least a year and apprentices were to serve seven years. A master who infringed this Statute was fined and a servant imprisoned. Hours of labour were fixed at 12 hours in the summer and all daylight in the winter. Unmarried women were liable for domestic work.

45 1747

Disputes between master and servant might be referred to the Justices. Legislation allowed for the cancellation of an apprentice's indentures if he was ill-treated.

46 1793

An Act was passed which permitted punishment of masters found guilty of ill-treatment.

47 1799 and 1800 Combination Acts

These prohibited the combination of workers. They were repealed 1824.

48 1801/2 Health and Morals of Apprentices Act

Workhouse apprentice children were to work no more than 12 hours a day and were to have cleaner and better ventilated accommodation. The Overseer of the Poor was to keep a register of apprenticed children and the magistrates (in the event, not very well), supervise the application of the Act. It was also laid down that the apprentices should receive elementary education.

49 1819 Factory Act

This Act, applicable only to cotton mills, prohibited children under 9 from working; those above that were restricted to a 12-hour day.

50 1831 Truck Act

This Act aimed to curtail the system whereby certain workers, in particular navvies, were paid partly in goods and partly in tokens exchangeable only at the employers' shops. The workers, other than domestic servants, were to be paid wholly in coin.

51 1833 Factory Act (Althorpe's)

This Act, applicable to textile mills, laid down hours of work for young people. Children aged from 9-12 to work a maximum of 9 hours a day, 48 hours a week, from 13-18 years up to 12 hours a day, 69 hours a week. Children were to have 2 hours' schooling a day. The first four factory inspectors were appointed.

52 1842 Mines Act

This Act followed a Royal Commission which discovered appalling examples of child exploitation. Instances of children as young as 4 being employed were cited, of children working 12 hours a day alone and in darkness, and of girls as young as 6 carrying coal on their backs.

This Act prohibited the employment of women in the mines and of boys under 10. It appointed mines' inspectors.

53 1844 Factory Act

This Act, applicable to textile mills, laid down that women were not to work more than 12 hours a day and that children were to spend half their day at school.

54 1853 Factory Act

This Act, applicable to textile mills, laid down that children were to be employed only from 6 a.m. to 6 p.m., with 1½ hours for meals.

55 1867 Factory Acts Extension

This legislation extended the various Factory Act provisions to other industries employing more than 50 people in one place.

56 1867 Workshop Regulation Act

This introduced inspection of workshops by local authorities. Employment of children under 8 was prohibited and those between 8 and 13 were to work only half a day. The employment of women and young people was to fall within the provisions of previous Factory Acts.

57 1874 Factory Act

The minimum working age was to be 9 (and in 1875, 10). Women and young people were to work no more than 10 hours a day, and

children up to 14 were to work only
half a day.

**58 1891 Factory and Workshop
Act**
   The minimum working age was
raised to 11.

59 1901 Factory Act
   The minimum workir.g age was
raised to 12.

60 1937 Factory Act
   It was laid down that young
people under 16 were to work no
more than a 44-hour week, those
between 16 and 18, and women,
48 hours a week.

SECTION S

BIBLIOGRAPHY

For Section A
Agricultural Records AD220-1958/
J.M. Stratton/1969.
Ancient Fields/H.C. Bowen/1961.
English Farming Past and Present/
Lord Ernle/rev 1936.
History of the English Agricultural
Labourer/W. Hasbach/1908.
History of the English Agricultural
Labourer 1870-1920/F. E. Green/
1920.
A History of Agricultural Science in
Great Britain/Sir E. John Russell/
1966.
The Evolution of the English Farm/
M.E. Seebohm/rev 1952.
A Short History of Farming in Bri-
tain/R. Whitlock/1964.
The Agrarian History of England
1500-1640/ed Joan Thirsk.
The Agricultural Revolution 1750-
1880/J.D. Chambers and G.E. Min-
gay/1966.
History of British Agriculture 1846-
1914/C.S. Orwin and E.H. Whetham/
1964.
Farmer's Tools/G.E. Fussell/1952.
Old Farm Implements/P. Wright/
1961.
Plough and Pasture/E.C. Curwen/
1946.
The Making of the English Land-
scape/W.G. Hoskins/1955.
The Land/John Higgs/1964.
The Marketing of Agricultural Pro-
duce (a section in The Agrarian
History of England 1500-1640) ed
Joan Thirsk.
The English Farmhouse and Cottage/
M.W. Harley/1967.
The English Countrywoman/G.E.
and K.R. Fussell/1953.
Country Relics/H.J. Massingham/
1939.
The Great Landowners of Great Bri-
tain and Ireland/John Bateman/
1876 reptd 1971.
Villainage in England/Sir Paul Vino-
gradoff/1892 reptd 1968.
English Land and English Landlords/
Geo. Brodrick/1881 reptd 1968.
Common Lands of England and
Wales/W.G. Hoskins and Sir Dudley
Stamp/1963.
The Enclosure and Redistribution
of our Land/W.H.R. Curtler/1920.
Common Land and Inclosure/E.C.K.
Gonner/1966.
English Village Community and En-
closure Movements/W.E. Tate/1967.

For Sections B and C
The Manor and the Borough/2 vols/
S and B Webb/1908.
Life on the English Manor/H.S.
Bennett/1948.
The Parish and the County/S and B
Webb/1906.
The Parish/J. Toulmin Smith/rev
1857.
Liberties and Communities in Med-
ieval England/Helen Cam/1963.
British Borough Charters 1042-1216/
A. Ballard/1913.
British Borough Charters 1216-1307/
A. Ballard and J. Tait/1923.
British Borough Charters 1307-1660/
H. Weinbaum/1943.
Borough Customs/M. Bateson/2
vols/Seldon Society 1904-6.
The Story of Early Municipal His-
tory/J. Tait/1932.
English Local Administration in the
Early Middle Ages/Helen Jewell/
1972.
The Medieval English Borough/J.
Tait/1936.
Town Life in the Fifteenth Century.
Alice Stopford/2 vols/1894.

Town Government in the Sixteenth Century/J.H. Thomas/1933.

A Century of Municipal Progress 1835-1935/eds H.J. Laski, W.I. Jennings, W.A. Robson.

A Short History of Local Government/K.B. Smellie/1954.

The History of Local Government in England/Joseph Redlich and Francis Hirst/rev 1970.

History of Local Rates in England/ E. Cannan/1927.

Local Government and Taxation in England/J.W. Probyn/1882.

The Burghs of Scotland/G.S. Pryde/ 1965.

The Story of the Shire/Fredk. Hackwood.

Town Hall and Shire Hall/N.R. Tillett/1949.

Medieval Panorama/G.G. Coulton/ 1945.

New Towns of the Middle Ages/ M.W. Beresford/1967.

Seventeenth Century Life in the Country Parish/Eleanor Trotter/ 1968.

A History of London Life/H.J. Mitchell and M.D.R. Leys/1958.

The English Village Community/ Fredk Seebohm/1883 reptd 1971.

Social Life in the Reign of Queen Anne/John Ashton/1882.

English Landed Society in the 18th Century/G.E. Mingay/1963.

London Life in the Eighteenth Century/M.D. George/1930.

Leisure and Pleasure in the Nineteenth Century/Stella Margetson/ 1969.

English Landed Society in the 19th Century/F.M.L. Thompson/1963.

Victorian Cities/Asa Briggs/1963.

The Victorian Underworld/Kellow Chesney/1970.

Life and Labour of the People in London/Charles Booth/1891-1903.

Life in Edwardian England/Robert Cecil/1969.

The English Provinces/D. Read/1964

Provincial England/W.G. Hoskins/ 1963.

The English Local Government Franchise/B. Keith Lucas/1952.

A History of Parliamentary Elections and Electioneering in the Old Days/ Joseph Grego/1886.

The Administration of the Window and Assessed taxes 1696-1798/H.R. Ward/1963.

English Land Tax in the 18th Century/H.R. Ward/1953.

Lay Subsidies and Poll Taxes/M.W. Beresford/1963.

History of Taxation and Taxes in England/4 vols/S. Dowell/1884.

For Section D

Approaches to Local History/Alan Rogers/1972 (BBC Publication).

Local History in England/W.G. Hoskins rev 1972.

Local History Objective and Pursuit/ H.P.R. Finberg and V.H.T. Skipp/ 1967.

The Local Historian and His Theme/ H.P.R. Finberg/1952.

Fieldwork in Local History/W.G. Hoskins/1967.

The Parish Chest/W.E. Tate/rev 1969.

Enjoying Archives/David Iredale/ 1973.

Sources for English Local History/ W.B. Stephens/1973.

Archives and Local History/F.G. Emmison/1966.

Historical Interpretation 1066-1540/ J.J. Bagley/1965.

Historical Interpretation 1540 to Present Day/J.J. Bagley/1971.

Local Records/L. Redstone and F.W. Steer/1953.

Texts and Calendars/E.L.C. Mullins/ 1958.

Record Repositories in Great Britain/Royal Commission on Historical Manuscripts/1971.

Guide to the Public Record Office Index to the Charters and Rolls in the Department of Manuscripts of the British Museum/ed F.B. Bickley and H.J. Ellis/1900.

County Records/F.G. Emmison and Irvine Gray/rev 1967 (Hist. Assoc.)

The Hundred and the Hundred

Rolls/Helen Cam/1930.
The Manor and Manorial Records/
N.J. Hone/1906.
The Manor and Manorial Records –
a list of those to be found at the
Public Record Office, British Mu-
seum, Lambeth Palace and Bodleian
Library/1925.
Village Records/John West/1962.
Domesday Book and Beyond/F.W.
Maitland/1960.
The Making of Domesday Book/
W.H. Galbraith/1961.
The Domesday Geography of Eng-
land: Eastern England/H.C. Darby.
Northern England/H.C. Darby and
I.S. Maxwell.
South West England/H.C. Darby and
R. Welldon Finn.
South East England/H.C. Darby and
E.M.J. Campbell.
The Records of the Established
Church in England, excluding paro-
chial records/D.M. Owen/1970.
Introduction to Ecclesiastical Re-
cords/J.S. Purvis/1953.
English Seals J. Harvey Bloom/1906
A Medieval Farming Glossary (Latin
and English)/John Fisher/1968
English Wills: probate records in
England and Wales/Peter Waine/
1964/NCSS.
Wills and Their Whereabouts/An-
thony Camp/1963.
How to Read Old Title Deeds XVI-
XIX Centuries/Julian Cornwall/
1964.
Title Deeds/A.A. Dibben/1971 (Hist.
Association).
Latin for Local History/Eileen A.
Gooder/1961.
Railway History in English Local
Records/J. Simmons/1954.
National Index of Parish Registers/
D.J. Steel/12 vols (Vols 1 and 5
published to date).
The Parish Registers of England/J.C.
Cox/1910.
Index to the Marriages in the Gentle-
man's Magazine 1731-1768/E.A. Fry.
Index to the Biographical and Obit-
uary Notices in the Gentleman's
Magazine 1731-1780.

Genealogical Gazetteer of England/
Frank Smith/1968.
In Search of Ancestry/G. Hamilton-
Edwards/1969.
Genealogy for Beginners/Arthur
Willis/1970.
Tracing Your Ancestors/Anthony
Camp/1964.
English Genealogy/Anthony Wagner/
1972.
Genealogical Research in England
and Wales/David Gardner and Frank
Smith/1956/3 vols.
Local History from Blue Books/
W.R. Powell/1962.
Guide to the Records of Parliament/
Maurice Bond/1971.
Journals of the House of Commons
from 1547.
Journals of the House of Lords from
1510.
Handwriting in England and Wales/
N. Denholm-Young/1954.
The Handwriting of English Docu-
ments/L. Hector/1958.
Catalogue of English Newspapers
and Periodicals in the Bodleian
Library 1622-1800/T. Milford and
D.M. Sutherland/1936.
Tercentenary Handlist of English
and Welsh Newspapers/The Times/
1920.
Hand List of English Provincial
Newspapers and Periodicals 1700-
1760/G.A. Cranfield.
Gentleman's Magazine 1731-1818
Notes and Queries.
The London Directories 1677-1855/
C.W.F. Goss/1932.
Guide to the national and provincial
directories of England and Wales,
excluding London, published before
1856/J.E. Norton/1950.
Brasses and Brass Rubbings in Eng-
land/Jerome Bertram/1971.
Beginners Guide to Brass Rubbing/
Richard Busby/1969.
A List of Monumental Brasses in the
British Isles/Mill Stephenson.
Maps/Geographical Magazine Vol 32
No. 11, April 1960.
Maps and Map Makers/R.V. Tooley/
1970.

Maps and Plans in the Public Record Office c1410-1860/HMSO/1967.
The Large Scale County Maps of the British Isles/E.M. Rodger.
The Early Maps of Scotland, with an account of the Ordnance Survey/ Royal Scottish Geographical Society.
The Road Books and Itineraries of Great Britain 1570-1850/H.G. Fordham.
Historian's Guide to Ordnance Survey Maps/J.B. Harley/1964 (NCSS).

For Section E
Archaeology
Collins Field Guide to Archaeology in Britain/Eric S. Wood/rev 1968.
An Archaeological Guide and Glossary/James Stewart/1960.
The Archaeologists Year Book 1973.
Guide to Historical and Archaeological Publications of English and Welsh Societies 1901-1933/E.L.C. Mullins.
Index of Archaeological Papers 1665-1890 (with annual supplements to 1909)/Sir G.L. Gomme.

Air Photography and the Evolution of the Cornfield/E. C. Curwen/rev 1938.
Archaeology in the Field/O.G.S. Crawford/rev 1960.
Beginning in Archaeology/K. Kenyon/1964.
Field Archaeology/R.J.C. Atkinson/ 1953.
Archaeology: Methods and Principles/R.J.C. Atkinson/1965.
Dating the Past/Fredk Zeuner/rev 1958.
Handbook of Scientific Aids and Evidence for Archaeologists/CBA/ 1970.
Field Archaeology: Notes for Beginners/Ordnance Survey/1963.
History on the Ground/M. Beresford/rev 1971.
Lower Paleolithic Archaeology in Britain/John Wymer/1968.
A Guide to Prehistoric Scotland/ Richard Feachem/1963.

A Guide to the Prehistoric and Roman Monuments in England and Wales/Jacquetta Hawkes/1951.
The Ancient Burial Mounds of England/L.V. Grinsell/1953.
Britain in the Roman Empire/Joan Liversidge/1968.
A Gazetteer of Early Anglo-Saxon burial sites/Audrey Meaney/1964.
Town Defences in England and Wales/Hilary L. Turner/1970.

Deserted Villages/K.J. Allison/1970
The Lost Villages of England/M.W. Beresford/1954.

The Archaeology of the Industrial Revolution/Brian Bracegirdle/1973.
Industrial Archaeologist's Guide/ David and Charles.
The English Windmill/Rex Wailes/ 1954.
Industrial Archaeology/K. Hudson/ 1966.
Industrial Archaeology in Britain/ R.A. Buchanan/1972.

The Treasure Diver's Guide/John Potter/1973.
Nautical Archaeology/Bill St John Wilkes/1971.

For Section F
Education
Four Hundred Years of English Education/W.H.G. Armytage/1970.
History of Education in Great Britain/S.J. Curtis/1948 rev 1967.
The History of Scottish Education/ James Scotland/1969/2 vols.
Blond's Encyclopaedia of Education/ ed Edward Blishen.
Educational Charters and Documents 598 to 1909/A.F. Leach/ 1911.
The Universities of Europe in the Middle Ages. Vol 3 — English Universities/Hastings Rashdall/1895 rev 1936.
English Schools at the Reformation 1546-8/A.F. Leach/1896.
The Schools of Medieval England/ A.F. Leach/1915.

The Educational Innovators 1750-1880/W.A.C. Stewart and W.P. Mc-Cann/1967.
The Educational Innovators 1881-1967/W.A.C. Stewart.
A History of English Education from 1760/H.C. Bernard/1961.
An Introductory History of English Education since 1800/S.J. Curtis and M.E.A. Boultwood/1960 rev 1966.
Hope Deferred (Girls' education)/Josephine Kamm/1965.
A History of Adult Education in Great Britain/Thos Kelly/rev 1970.

For Section G
Social Welfare
History of the English Poor Law:
Vol 1 924-1714/G. Nicholls/1898.
Vol 2 1714-1853/G. Nicholls/1898.
Vol 3 1834-1894/T. Mackay/1899.
English Poor Law History/S. and B. Webb/1927-29.
The Anti-Poor Law Movement 1843-44/Nicholas Edsall/1971.
The English Poor Law 1780-1930/Michael Rose/1971.
A History of Vagrants and Vagrancy/C. Ribton-Turner/1887.
London Labour and the London Poor/Henry Mayhew/1861.

History of English Public Health/I.M. Frazer/1956.
The Sanitary Condition of the Labouring Population of Great Britain/ed M.W. Flinn/1965.
Edwin Chadwick and the Public Health Movement 1832-1854/R.A. Lewis/1952.
A Century of Public Health in Britain 1832-1929/J. Harley Williams/1932.
History of Epidemics in Britain AD 64 to Extinction of the Plague/C. Creighton/1891-94/2 vols.
Fifty Years in Public Health/Sir Arthur Newsholme/1935.
English Sanitary Institutions/John Simon/1890.

Doctors and Disease in Tudor Times/
W.S.C. Copeman/1960.
The Hospitals/Brian Abel-Smith/1964.
The Medieval Hospitals of England/Rotha Mary Clay/1909.
A History of the Nursing Profession/Brian Abel-Smith/1960.
The Story of the Growth of Nursing/Agnes Pavey/rev 1959.
Mr Guy's Hospital 1726-1948/H.C. Cameron/1954.
History of St Thomas's Hospital F.G. Parsons/1932/3 vols.
The History of the Royal College of Surgeons of England/Z. Cope/1959.
A History of the Royal College of Physicians/Sir George Clark/1964/2 vols.
The Trade in Lunacy/William L1. Parry-Jones/1972.
A History of the Mental Health Services/Kathleen Jones/1972.

History of English Philanthropy/B.K. Gray/1905.
English Philanthropy/David Owen/1964.
The Charities of London 1480-1660/W.K. Jordan/1960.

For Section H
Law and Order
Elizabethan Life: Disorder/F.G. Emmison/1970.
Guardians of the Queen's Peace/George Howard/1953.
The Thief Takers/Patrick Pringle/1958.
A History of Police in England and Wales 900-1966/T.A. Critchley.

Imprisonment in Medieval England/R. Pugh/1968.
The English Prisons/D.L. Howard/1960.
The Criminal Prisons of London/Henry Mayhew/1872.
English Prisons under Local Government/S. and B. Webb/1922.
The English Prison Hulks/W. Branch Johnson/rev 1970.

A History of English Law/Sir W.S. Holdsworth/1903-66.

English Courts of Law/H.G. Hanbury/1967.

The Courts of Law/Peter Walker/1970.

The Justices of the Peace in England 1558-1640/J.H. Gleason/1969.

A Concise History of the Common Law/T.F.T. Pucknett/rev 1961.

Historical Introduction to the Land Law/Sir W.S. Holdsworth/1927.

Contracts in Local Courts of Medieval England/R.L. Henry/1929.

Oxford Studies in Social and Legal History/Sir Paul Vinogradoff/1921.

For Section J
Public Utilities and Services

British Gas Industry before 1850/Economic History Review Vol 20 1967/M.E. Falkus.

The Victorian Celebration of Death/James Stevens Curl/1972.

The Electric Revolution/R.A.S. Hennessey/1972.

A History of the British Fire Service/G.V. Blackstone/1957.

British Fire Marks from 1680/G.A. Fothergill/1911.

Fire Marks and Insurance Office Fire Brigades/B. Williams/1927.

The History of Water Supply/F.W. Robins/1949.

Water in England/Dorothy Hartley

English Spas/William Addison/1951.

The Lost Rivers of London/Nicholas Barton/1962.

History of the Public Library Movement in Great Britain/J. Minto/1932.

The Penny Post/Frank Staff/1964.

History of the British Post Office/J.G. Hemmeon/1912.

The British Post Office to 1925/C.F. Dendy-Marshall/1926.

The Post Office — an Historical Survey/HMSO/1911.

The British Post Office/Howard Robinson/1948.

The Letter Box/Jean Farrugia/1969.

For Section K
Transport

Roman Roads in Britain/Ivan Margary/rev 1967.

Roman Ways in the Weald/Ivan Margary/rev 1956.

Roman Roads in the South East Midlands/The Viatores/1964.

Ancient Trackways of Wessex/H.W. Timperley and Edith Brill/1965.

A History of Roads/Geoffrey Hindley/1971.

The King's Highway/Rees Jeffreys/1949.

The Story of the King's Highway/S. and B. Webb/1913.

British Roads/A.E. Boumphrey/1939.

Ancient Bridges of England/S. Jervoise/1930-36/4 vols.

The Drove Roads of Scotland/A.R.B. Haldane/1952.

The Road System of Medieval England/Economic History Review Vol 7 1936/F.M. Stenton.

Great Britain, Post Roads, Post Towns and Postal Rates 1635-1839/A.W. Robertson/1961.

English Wayfaring Life in the Middle Ages/J.J. Jusserand/rev 1950.

Roads and Their Traffic 1750-1850/John Copeland/1968.

Roads and Vehicles/Anthony Bird/1969.

The Mail-Coach Men of the Late Eighteenth Century/Edmund Vale.

Stage Coach to John O'Groats/Leslie Gardiner/1961.

A Century of Traction Engines/W.J. Hughes.

The Story of the Bicycle/John Woodforde/1970.

A History of London Transport — the 19th Century/T.C. Barker and Michael Robbins/1963.

The History of British Bus Services/John Hibbs/1968.

The Omnibus/ed John Hibbs/1971.

London United Tramways/Geoffrey Wilson/1971.

Great British Tramway Networks/Wingate Bett and John Gillham/1962.

Steam Cars 1770-1970/Lord Mont-

ague and Anthony Bird/1971.
English Pleasure Carriages/W. Bridges
Adams/1837 reptd 1971.

Historical Geography of the Railways of the British Isles/E.F. Carter/1959.
A Regional History of the Railways of Great Britain:
Vol 1 The West Country/David St John Thomas.
Vol 2 Southern England/H.P. White.
Vol 3 Greater London/H.P. White
Vol 4 The North East/K. Hoole
Vol 5 The Eastern Counties/D.I. Gordon.
Vol 6 Scotland (Lowlands and Borders) John Thomas.
British Railway History 1830-1876/Hamilton Ellis/1954.
British Railway History 1877-1947/Hamilton Ellis/1959.
The Railway Mania and its Aftermath/Henry Grote Lewin/1938 reptd 1968.
Midland Railway/Fred Williams/1876 reptd 1968.

The North Western/O.S. Nock/1968.
London Midland and Scottish/Hamilton Ellis/1970.
LMS Steam/O.S. Nock/1971.
History of the Southern Railway/C.F. Dendy-Marshall and R.W. Kidner/1963/2 vols.
Railway Stations — Southern Region/Nigel Wikeley and John Middleton/1971.
London Railways/Edwin Course/1962.
London's Underground/H.F. Howson/1951 rev 1967.
The Railway Clearing House Handbook of Railway Stations 1904/reptd 1970.
Bradshaw's Railway Timetable/first published 1839.
The Railway Navvies/Terry Coleman/1965.

British Canals/Charles Hadfield/1969.
The Canal Age/Charles Hadfield/1968.
Lost Canals of England and Wales/Ronald Russell/1971.
The Canals of North West England/Charles Hadfield and Gordon Biddle/1970/2 vols.
The Canals of the West Midlands/Charles Hadfield.
The Canals of South West England/Charles Hadfield.
The Canals of South Wales and the Border/Charles Hadfield.
The Canals of South and South East England/Charles Hadfield.
The Canals of Scotland/Jean Lindsay.
The Canals of the East Midlands/Charles Hadfield.

For Section L
Religion

A Handlist of Medieval Ecclesiastical Terms/NCSS
Oxford Dictionary of the Christian Church/ed F.L. Cross
Ecclesiastical History of England/ed J.C. Dickinson:
Vol 1 The Pre-Conquest Church in England/M.Deanesley/1961.
Vol 5 The Victorian Church, Parts One and Two/W.O. Chadwick/1966 and 1970.

Pelican History of the Church/ed by W.O. Chadwick.

Vicarages in the Middle Ages/R.A.R. Hartridge/1930.
English Dioceses/G. Hill/1900.
History of the English Clergy 1800-1900/C.K.F. Brown/1953.
Origin of the Office of Churchwarden/C. Drew/1954.

Five Centuries of Religion/G.G. Coulton/1923-50/4 vols.
Parish Priests and their People in the Middle Ages/E.L. Cutts/1891.
The Country Clergy in Elizabethan and Stuart Times/A.T. Hart/1958.
Church Life in England in the 13th Century/J.R. Moorman/1934.

The English Reformation/A.G. Dickens/1964.

Sources for the History of Roman Catholics in England/J.H. Pollen/ SPCK 1921.
Catholics in England/1559-1829/ M.D.R. Leys/1961.
Recusant Records/ed C. Talbot/ Catholic Records Society Vol 53 1961.

History of Presbyterianism in England/A.H. Drysdale/1889.
Origins of the Plymouth Brethren/ H.H. Rowden/1965 (Ph.D).
History of English Congregationalism/R.W. Dale/1907.
The Beginnings of Quakerism/W.C. Braithwaite/rev 1955.
History of the Salvation Army/R. Sandall/1947.
History of English Baptists/A.C. Underwood/1947.
New History of Methodism/W. Townsend, W.J. Workman and G. Hayes/1909/2. vols.
The Moravian Communities in Britain/W.H.G. Armytage/Church Quarterly Review No. 158.

The Churches and the Working Classes in Victorian England/K.S. Inglis/1963.

For Section M
The Militia
Elizabeth's Army/C.G. Cruickshank/ 1946.
The Elizabethan Militia 1558-1638/ Lindsay Boynton/1967.
Cromwell's Army/Charles Firth/ 1902 rev 1962.
History of the Uniforms of the British Army/Cecil Lawson/5 vols.
A Register of the Regiments and Corps of the British Army/ed Arthur Swinson/1972.

A Naval History of England/G.J. Marcus/1961/2 vols.
A Social History of the Navy 1793-1815/Michael Lewis/1960.
The British Seaman/Christopher Lloyd/1968.

For Section N
Architecture
Local Style in Architecture/T.D. Atkinson/1947.
English Medieval Architecture/C.E. Power/1923/3 vols.
Architecture in Britain 1530-1830/ Sir John Summerson/1953.
Buildings of England/N. Pesvner/ Penguin series.
Early Victorian Architecture/H.R. Hitchcock/1954/2 vols.
Collins Guide to English Parish Churches/ed John Betjeman.
The English Medieval Parish Church/ G.H. Cook/1954.
Introduction to Tudor Architecture/ J.H. Harvey/1949.

History of Building Materials/N. Davey/1961.
History of English Brickwork/N. Lloyd/1925.
Building Stones/A.R. Warnes/1926.

Form Section O
Names
Oxford Dictionary of English Place Names/E. Ekwall/rev 1960.
English Place Name Elements/A.H. Smith/1956/2 vols.
The Origin of English Place Names/ P.H. Reaney/1960.
English Place Names and Their Origins/G.J. Copley/1968.
The English Place Name Society series.
The English Hundred Names/O.S. Anderson/1934-39/3 vols.
English Field Names/John Field/ 1972.
English River Names/E. Ekwall/ 1928.
A Dictionary of British Surnames/ P.H. Reaney/1958.
The Oxford Dictionary of English Christian Names/E.G. Withycombe.
Penguin Dictionary of Surnames/ 1966.

For Section P
Coins and Tokens
English Coins from the 7th Century

to the Present Day/G.C. Brooke/ 1932.

Story of the English Coinage/P.J. Seaby/1952.

Anglo-Saxon Coins/ed R.H.M. Dolley.

The Scottish Coinage/I.H. Stewart/ 1955.

Kenyon's Gold Coins of England/ R.L. Kenyon/1884 reptd 1969.

Trade Tokens Issued in 17th Century England/W. Boyne/rev 1892/2 vols.

English Trade Tokens: Industrial Revolution Illustrated/P. Mathias/ 1962.

19th Century Token Coinage of Great Britain and Ireland/W.J. Davis/ 1904.

For Section Q
Heraldry
An Encyclopaedic Dictionary of Heraldry/Julian Franklyn and John Tanner/1970.

Boutell's Heraldry/rev 1970.

Heraldry Simplified/W.A. Copinger/ 1910.

For Section R
Trade, Commerce and Industry
The Livery Companies of the City of London/William Hazlitt/1892.

The Guilds and Companies of London/George Unwin/1963.

The Early English Trade Unions/A. Aspinall/1949.

The History of Trade Unionism/ S. and B. Webb/1894.

A History of British Trade Unionism/Henry Pelling/1963.

The Making of the English Working Class/E.P. Thompson/rev 1968.

English Fairs and Markets/William Addison/1953.

Discovering English Fairs/Margaret Baker.

Royal Commission on Market Rights and Tolls/1889/2 vols.

Markets of London/Cuthbert Maughan/1931.

A History of the English Public House/H.A. Monckton/1969.

Old Inns of England/C.G. Harper/ 1906/2 vols.

The History of Liquor Licensing in England 1700-1830/S. and B. Webb/1903.

The Brewing Industry in England 1700-1830/Peter Mathias/1959.

English Inn Signs/J. Larwood and J.C. Hotten/1951.

Some Sources of Inn History/W.B. Johnson/Amateur Historian Vol 6 No. 1 1963.

Drink and the Victorians/Brian Harrison/1971.

The Stannaries/G.R. Lewis/1934.

The Rise of the British Coal Industry 1550-1700/J. H. Nef/1966/2 vols.

Glassmaking in England/H.J. Powell/ 1923.

Furniture Making in the 17th and 18th Centuries in England/R.W. Symonds/1955.

The Wool Trade in English Medieval Industry/E. Power/1941.

The Wool Trade in Tudor and Stuart England/F.J. Bowden/1963.

The Village Carpenter/W. Rose/ 1937.

Village Labourer 1760-1832/ J.L. and B. Hammon/1948.

The Story of the Smith/F.W. Robins/1953.

The Medieval Mason/Douglas Knoop and G. Jones/1949.

The Porters of London/Walter M. Stern/1960.

The London Tradesmen/R. Campbell/1747 reptd 1969.

English Trade in the Middle Ages/ L.F Salzman/1964.

English Industries of the Middle Ages/L.F. Salzman/1964.

Economic History of England/(18th Century)/T.S. Ashton/1955.

The Industrial Revolution/T.S. Ashton/1948.

Retail Trading in Britain 1850-1950/ James Jeffreys/1954.

A History of Shopping/Dorothy Davis/1966.

Abacus N1
Abjuration of the Realm H43
Abutment N2
Acanthus N3
Accapitare C1
Achievement Q7
Acre (measure) A2
Acre A249
Acreland A3
Acreme A4
Act of Association 1696 D67
Ade A250
Adjustment of Rights A329
Administration Act Books D162
Administration Bond D139
Adopted Children — registration
    D35
Advowson L38
Advowson Appendant L39
Advowson in Gross L40
Adult School Movement F12
Adze E84
AE P32
Aerial Photography E74
Affeerers B79 H44
Agger E1 K40
Agist A370
Agister B80
Agricultural History A455
Agricultural History Societies D254
Agricultural Organisations A456
Aid A250
Aids C2 C72
Aisle N105
Ait A51
Alderman B81
Aleconner B82 R5
Alefounder B82 R5
Alehouse Act 1552 D115
Alehouse Act 1828 R23
Alehouse keepers — licensing of
    D115
Alehouses R13
Ale Silver R25
Ale stake R26
Aletaster B82 R5 R26
Alien B170

Alienation A421
Alienation Office A421
Aliens, Returns of D66
Allegiance B203
Al(l)odium A371
Allotment A372
Almanac Man B83
Almsgiving G5 G6 G7
Almshouses G23
Altar N106
Altarage C80
Althorpe's Factory Act 1833 R51
Amad A52
Amen Clerk B84
Amercement B204 H45
Amober C3
Anabaptists L20
Ancaster Stone N150
Ancient Demesne A373 C72
Ancient Messuage A457
Ancient Monuments Consolidation
    and Amendment Act 1918 A483
Ancient Monuments Preservation
    A483
Ancient Monuments Protection
    Act 1882 A483
Ancient Monuments Protection
    Act 1900 A483
Ancient B68
Angel P1
Angel Beam N4
Anglesey —
    Probate Courts D138
    Baptist Registers D44
    County Record Office D246
    Police H9
    Fairs/Markets charters R11
    Fairs/Markets 1792 and 1888
        R12
Annates C81
Annulet Q8
Applegarth A53
Apprenticeship Records D118
Appropriation C82
Approvement A251
Approvers H46
Apse N107
Archaeological Periods E73

Archaeological Publications D247
Archaeological Societies D247
Archaeology Section E
Archaeomagnetism E75
Archdeacon L10
Architecture Section N
Architrave N5
Archives Section D
Argent Q9
Armed (Heraldic) Q10
Armory Q1-76
Arpen(t) A5
Armorial Bearings, Tax on C115
Army Historical Societies D248
Army Lists D179
Army Records D179-189
Army Registers D43
Army Registers after 1880 D189
Arras Culture E2
Arrentation C4
Arrowhead E85
Artisans & Labourers Dwellings
    Improvement Act 1875 G38
Ashlar N151
Assart A54
Assessed Rates Act 1869 B225
Assize H47
Assize of Arms 1181 M3
Assize of Arms 1285 H1
Assize of Bread and Ale R15, R26
Assize of Clarendon 1166–View of
    Frankpledge H25
Assize of Darrein Presentment H31
Assize of Mort d'Ancestor H30
    A445
Assize of Novel Disseisin H29
Association Oath Rolls D167 D67
Atcheson P2
Atheling B171
Atrium N6
Attainder H48
Augmentations (Heraldic) Q12
Aulnager B85 R6
Avenage C5
Average C6
Awl E86
Aylesford Culture E3
Azure (Heraldic) Q13

Bache A55
Badgers G24
Badgers, licensing of D68
Badges Q14

Bailey N135
Bailie-days C7
Bailiff B86
Bailiffs, record of names D70
Bailiwick B1
Bairman G25
Balfour's Education Act 1902 F9
Balk A252
Baluster N7
Balustrade N8
Band of Hope R39
Bang A56
Bang-Beggar B87
Bank A56
Bannering B205
Baptist Registers & Records D44
Baptists L21
Bar (Heraldic) Q15
Barbican N136
Bareman N25
Barge Board N9
Barges, registration of D69
Barken A57
Barmote B2
Barn A458
Barony B3
Barrow A58
Barrowists L22
Barrows E4
Barry (Heraldic) Q16
Barth A59
Barton A60
Bartizan N10
Basket Tenure A374
Bas-Relief N11
Bastardy Legislation G26
Bastardy Returns D71
Bastion N137
Batch A61
Bath Stone N152
Battle, Trial by H76
Battlement N138
Baulk A252
Baulk (Archaeology) E5
Bawn A62
Beaconage C8
Beadhouse G27
Beadle B88
Beadman B88
Beagle B88
Beaker People E6
Bearing Q17
Beastgate A332
Beating the Bounds B206

Beck A63
Bede C9
Bede ales R27
Bedehouse G27
Bedell B88
Bedellary B4
Bedemad C9
Bederepe C9
Bedewed C9
Bedewick B5
Bedfordshire —
  Probate Courts D138
  Baptist Registers D44
  Congregational Registers D48
  Methodist Registers D55
  Moravian Registers D56
  County Record Office D246
  Schools F31
  Police H9
  Prisons H14
  Fairs, Markets, charters R11
  Fairs and Markets in 1792 and
    1888 R12
  Mints P31
Bedman B89
Bedral B90
Beerhouse Act 1830 R24
Beggar-Banger B91
Beighton, Henry D232
Belfry N108
Bell Barrow E7
Bell Gable N109
Bellman B92
Bell Pit E8
Belvedere N12
Bench Ends N110
Bend (Heraldic) Q18
Bend Sinister Q19
Benefice L41
Benefit of Clergy H49 L42
Benerth C10
Berbiage C11
Berewick B5
Berkshire —
  Probate Courts D138
  Baptist Registers D44
  Congregational Registers D48
  Countess of Huntingdon's
    Connection Registers D49
  Methodist Registers D55
  Presbyterian Registers D60
  County Record Office D46
  Schools F31

  Police H9
  Prisons H14
  Gas Companies J9
  Fairs/Markets — charters R11
  Fairs/Markets 1792 and 1888
    R12
  Mints P31
Berm E9
Berneshawe A64
Berton A65
Bercia A6
Besswarden B93
Beveches C12
Bible Christian Registers D45
Bible Christians L32
Bibliography Section S
Bield A459
Bierbalk L43
Biggin A460
Bills of Mortality D119
Bind Days C13
Birth Certificates D34
Births and Deaths on HM Ships
  D190
Births and Deaths on Merchant
  Ships D191
Biscot B207
Bishops' Transcripts D203 D42
  D22
Blancheferme C14
Blind House H22
Board of Education F7
Board Schools F13
Boards of Guardians — records
  D120
Bona Notabilia D140
Bondage C15
Bond of Indemnification G28
Bond Tenants A375
Bong A66
Bookland A376
Booley A67
Booly A67
Boon C16
Boonmaster B94
Boonwork C17
Boor B181
Booth A461
Borchalpening B208
Bordar B172
Border/Bordure Q20
Bord Lode C18
Borough B6

Borough Charters B224
Borough English A422 A377
Borough Sessions H38
Borsholder B95
Borstal K9
Bosing E76
Boss N13
Bote A330
Bottle A462
Bottom A68
Boundary Banks E10
Bounty Papers D192
Bourne A69
Bovate A7
Bow A463
Bowen, Samuel D233
Bowl Barrow E11
Bozzler B96
Bracket N14
Brake A70
Brasses N111
Breach A71
Breck A72
Breconshire —
    Probate Courts D138
    Baptist Registers D44
    Police H9, H11
    Fairs/Markets — charters R11
    Fairs/Markets 1792 and 1888
        R12
Breech A71
Brewcreech R30
Brewers Company R28
Brew Farm R31
Brewing and Public Houses R13-40
Brewing — ecclesiastical R17
Brewster Sessions D115 R21
Bride-ales R29
Bridewell H15
Bridges, county rate K2
Bridges, repair of K2
Bridge-bote C75
Bridle-path K10
Brigbote C19
British and Foreign School Society
    F14
British and Foreign Temperance
    Society R39
British Schools F14
Broad A253
Broad Oxgang A8
Broch E12
Broke Money P33

Brownists L23
Buckinghamshire —
    Probate Courts D138
    Baptist Registers D44
    Congregational Registers D48
    Methodist Registers D55
    County Record Office D246
    Schools F31
    Police H9
    Prisons H14
    Gas Companies J9
    Fairs/Markets — charters R11
    Fairs/Markets 1792 and 1888
        R12
    Mints P31
Burgage A73 A378
Burgage Holding A378
Burgh B7
Burgbote C20
Burghbote C75
Burgmotes B52
Burh B8
Burial Acts 1852/3 J6
Burial Boards — franchise B242/3
Burial Boards J6/7
Burial in Wool Acts D25
Burin E87
Burleyman B97
Burn A75
Burton A74
Buses K56
Butchers — licensing D89
Building Materials N150-168
Butland A76
Butt A254
Buttress N112
Bydel B88
Byes A77
Byrlaw B9

Cadency Q21
Cadet (Heraldic) Q22
Caernarvonshire —
    Probate Records D138
    County Record Office D246
    Police H9
Cage H16
Cagge H16
Cairn E13
Calendar, The D257/258
Calendar (Archive term) D1
Cam A78

Cove N30
Cove (Archeological) E22
Cowgate A342
Cow Leaze A343
Crescent Moon (Heraldic) Q33
Cressets N118
Crest Q34
Crew(e) A92
Criminal Records D173
Croat A93
Crocket N31
Croft A93
Cromlech E23
Crop Marks E24 E74
Crossing N119
Croud A93
Crowd A93
Crown P3
Crowned (Heraldic) Q35
Crucifixion Chamber E25
Crucks N32
Crypt N120
Cumberland —
    Probate Records D138
    Baptist Registers D44
    Congregational Registers D48
    Countess of Huntingdon's
    Connection Registers D49
    Methodist Registers D55
    Presbyterian Registers D60
    County Record Office D246
    Schools F31
    Police H9
    Prisons H14
    Fairs/Markets — charters R11
    Fairs/Markets 1792 and 1888
      R12
Cunner A90
Cup and Ring Marks E26
Cupola N33
Curate L11
Curation D144
Currency Bar E27
Cursus E28
Curtain Wall N139
Curtesy of England A425
Curtilage A469
Cusps N34
Custom Pottes R32
Customals B211
Customary Court Baron B21
Customary Freehold A383
Custos Rotulorum B19 B125 D64

Dado N35
Dales A261
Dalt A262
Dame Schools F19
Dandiprat P4
Danegeld C119
Danelaw Counties B28
Danish Forts E29
Darrein Presentment, Assize of
    H31
Davoch A11
Day-Math A12
Day-Work A13
Dean L12
Death Certificates D34
Decimer B108
Decree D145
Deed Land A384
Deed of Gift A418
Deed of Grant A418
Deed Poll D4
Deer Roast E30
Dell A263
Demesne A94 A385
Demise A426
Denbigh —
    Probate Records D138
    Baptist Registers D44
    Police H9
Dendochronology D77
Denn A95
Deodand H52
Deputy Mayor B127
Derbyshire —
    Probate Records D138
    Baptist Registers D44
    Congregational Registers D48
    Countess of Huntingdon's
    Connection Registers D49
    Methodist Registers D55
    Moravian Registers D56
    New Jerusalemite Registers D57
    Presbyterian Registers D60
    County Record Office D246
    Schools F31
    Police H9
    Prisons H14
    Fairs/Markets — charters R11
    Fairs/Markets 1792 and 1888
      R12
    Mints P31
Description Books (Army) D184
Description Books (Navy) D193

Ealdorman B111 B156
Easter Dues C85
Ecclesiastical Brewing R17
Ecclesiastical Courts H26 L8
Eddish A99
Edge A265
Edition (Maps) D217
Education   Section F
Education Act 1870 F4 B244
Education Act 1880 F6
Education Act 1889 F7
Education Act 1902 F9 F22
Education Act 1944 F11 F22
Elders B68
Electioner B176
Electrical Resistivity E78
Electricity Supplies J10
Embrasure N141
Employment Legislation R42-60
Enclosure Act 1607 A361
Enclosure Act (General) A363
Enclosure Acts 1760-1797 A362
Enclosure Act 1845 A365
Enclosure Award Maps D218
Enclosure Awards D76
Enclosure by Consent A364
Enclosure Commissioners A365
Enclosure Legislation A359-369
Enclosure Roads K17
Enclosures — curtailment 1876
   A366
End A100
Enfeoff A428
Englescherie H67
Englishry H67
Engraver (Maps) D219
Engrossment A266
Entailed land — conveyancing
   A419
Entablature N41
Entasis N42
Eorl B177
Erding A470
Ermine Q39
Ermines Q40
Ersh A101
Erws A14
Elementary Education —
   1876 legislation F5
   1891 legislation F8
Escheat A429
Escheators A429
Escuage C121

Escutcheon Q50
Essart A102
Essex —
   Probate Records D138
   Baptist Records D44
   Congregational Records D48
   Countess of Huntingdon's
   Connection Records D49
   Methodist Records D55
   New Jerusalemite Records D57
   Presbyterian Records D60
   County Record Office D246
   Schools F31
   Police H9
   Prisons H14
   Gas Companies J9
   Fairs/Markets — charters ?11
   Fairs/Markets 1792 and 1888
      R12
   Mints P31
Essoin B213
Estate Maps D220
Estate Papers D122
Estovers A345
Estray B214
Estreat D6
Etch A103
Extents B215
Extra-Parochial B24
Eyre, Justices on H32

Fabric Lands C86
Factor B112
Factory Act 1819 R49
Factory Act 1833 R51
Factory Act 1844 R53
Factory Act 1853 R54
Factory Act 1874 R57
Factory Act 1901 R59
Factory Act 1937 R60
Factories Acts Extension 1867 R55
Factory and Workshop Act R58
Factory Schools F21
Faience E36
Fairs and Markets R2-12
   Charters R11
   Legislation R3
   1792 and 1888 R12
   Administration R4
Faitours H57
Falcage A346
Fan Vault N43
Fardel A15 A267

Farleu A430
Farley A430
Farm A386
Farm C32
Farm Buildings A450-472
Farren A268
Farrow K18
Farthing P6
Farthingdale A16
Farthinghold A16
Fee A387
Fee Simple A419
Fee Simple Conditional A419
Fee-Farm Rents A388
Feet of Fines D171
Female Servants — Tax on C122
Feodary A431
Feoffment A418
Ferbote A347
Ferendell A17
Ferling A18
Fesse Q41
Fesse Point Q42
Feudal Aids C2
Feudal Incidents C33
Ffridd A104
Fief B25
Field A269
Field (Heraldic) Q43
Field Garden Allotments A270
Field Jury B26
Field Master B113
Field Names A51-247
Field Reeve B113
Fieldman B113
Fifteen B27
Fifteenth C123
Fillet N44
Fine A432
Fine Rolls D172
Fines C34
Finial N45
Fire Brigades J1 J2
Fire Insurance Companies J1 J2
Firebote A347
Fit A105
Five Boroughs B28
Fixed Feasts D258
Flash A106
Flat(t) A19 A271
Flintshire —
   Probate Records D138
   Baptist Records D44

County Record Office D246
  Police H9
Flockrake A107
Flonk A108
Florin P7
Fluorine Measurement E78
Fluting N46
Fogous E37
Foils N47
Fold A109
Fold Course C36
Foldage C35
Foldbote A348
Folio D7
Folkland A272
Folklore Societies D249
Food Rents C124
Footpaths K19
Ford K20
Fordraught K21
Fore-Acre A273
Foreman of the Fields B113
Forests — administration B164
Forfal B216
Forfang H58
Forfeiture H59
Forical A273
Forschel A110
Forstal A111
Forsters Education Act 1870 F4
Foss(e) A112
Fother A274
Franchise B225-244
Frank Fee A390
Frank Tenement A392
Frank Tenure A383
Frankalmoin A389
Franklin B116 B178
Frankmarriage A391
Frankpledge B29
Free Church of England L26
Free Church of Scotland L27
Free Peasant B179
Free Services C37
Free Socage A395 A413
Free Warren A396
Freebench A433
Freedom A349
Freehold A393
Freehold Tenures — conveyancing
  A418
Freeland A394
Freeman B179 B180

Freemasons — returns of D77
Freemen's Rolls D123
Freeth A113
Friendly Societies — registration
  D78
Frieze N48
Frith A114
Fumage C125
Furhead A275
Furlong A20 A276
Furnage C38
Furrow A115
Fyrd M1
Fyrd-bote C75 M1

Gable C39
Gable (Architecture) N49
Gafol C39
Gainage A116
Gair A117
Gait A277 A350
Gale C40
Gall A118
Gallery Graves E38
Gallets N158
Game Duty C126 D79
Gaol Delivery D80
Gaol Delivery, Commission of H35
Garb (Heraldic) Q44
Garderobe N50 N142
Gargoyle N51
Garston A119
Garth A471
Garthstead A472
Gas Companies J9
Gas Light and Coke Co. J8
Gas Supplies J8
Gasworks Clauses Act 1847 J8
Gate A277 A350
Gate (Path) K22
Gatehouse N143
Gatrum K23
Gauger B114
Gavel B10
Gavelacre C41
Gavelerthe C42
Gavelkind A434
Gavelsed C43
Gavol C39
Gazebo N52
Gebur B181
Geld C44 C127
Gemote B30

Genealogical Societies D250
Geneat B182
General Musters M6
Gennell K24
General Turnpike Act 1773 K4
Gentleman (Vestry) B68
Geochronology E80
Geographical Features A51-247
Geological Maps D221
George Rose's Act 1812 D30
Gesith B183
Gilbert's Act 1782 B237 G14
Gill A120
Gin Act 1736 R22
Glamorgan —
  Probate Records D138
  Baptist Records D44
  County Record Office D246
  Police H9
Glebae Adscriptitii B184
Glebe A397
Glebe Terriers D204
Gloucestershire —
  Probate Records D138
  Baptist Records D44
  Congregational Records D48
  Countess of Huntingdon's
  Connection Records D49
  Methodist Records D55
  Moravian Records D56
  Presbyterian Records D60
  County Record Office D246
  Schools F31
  Police H9
  Prisons H14
  Gas Companies J9
  Fairs/Markets — charters R11
  Fairs/Markets 1792 and 1888
    R12
  Mints P31
Godbote C87
Gore A121
Gospel Tree A122
Gracious Aids C2
Grades of Coin P35
Grammar Schools F22
Grammar School Act 1840 F22
Grand Assize H37
Grasson A435
Grassum A435
Graver E89
Great Tithes C88
Gr(e)ave A123

Green Lane K25
Green Village B31
Greenwich Hospital Records D194
  D50
Greenwood, Christopher D237
Greeve A123
Grip A124
Groat P8
Ground A125
Groundage C45
G(u)ardant Q45
Guardians of the Poor B115 G18
  G19
Guild Records D205
Guinea P9
Gules Q46
Guns, Tax on C128
Gut A126
Gypsey A127
Gyronny Q47

Hachuring D222
Hade A128
Hafod A129
Hag(g) A130
Hair Powder Duty C129
Halberd E90
Hale A131
Half A132
Half-crown P10
Half-penny P11
Half Ryal P12
Half-year close A133
Half-year land A278
Hall A131
Hallhouse A473
Hallstatt Culture E39
Halmot B32
Hallmoot B32
Hallmote B32
Halter Path K26
Ham A134 A279
Ham B33
Hamil B34
Hamlet B35
Hammer Beams N53
Hammerponds E40
Hampshire —
  Probate Records D138
  Baptist Records D44
  Bible Christian Records D45
  Congregational Records D48
  Countess of Huntingdon's

Connection Records D49
Methodist Records D55
Presbyterian Records D60
County Record Office D246
Schools F31
Police H9
Prisons H14
Fairs/Markets — charters R11
Fairs/Markets 1792 and 1888
  R12
Mints P31
Hamstal A135
Handwriting D262
Hanger A136
Hanging Field A137
Hansard D206
Hant A138
Harden A139
Hardwick B36
Hardwicke's Marriage Act 1754
  D28 D33
Harrage C46
Harrial A436
Harve A140
Hatch A141
Hatchet A142
Hatchment Q48
Haughland A143
Haw A144
Hawgable A378 C47
Hay A145
Haybote A351
Hayward B117
Headborough B118
Headland A280
Headsilver C27
Heaf A147
Health & Morals of Apprentices
  Act 1801/2 R48
Hearth Penny C89
Hearth Tax C130 D81
Heater A148
Hedgebote A351
Hedge-looker B119
Helm P13
Hempland A149
Hendre A150
Henge E41
Heraldic Societies D250
Heraldry Section Q
Herefordshire —
  Probate Records D138
  Baptist Records D44

D99
Police Act 1946 H11
Police Acts, Local H4
Police in Scotland H12
Poll Books D100
Poll Tax C139
Pond Barrows E55
Ponderator B143 R10
Pontage C62
Poor Law — franchise B237-240
Poor Law Act 1563 B104
Poor Law Act 1601 G9
Poor Law Act 1844 F2
Poor Law Act 1930 G20
Poor Law Amendment Act 1834
B115 B239 G18
Poor Law Amendment Act 1844
B240 D71
Poor Law Commissioners G18
Poor Rate Returns D101
Poor Relief Act 1819 B231
Poorhouses G8 G9
Port B59
Port Way K35
Portcullis N148
Portico N80
Portland Stone N164
Possessioning B220
Possessory Assizes H28
Post Hole E56
Post Mills E99
Post Office J3 J4
Post Offices, old J4
Pound P19
Pounds B221
Poundkeeper B144
Praedial Tithes C102
Prebend L52
Precentor B145
Prerogative Court of Canterbury
D135 D137 D158
Prerogative Court of York D159
Presbyterian Registers D60
Presbytery N128
Presentation L53
Presentment H71
Preservation of Historic Buildings
A476
Preservation Societies D252
Primer Seisin A446
Primogeniture A447
Principal Probate Registry D135
D163

Printing Presses — licensing D102
Prison Registers D58
Prisons D103 H13-23
Prisoners — returns of D104
Probate Act D153
Probate Act Books D161
Probate Records D135-166
Probing E81
Process Registers D105
Processioning B220
Proper (Heraldic) Q63
Protestant Methodists L32
Protestation 1641 D177
Provincial Constitution of Can-
terbury 1598 D22
Provost B146
Public Health Act 1848 B241
Public Health (Water) Act 1878 J5
Public Houses and Brewing R13-40
Public Libraries J11-15
Public Libraries Act 1850 J11
Public Libraries Act 1854 J12
Public Libraries Act 1855 J13
Public Libraries Act 1892 J14
Public Libraries Act 1919 J15
Public Schools F25
Public Schools Act 1868 F25
Public Undertakings — county
records D106
Punder B147
Purbeck Marble N165
Purlieu A207
Purpresture A406
Purpure Q64
Purveyance C140

Quadrant System E82
Quaker Records and Registers D59
Quakers L35
Qualification of Women (County
& Borough Councils) Act 1907
B236
Quarentena A39
Quarter A208
Quarter B60
Quarter Sessions B20 H38
Quarter Sessions Records D64-117
Quarterage C63
Quarterings Q65
Quarterly (Heraldry) Q66
Quatrefoil N81
Queen Anne's Bounty C103
Querns E93

Quia Emptores A448
Quillet A209 A304
Quit Claim H72
Quit Rent C64
Quoin N82

Race-courses — licensing D89
Racehorses, tax on C141
Radio-carbon dating E83
Radknight B193
Radnorshire —
    Probate Records D138
    Police H9 H11
Ragged Schools F26
Ragman D15
Raik K36
Raikes, Robert F28
Railways K53
Rake K36
Rampant (Heraldic) Q67
Rand A210
Rap A211 A305
Rape B61
Rath E57
Ravelin N149
Reading A212
Rean A306
Recognizances D107
Recto D16
Rector L16
Rectorial Tithes C104
Recusants D108 L54
Red Flag Act 1865 K57
Reeding A212
Reen A213
Reeve B148
Regality B62
Regardant Villein B194
Regimental Registers D188
Registrar of Friendly Societies D78
Registration of Births, Deaths and
    Marriages in England and Wales
    D34
Registration of Births, Deaths and
    Marriages in Ireland D38
Registration of Births, Deaths and
    Marriages in Scotland D37
Registration Tax C142
Regnal Years D259
Regrant A449
Reguard B63
Release A418
Releet K37

Relict D154
Relief A418
Religion Section L
Religious History Societies D253
Religious Sects L20-37
Removal G34
Removal orders for paupers D109
Rents Section C
Replevin H73
Representation of the People Act
    — 1867 B225
    — 1918 B226
    — 1928 B227
    — 1945 B228
Reredos N129
Reveland A407
Reverse P44
Reversion A418
Revet N83
Revetment E58
Rib N84
Ridding A212
Ridding K38
Ridge A307
Ridgeway K39 E59
Riding B64
Rig and Rennal A308
Rigg A307
Ring Barrows E60
Roads K1-52
Rocque, John D242
Rogue Money H21
Roll D17
Roman Catholic Registers D21
Roman Roads K40
Romescot C105
Rood N130
Rose Window N85
Rotation Meadow A309
Rotunda N86
Round House H22
Roundels Q68
Royal Lancastrian Society F14
Royal Peculiar L55
Royalty (area) B65
Royd A214
Rural Dean L17
Rural District Councils B234
Rustication N87
Rutland —
    Probate Records D138
    Baptist Records D44
    Congregational Records D48

306

— Highways K1
— Law and Order H1
Stetch A317
Steward B159
Stint A318 A357
Stitch A317
Stitch-meal A319
Stocks H75
Stoneman B157
Stonewarden B157
Stray A358
String Course N94
Strip Farming A320
Stubb A231
Stubbing A231
Sturges Bourne Acts 1818 and 1819
   B54 B230 B231
Swale A232
Swainmoot B71
Swanimote B72
Swedenborg Registers D61
Swineherd B160
Subsidy Rolls D178
Suffolk —
   Probate Records D138
   Baptist Records D44
   Congregational Records D48
   Methodist Records D55
   Presbyterian Records D60
   County Record Office D246
   Schools F31
   Police H9
   Prisons H14
   Fairs/Markets — charters R11
   Fairs/Markets 1792 and 1888
     R12
   Mints P31
Suit of Court B223
Suit of Mill C71
Sulung A43
Sunday Schools F28
Supporters (Heraldic) Q73
Surcharge A321
Surplice Fees C111
Surrender A420 A452
Surrey —
   Probate Records D138
   Baptist Records D44
   Bible Christian Records D45
   Congregational Records D48
   Irvingite Records D53
   Methodist Records D55
   County Record Office D246

Schools F31
Police H9
Prisons H14
Gas Companies J9
Fairs/Markets — charters R11
Fairs/Markets 1792 and 1888
   R12
Mints P31
Surrogate L18
Surveyor of Highways B158 K3
Sussex —
   Probate Records D138
   Baptist Records D44
   Bible Christian Records D45
   Congregational Records D48
   Countess of Huntingdon's
   Connection Records D49
   Methodist Records D55
   Presbyterian Records D60
   County Record Offices D246
   Schools F31
   Police H9
   Prisons H14
   Fairs/Markets — charters R11
   Fairs/Markets 1792 and 1888
     R12
   Mints P31

Tallage C72
Tail-race E96
Tallet A477
Taverns R13 R19 R20
Taxes Section C
Tealby P46
Team B73
Teinds C90
Temperance Movement R39
Temporalities C112 L56
Tenancy at Will A414
Tenant by Copy A415
Tenant by the Verge A416
Tenant-in-Chief A417
Tenants A370-417
Tenantry Acre A44
Tenantry Field A322
Tenantry Road K45
Tenth C146
Tenures A370-417
Tenures Abolition Act 1660 A400
Terra Regis A373
Tessellated Pavement N95
Testamentary Peculiar D137 D155
Testoon P25

Tewer K46
Thane B196
Theam B73
Thegn B196
Theow B197
Third Penny C73
Thirdborough B161
Thirling Mill C54
Thrall B198
Three Farthings P26
Threepenny Piece P27
Thrymsa P28
Thwaite A233
Tide Mills E98
Tie Beam N96
Tile Hanging N97
Tippler R40
Tippling Houses R13
Tithe Act 1925 C113
Tithe Act 1936 C113
Tithes, Commutation of D73
Tithe Commutation Act 1836
    C113 D73 D132
Tithe Maps D230
Tithe Redemption Commission
    D230
Tithe Records D132
Tithes C113
Tithing B74
Tithingman B162
Title Deeds D133
Toft A478
Tokens P47
Toll C74
Toll Booth H23
Torteaux Q74
Tower Mills E100
Town and Country Planning Act
    1944 — preservation A483
Town Husband B163
Town Place A479
Townbalk A252
Townland A234
Township A235 B75
Tracery N98
Trade History Societies D254
Trained Bands M6
Tramways K55
Tramways Act 1870 K55
Tranchet E94
Transept N133
Transfer of Land A418-447
Transom N99

Transport Section K
Transport History Societies D255
Transport Maps D231
Transportation D114
Treasure Trove E65
Treatment of the Poor G1-20
Trev B10
Trial by Battle H76
Trial by Ordeal H77
Trick (Heraldic) Q75
Trinity House Records D201
Trinoda Necessitas A389 C75 M1
Truck Act 1831 R50
True Bill H78
Tuition D156
Tump E66
Tumulus E67
Turnpike Roads K4 K47
Twelve B68
Twenty B68
Twissell K48
Twitchell K48
Twopenny Piece P29
Tyburn Tickets D116
Tye A236
Tye A323
Tympanum N100
Tyning A237

Under Sheriff B19
Union G36
Unitarians L36
Unitarian Registers D62
Unite P30
United Free Church of Scotland
    L37
United Kingdom Alliance R39
United Methodist Free Churches
    L32
Universities — foundation F32
Urban District Councils B234

Vaccary A238
Vagrancy G1 G3 G4 G5 G6 G9
    G10 G12
Vault N101
Vavassor B199
Velge A239
Verderer B164
Verge A45
Verso D19
Vert Q76
Vestries — close/select B229